MODERN ARCHITECTURE IN MEXICO CITY

CULTURE, POLITICS, AND THE BUILT ENVIRONMENT

DIANNE HARRIS, EDITOR

MODERN ARCHITECTURE IN MEXICO CITY

HISTORY, REPRESENTATION, AND THE SHAPING OF A CAPITAL

KATHRYN E. O'ROURKE

UNIVERSITY OF PITTSBURGH PRESS

Graham Foundation

This publication has been supported by a grant from the
Graham Foundation for Advanced Studies in the Fine Arts.

Published by the University of Pittsburgh Press, Pittsburgh, Pa., 15260
Copyright © 2016, University of Pittsburgh Press
This paperback edition, copyright © 2022
All rights reserved
Manufactured in the United States of America
Printed on acid-free paper
10 9 8 7 6 5 4 3 2 1

ISBN 13: 978-0-8229-6699-9
ISBN 10: 0-8229-6699-9

Cataloging-in-Publication data is available from the Library of Congress

Cover photo: AHUNAM, photograph by Ricardo Salazar, Fondo Construcción de la
Universidad, 3020.

Cover design: Alex Wolfe

For Curtis

And for Patrick,
who arrived between chapters four and five
and put everything into perspective

CONTENTS

CONTENTS

ACKNOWLEDGMENTS

My debts to friends, family, and colleagues for their help in realizing this book are many. It is difficult to overstate the one owed to David Brownlee. With his unique combination of tenacity and tenderness, he sharpened my mind, improved my writing, and taught me how to be an architectural historian. His encouragement, friendship, and deep wisdom about life inside and outside the academy have been my companions throughout the many phases of research and writing.

At Wellesley College I had the great fortune to learn from four scholars who started me on the path that led to this work. James Oles's mentorship and generosity began then and have continued in ways small and large ever since. No one has taught me more about Mexico or made learning about it more fun. Alice T. Friedman opened my eyes to architectural modernism and profoundly shaped the way I think about architect–client relationships and houses. I treasure her life lessons and friendship. James F. O'Gorman taught me the fundamentals of architectural history and helped shape my understanding of nineteenth-century U.S. architecture; Peter Fergusson introduced me to the study of landscape architecture.

In courses and conversations the late Detlef Mertins enriched my understanding of modernism and encouraged and challenged me in ways that continue to resonate in my work. I am grateful to Keith Eggener for his support and particularly for sharing his insights into Luis Barragán. Barbara Miller Lane, whose work on architecture and nationalism I admire tremendously, humbled me with her interest in my research and helped me in critical ways in a seminar at Bryn Mawr.

In 2010 I had the privilege of leading an architecture tour of Mexico City for the Society of Architectural Historians (SAH), and thereby of spending a week with some of the field's top scholars at a crucial point in the research and writing of this book. I am deeply grateful to the SAH for that opportunity and to the tour participants, especially Abigail Van Slyck, Richard Longstreth, Dietrich Neumann, Kenneth Breisch, Carol Willis, and the late William Stern, for sharing their insights and encouraging my scholarship.

Conversations with Luis Castañeda, Patricio del Real, Helen Gyger, David Rifkind, Winifred Newman, Peter Clericuzio, and Catherine Ettinger McEnulty were extremely helpful as I worked through material that became part of chapter 5. I thank George Flaherty for his observations on and encouragement of my reading of Barragán, and his students at the University of Texas in the Permanent Seminar on Latin American Art at the Center for Latin American Visual Studies for sharing their knowledge and perspectives as I wrote chapter 6. Two anonymous readers of the manuscript helped me to improve it dramatically and I thank them heartily for their generosity. At the University of Pittsburgh Press, Abby Collier's steady guidance, encouragement, and attention to detail has enriched the book immeasurably. I am also grateful to Dianne Harris for her enthusiasm for the project and to Alexander Wolfe for his assistance in bringing the book to completion.

In Mexico City many people helped make research possible and pleasurable. Foremost among them are Miguel Legaria and Cuca Valero, who have made the city feel like home since my college days. Enrique and Cathie Pani welcomed me to their home and shared their memories of Mario Pani, Luis Barragán, José Clemente Orozco, Juan O'Gorman, and José Villagrán García. I thank them most warmly.

My friend and Trinity colleague Aaron Navarro graciously arranged for me to meet the Panis; I thank him for that and for our conversations on modern Mexico. I am grateful to my colleagues in the Department of Art and Art History for their support, and especially my comrades, Douglas Brine and Michael Schreyach, with whom I have had the pleasure of sharing the trials and triumphs of life as a junior faculty member. Hearty thanks go to Holly Goeckler for her help in securing and preparing illustrations. Ann Mueller and Denise Wilson attended to a thousand tiny logistical details of research and publishing and made anxieties evaporate. There would be no book without the staff of Trinity's Interlibrary Loan department, and I am particularly grateful to Maria McWilliams for tracking down obscure texts and, as if by magic, making them appear in my office. Benjamin Harris is the best research librarian with whom a scholar could hope to work.

Conversations about Mexico and architecture with friends and colleagues in Texas have helped propel the project. I am especially grateful to Tomás Ybarra-Frausto for his interest, support, and friendship, and to Marion Oettinger, who welcomed me from day one into San Antonio's community of people who love Latin American art. My appreciation also goes to Stephen Fox and Kathryn Holliday for their encouragement and insights about writing and publishing. It seems unlikely that the book would have been finished without my friend Anadelia Romo. Our weekly conversations on scholarship, modern Latin America, teaching, and parenthood have kept me on course and sustained me through the end. I thank Patrick Keating and Lisa Jasinski for their steadfast friendship, enthusiasm, and wisdom. Much farther afield, treasured friends Megan Haseltine, Dana Rooney, Emily Heersink, and Tara Brennan have nurtured me and my work in countless ways for many years.

A grant from the Graham Foundation for Advanced Studies in the Fine Arts has supported this publication. I am also grateful to Trinity University, which has supported my research through two Berger Junior Fellowships and additional monies for the publication, and to the Mexico Americas Spain Program at Trinity, which also provided research funding. I thank as well the many individuals and institutions that assisted in securing reproductions and publication permissions.

My parents, Joanne Edmundson and Terence O'Rourke, each in different ways have been contributing to the realization of this book for decades. With my mother, as a child in Houston I first began to appreciate the long reach of Mexican colonial architecture's influence. Mexico started to imprint itself on me during a childhood trip to San Miguel de Allende with my father. Both of them encouraged my study of Spanish, nurtured my love of architecture from an early age, and supported my travels in Latin America. I am deeply grateful for their unwavering interest in my work and for their love. The encouragement and good-natured humor that members of my extended family, especially my aunts and uncles, have offered for years has buoyed me in countless ways.

Finally, no one has been more important than Curtis Swope. He has visited buildings, combed bookstores, met me outside of archives, pulled me and my computer from a jam-packed Mexico City subway car, climbed pyramids, read drafts, talked through ideas, and to our children is the greatest father I could imagine. He makes each day a joy.

INTRODUCTION

In 1680 Carlos Sigüenza y Góngora, one of colonial Mexico's foremost intellectuals and one of its first historians, was asked by the city council of Mexico City to design the triumphal arch under which the new viceroy, the Marquis of La Laguna, would walk during his ceremonial entrance to the city. For the occasion Sigüenza y Góngora created a monumental gateway ninety feet high and fifty feet wide that resembled a classical triumphal arch. Organized into three stories, with each entablature supported by Corinthian columns or pilasters, the gate had sixteen niches for figural sculptures. Instead of depicting Christian saints, holy figures, or imperial leaders, the statues represented twelve Mexican rulers, including three Aztecs: Huitzilíhuitl, the lawgiver; Moctezuma Ilhuicamina, the warrior and protector of religion; and Cuauhtémoc, the last Aztec leader and the most celebrated resistor of the Spanish conquest. Sigüenza y Góngora's monument was perhaps the first major public architectural work to honor Mexico's Aztec past and to link pre- and postconquest history. By combining the language of classicism and references to Mexican historical figures, Sigüenza y Góngora created a work that deliberately revealed Mexico's bicultural influences and relied on them for meaning in the service of a modern political event.

Nearly three hundred years later, in 1950, Juan O'Gorman designed one of twentieth-century Mexico's most famous buildings, the Central Library of the National Autonomous University (UNAM) in Mexico City. His fourteen-story slab towered over a campus that resembled modernist urban planning schemes envisioned by the members of the International Congress on Modern Architecture but made use of the native volcanic rock at the site and opened the campus to views of the distant mountains and volcanoes that ringed the valley of Mexico. The library would have looked like the university's other International Style buildings had it not been for its cladding. O'Gorman wrapped the ten nearly windowless upper stories in a four-thousand-square-meter multicolored mosaic on the theme of Mexican history and depicted buildings and figures associated with Mexico's pre-Hispanic, colonial, and modern periods (plate 1). It was the most famous of many modern buildings in Mexico City whose facade, like Sigüenza y Góngora's, was fully legible only to those with knowledge of some aspect or aspects of Mexican architectural or cultural history. To those unfamiliar with that history it looked decidedly different from modern works elsewhere, and its many specific pictorial references were recognizable in only a general way. The foreign visitor to the UNAM campus, for example, might recognize on the south facade a Spanish colonial church, but he or she would be unlikely to identify in the pair of giant blue orbs the allusion to the eyes of the preconquest god Tlaloc, an easily recognizable reference for students of the architectural sculpture on the Pyramid of the Feathered Serpent at Teotihuacan. Only with close study would he or she notice that the church and its pendant, a colonial palace, both stood atop the bases of pre-Columbian pyramids, just as many actual colonial buildings in downtown Mexico City were built on the ruins of Tenochtitlan. O'Gorman's was one of many modern buildings that prioritized legibility and recognizability, whether of architectural elements, relief sculpture, cladding material, or images, and whose facades and wall surfaces—to a far greater extent than their plans or sections—were central to their meanings.

Photographs of the library appeared near the beginning of the final section of *4,000 Years of Mexican Architecture*, a book published in 1956 by the Society of Mexican Architects, which dedicated an entire chapter to the campus and also published numerous photos of preconquest and colonial buildings (figure I.1). Opposite a picture of the library, the authors wrote that "architecture is called upon to express national ideals in concrete form," and "we feel ourselves to be the heirs to *4,000 years of architecture*, a synthesis of the highest cultural tradition of the *American Indian* and one of the most highly developed aspects of *Western Culture*; our work in the future must be worthy of such origins."[1] The authors of this monumental history were, like those of many histories of Mexican architecture, practicing architects. Like O'Gorman, they understood the problem of modern design in relation to Mexican architectural history—or at least its image—and to a host of cultural associations that history carried.

FIGURE I.1. Sociedad de Arquitectos Mexicanos, *4000 años de arquitectura mexicana*, cover, 1956.

Modern Architecture in Mexico City: History, Representation, and the Shaping of a Capital examines O'Gorman's library and the campus where it was built, along with a government ministry, a park and schools for the working class, and several private houses designed between 1925 and 1952 by some of Mexico's most famous and lesser known architects: Carlos Obregón Santacilia, Juan Segura, Enrique del Moral, Mario Pani, Alberto Arai, and Luis Barragán. It argues that the intellectual origins of Mexican modernism lay in the first texts on colonial architectural history and that architects' continuing engagement with

Mexican architectural history throughout the first half of the twentieth century defined their buildings. Because Mexican architectural history (but not archaeology) and the idea of a nationally distinctive modern architecture were invented at the same time, by many of the same people, beliefs about history and nationality often entwined in new works. Architects' attention to history took many forms: it manifested as research and writing on colonial, vernacular, pre-Hispanic, and eventually twentieth-century buildings; as personal contact with historical works in provincial towns and remote archaeological sites; and in the daily experience of living and working in Mexico City, surrounded by extraordinary buildings from the colonial era and remnants and reminders of the Aztec capital. Some assisted the Mexican government in preserving and documenting old buildings at the same time they designed new ones that expressed collective aspirations to make Mexico a respected member of a modern, cosmopolitan community of nations. However they encountered or imagined Mexican architectural history, architects derived from it the principle that became the foundation on which they based their work: that in conjunction with the other arts, buildings' facades and surfaces could be used as representational spaces capable of conveying ideas about Mexico's cultural character.

Architects distilled this idea from the claim made in the first histories of colonial architecture written around 1900 that a nationally unique architecture had existed since the sixteenth century, and that its uniqueness was carried on facades in elements and decoration, which themselves reflected Mexico's history of cultural and racial mixing. Historiographic and pedagogical structures helped transmit these ideas to two generations of architects and influenced accounts of Mexican modernism starting in the 1930s. In the 1920s, as architectural education began to present Mexican as well as European models, texts on colonial architecture became important sources for young architects. At the same time, a new cultural patriotism rooted in the revaluation of indigenous culture and embodied by Diego Rivera's famous murals swelled, even as architects' training emphasized principles associated with the École des Beaux-Arts. Chiefly these were complex, rigorous facade composition, hierarchical planning, and attention to program. These characteristics defined many new works, even as information about the radically new architecture being built in Europe arrived beginning in the mid-1920s.

In practice, the influence of an architectural history that interpreted buildings in terms of national exceptionalism, but as being closely related to European models, and the emphasis on the facade as an expressive site, gave rise to a modern architecture marked not by its innovative spatial planning or responsiveness to a long theoretical tradition (as in Europe), but one in which representation was paramount. Mexico's modern buildings were profoundly visual and they were charged with enormous cultural work. From Carlos Obregón Santacilia and Juan Segura's representations of colonial elements on facades, to Juan O'Gorman's architecture of images—first of industrial objects, and then, in mosaic, of old buildings and cultural icons—to Alberto Arai's repurposing at UNAM of the inclined walls of ancient pyramids, and finally to Luis Barragán's vivid geometric abstractions from provincial works of art and architecture, these buildings were meant to be seen and "read." They addressed local and international audiences and, over time, helped create one of the most complex systems of visual culture in the twentieth century.

With the significant exception of Barragán, these architects' most important patron was the Mexican government, which, from the mid-1920s on, skillfully enfolded its new buildings in a narrative that fused history, politics, and national character. It accomplished this through statements by politicians and their agents, by funding exhibitions and publications on new and historical buildings, and in the research and presentation of archaeological sites and colonial buildings for tourists. With breathtaking thoroughness, through several offices within the Ministry of Education, as the century went on the Mexican government choreographed an extraordinary presentation of a modern, progressive country that was unified culturally and historically. Architecture was at the heart of this image.

For a variety of reasons, including the influence of early histories of postconquest architecture, scholarship of modern Mexican architecture has tended to emphasize the ways that buildings carried ideological meaning or responded to the political concerns of their patrons, rather than problems particular to architecture—the shaping of elements, the treatment of walls, and responsiveness to site and context—despite the highly formalist approach that many architects took to their designs.[2] Architecture and politics were entwined in Mexico long before 1900, but their enmeshment became particularly notable with the construction of the new university campus, where the urban planner and bureaucrat Carlos Lazo oversaw the plan and Mario Pani, the nephew of a powerful political figure, was one of two leading architects. It came into full bloom even later, in the mid-1960s, in the person of Pedro Ramírez Vázquez, who was president of the Society of Mexican Architects when *4,000 Years of Mexican Architecture* was published.[3]

Many of the architects, buildings, and even texts discussed here will be familiar to historians of modern Mexican art and architecture, but the book endeavors to deepen and widen the understanding of the intellectual and cultural contexts in which modernism arose in Mexico. It also aims to recentralize architects in the making of architecture. For example, many scholars have emphasized the importance of education minister José Vasconcelos in establishing the theoretical framework in which the radical innovations in 1920s art occurred and stressed his significance as a patron of art and architecture. His influence in many realms is indisputable. *Modern Architecture in Mexico City*, however, foregrounds the work of architects and historians—people who had far more immediate influence on Mexican architectural design and history—as shapers of modern architectural culture in the first decades of the century. Recently, scholars, most notably Johanna Lozoya, have begun to interrogate the history of Mexican architectural history to reveal its assumptions and their sources,[4] while others, such as María Fernández and George F. Flaherty have begun to locate Mexican modern architecture in wider, international networks of images and ideas.[5] In his study of the architecture and allied arts created for the 1968 Mexico City Olympics, Luis M. Castañeda has shown how architects' very close connections to bureaucrats and politicians gave rise not only to visually "spectacular" buildings designed to convey nationalistic messages to Mexicans and foreigners, but functioned within what he calls an "image economy," in which buildings, infrastructure projects, and graphic design produced multiple kinds of benefits for those who helped realize them.[6] As he noted, the roots of this intimate relationship between architecture and politics lay in works of preceding decades. Like these scholars, I am interested in the many and varied ideas that shaped buildings and the constructs that have occluded certain ways of understanding them, as well as in why architects made the formal decisions that they did. In some instances the book offers perspectives on Mexican buildings' differences from canonical avant-garde modern works abroad. However, my interest is not so much in disproving the idea that Mexican modern architecture was derivative, as in illuminating the ways that Mexican architects' privileging of histories and visual systems internal to Mexico shaped architectural modernism there.

ARCHITECTURAL HISTORY AND MESTIZAJE

Architects and their patrons became preoccupied with the idea of a distinctively Mexican architecture in the last quarter of the nineteenth century, when they usually turned to pre-Columbian buildings as sources for nationally specific forms. Antonio Peñafiel and Antonio María Anza's Mexican Pavilion at the 1889 World's Fair in Paris, which evoked pre-Columbian temples on a Beaux-Arts plan, is perhaps the best-known nineteenth-century example.[7] Although archaeological discoveries and research into pre-Columbian art and architecture was vital to the development of Mexican modern art, the intellectual and theoretical underpinnings of modern architecture in Mexico lay in histories of colonial buildings. Many of these and, later, histories of 1920s and 1930s modernism, were written by Mexican architects as they were designing pathbreaking buildings, or just before their students did. The authors of these accounts believed that a distinctive Mexican architecture came into being during the colonial period and suggested that its characteristic forms, which they identified as having European antecedents and indigenous influences, had been shaped by conflating forms and techniques particular to western Europe and to Mexico, broadly understood. By midcentury, as early modernism became historical, architect-historians sought to link their work not just to the colonial past, but, increasingly to pre-Columbian architecture and vernacular buildings, about which they also wrote. Other influential authors of Mexican architectural history, or of important catalogs of modern Mexican architecture that linked new buildings to old ones, were U.S. historians including Baxter, Esther Born, I. E. Myers, and Esther McCoy who, looking at Mexican buildings as outsiders, helped further solidify the idea that they expressed national character.

Undergirding the designs of many major new works was a robust debate about the idea of mestizaje, the racial and cultural mixing of Europeans and indigenous Mexicans that followed the Spanish conquest in 1521, and that was widely regarded as Mexico's chief cultural characteristic. The focus on mestizaje was closely related to what was often later described as a preoccupation with national identity. Beliefs about cultural mixing, and the significance and proper place of indigenous people in modern Mexico animated philosophical, literary, and artistic discussions before the revolution of 1910–17 and helped shape much of Mexican social policy thereafter.[8] Significantly, intellectual genesis of the problem of "Mexicanness" in architecture and architect-historians' assertions about mestizaje in buildings preceded the postrevolutionary enshrining of the idea as a cultural ideology, and long predated the implementation of social and legal reforms designed to improve the welfare of indigenous and mixed-race Mexicans.[9] The architectural result was a diverse group of buildings that bore many hallmarks of modern architecture elsewhere, but were distinguished and linked by their architects' deep engagement with forms, materials, and, in some cases, images that awakened associations with older buildings and native culture. Early architectural historians' consciousness of mestizaje as a historical process shaped the interpretive framework they developed to describe colonial buildings. They fused analysis of buildings' visual characteristics and historical contexts with descriptions of the sociocultural character of the period as they imagined it, and described the synthesis of these things as "Mexican." They found evidence for their claims on facades and in works of painting and sculpture that were integrated into wall surfaces. The first generation of Mexican modernists, who were trained in the early 1920s, inherited this way of understanding buildings. Having absorbed what was fundamentally a mode of historical interpretation from books and from their teachers, younger architects transformed it into an approach to design that focused on the communication of historicity though surfaces.

RATIONALISM AND REPRESENTATION

Preference for historicist schemes dominated architecture in the early 1920s, but two students trained in these years, José Villagrán García and Carlos Obregón Santacilia, led the movement away from historicism beginning in 1925. At the start of their careers, they embodied two different strands of modernism: rationalist classicism in the case of Villagrán, and a more historically evocative, representationally rich modernism in the case of Obregón Santacilia. In part because of his influential position as a professor of architectural theory at the national school of architecture for many decades, and because of rationalism's apparent suitability to the ideals of economic austerity and rigorous reform espoused by government patrons in the 1930s, as well as for the ways it seemed to anticipate the language of International Style modernism that came to dominate architecture by midcentury, Villagrán has long eclipsed Obregón Santacilia in histories of Mexican modernism. But in the 1920s, although both architects received important commissions, it was Obregón Santacilia who designed the most symbolically important and widely admired works. It was he who was invited to design the Mexican Pavilion at the Centennial Exposition in Rio de Janeiro in 1922, and he who designed the most important new school for the Ministry of Education in 1923. In 1925 he created the new headquarters of the second-most important federal agency, the

Ministry of Health, which stood on the Paseo de la Reforma, the most important street in the entire country, and at the edge of Chapultepec Park, Mexico City's largest, oldest, and most beloved public park. The building included stained glass and murals by Diego Rivera, who was by then the most important artist in the hemisphere and one of the most famous in the world. Although Villagrán's National Stadium had considerable symbolic significance, he was often tasked with designing more utilitarian and less visible buildings: a remote vaccine laboratory and a tuberculosis sanatorium on the distant edges of the capital, which few people other than scientists, a few doctors and nurses, and indigent consumptives saw. Obregón Santacilia's ministry building, by contrast, appeared in the pages of *Architectural Record*, and in 1929 he was the lone architect identified, along with Rivera, José Clemente Orozco, and three others, as "six figures in a Mexican Renaissance."[10] O'Gorman and del Moral, who would go on to design some of the most important buildings of the middle of the century, both worked in his office at the beginning of their careers and at a pivotal point in his. Under Obregón Santacilia's guidance, the younger architects drew colonial buildings and assisted in designing ones that marked the transition away from historicism. This book is concerned with the buildings that belong more to his branch of Mexican modernism than to Villagrán's but also shows the ways in which those branches entwined starting in the 1930s, first in O'Gorman's work. The three other figures in the "Renaissance" were a bureaucrat, Moises Saenz, who oversaw important architectural commissions from several different posts in the federal government; the painter-historian Dr. Atl, and Frances Toor, the publisher and editor of the bilingual journal *Mexican Folkways*, which presented information about the folk art and customs of Mexico. It was in this context—one that was predominately shaped by architects, artists, and intellectuals interested in history and culture, but supported by government—that I position the development of Mexican modern architecture.

Representation—on facades, in photographs, and in texts—was the chief means by which architects communicated their buildings' relationships to history and indigenous culture and endeavored to fulfill the mandate that histories of colonial architecture seemed to impose. Ideas and forms were represented in many ways: pictorially, in figural sculptures, paintings, and mosaics; abstractly, in representations of architectural elements; photographically, in carefully composed images that contrasted old and new buildings, suggested parallels to famous works elsewhere, or proposed a distinctive kind of Mexican

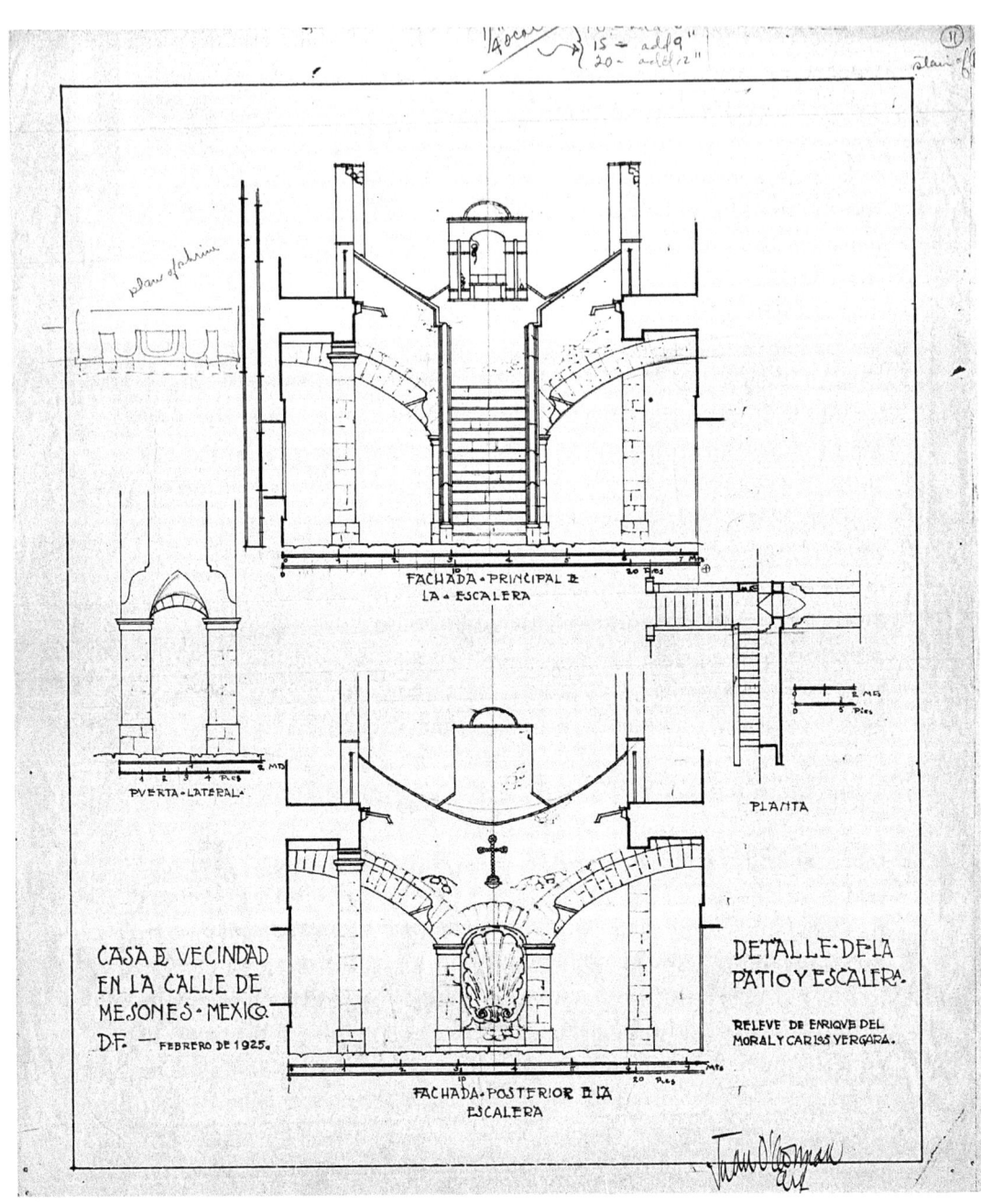

FIGURE I.2. Juan O'Gorman, with Enrique del Moral and Carlos Yergara, *Casa de Vecindad en la Calle de Mesones, México D.F., detail of patio and stairs*, February 1925. Drawing made when all three architects were employed by Carlos Obregón Santacilia.

architectural subject; or, textually, in writings and statements about new buildings, Mexican architectural history, and about the architects themselves. Architects frequently relied on representations of and allusions to folk art, which Mexico City intellectuals and artists began to collect and exhibit in the 1920s, and to vernacular provincial architecture, to bridge the perceived divide between formal characteristics that read as international and the social concerns that clients articulated in national terms. Because folk art and vernacular architecture were created by indigenous people, or showed native influences, they were imagined to represent continuity with history and connection to indigenous Mexicans. Including references to folk art allowed architects to acknowledge present-day sociopolitical ambitions to integrate indigenous people into mainstream culture, symbolically unite rural and urban Mexico, and relate modern architecture, like the historical buildings they admired, to ideas about native influence. It also provided a way to acknowledge indigenous Mexicans that emphasized their artistic talents rather than their enormous deficits in education, access to health care, and civic participation, which the government attempted to address in its reform programs. Allusions to vernacular architecture provided a culturally appealing way to distinguish Mexican architecture from buildings elsewhere and to link new works to "old" ones, or ones associated with vanishing ways of life, without using historicist elements.

Although it became one of the central concerns of Mexican modernism, the question of what buildings should represent and how was not particular to Mexico and had engaged architects in Europe for several centuries by the time it emerged as a major concern in Obregón Santacilia's Health Ministry. Stemming from debates about buildings' relationships to history and nature, European discussions of representation in architecture touched on a wide variety of issues including building materials, ornament, and abstraction, and the question of whether it was possible for buildings to represent ideas outside the traditional boundaries of architecture.[11] In Mexico, the problem of representation and its relationship to materials, ornament, and abstraction was also at the heart of modern architecture, but whereas European architects had largely been concerned with representation as it dealt with issues internal to an architectural theory that was derived from classicism and increasingly concerned with rationalism, in Mexico architects focused primarily on the potential of buildings to represent ideas about the character of the country.

HISTORY AND REPRESENTATION IN CONTEXT

In the late 1920s or early 1930s a person in downtown Mexico City might not only encounter extraordinary colonial and neoclassical buildings but also see in magazines images of new works by French rationalist architect Auguste Perret and Le Corbusier, watch shiny new automobiles zoom past, buy ceramic pottery or a handmade textile from a distant state, and encounter in the street the peasants, recently arrived from the countryside, wearing the straw hats, white linen pants, and sandals that inspired Rivera's new indigenist iconography. In this way images and objects from the real past, those nostalgically imagined to embody a fading one that was also geographically distant, and those associated with the very latest thinking in Mexico and abroad, existed together in real space and real time in the capital.

Because of its slower pace of economic, technological, and educational development relative to industrialized European countries and the United States, and its abundant supply of laborers, as in many non-industrialized countries, in Mexico architecture followed a somewhat different timeline than that in European centers, but there were significant parallels in the evolution of architectural modernism on both sides of the Atlantic. In Mexico formal allusions to industrial modernity were aspirational expressions rather than responsive references to new conditions. But Mexican architects' preoccupation with architectural history, and their interest in craft (embodied by folk art), vernacular architecture, painting, or architecture's role in reflecting and shaping society, was not unique. Indeed, their attention to these things resonated with quintessentially modern themes—an interest in origins and foundations, the tensions between abstraction and representation, the changed relationship between city and country and the transformation of individual experience and social interaction in the wake of the rise of new technologies—evident in architecture in many countries, beginning, in some places, as early as the mid-eighteenth century.[12] Discernible in the statements and writings of the architects considered here are echoes of major currents of French architectural theory, including Jean-Nicolas-Louis Durand's emphasis of architecture's social significance, Eugène Emmanuel Viollet-le-Duc's linking of historic preservation, architectural history, and nationalism, and a Henri Labroustian interest in representation and the creation of an architecture legible to a particular audience.[13] Even before Mexican independence from Spain in 1821, French architecture and theory provided the most important cultural model for Mexican architects. They learned of it just as colonial architects and builders had learned of Renaissance and Baroque architecture in Italy and Spain—through illustrated books and, occasionally, by traveling to Europe. Although overt Francophilia in Mexican architecture, as it manifested in ornate second-empire style and neoclassical buildings built in the colonial center during the long rule of Porfirio Díaz (1884–1911), was widely decried by many architects and critics after the revolution, the legacy of francophone theory, particularly that of the influential turn-of-the-century theorist and professor at the École des Beaux-Arts, Julien Guadet, and Le Corbusier, remained strong well into the century.

The many overlapping concerns and formal similarities to modernisms elsewhere, coupled with the very different economic and technological context in which Mexican architects worked, make it especially important to understand the centrality of representation to this architecture. As Edward Burian has noted, "one of the most fundamental dichotomies . . . [of Mexican modern architecture] is that between the technological *image* of a machine age and the handcrafted *reality* of Mexican production. This has resulted in a profound discontinuity of means and ends."[14] Indeed, although they were intended to be seen as emblems of an up-to-date midcentury modernity, many of the buildings at the National University, for example, were constructed by peasants who laid block into concrete frames. At midcentury some of the most astute minds in Mexican architecture began to dwell on the gaps between representations and realities, between the experience of twentieth-century cosmopolitan people and ancient (and modern) indigenous ones, and between individuals themselves. In seemingly very different works, Arai and Barragán, in the fronton courts at the National University and Barragán's house, as well as in their own writings and interviews, used representation and architectural history to examine the problems of subjectivity and the assumptions about national culture at the core of the idea of national architecture as they helped shift modern design decisively away from reliance on figuration.

Understanding modern architects' deep engagement with history, representation, and national specificity is critical because the facadism these preoccupations helped motivate is one of the chief characteristics that makes Mexican buildings seem so strikingly different from works of avant-garde European architects or Frank Lloyd Wright. Several of the buildings presented here do not look "modern" in the sense that they do not obey the rules of International Style modernism enumerated by Henry-Russell Hitchcock and Philip Johnson in 1932 in their transformative exhibition at the Museum of Modern Art in New York, nor do they all look alike. Hitchcock's and Johnson's statements were only some of many about what modern architecture was, but they were uniquely influential. They were also highly art historical and written to describe buildings that, with a few exceptions, had been created in or near places where cubism and nonfigurative painting flourished.

That 1900s–1910s histories of architecture would focus primarily on facades seems obvious—in the first two decades of the twentieth century the radical reconceptualizations of plan and architectural space that helped shape modern architecture elsewhere were only in germinal stages. In the 1910s Mexican architects apparently had no knowledge of Frank Lloyd Wright's revolutionary reordering of plan and interior space nor of Viennese architect Adolf Loos's theory of spatial organization, the *Raumplan*. Although photographs and texts of avant-garde European buildings circulated in Mexico City in the 1920s and 1930s, the intellectual and aesthetic processes and milieu out of which those buildings emerged could not be replicated. Far from Vienna, Paris, Dessau, Utrecht, and Oak Park, architects in Mexico learned about the new modern architecture in Europe and the United States from black-and-white pictures—usually of facades—and descriptions, just as they had learned about many Mexican colonial buildings far from the capital.

Scholarly emphasis on facades was particularly consequential in Mexico, where architects, working at great distance from the places where avant-garde European architecture matured, had little opportunity to contemplate the revolutionary implications for designing in plan and section suggested by Cubism and De Stijl. Le Corbusier's work as a painter, the connections of Ludwig Mies van der Rohe and Walter Gropius to painting and two-dimensional design and sculpture through the G Group and the Bauhaus, and the very close links between Piet Mondrian, Theo van Doesburg, and Gerrit Rietveld were critical to these architects' approaches to shaping space and their new conceptualizations of the interplay of plan, section, and elevation. In Mexico, painterly abstraction had little influence until much later in the century, not because Mexican artists were ignorant of it, but because in the 1920s they chose to work in figurative styles more suited to narrative and history painting. In the 1910s Rivera lived in the same building as Mondrian in Paris and was an accomplished cubist. In many of his groundbreaking murals David Alfaro Siqueiros used principles he learned from Italian Futurism.

Mexican architects' preoccupation with architecture's national qualities also distinguished them from most avant-garde European architects, but did link them to Wright and back to Louis Sullivan in the United States. Support for such an approach was abundant from Mexican governmental clients, but that was not the only reason for it. It also had to do with a hemispheric awareness of difference and distance from, and yet reliance on, cultural centers across the Atlantic that had seemed to define architecture in the Americas since the sixteenth century and was confirmed visually by colonial buildings. In Mexico in 1900, the lived reality and cultural construct of mestizaje and the extraordinary eighteenth-century architecture of the Churrigueresque style, in addition to eighty years of independence, provided evidence that Mexico City, rather than being the victim of a culturally stultifying imperial power, was in fact a place of innovation, but one that, for a variety of reasons, was not quite on par with admired centers elsewhere. Despite their many differences, the designs of Sigüenza y Góngora and O'Gorman evinced a consciousness of distance, difference, and connection to European precedent. This awareness crystallized in its modern incarnation in the late nineteenth and early twentieth centuries, at the same time that Mexican architectural history was invented.

By examining buildings from the perspective of Mexican architectural history and visual culture, instead of relying on a framework that has defined modern architecture in terms of art historical and technological developments in western Europe, this book attempts to add to the story of architecture in one of the centers of modernism in the Americas by more fully illuminating what was distinctive and particular about it, and at the same time to contribute to the shaping of a more nuanced, inclusive history of modern architecture. In the past twenty years that history has included more countries, problems, influences, and, to a lesser extent, forms that had long been relegated to the margins of modern architecture at best, and in some cases not considered at all. Today histories of modern architecture in Mexico are more international than ever. Along with scholarship on modernism in other major, but long-marginalized countries, recent accounts contribute to new understandings of what "modern" architecture is and was, and inform the writing of "global" architectural histories. Questions of how Mexican architecture relates to that of other Latin American countries persist, although new treatments dealing with the region as a whole have emphasized coexistence rather than comparison.[15]

In 2010 Mexico City hosted the eleventh annual meeting of the international group DOCOMOMO, which is dedicated to the "Documentation and Conservation of the Modern Movement." Among its keynote speakers were Barry Bergdoll, then the curator of architecture at the Museum of Modern Art in New York, who was preparing a major exhibition on Latin American architecture from 1955 to 1980 that picked up where Henry-Russell Hitchcock's groundbreaking *Latin American Architecture since 1945* show (1955) left off, and Mexican architect Ricardo Legorreta, whose work in many respects carried on the legacies of those architects addressed here. Legorreta's topic was the architecture of Barragán and Villagrán but he began his talk with a discussion of the enduringly powerful architecture of Teotihuacan and Monte Alban.[16] Moving to colonial buildings, of which he was equally admiring, with a slide of the Royal Chapel at Cholula behind him, Legorreta claimed that colonial architecture was distinguished not by the twin influences of European and indigenous art as early historians would have it, but, unsurprisingly perhaps for an architect with major clients in Qatar, by "Hispanic" and "Islamic" forms. Legorreta's replacement of indigenous Mexicans with Muslims as the shapers of a distinctive colonial idiom echoed nearly five-hundred-year-old claims about the parallel relationships these groups had with Spain. That in the twenty-first century one of the country's foremost architects opened a lecture to an international audience in much the same way his predecessors would have one hundred years before, shows the enduring power of the framework for defining national architecture they established.

INVENTING MEXICAN ARCHITECTURAL HISTORY

In 1901 Sylvester Baxter published the first major illustrated history of Mexican colonial architecture, the monumental, ten-volume *Spanish-Colonial Architecture in Mexico.* As a Bostonian, Baxter was an unlikely pioneer in the new field of Mexican architectural history, but his book, which was illustrated with photographs by Henry Greenwood Peabody and architectural drawings by Bertram Grosvenor Goodhue, not only presented the major works of colonial Mexico to U.S. readers, but quickly became an authoritative source for Mexican scholars.[17] It was one of several important works on Mexican colonial architectural history and was followed in the early 1910s by scholarship by Mexicans Federico Mariscal (who helped translate Baxter's text in 1934), Genaro García, Jesús T. Acevedo, and Manuel Álvarez. These illustrated histories emphasized three main ideas: that Churrigueresque architecture represented the fullest efflorescence of "Mexican" architecture; that indigenous artists had helped shape distinctive buildings beginning in the sixteenth century; and that Mexican architecture evolved against the backdrop of the cultural melding that followed the conquest. In

FIGURE I.3. Henry Greenwood Peabody, *Church of Santísima Trinidad*, Mexico City (eighteenth century), in Sylvester Baxter, *Spanish-Colonial Architecture in Mexico* (1901).

addition to documenting the architecture of their country, Mexican architect-historians hoped to formalize and discipline the profession of architecture. They defended it and its institutions, claiming repeatedly that architecture and art did special cultural work. Mariscal went furthest of all, emphatically linking "national" architectural history and the concept of "patria," or "fatherland," which connoted a deep feeling of connection to the place, people, and idea of Mexico. The association Mariscal proposed between Mexican architectural history and national sentiment was influential for decades to come, and the flexibility and ambiguity inherent in the idea of patria and the word "Mexico" made the concepts enduringly useful to architects and their clients.

Pioneered by Guillermo Kahlo and Antonio Cortés, in Mexico modern architectural photography emerged in tandem with written histories of colonial architecture, following the precedent set by Peabody. Since the middle of the nineteenth century foreigners had been fascinated by Mexican buildings and documented them in prints and photographs. Frederick Catherwood's lithographs of Maya ruins and Désiré Charnay's photographs of archaeological sites are perhaps the best known. While these traveler-artists' images of ancient Mexican architecture helped foment interest in preconquest cultures and monuments among artists and intellectuals in Mexico and abroad, colonial architecture had been documented photographically only minimally, and since the late nineteenth century preconquest buildings had been most often presented by the Mexican government as examples of and sources for a truly Mexican architecture.[18] In 1904 Mexican finance minister José Yves Limantour hired Kahlo to document all the buildings owned by the federal government, which included a great many colonial Mexican churches seized during the Reform period after 1857, and numerous eighteenth-century palaces in Mexico City that were used as government offices. Kahlo devoted most of his attention to the architecture of the capital, but also traveled to cities and towns throughout the country. In addition to rapidly and systematically increasing the number of images of colonial buildings, Limantour's commission strengthened the already close connections between the government and architecture that had been established through archaeology, and presaged the federal government's close involvement in architecture in decades to come, when it became the most important patron of modern buildings. In roughly the same years that Kahlo worked for Limantour, Antonio Cortés photographed the works that appeared in Genaro García's book, *La arquitectura en México: Iglesias,* documenting in extraordinary detail the forms of provincial colonial churches. Together, the photographs by Kahlo and Cortés constituted the single-most important body of images of colonial Mexican buildings.

In Mexico City in the first half of the twentieth century architects were literally surrounded by colonial buildings in the downtown, where most of them were trained, but they also watched as the capital's colonial center was transformed. The destruction of colonial buildings, the creation of new ones in colonial-revival languages, which were sometimes nearly indistinguishable from their predecessors, and the removal of commercial signage and plant material from the buildings and facades drew attention to Mexico's colonial past. Beginning in the 1910s, concerned about the demolitions and cultural losses inflicted by the secularization and neoclassicization of eighteenth-century church-es, Mariscal and others began campaigns that lasted for decades to save and restore buildings that had survived but, in many instances, had been allowed to deteriorate.[19] The ambition to beautify the downtown was also spurred in part by anticipation of the 1910 centennial celebra-tions, but continued long after and helped generate a building boom of colonial revival buildings.[20] In the 1920s, thanks to cars and improved infrastructure, architects could relatively easily visit the provincial cit-ies and towns where other great colonial churches and palaces stood. The ongoing reconstruction of preconquest ruins throughout the first half of the century, their promotion as tourist destinations, and classi-fication by the government as national patrimony further strengthened the idea that there was a nationally distinctive architecture, and that it was historical.

These three related developments—the rise of written histories of colonial architecture, the representation of it in widely circulated photographs, and the destruction and restoration of colonial buildings downtown—contributed to the new awareness of Mexico's architectur-al history. Underlying the growth of interest in colonial architecture was the belief that modern Mexico had come into being during the colonial period when its modern character as a country defined by Eu-ropean and indigenous cultures was fixed, and that Mexican colonial architecture was unique and was the finest in the Western Hemisphere. The entwined ideas about history, culture, and singularity, and the ways that buildings related to the other arts and to representation in general pervaded Mexican architectural culture throughout the twen-tieth century. Although Baxter addressed a U.S. audience and Mariscal spoke primarily to Mexicans, both writers defined their subjects with reference to these ideas. That they felt compelled to defend the value of even looking seriously at colonial buildings (much less to make arguments about them) gives some indication of how marginalized this architecture was at the turn of the century when Renaissance Revival buildings increasingly dominated the downtowns of major cities of the Americas and a focus on pre-Columbian buildings defined architectural historical research in Mexico.[21]

Since the middle of the nineteenth century indigenous Mexico had been a source of fascination for artists and intellectuals, and the government had supported excavations of pre-Hispanic archaeological sites as well as public monuments commemorating indigenous Mexico. Baxter and Mariscal sought to shift attention to the colonial period, although Baxter especially emphasized the influence of indigenous technique and imagery on colonial forms. Implicit in the histories was the idea that modern Mexico had been formed fundamentally by Europeans. While not inherently political, this belief resonated in twentieth-century Mexico and informed its politics in critical ways. In a nation that was still overwhelming agrarian and peopled by indigenous or mixed-race peasants and workers who did not participate fully in mainstream political and economic systems, efforts to reform society and change individual behaviors that were not consistent with European (or U.S.) norms could be justified when coupled with an understanding of national history that privileged European habits and financial structures. While by no means inherently anti-indigenous in sentiment, in the climate of highly charged left-wing politics of the late 1920s and early 1930s, twentieth-century interest in colonial architecture was sometimes construed as conservative, particularly because it necessarily emphasized the role of the Catholic Church in the development of "national" architecture. At no point in their texts, however, did the authors refer to politics, a point that is particularly striking in the case of the Mexican writers who worked on the eve of and in the midst of the Mexican Revolution.

Although Mariscal stressed the national character of colonial architecture more emphatically than other historians did, they all helped establish a mode of viewing and thinking about architecture, old and new, in national terms—precisely the opposite of the way Hitchcock and Johnson would frame the new antihistoricist architecture appearing throughout Europe that they cataloged in 1932. The effect of this difference was enormous: unlike their avant-garde colleagues in Europe, after 1920, and for decades to come, Mexican architects sought to connect their work to nationalist beliefs and historic buildings, rather than distance it from these things. This difference helps explain Mexico's still marginal position in most histories of modern architecture, the authors of which, for a variety of historical reasons, have privileged abstract, supposedly universal forms and aspirations over those with nationalistic undertones.

STRUCTURE AND SCOPE

Although *Modern Architecture in Mexico City* in some respects reads as a series of case studies, its narrative arc begins with the ascendancy of entwined beliefs about nationally specific and historical forms in the first two decades of the century, follows the rejections of historicism and historical allusion in the 1920s and 1930s, and concludes with the writings of the first histories of modern architecture around 1950, and the new uses of history in buildings whose architects explored subjectivity, alienation, and privacy, and, in the case of Barragán, challenged the idea of a nationally distinctive architecture altogether. The book's six chapters are organized into two parts in order to illuminate this trajectory. Analysis of buildings and texts written before the Mexican Revolution began in 1910, through the tumultuous postrevolutionary 1920s and 1930s, and into the middle of the century—periods that have often been separated historiographically—demonstrates the coeval development of the principles that undergirded modern architectural design and the preoccupation with national distinctiveness, and shows how representation advanced architects' aims. Parallel examination of built and written works reveals the ways in which architects explored ideas developed in texts, while the dialogue between the two media reveals the tensions in and tenuousness of the concept of nationally specific architecture as it evolved over five decades.

Chapter 1 establishes the historical and intellectual foundations of Mexican architectural modernism before 1920 by analyzing the writings of leading architects and their contributions to the invention of a national architectural history in the fifteen years after 1900. It provides the historiographical umbrella under which the buildings discussed in chapters 2 and 3 should be understood. Chapter 2 focuses on two works by Carlos Obregón Santacilia from the 1920s: the Mexican Pavilion at the 1922 International Exhibition in Rio de Janeiro and the Ministry of Health Building in Mexico City (1925–29). It examines Obregón Santacilia's pioneering transition away from historicism to an approach characterized by the manipulation of architectural elements to consciously represent forms associated with older buildings in compositions that were unambiguously new. The chapter argues that Obregón Santacilia established the pattern of conveying architectural Mexicanness by representing architectural elements associated with Mexican colonial buildings. Through his collaboration with the sculptor Hans Pillig and the painter and folk art promoter Roberto Montenegro, Obregón helped create in architecture a distinctively national iconography, which, by being full legible only to an audience knowledgeable about "Mexican" forms, advanced the idea of national distinctiveness in Mexican architecture.

Chapter 3 examines the ways that Juan Segura, at his enormous Venustiano Carranza Workers' Park and recreation center (1929), refined Obregón Santacilia's approach by using colonial architectural elements pictorially and explicitly as ornament, advanced the development of the modern facade as a representational site, and revealed a nascent, collective doubt about the project of creating a national modern architecture. The chapter positions the park in relation to one of Mexico's major histories of architecture, *Iglesias de México* (1924–27), which was a collaborative work undertaken by artists, historians, and photographers and funded by the federal government, as well as to debates about the proper style for the 1929 Mexican Pavilion at the Ibero-American Exposition in Seville. Considering the park in the context of the nationalistic performances that took place there, it also shows how beliefs about a national architecture came to be associated with reform programs aimed at the urban working class and indigenous groups.

In many ways 1929 marked a turning point in Mexican architecture, and it is a turning point in *Modern Architecture in Mexico City*. Thereafter, many new buildings in the capital were notable for their designers' apparent rejections of architectural history. Chapter 4 examines Juan O'Gorman's replacement of historical references with allusions to vernacular and popular forms and his pictorial repurposing of elements in Le Corbusier's buildings and responses to his writings in the pair of houses for Diego Rivera and the elementary schools he designed for the Ministry of Education. Although in some respects these buildings marked a dramatic break with precedent, they also bridged works of the 1920s, with their colonial allusions, and the celebrated projects of midcentury, when abstraction became more important and references to pre-Hispanic architecture increased. Exploring O'Gorman's work as a painter, his personal connections to colonial buildings, his response to landscape, and the influence of his mentor, the chapter analyzes the key publication on the elementary schools, *Escuelas primarias* (1933), to show how O'Gorman's buildings were constructed symbolically by photographers and their patron with respect to issues of modernization, architectural history, and rural landscapes. The chapter also examines the schools' links to high Mexican muralism and to popular *pulquería* (working-class bars that served pulque) painting, which was itself understood as a product the country's bicultural history.

Chapters 5 and 6 deal with what many architects and critics regarded as the long-awaited, full flourishing of modern architecture in Mexico around midcentury in two very different projects—the enormous campus of the National Autonomous University of Mexico (UNAM; 1948–53) and Luis Barragán's house for himself (1947)—and with architects' reactions to modernism as historical. Together they present the climax of the story—at UNAM, where many of the problems examined in earlier chapters of *Modern Architecture in Mexico City* coalesced—and its denouement—evident in the doubts about "Mexican" architecture that del Moral and Arai expressed as they worked on the campus, and the complete rejection of the idea of national architecture in Luis Barragán's house. Chapter 5 considers UNAM in the context of the rise in the 1940s of interest in the symbolic potential of landscape to convey nativism and to the robust debate about the relationships between architecture and the other arts. It also examines the campus in relation to the first histories of modern architecture, published around 1950, which codified José Villagrán García as the "father" of Mexican modernism. This new historiographical context serves as the background against which, in chapter 6, I analyze Barragán's house. Considering the building experientially, along with the architect's own statements about his work (which he claimed was autobiographical), and the responses of friends, critics, and historians to it, the chapter foregrounds his status as both an insider and outsider of the profession, and discusses the tremendous popularity of his work internationally in order to show the limits of the multidecade project of grafting "national" meaning onto historically evocative forms.

Doubts about how modernism, politics, and the core cultural narrative of mestizaje could entwine in architecture were evident in O'Gorman's work in the 1930s. They became clear in the late 1940s and early 1950s, particularly in historical and theoretical essays by del Moral and Arai, who concluded that some of the central assumptions on which explanations of national exceptionalism and cultural fusion rested—notably artistic integration and harmonious connectedness of modern people to ancient indigenous culture—were tenuous at best. Calling for deeper inquiry into the nature of history, with their perceptive reflections on modern Mexicans' connections to and differences from both Europeans and preconquest people, Arai and del Moral, perhaps without meaning to, threatened the foundations on which the project of twentieth-century Mexican cultural nationalism was based. The comparably minor place these two architects have occupied in histories of Mexican architecture until now becomes notable when viewed in this light. Barragán's refusal to participate in the nationalization of modern architecture—his disavowal of national specificity in architecture, his very limited involvement with public projects, his self-promotion in foreign venues, combined with his close study of colonial and vernacular precedents, and a house that, in the way it materialized the dynamics of disappearance, invited viewers to think about image-making and self-presentation—challenged the idea of "Mexican" architecture even more deeply.

PART I

COLONIAL CONCEPTS FOR MODERN MESTIZOS

FIGURE 1.1. Henry Greenwood Peabody, *House of the Count of Santiago*, published in Sylvester Baxter, *Spanish-Colonial Architecture in Mexico* (1901).

CHAPTER ONE

HISTORY, PHOTOGRAPHY, AND THE INVENTION OF MEXICAN ARCHITECTURE

> The Spanish-Colonial architecture of New Spain represents not only the first, but the most important development of the depictive arts in the New World. . . . With its auxiliary arts, Sculpture and Painting decoratively employed, the architecture of Mexico illustrates the richest aesthetic movement that has yet had its course in the Western Hemisphere.
> —Sylvester Baxter, *Spanish-Colonial Architecture in Mexico*, 1901

Drawing attention to the singularity and quality of Mexican colonial architecture, and its close relationship to the other arts, Sylvester Baxter thus began the first major illustrated history of Mexican colonial architecture. In it he documented buildings in twelve states built between the sixteenth and early nineteenth centuries, cataloged works at the edge of Mexico City, and many in the capital's historic center at a time when architects feared for its survival as they saw its buildings demolished and decay. Architectural drawings by the U.S. architect Bertram Grosvenor Goodhue appeared alongside Baxter's analysis and filled the first of the book's ten volumes; the other nine consisted of 150 individual plates of photographs by Henry Greenwood Peabody.[1] Peabody's images of Mexico City showed a metropolis that differed dramatically from the one that came into being just a few decades later, when skyscrapers began to dwarf restored eighteenth-century palaces and the historic center was eclipsed as the locus of pioneering architecture and planning that it had been for centuries by new suburbs to the south and west. While Peabody's photographs bolstered Baxter's claims they also revealed that the owners of great colonial works did not hold them in the high esteem that Baxter did. His pictures of the House of the Count of Santiago de Calimaya, a splendid work by Francisco Guerrero y Torres south of the main plaza, or Zócalo, revealed a building partially covered in nineteenth-century commercial signs (see figure 1.1). Inside, temporary structures with variegated metal roof panels cluttered the central patio, obscuring the ground-level arcade and making it impossible to see the space as a whole (see figure 1.2). In another image taken at the corner of Monterilla and Don Juan Manuel streets a large sign

FIGURE 1.2. Peabody, *House of the Count of Santiago.* View of the patio.

reading "El Lazo Mercantil" wrapped around the corner of the once-splendid palace; large awnings obscured nearly all of the ground floor on one side of the building; and a tangle of telegraph and electrical wires, poles, and a lamp hung above the street (see figure 1.3).

In nearly every instance, Peabody's photographs were highly detailed, technically excellent, and unsentimental. Closely keyed to Baxter's text, they recorded facades and patios; naves, domes, and towers; and exceptional interior works including altarpieces, pulpits, choir stalls, tapestries, and paintings (see figure 1.4). Each plate included on the back a label that identified the building, the approximate date of its construction, its style, the name of its architect, and a brief explanation of the building's significance. This organization made it possible to learn a great deal about many Mexican colonial buildings by looking only at the plates and turning them over in a far quicker process—which would likely have appealed to architects and readers whose native language was not English—than reading Baxter's long paragraphs. The publication of the photographs as discrete plates with

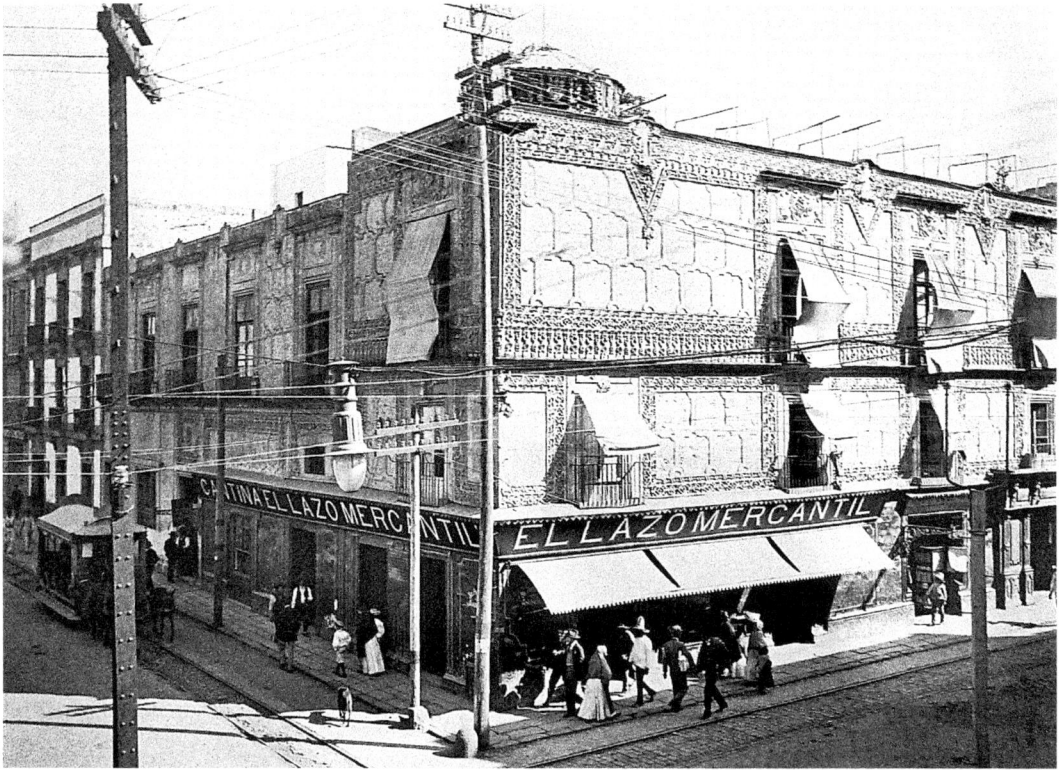

FIGURE 1.3. Peabody, *House in the Calle de Monterilla.*

detailed identifications reinforced the singularity of each building, but as a group the plates implied the relatedness of very different buildings to one another, whether they stood in the same city or were even built in the same century. In this way the plates functioned as a mini-collection of Mexican colonial works. Furthermore, because it cataloged buildings throughout the country, Baxter's book made it possible for architects in Mexico City to see buildings in places that they could not visit easily. As a work that consisted of many physical parts, in the way that it brought together in one place images of buildings that were hundreds of miles from one another and from Mexico City, it helped centralize symbolically the nation's architectural history and participated in the project of consolidating and recording national history that had begun even before independence.

In the Mexico City that Baxter and his associates chronicled, juxtapositions of class and culture were vivid and commonplace, facts of daily life in the capital. Although people rarely appeared in Peabody's photographs, when they did they served as striking reminders of the

FIGURE 1.4. Peabody, *The Pulpit, The Convent Church of Santa Clara*, Querétaro.

social differences that defined Mexico in 1900. In one particularly evocative detail, two men, walking in opposite directions along the sidewalk
in front of Number 5 Monterilla, passed at close range, one wearing a
modern European-style suit and bowler hat and the other the distinctive
white cotton shirt and wide-brimmed straw hat worn by Mexican peasants (see figure 1.5). In a city dotted with colonial palaces, cluttered with
the hardware of modernity, and controlled by a largely white elite that
admired European customs and forms, the presence of peasants—most
of whom were mixed-race or indigenous—literally and symbolically
challenged linear notions of history and progress. Multiple pasts, objects
that signified modernity, rural and urban clothing and customs, and
poor and rich people existed simultaneously and often side by side in the
same visual frame. Although Peabody did not exploit these evocative
juxtapositions to romanticize or comment on them, unlike many of the
photographers who flooded the city and countryside in the 1920s and
1930s in search of pregnant, picturesque, or avant-garde shots of peasants
and the objects of technological modernity, he nevertheless captured the
urban circumstances in which Mexican modern architecture was born.
The themes his pictures suggested—racial and social difference and
modernization against the backdrop of a rich cultural inheritance—
ran through discussions of modern architecture throughout the first
half of the century and animated Mexican visual culture generally.

Into the 1930s Mexican scholars considered Baxter's book the authoritative source on their country's colonial architecture and often
reproduced Goodhue's detailed plans of churches and convents in their
own texts. *Spanish-Colonial Architecture in Mexico* established the
approach adopted by other historians and architects who, like Baxter,
prioritized buildings' formal qualities, interpreted or meant them to
be culturally distinctive, and believed that an inherent flexibility of
meaning defined the use and reuse of architectural elements in Mexico. His text also suggested that representation—on buildings' facades
and wall surfaces, and in painting and sculpture—had defined colonial
works. The quantity and quality of Peabody's plates also showed how
photography could serve architecture and shape interpretations of it.
In later decades, as architects designed works that they and their patrons claimed were nationally distinctive, they reinterpreted many of
the characteristics that Baxter and the scholar-architects who followed
him in the 1900s identified in colonial buildings. Along with the new
histories, two other developments before and just after 1920 recentralized colonial architecture in discussions of Mexican architecture early
in the century: the rise of a preservation movement focused on colonial

FIGURE 1.5. Peabody, *House No. 5 in the Calle de Monterilla*. Detail with pedestrians.

buildings downtown and, following calls to create a "national" architecture, the ascendency of colonial revival–style architecture. All three endeavors were led by the architects who taught or influenced the creators of Mexico's first modern buildings in the mid-1920s.

ART AND INDIGENOUS MEXICO: HISTORY, REPRESENTATION, AND THE SHAPING OF A CAPITAL

Spanish-Colonial Architecture in Mexico was notable not only for its photographs and its form, but because its author attempted to define the character of Mexican colonial architecture in terms of social history and argued for architecture's relatedness to painting and sculpture. Baxter believed that colonial Mexican architecture was distinctively different from the buildings of peninsular Spain and those of the English colonies in North America, and that it was qualitatively and quantitatively more significant than that of any other country in the hemisphere. His claims also reflected concerns that had been central to Mexican architecture since the sixteenth century. Foremost among them was an awareness of geographical distance from Spain (and, later, France or Europe in general). From the earliest days of its colonial existence, through the boom decades in the eighteenth century, Mexico was necessarily understood by its Creole elite as other than Spain, but part of it, because of the political and economic disadvantages that its members experienced as residents of the colony.[2]

According to Baxter, Mexican colonial architecture reflected the political and cultural changes that occurred between the conquest and independence and he argued that these changes were visible in the fusion of Spanish forms and indigenous techniques (what some scholars later called "tequitqui"). At the core of his interpretation lay the idea that "indigenous" characteristics differentiated Mexican colonial visual culture fundamentally from that of Spain. Baxter noted that "the dominance of ideas, political and religious . . . naturally found realization in rich and impressive artistic shapes" and registered the distinctive transformations of European forms in the hands of indigenous craftspeople who "interpret[ed]" the foreign models even as they "retained more or less of the native dexterity, the manner of handicraft, and even the traditions of form that had been employed in their own peculiar types of architectural ornamentation."[3] Baxter identified the dome as the most obvious and widely adopted European element and the use of painted tile as a surface material as the most significant example of imported decoration. Like Spanish buildings, those in Mexico that were shaped by native "artist-artisans" had "a decided individuality" and "definite charm" that kept them from being "mere cop[ies] of the art of the Peninsula." Baxter argued that colonial art was "based upon a pre-existent aboriginal handicraft" that he viewed as "a most interesting phase of the spirit that pervaded the medieval handicraft of Europe." Claiming to see in such work the expression of "racial character," the author suggested that indigenous stonecutters, wood-carvers, metalworkers, tile makers, and potters "imparted to their work a palpable flavor of the native spirit." Baxter saw this "spirit" as a legacy of Aztec sculpture that he considered notable for its "excellent technique" and "bold freedom in design, with a large sweep in flowing movement as a conspicuous trait." Although he struggled to define the characteristics of Aztec-influenced colonial art formally, he spoke of the nature of indigenous Mexicans, who were "by no means savages, but belonged to a race that had advanced to a certain degree of civilization" and who had a "docile and adaptable nature."[4]

Baxter further claimed that the legacy of preconquest artistic culture was evident in the work of modern craftspeople, and that despite what he saw as a general decline in Mexican art (which he believed was controlled by "philistine[s]"), the endurance of indigenous artistic skill would shape a new era in Mexican art. He wrote of the present day: "There still survive the intelligence and the fine feeling with which so many workmen give themselves to their tasks, in spite of the scanty hire and slight appreciation—animated solely by the pleasure of producing something beautiful, even though of lowly utility. This indicates that when a new Renaissance at last dawns in Mexico—as some day it must . . . there will be ready at hand a fine body of skilled and tasteful workers."[5] Baxter did not suggest that the "Renaissance" would be led by indigenous or mixed-race craftspeople, but he did imply that these artisans were motivated by an inherent understanding of and yearning for artistic beauty. He envisioned a future that would, like the sixteenth century, be shaped by craftspeople whose ancestors were more likely to have been Aztecs than Spaniards.

THE IDEA OF CHURRIGUERESQUE ARCHITECTURE

The formal fusion that so intrigued the historian had a parallel, he suggested, in the architecture of Spain, which, at the time of the conquest, was itself characterized by "irregularity," or a "manifest lack of purity," and was notable for its "individuality, a strength of character."[6] Such language echoed closely sociological descriptions of Mexico's racial and cultural composition. Relying on the characterizations of seventeenth-century colonial baroque art by Mexican art historian Manuel G. Revilla, Baxter suggested that the Spanish facility in integrating forms typically viewed as stylistic opposites explained the formal success of the cathedrals of Mexico and Puebla.[7] But the most important manifestation of stylistic synthesis in Mexico was found in Churrigueresque architecture. Long before Baxter wrote, the ornamental eighteenth-century style had inspired strong reactions in peninsular critics who saw it as uncontrolled and subversive. After 1900 it regularly attracted special attention and even enraged some architects and critics because of its characteristic prioritization of the

FIGURE 1.6. Lorenzo Rodríquez, Sagrario Metropolitano, ca. 1749–69.

visual effects of surface decoration over ornament used intentionally to emphasize structure. The typical Churrigueresque altarpiece, such as the Altar of the Kings in the Mexico City Cathedral (ca. 1725), was made of carved gilt wood, covered in sculptural decoration, had inverted pyramidal piers (*estípites*), niches, and was lavishly decorated with figural sculptures (plate 2). Mexico City's most important Churrigueresque facade was that of the Sagrario Metropolitano (ca. 1749–69; figure 1.6), and while it was not gold, it was as ornamental and unconcerned with structural logic as any altarpiece. Although adjoined to it, the Sagrario departed radically in form and color from the cathedral, whose "correctly" used elements seemed stiff and unimaginative in comparison (plate 3). Conflating the Churrigueresque style's all-over decoration, which occasionally had vegetal motifs, with a fantasy of tropical Mexico, Baxter linked the style to the natural setting foreigners often associated with the country, and to its people. Explaining objections to the style he wrote that the "riotous luxuriance of its imaginative quality—akin to the entangled profusion of a tropical forest where the interlaced vegetation is starred with vivid blossomings, fantastically adorned with clinging orchids, and the air is heavy with rich perfumes—was followed early in the present [nineteenth] century by what seems to have been almost a fanatical rage for its extermination."[8]

Following the establishment of the Academy of San Carlos in 1783, and the ascendancy of officially sponsored neoclassicism, many Churrigueresque buildings were destroyed. In condemning their loss and replacement with "lifeless altars of affectedly classic form whose air of tawdry decorum has destroyed all the charm of church interiors in Mexico today,"[9] Baxter drew attention to the first systematic campaign of architectural demolition since the conquest. Led, Baxter believed, by Manuel Tolsá, Mexico's most celebrated neoclassical architect and one of the founders of the academy, the anti-Churrigueresque crusade nearly amounted to an attack on colonial Mexico itself, Baxter implied. The association of the style with the country went even deeper in Revilla's estimation. According to him Churrigueresque architecture had "its birth among a people profoundly religious, and in an epoch where faith was still intense . . . to an extraordinary degree it became an expression of Catholic mysticism, as did the Gothic in the middle ages."[10]

Baxter's readers learned that the Churrigueresque was a national style characterized by a profusion of surface decoration and dependent on the other arts for dramatic effects, and that it emerged from and flourished in a country with distinctive culture and nature. Baxter seized upon Revilla's notion of the ensemble and used it to help explain the relationships between architecture, painting, and sculpture in colonial buildings.[11] Individual artworks were subsumed into a stunning, visually unified architectural surface so ornate that it could be difficult even to differentiate sculpture and architecture. At its finest, a Churrigueresque altarpiece created a totalizing visual experience: "when ornament is lavishly employed, the impression made is largely due to the effect of the decorated surface as a whole."[12] He remarked on the static, conventionalized forms of colonial sculpture and devoted twenty-six pages to painting, reproducing from Revilla's book a long list of the names of colonial artists. In Baxter's view, mural-scaled colonial painting was site-specific and architectural, and he wrote that "these huge pictures were usually designed with special reference to some definite wall surface to be covered, and the effect was consequentially architectural, rather than that of arbitrary embellishment with 'hung' pictures."[13] Peabody, and later Guillermo Kahlo and Antonio Cortés, captured the effects Baxter described in several of their photographs, most notably those of the sacristies and the choir in the Mexico City Cathedral. Twice in his discussion Baxter conflated the wall with architectural or painterly elements—space and surface. In his reading, colonial walls were most often "covered," in a process in which painting transformed implicitly "empty" spaces or blank surfaces into parts of a vibrant ensemble that was simultaneously architectural, sculptural, and painterly. His assessment subordinated the other arts to architecture, but made them all mutually dependent, and his argument anticipated by fifty years those that artists and architects made about artistic integration.

ARCHITECTURE WORTHY OF THE *PATRIA*

In the decades after Baxter's book appeared Federico Mariscal, a Mexican architect, professor, theorist, and the most influential architectural historian of his time, further nationalized and extolled colonial buildings. In the 1910s he introduced a generation of architects to their country's colonial architectural history, urging them to study it as closely as they examined the Renaissance and Beaux-Arts buildings that were the focus of nearly all their training. Mariscal was also one of the first and most forceful advocates for the preservation of colonial buildings. Under his tutelage architects who would radically transform Mexican architecture in the decades to come, most notably Carlos Obregón Santacilia, learned to copy colonial elements and ornament.

In October 1913, Mariscal gave the first of eleven lectures at the Universidad Popular Mexicana in Mexico City on colonial architecture. They were published in 1915 as a single volume, *La patria y la arquitectura nacional*, in which Mariscal explained why colonial architecture constituted "national" art, and linked it to the social and cultural development in Mexico. Rooted in his readings of Baxter, Revilla, and scholars of national history, geography, and art, but motivated by the demolition of colonial buildings in Mexico City, Mariscal described the evolution of building types, discussed the formal and spatial arrangements of exemplary works, and implored his audience to join in the effort to save them. Over the course of the lectures he showed 550 slides, but relatively few images were published in the book, and most that were illustrated facades. In his text, Mariscal classified buildings typologically—"from the *casa de vecindad* [a modest multifamily residential building] to the palace"—and he included buildings' addresses, making the book usable as a guide.[14] An appendix listed the names of the architects, sculptors, and painters who worked in the cathedral and Sagrario.

Mariscal hoped that his talks and the book would inspire in his audience "love" of colonial architecture and the study of national architectural history. In his emotional appeal he linked architecture to patriotic sentiment claiming that "among the elements that constitute *la Patria* are surely the house in which we live and those in which our parents live, our friends, the representatives of our Government and all our citizens." He urged Mexicans to "love the buildings of the soil on which we were born," and defined national architecture, which he referred to as "national architectonic art," as buildings that were "faithful expression[s] of our life, our customs, and in sympathy with our landscape . . . our soil and our climate."[15] Notably, Mariscal did not explain "national architectonic art" in specifically architectural terms beyond suggesting that buildings in this category were suitable to Mexican culture, customs, and climate. "National architectonic art" was thus an extraordinarily broad term, potentially encompassing an enormous variety of buildings and styles. By failing to specify what formal characteristics made a building "Mexican," Mariscal opened the door to a nearly infinite number of interpretations of what national architecture was.

Eliding national character and architectural history, Mariscal argued that colonial architecture had emerged in tandem with postconquest Mexican culture. He wrote: "The Mexican citizen of today, he who forms the majority of the population, is the result of a material, moral, and intellectual of mix of the Spanish race and the aboriginal races that populated Mexican soil. Thus, Mexican architecture must be that which grew and developed during the three viceregal centuries in which 'the Mexican' was constituted and which was developed later in independent life."[16] In linking architecture, national history, and the emergence of the mestizo, Mariscal articulated a new theory of architecture that proceeded from Mexican circumstances, drew attention to a cultural condition that was distinctive to Spanish-speaking America (and pronounced in Mexico), and, for the first time, suggested a redirection away from Renaissance and Baroque models. Like his avant-garde colleagues in Europe he sought to deemphasize academic classicism in order to promote the design of buildings that were better suited to circumstances different from those of Renaissance Italy and nineteenth-century France. While most progressive architects in western Europe in the 1910s and 1920s attempted to key their buildings to industrial modernity and rejected historicist styles, for Mariscal updating architecture required reconnecting with historical forms.

The destruction of colonial works in the center of the capital and their replacement with Renaissance Revival– and Second Empire–style buildings motivated Mariscal's injunctions to study, love, and save old buildings. In the first decade of the twentieth century countless colonial palaces and some churches were leveled to make way for modern department stores, banks, theaters, and office buildings. A new taste among the ruling class for the forms and fashions of industrialized countries, especially France, and the arrival of foreign architects who received important commissions from the Mexican government accompanied rapid industrialization in Mexico and the influx of international capital from western Europe and the United States in the late nineteenth and early twentieth centuries. Mariscal lamented what he viewed as the ascendancy of "exotic influences" in architecture and the construction of buildings that could stand anywhere.[17] Among such works were two unfinished monumental modern palaces, the Palace of Fine Arts (see figure 1.7; Palacio de Bellas Artes) designed by Italian architect Adamo Boari (with whom Mariscal studied), which, despite having "localizing" decorative details, recalled vividly the Petite Palais at the 1901 Paris Exposition, and the new Legislative Palace, Émile Bernard's giant domed classical building, which was obviously modeled on the United States capitol. The architect's concern about the disappearance of colonial buildings was also tinged with nostalgia and the anxiety that as new forms and institutions appeared some aspect of what was essentially "Mexican" about the country was slipping away. He claimed that he and his contemporaries had an "obligation to leave to our children" their "heritage," and he called on people in many fields—"the worker, the businessman, the proprietor, and more than they, the builder, and even more still, the architect"—to preserve the past. To their efforts would be added those of the "artist, painter, sculptor, musician or poet" who would keep from "being lost completely" those things that "of all the constitutive elements of the Patria, [were] perhaps the most difficult to recover." Furthermore, he claimed, "the architect himself must recognize . . . the necessity of acquiring philosophical-social knowledge in order to realize fully his mission."[18]

Long before the social tenets of the Mexican Revolution were clear, codified, or propagated, Mariscal linked architecture and society, not out of fealty to a specific political agenda, but because of his belief that architecture reflected distinctive social and cultural characteristics—an idea that he may have absorbed from his reading of European architectural theory and Baxter's history. National architectonic art

FIGURE 1.7. Adamo Boari, Palacio de Bellas Artes, begun 1904.

included, he claimed, "the great constructions destined for the education of the new race that was emerging: the Mexican." Although
the "new Mexican" was a product of the blending of two races, it was
Spanish colonial educational institutions that formed fundamentally
the character of the new culture, instilling "the religion and morality of
Christ, and individual initiative."[19] Mariscal's ideas paralleled and were
informed by discussions he and other members of the group of intellectuals, the Ateneo de la Juventud (Athenaeum of Youth), had about
the cultural rejuvenation of Mexico through humanistic pursuits, in
opposition to what they regarded as the stultifying effects of positivism
associated with the regime of President Porfirio Díaz.[20] Embedded in
Mariscal's formulation was the issue at the heart of postrevolutionary
social theory, which many architects would consider later—the question of how to acknowledge and integrate indigenous culture while
promoting the habits and customs inherited from Europe. The two
realms that Mariscal linked—the national and the social—would remain entwined in Mexican architectural culture for decades.

ART AND ARCHITECTS

Also embedded in *La patria y la arquitectura nacional* was an ambition to order and strengthen architecture as a profession. Mariscal hoped that architects would use their knowledge of architectural history to improve their own work and thereby raise the status of architects. His attempt to discipline history and his colleagues echoed long-standing efforts by his architect brother, Nicolás (who was also a member of the Ateneo de la Juventud), to regulate and promote architecture in the face of what they felt to be public misunderstanding of the special work architects did. In his 1901 lecture, "The Development of Architecture in Mexico," Nicolás discussed nineteenth-century Mexican architecture, paying special attention to the evolution of architectural training, the influence of European architects, and the works of the greatest architects of the century. At the core of his argument was an attempt to distinguish architecture and engineering by defining architecture as an art. Interested in and respectful of science, Nicolás was especially troubled by the confusion of architecture and engineering that emerged in the 1870s, when the title "engineer architect" was used to refer to professionals who at other times were known as architects.[21] The conflation of the terms stemmed from shifting academic norms, which had been resolved by the turn of the century, but Nicolás perceived disastrous long-term consequences of the elision of the two concepts. At stake in the confusion, he felt, was the concept of art and its role in society. Nicolás defended architecture by insisting that it, unlike engineering, was art. While he acknowledged the close relationship between architecture and engineering, which he said were linked by mathematics, he claimed that they were fundamentally different because "beauty constitutes the essence of architecture as a liberal art." In other parts of his essay he linked architecture with poetry, music, painting, and sculpture, all of which had at their cores the capacity to "influence" the spirit and provoke "aesthetic emotion." Art was the "mirror of a civilization."[22] The Mariscal brothers' eagerness to raise the status of architectural practice and to save historical buildings explains why both often used the term "architectonic art" rather than just "architecture." Shaped by the study of colonial buildings in which architecture, painting, and sculpture were integrated, and having emerged in response to concerns about preservation and the public perception of architecture, the Mariscals' emphasis on the art of architecture further laid the groundwork for the postrevolutionary impulse to closely link architecture with other arts, especially in ways that were easily visible on buildings' facades, and anticipated the fiery debates about architectural "functionalism" in the 1930s.

Just as Federico later linked architectural history with the nation, Nicolás joined art and architecture to a concept of nationality that was exceptionally fluid and far-reaching. Like his brother, Nicolás urged architects to shape a new and vital "national" art and to work to instill in the public "good taste . . . for the progress of architecture for the good of society and la patria."[23] Ten years later, as the Mexican Revolution was beginning, Nicolás spoke with frustration about the absence of a national art and called on his colleagues to forge one. Using "nation" to refer to political nationhood in Mexico, rather than all of Mexico since the conquest or before, he said, "we have no national art, there is no Mexican art, just as there is no Danish art, nor Canadian, nor Chilean, nor Guatemalan art. The nation of Mexico is essentially a disciple of the great teachers of history." Nicolás linked the failure to create a true national art to a variety of political and social conditions and ultimately called on his colleagues, in opposition to "aristocratic favoritism," to become "apostles of national aesthetic culture" and to "give all glory to our patria."[24] The distinction he made between "nation" and "patria," like the close link drawn between architecture and the other arts, would have profound consequences for subsequent generations of architects. Whatever the failures of the politicians and political structures of Mexico since 1810, and despite its failure to create "national" art, architects could still commit themselves wholeheartedly to patria—to a concept that encompassed far more than 100 years of borrowed artistic and political forms. Broad and flexible, "patria" could fold into "Mexico," any number of ideas, influences, and forms.

Together, in their lectures and writings in the first fifteen years of the twentieth century, Federico and Nicolás Mariscal articulated six concepts that would inform Mexican architecture starting in the 1920s: that national architecture was colonial architecture; that the modern character of Mexico was born during the colonial period, when Spanish and indigenous cultures met and mixed; that architecture was an art, related in significant ways to painting and sculpture; that architecture reflected society; and that despite the weakness of the nation as a political construct, architects should aspire in their work to serve la patria. This potent group of ideas inspired some of Mexico's foremost modern architects and, although in some respects it was like modernist ideas about architecture elsewhere, it distinguished Mexican theory and provided architects an intellectually robust, but highly flexible, nationally specific basis from which to work.

COLONIAL FORMS AND CLASSICAL LESSONS

In his prologue to a collection of Jesús T. Acevedo's writings, published posthumously in 1920 as *Disertaciones de un arqitecto*, Federico Mariscal said of his late colleague that despite having built and written very little, he "influenced decisively the transformation and progress of Architecture in Mexico."[25] In several lectures delivered before his death in 1918, and in the drawing courses he taught at the National Preparatory School, Acevedo, the most eloquent of colonial architecture's defenders, amplified the Mariscals' calls for its preservation and its value to architects as they created new buildings. He stressed as well architecture's embeddedness in Mexico's social and even racial histories. In romantic tones he encouraged architects to look admiringly at buildings from different eras and discover in them principles that might inform modern design.

Like Mariscal, Acevedo linked architecture to its historical context and insisted on the importance of understanding the conditions that gave rise to colonial buildings. Poetically framing Mexico's colonial past, in a 1914 lecture he evoked Felix Parra's two famous oil paintings, *Episodes of the Conquest* (1877) and *Friar Bartolomé de las Casas* (1875) as he explained that early colonial Mexico's relationship to architecture was defined first and foremost by destruction. He celebrated the transmission of European artistic techniques to indigenous Mexicans shortly after the conquest and the infusion of indigenous forms into an emergent colonial art. Observing that although the new art was based on foreign models, he wrote that it contained "a new gesture, an unexpected mold, a special color" and that during the colonial era "our Mexico noted its [own] idiosyncrasy."[26] As if anticipating the elision of workers and peasants in postrevolutionary ideology, Acevedo referred to the indigenous artist as a "Mexican worker" and believed that he had "an exquisite ability to work with refinement and delicacy," characteristics he linked to Asia, presumably thinking of the long history of human migration to the Americas. Like Baxter he traced facility with ornament and decoration to modern workers and native people who made folk art: those who with "brown hands paint jugs and ceramic dishes."[27]

Acevedo also addressed the legacy of classicism in Mexico, the character of architecture inherited from Spain, and went further than any of his colleagues in suggesting that the study of Mexican colonial buildings might help give rise to a new formal language. Of classical architecture he observed, "the examples that the conquistadors were able to bring were very far from those that made of Rome the first museum of classical architecture. The orders did not arrive in these lands with their original purity."[28] Acevedo used the notion of distance metaphorically and literally to emphasize formal and geographic difference. In Mexico the orders were literally far from Rome and looked different from those in that city. Not only had European forms arrived in Mexico already "impure," as Baxter had also observed, but the architecture that emerged in early colonial Mexico was shaped by radically different conditions from those that had given rise to buildings in Europe.

Acevedo's understanding of classicism was more nuanced than that of most twentieth-century Mexican architects. His teacher, Emile Bernard, taught him to regard architectural history in the ways that many European modernists did, and like them, to appreciate the principles of classical architecture rather than attempt to replicate its forms. More explicit in his discussion of historical time than any of his Mexican colleagues, Acevedo believed in the importance of understanding, almost abstractly, the relationship between past and present. Explaining the importance of studying history, he wrote, "rare are those who live in accordance with their time, those who, filled with living curiosity, are interested in the present time of the world, always related, although in fugitive apparitions, to epochs of greater or less distance."[29] Responding to those who, already in the early 1910s, criticized the study of classical models Acevedo observed: "No danger exists, as has been childishly suggested by some, that the imitation of classical works will detract from the distinction of the devoted student. Learn in order to measure and compare; to awaken a love of sobriety and of sound judgment; to take pleasure in study from the first day and for all of life the delicate transitions of form in each being and each thing."[30] As nineteenth-century European architectural theorists had, Acevedo recognized in the study of history the potential to gain insight into the nature of change. Architectural history could be mined for its insights into evolution; it showed that just as classicism was different in Spain than it had been in Rome, it was yet again transformed in colonial Mexico. In the 1920s Obregón Santacilia would be the first to realize the formal implications of that way of understanding history. Decades later, as they considered the relationship between history and new designs, Enrique del Moral and Alberto Arai would return to the themes of temporality and geographical difference that Acevedo had raised.

Attuned to change as a consequence of cultural and territorial difference, like others Acevedo saw in colonial Mexican buildings the inheritance of formal blending: "Spain could not give us a single pure style because it had imported all styles." In Mexico this situation gave rise to a "picturesque mishmash of styles, a respectable and [an] exemplary knowledge of the art of building." Architects should study colonial buildings and the conditions in which they emerged, he said, "in order to be prepared to continue some day so noble a tradition." Vividly and tenderly describing his own encounters with Mexican colonial buildings in the capital, he suggested that they might be the source of a new architecture: "Passing through the streets of the city of my birth, in the silence of the night, when you can best see the silhouettes of buildings and arrangements of composition, I have asked myself if our colonial style, made of bits and pieces, could in turn constitute an exemplary style, if its study could become an indispensible discipline and if through that, not withstanding the changes of customs since the beginnings of the nineteenth century, it could provide the substance of evolution and ultimately current application."[31] For Acevedo, thorough appreciation of colonial architecture was deeply experiential and even personal, just as pre-Columbian architecture would be for Arai decades later. He urged architects to look at the city, and especially the eighteenth-century churches and squares around them, and he privileged looking at the buildings themselves over reading architectural theory or even studying drawings: "the pinnacles of the Sagrario, the walls of the Enseñanza, the plazas of Santo Domingo, Vizcaínas and of Regina say more than all of our books. Our admirable Sagrario Metropolitano, masterpiece of architecture, as much for its skillful disposition, as for the delicious ornamentation of its facades, enthralls profoundly."[32]

DOCUMENTATION AND DEMOLITION

Other than through the efforts of architect-historians, knowledge of colonial architecture expanded prior to 1920 through the work of the National Museum and in scholarship commissioned by the government. In the first decade of the century, federal institutions and the documents they produced helped lay the groundwork for preservation programs and contributed to the development of architectural history as a discipline. Federico Mariscal's entwined projects of education and preservation were taken up by a variety of government entities and helped along by the work of two important architectural photographers.

Although colonial buildings were not fully protected with meaningful legislation and oversight until 1938, efforts to preserve them were under way in the 1910s when the federal government created the first of several new institutions to safeguard buildings. In 1914 the Law on the Conservation of Historical and Artistic Monuments and Areas of Natural Beauty was passed, which kept publicly owned buildings from being acquired by private entities and required that private owners receive permission from the National Inspectorate of Artistic and Historical Monuments, a division of the Ministry of Education, before modifying their buildings.[33] More stringent regulations were not passed until the 1930s when a series of laws gave increasing authority to departments within the Ministry of Education and gave more specific protections to colonial architecture.[34]

As early as the mid-nineteenth century, architectural and cultural history in Mexico had been closely tied to images. The first efforts to preserve buildings had focused on preconquest architecture and archaeological sites and were often directed by the National Museum. Founded in 1825 by the federal government of the newly independent nation, the museum had several names over the course of the nineteenth century, but during that time became an important repository of information on images of the nation's architectural history. In the 1860s researchers used photographs to document Mexico's pre-Hispanic architecture and its indigenous people, and the National Museum displayed many of these pictures, often in cases alongside artistic and ethnographic objects.[35] Scholars in the museum used photographs in their research on codices, manuscripts, and various objects, and museum activities were often documented photographically. In 1880 the museum created the position of draftsman-photographer, which was held for some time by the famous landscape painter José María Velasco who, along with outside photographers, documented the museum's collections. The result was a large number of photographs, including postcards, of Mexican art historical and archaeological objects in the museum's collection that circulated in Mexico around the turn of the century.

In part because there was simply so much to document, particularly the many major archaeological sites far from Mexico City, photographs and drawings provided a valuable means of cataloging and consolidating knowledge of the country's architectural past in the capital. Although the federal government funded such projects, they were not necessarily propagandistic or conceived of as nationalist endeavors. In the late nineteenth and early twentieth centuries many were carried out by professional historians, curators, and photographers who, in the absence of reliable alternative sources of funding, had to rely on government sponsorship to complete their research. As influential in shaping professional and public perceptions of colonial architecture as the works of Baxter and Mariscal, were the photographs taken by Guillermo Kahlo and those shot by photographers employed by the National Museum in preparation for exhibits and publications for the 1910 centennial celebrations. In addition to the museum's regular photographers, beginning in 1907 Antonio Cortés, curator of Industrial Art at the museum, took nearly six hundred photographs of colonial churches in six states. While Kahlo's are most significant for their breadth and number, those by Cortés published by the National Museum in 1914 in *La arquitectura en México: Iglesias* are remarkable for the ways they emphasized architectural detail, surface, and the relationships between architecture, painting, and sculpture.

Long overshadowed by his famous daughter, Frida, Guillermo Kahlo was the most important architectural photographer in Mexico in the early twentieth century. Having begun his career documenting new construction, from 1904 to 1908, at the direction of the finance minister, José Yves Limantour, Kahlo visited twenty-six towns in thirteen states methodically documenting churches, convents, and palaces, all owned by the federal government. From his travels Kahlo printed 1,926 photographs, many of which were reproduced in the monumental twenty-two-volume work, *Templos de propiedad federal*, which appeared in 1909. It is likely that given the extraordinary cost and exceptional size of the book, very few copies were made and that its circulation was limited to the very wealthy; however, a greatly condensed and presumably more accessible version, *Fotografías de templos de propiedad*, was published as well.[36]

The sheer number of photographs Kahlo took and the distances he covered distinguished his work. However, his oeuvre was not limited to colonial architecture, and his photographs of it were not as immediately influential as those of his colleagues nor did they participate as fully in constructing a narrative of Mexican architectural history. *Templos de propiedad federal* did not include an index or an explanatory introduction. Fundamentally a documentary work intended to inventory federal property, the project was apparently neither shepherded nor reviewed by architects or historians.[37] Seen in relation to Kahlo's total body of work in the first twenty years of the century, the images of colonial buildings are but one (especially important) group of photographs among many that document new and old architecture and industry in Mexico. In 1909–10 Kahlo worked for the Compañía Fundidora de Fierro y Acero de Monterrey shooting factories, mines, and industrial sites. Beginning in 1905 his photographs appeared in mainstream illustrated periodicals and helped introduce the general public to architecture of many different kinds. His pictures of colonial buildings did not reach a wide audience until the 1930s, when Manuel Toussaint and Dr. Atl published them in their six-volume *Iglesias de México*. In some respects Kahlo's photographs closely paralleled Peabody's and it is likely that Kahlo consulted Baxter's work as he prepared his own project. Unsurprisingly, many of the same buildings appear in the works of both photographers and in several cases the same buildings are shot from similar angles. Emphasizing facades, domes, and towers, and by framing most shots from a distance, both photographers created compositions that provided a general sense of a building rather than focusing on details.

More easily available and useful to Mexican architects in the 1910s than Kahlo's photographs were those of colonial churches taken by Antonio Cortés that were meant to be included in a book to be published by the National Museum as part of the Centennial Celebrations. Cortés began the project in 1907, but the volume was not ready in time for the Centennial. When it did appear in 1914 as *La arquitectura en México: Iglesias*, it broke new ground in the historiography of Mexican colonial architecture by being the first illustrated history published in Mexico devoted exclusively to buildings. Although it dealt with only seven religious buildings or complexes, the book presented them in exceptional photographic detail and included building histories and an overview of Mexican architectural history written by Genaro García, one of Mexico's foremost historians. As director of the National Museum, García continued to build the institution's impressive collection.

Under García's direction, Cortés visited the states of Queretaro, Guanajuato, Guerrero, Puebla, Oaxaca, and Mexico—all sites of exceptional ecclesiastical buildings—on three trips. He took 590 photographs, 130 of which were included in the book. In his introduction he explained that the volume was intended to improve "national education" and showed "our most characteristic buildings."[38] He described architectural forms far more precisely than Mariscal did but, like the architect, he framed colonial architectural history in social terms. Unlike his colleague, he did not find in them evidence of cultural mixing. The first sentence of his introduction included no mention of architecture, but offered an interpretation of postconquest history that was the opposite of Mariscal's: "The Spanish conquest destroyed not only the autonomy of the indigenous races that then populated our patria, but also their entire civilization: religious, political and civil institutions, customs, arts, and sciences were supplanted by European civilization: there was not, strictly speaking, a mixing of both cultures."[39] García spoke from the perspective of the dispassionate historian who saw little around him, in the built environment, in social structures and norms, and in numerous postconquest texts, that suggested true cultural blending. The museum he ran documented ruins and traces of cultures that had disappeared or, at best, were so thoroughly marginalized as to be insignificant as cultural drivers.

FIGURE 1.8. Antonio Cortés, San Francisco Acatepec, Puebla, eighteenth century, from Genaro García, *La arquitectura en México: Iglesias.*

García welcomed indigenous influence but he did not romanticize it. Struck by the "extraordinary solidity and colossal proportions" of preconquest buildings, he linked them to the landscape, claiming "that each temple resembled a small, truncated pyramidal mountain." His description calls to mind, as he surely intended, the great temples of the Sun and Moon at Teotihuacan, whose architects positioned them in provocative formal and spatial dialogue with the nearby mountains and volcanoes. There, solid and void (in the form of regular plazas and sky) were arranged in ways that powerfully dramatized humans' relationship to architecture and nature. Like his colleagues, he also emphasized the importance of the Churrigueresque style, and noted the significance of surface in it, the style's seeming "arbitrariness" and "hybrid character," as well as what he called Mexico's "immoderate love of ornament." He drew attention to Islamic influences on colonial architecture and praised "true originalities, like our Church of San Francisco in Acatepec,"[40] a church famous for its painted tile facade in the state of Puebla (figure 1.8; plate 4).

Cortés's photographs extended and elaborated García's argument and, unlike those by Peabody and Kahlo, were framed and selected not only for documentary purposes but also for focused study. Although the format of Peabody's plates made them suitable for studying many buildings rather generally, Cortés's focus on architectural detail and the number of images of each building included in the book made in-depth examination of the churches possible in an entirely new way. The relatively small parish church at Acatepec was documented in twenty-two photographs; thirty were devoted to the complex at Tepotzotlán; the church and chapel of Santo Domingo in Oaxaca was recorded in thirty-three (figure 1.9). The sheer number of images, many of them of the same object or part of the church, but taken from different angles or distances, suggested that they were shot and ordered by and for architectural experts attuned to the challenges of conveying completely a single building in one or a few photographs. Whether intentionally or not, by including in the final publication so many images of so few buildings, García powerfully affirmed the special status of architecture. Unlike painting, buildings could be known fully in photographs only gradually and through multiple images that conveyed their many parts. Because architectural knowledge required moving through a building and seeing its elements from different angles, it emerged, the book argued implicitly, differently from the way that knowledge of painting does. Furthermore, and in marked contrast to Kahlo's brief from Limantour, *La arquitectura en México: Iglesias* positioned the nation's colonial buildings not as pieces of real estate or state possessions, but as singular, multilayered works that were shaped by architects and sculptors, had their own histories, and belonged to recognizable national styles.

Photographs by Cortés and his colleagues enabled architects in the early twentieth century to see Mexican architecture in new ways. What they saw, primarily, were facades and the surfaces of walls, towers, and domes, enlivened by and inseparable from painting and sculpture. They saw in the great Churrigueresque buildings of the eighteenth century splendid altarpieces and retablo facades covered in superficial sculptural decoration. Images of sacristies and choirs showed magnificent wall-sized paintings fit into architectural frames arranged such that the picture and wall surface appeared to be one. A stunning fresco painted inside the dome of the Mexico City Cathedral seemed to fully meld to it. Towers and domes were clad in tile, which they knew from experience was painted in bright colors. While some early images do suggest spatial plasticity, such as Peabody's of Manuel Tolsá's magisterial staircase at the Palacio de Minería, the vast majority emphasized

FIGURE 1.9. Cortés, Church of Santo Domingo, Oaxaca, vault above the choir, eighteenth century, from García, *La arquitectura en Mexico: Iglesias*.

buildings' surfaces. Along with the texts of *La arquitectura en México: Iglesias*, *La patria y la arquitectura nacional*, and *Spanish-Colonial Architecture in Mexico*, the photographs encouraged architects to look at architecture around them in new ways and directed their looking. Those wandering around Mexico City and sympathetic to Mariscal's warnings about "imported" architecture would have registered that national specificity was communicated most effectively on buildings' exteriors. The nuances of species of classical revivals or eclectic combinations transforming downtown Mexico City might be discernible only to specialists, but nearly anyone with basic knowledge of Mexican colonial architecture would be able to differentiate the *tezontle* and *chi-*

luca palaces and churches of the eighteenth century from later works that could stand as comfortably in London, Paris, or New York.

Documenting, interpreting, and representing Mexico's colonial buildings as the first examples of real "Mexican" architecture, the first historians unintentionally provided a theoretical framework that politicians, mostly after the Mexican Revolution, could use to shore up their claims of advancing revolutionary national interests by sponsoring building projects. Of greater significance to the intellectual history of Mexican modernism was the influence of their histories on the pioneers of modernism in the 1920s, and later, on architects at mid-century, who, as the first generation of modern buildings became historical, reinvigorated Mexican architectural theory with writings that developed and departed from the early works in innovative and influential ways.

TRANSFORMING THE HISTORIC CENTER

In the first twenty-five years of the twentieth century, colonial buildings were recalled for architects and the public not only in photographs and texts but also by new buildings themselves. Having been inspired by histories of colonial architecture, and hired to design new buildings on sites in downtown Mexico City by government clients even before the end of the Díaz regime and the official preference for colonial revival architecture emerged in the early 1920s, architects created historicist buildings that in many cases so closely resembled their eighteenth-century neighbors that it was difficult to differentiate the old and new. Particularly notable was the addition to the Colegio de San Ildefonso by Samuel Chávez and Manuel Torres Torrija (1906–11). Housing the National University and the Bolivar Theater, with its red tezontle facade, multifoil window and door frames, and pairs of estípite columns framing the entrances, the building was nearly indistinguishable from its colonial neighbors. Around the same time, Manuel Gorozope undertook the renovation and expansion of City Hall (1906), which stood on the south side of the Zócalo (figure 1.10) Although its foundations dated to 1527, the building had been modified substantially in 1574 and almost entirely rebuilt in 1720–24 after having sustained considerable damage in the Corn Riots of 1692.[41] In 1900 the building had two stories, including a ground-level arcade. The fenestration pattern on the upper floor resembled that of other eighteenth-century palaces but was enlivened by pilasters that divided it into bays. Gorozope retained the ground-level arcade, added two stories, and used historicist ornament

FIGURE 1.10. City Hall, Mexico City, with addition and renovation by Manuel Gorozope, 1906. Photograph by Guillermo Kahlo.

to embellish the facade, creating a building that was considerably more ornate and imposing than it had been in the eighteenth century. As if to acknowledge the building's links to the early colonial period and its remaking two hundred years later, the architect alluded to sixteenth- and eighteenth-century forms: the uppermost included a gallery that opened to the plaza and evoked Mexican plateresque designs, but Gorozope dressed up the facade of the lower stories in gray Churrigue-resque-revival pilasters and window frames.

The City Hall was only the first important building on the Zóca-lo to receive a makeover in the twentieth century. In the next thirty years architects transformed the buildings around the square to create an even more visually coherent and monumental urban center. The re-made plaza was defined by its enormous scale and by the relative formal consistency of the buildings that surrounded it. By 1940 nearly all of the Zócalo's buildings were either actual colonial buildings or evocations of them. One of the most important changes took place in 1926–27, when Augusto Petriccioli added a third story to the National Palace, capped each of the three portals with a Churrigueresque-revival parapet, and refaced the building, restoring ornament that had been removed in the nineteenth century. On the ground level of the building, which runs the entire length of the east side of the Zócalo, Petroccioli retained the severe, unornamented wall surface and regular rectangular windows typical of the sober sixteenth-century Spanish style associated with architect Juan de Herrera. Like Gorozope's modifications, Petroccioli's evoked two distinct centuries of Mexican colonial history—the one in which the conquest occurred and that during which viceregal Mexico was at the height of its administrative power, flush with wealth from provincial mines, and during which collective consciousness of Mexico's cultural separateness from Spain became acute.

By raising the height of the buildings that framed it and reusing historical forms, architects made the Zócalo more monumental than it had ever been. They created a strongly defined center where several major buildings looked older than they were. Here national architectural history, interpreted in built form, was used to convey political power and create one of the most affecting urban spaces in the world. Notably the buildings around the Zócalo, although they are consistent in many ways, are not stylistically uniform, as the north side of the plaza, where the Cathedral and Sagrario stand, reveals most vividly. The viewer's sense that the buildings are truly colonial comes in part from their differences. By combining historical styles in individual buildings and shaping others in ways that put them in dialogue with existing ones but did not copy them exactly, the architects of the modern Zócalo created a space that was varied enough that it did not look like it had been designed all at once. More compelling than uniformity, difference was critical to the success of the remade space.[42] As if in response to Acevedo's assertion that Mexican architecture, and Spanish architecture before it, was characterized by accretion and modification, not purity, the modern Zócalo suggested gradual, but historic accumulation.

Federico Mariscal was one of the first architects to use colonial revival forms on new buildings in and near the center of the city. In 1917 he designed the Sostres y Dosal building (figure 1.11), a department store at the corner of Correo Mayor and the street now called Venustiano Carranza, two blocks southeast of the Zócalo. In its massing and pronounced rounded corner, the five-story building recalled Art Nou-

FIGURE 1.11. Federico Mariscal, Edificio Sostres y Dosal, 1917.

veau Porfirian shopping palaces, and its ground-level rustication and classicizing west portal echoed their Renaissance Revival counterparts. But Mariscal referred to eighteenth-century buildings in his treatment of the facade surface. He used H-shaped window frames familiar from baroque palaces, topped the building with a mixtilinear parapet, and between the third and fourth stories ran a course of blue and white tiles arranged in a zigzag pattern, which was repeated on the rounded portion of the uppermost story. There Mariscal placed three colonial revival windows, the central one of which was shaped like a six-pointed star.

The form of the window frames, the tile pattern, and the mixtilinear parapet strongly evoked the famous Chapel of the Well, known as El Pocito, designed by Francisco Guerrero y Torres in 1777–91 to mark the place where a well sprang up after the apparition of the Virgin of Guadalupe in Mexico City in 1531 (figure 1.12). The small, nearly circular chapel is one of the finest of all Mexican baroque buildings, and Mariscal had included a photograph and a plan of it that he reproduced from Baxter in his chapter on chapels in *La patria y la arquitectura nacional*. Made of tezontle and chiluca, the building was famous for the blue-and-white zigzag tile pattern that decorated its large dome, cupola, and parapet, as well the smaller versions of these elements on the rounded antechamber. Six windows framed in six-pointed stars enlivened the facade of the antechamber. At the Sostres y Dosal building Mariscal reinterpreted the rounded Porfirian corner—one of the most distinctive forms in the turn-of-the-century historic center—with reference to El Pocito. The architect drew further attention to the corner by flanking it in vertically running patterns of blue, yellow, and white tiles. Decorative sculpture, generally evocative of eighteenth-century architectural ornament, appeared beneath the windowsills. The Sostres y Dosal building was the first instance in Mariscal's built work that he synthesized the modern and cosmopolitan with formal references to Mexican architectural history, which appeared exclusively, but unmistakably, on the surface of the building.

Angel Torres Torija also used the facade of his 1922 Gaona Apartment Building to recall colonial architecture, but did so using historicist forms and explicit pictorial references to national political history (figure 1.13). Built just outside the historic center, near many of turn-of-the-century Mexico City's most fashionable residences, the Gaona Building was one of the capital's most impressive and earliest purpose-built apartment buildings. It wrapped around the southeast corner of Bucareli Avenue and Emilo Donde Street, echoing the form of the traffic circle at the intersection and extended south for nearly a

FIGURE 1.12. Peabody, *El Pocito* (Francisco Guerrero y Torres, 1777–91).

FIGURE 1.13. Angel Torres Torija, Edificio Gaona, 1922.

block on the east side of Bucareli. Torres faced the facade in tezontle and adorned it with ornate neobaroque ornament, window frames, courses, and quoins. The main entrance was at the corner and was capped with a mixtilinear parapet faced with blue and white tiles on which "Edificio Gaona" was painted in stylized letters. Blue and white tiles, arranged in a zigzag pattern like that at the Sostres y Dosal building also covered the wall surface above the paired doors along the Bucareli and was repeated in an eight-pointed star high above the main entrance. In the large planes where the building's neobaroque parapet rose, Torres placed rectangular tile panels with the shields and names of Mexican states and major cities. Below, on the wall plane between the second and third stories and between the window ledges and quoins, were tile portraits of Hernán Cortés and Mexican viceroys.[43]

Torres appears to have been the first twentieth-century Mexican architect to incorporate pictures into a wall surface. His building evoked eighteenth-century architecture formally and materially, while it recalled political history pictorially and alluded to Mexico's territo-

FIGURE 1.14. Advertisement for the Taller Tostado (F. Mariscal, 1923).

rial breadth and diversity by referencing Mexican states. Standing opposite a comparably sober 1903 neoclassical mansion built for Feliciano Cobián (Rafael García Sánchez Facio; later used as the Secretaría de Gobernación) across the street, and just three blocks north of Miguel Angel de Quevedo's unflinchingly neoclassical La Mascota apartment block (1912), which could almost have stood in London, the Gaona Building was resolutely different, distinguished formally by its materials, decoration, and explicit references to the history and territory of Mexico.

In the same year that Torres designed the Gaona, Federico Mariscal was at work on another building, a large workshop for the Tostado photography and printmaking firm on the edge of downtown (figure 1.14). The building was commissioned by Ezquiel Álvarez Tostado, one of early twentieth-century Mexico's leading photojournalists, as the workshop and headquarters of his growing business. There Álvarez Tostado and his sons printed photographs on large, modern machines and did photoengraving and graphic design for a variety of clients, including major Mexico City newspapers.[44]

As he had at the Sostres y Dosal building, Mariscal referred to colonial architecture, but unlike Torres he did so abstractly and integrated these references with allusions to modern industry. Here the colonial evocations acknowledged not just history, but the neighborhood; the new workshop stood directly behind the Church of San Fernando (1735–55), a notable baroque building of tezontle and chiluca, with a single ornate tower, an octagonal rose window, and a framed relief of Santiago Matamoros between restrained estípites. The sculptural treatment of the door, the broken pediment atop the church, and the prominent quoins further distinguished the building. Rather than shaping the Taller Tostado to mimic the forms of its neighbor as he had at the Sostres y Dosal building, Mariscal alluded to it.

With its enormous floor-to-ceiling industrial windows and expressed piers, the Taller Tostado building was well suited to its purpose and acknowledged the principles of international rationalist modernism. But the bands of painted tiles that clad the facade between the first and second and second and third floors and the undulating parapet evoked colonial buildings. Mariscal treated the stacked oriel windows as a single vertical volume that culminated in a domical attic that he clad in zigzag-patterned tile and opened with a quatrafoil-shaped window. Here the architect transformed the oriel window—so strongly associated with Chicago skyscrapers—into a form that simultaneously recalled Mexican baroque architecture while retaining its connection to one of the signature forms of modern, industrial capitalism. The association was particularly appropriate for a large, successful company eager to convey its currency and competence. Originally a continuous course, presumably of tile, ran across the facade beneath the uppermost windows with the words "Tostado Grabador" (Tostado Printer). Although the building is in poor condition today, it is possible to see where, on the westernmost bay, a nameplate that extended nearly from the cornice to the base of the building like a giant vertical billboard was set into the surface of the facade.[45]

The Taller Tostado helped set the precedent in built form of expressing on the exterior its architect's conversance with up-to-date architectural thinking, and signaling difference from international norms visually by attaching to the facade a formal reference to an architectural history specific to Mexico. Its industrial aesthetic linked it to architecture elsewhere that referenced modern machines and technology. As one of the first buildings in twentieth-century Mexico in which form and program were allied so explicitly, the Taller Tostado helped lay the groundwork for an architecture in which program or purpose was expressed on the facade. In contrast, colonial revival forms in the Gaona Building and the countless new colonial revival houses, stores, and office buildings designed or built in Mexico City between 1920 and 1925 seemed arbitrary.[46] Against Mariscal's design and detached from his sophisticated engagement with history, form, and purpose, they read as faddish.

In the years immediately after the end of the Mexican Revolution, key leaders in the Mexican government, having absorbed ideas from architects and historians who worked before the war, promoted the colonial revival style in a variety of ways. The government of President Venustiano Carranza (1917–20) gave federal tax exemptions to people who built colonial revival–style houses.[47] Several administrations sponsored the transformations in the historic center. Most famously, education minister José Vasconcelos oversaw the design and construction of several major buildings in that language. These were the first of many instances of postrevolutionary governments appropriating the forms of leading twentieth-century architects, federalizing them in various ways, and using them in the service of an agenda that was nearly always framed in nationalistic terms. The rhetoric of nationality and patria that appeared in the first histories of Mexican colonial buildings and the flexibility of these concepts in those texts helped make the politicization of architecture possible, although the authors could not have foreseen the ways that their ideas would be made to fit a variety of agendas. Using a technique perfected over decades, bureaucrats appropriated art of many kinds to craft an image of the country for Mexicans and foreigners alike throughout the twentieth century.[48] After the Revolution, as the most important client of modern architecture in Mexico, the federal government was also its most voracious, attempting to imprint itself rhetorically on new buildings of all kinds.

Although it was later absorbed and manipulated by the government, private developers, and the middle class as a useful or fashionable revival style, in the first two decades of the twentieth century Mexican colonial architecture was at the heart of a complex and richly nuanced dialogue about the nature of Mexican architecture and culture. Some of the best minds in the country concerned themselves with it and with the changing form of the capital. To varying degrees individually and together Baxter, the Mariscals, Acevedo, García, and their collaborators sought to order the history of Mexican architecture, better define the profession, protect colonial buildings, reform the teaching of architecture, expand knowledge of the nation's extraordinary architectural history, and stimulate the creation of new forms. These scholars and architects and the photographers they worked with invented the idea of Mexican architecture by fusing architectural history with beliefs about the cultural conditions of nation, formal multiplicity and fusion, the relative contributions of indigenous Mexicans to colonial architecture, and a profound engagement with the visual effects of the surfaces and facades of Churrigueresque and baroque buildings. These were the roots from which Mexican modern architecture grew.

CHAPTER TWO

REPRESENTATION AND REFORM
AT THE MINISTRY OF HEALTH

The three most important themes to emerge from the early histories of colonial Mexican architecture—architecture's dependence on the other arts, its capacity to convey aspects of social history and cultural character on wall surfaces, and the uniqueness understood to be endowed by its connections to indigenous Mexicans—shaped the work of a new generation as it took up Jesús Acevedo's call to create a new national architecture in the 1920s. New texts including José Juan Tablada's *History of Mexican Art* (published in Mexico City in 1927) echoed many of the themes in prerevolutionary works, but, unlike books by Mariscal, Acevedo, and Baxter, positioned colonial buildings in a broader history that included not only major works of preconquest architecture but also vernacular, even "primitive" buildings, and "minor arts" from the colonial era, such as ceramics, works of iron and metal, and textiles. In a scholarly shift that paralleled politicians' attempts to create a unified but more inclusive narrative of national culture, as the canon of "Mexican art" expanded, its protagonists became more diverse. Tablada's text also enfolded contemporary painting into the new Mexican art history. Among the artists whose work he examined were muralists Diego Rivera, Roberto Montenegro, and painter Adolfo Best Maugard, whose influential drawing manual for school children, *Método de dibujo: Tradición, resurgimiento y evolución del arte mexicano*, the Ministry of Education published in 1923.

The artistic efflorescence in the other arts that Rivera, Montenegro, and Best Maugard personified in the 1920s was dominated by a new attention to indigenous traditions and folk art. With the backing of the federal government, artists painted the first famous murals and

FIGURE 2.1. Carlos Obregón Santacilia, Ministry of Health, 1925–29. Photograph by Guillermo Kahlo.

created a vast visual lexicon dominated by images of peasants, folk customs, indigenous cultures, or the working class that was so robust that subsequent generations would continue to rely on or resist it well into the twentieth century. At the same time, the connections between architecture and the other arts began to grow, even as architects became increasingly interested in architectural history. As the range of sources and associations expanded, buildings became increasingly abstract, complex bearers of meaning.

Carlos Obregón Santacilia's new Ministry of Health Building (1925–29) was the first major work in which the core ideas suggested by colonial histories manifested in a modern idiom. By treating the facades of his building representationally, Obregón Santacilia linked the ministry to the theoretical principles suggested by the histories of colonial architecture written in the two previous decades and gave form to his generation's ambition to design buildings that were not historicist, but that clearly belonged to a new era *and* a long history of Mexican architecture. As the first major government building constructed outside the capital's historic center, at the edge of Chapultepec Park along the Paseo de la Reforma, the new ministry metaphorically embodied the postrevolutionary expansion of the regulatory reach of the federal government beyond its historic limits and anticipated Mexico City's continued growth south and west of the center (figure 2.1). It acknowledged the aspirations of the agency and the indigenous people it sought to help most pictorially and metaphorically—using representational sculpture and cladding materials—and spatially evoked colonial palaces. But its disposition was essentially classical.

Often neglected or marginalized in histories of Mexican architecture, perhaps because it more closely resembled the great modern classical buildings of federal bureaucracy in France and the United States than the unadorned, asymmetrical new houses and apartments in continental Europe or the glass-and-concrete Mexican buildings that followed it beginning in the 1930s and were eventually canonized as works of "real" modern Mexican architecture, the Ministry of Health nevertheless provided the vital link between the architectural debates of the 1910s, the initial, tentative built responses to them in the early 1920s, and the most celebrated works of Mexican architecture from mid-century. Obregón Santacilia refined the techniques Federico Mariscal and Manuel Torres Torija had developed in their buildings near the historic center to allude to colonial history and architecture, but in a more muscular and symbolically rich work than any of theirs. The differences between his designs for the Health Ministry and the slightly earlier Mexican Pavilion at the 1922 Exhibition in Rio de Janeiro encapsulated the dramatic transformations in his thinking in just three years and reveal how innovative the Ministry of Health was. Well aware of the long shadow cast by Mexico's preconquest and colonial buildings and sensitive to the needs of his clients, with the Ministry of Health Obregón Santacilia helped establish the precedent of conveying Mexicanness in public buildings by representing or picturing, but not copying, historical forms and objects or elements associated with indigenous Mexican culture. The Ministry of Health building was the first to make explicit references to folk art, and with forms drawn from the languages of modern classicism and Art Deco, introduced the possibility that references to Mexican architectural history and international modernisms could coexist.

The flexible, formal approach to architectural elements that historians identified in the architecture of Spain and colonial Mexico was partially discernible in the design, which seemed to defy straightforward stylistic classification. But the U.S. architect William Spratling called the ministry "the finest example of modern architecture in th[e] country . . . [and was] perhaps the most Mexican building which has been done in Mexico since the Conquest."[1] Most famous for his work as the designer of silver jewelry with motifs inspired by indigenous patterns, Spratling was an important figure in the cultural renaissance that began in the 1920s and helped bring news of it to the United States. His assessment of the Ministry of Health appeared in the pages of a 1931 issue of *Architectural Forum* accompanied by photographs by Guillermo Kahlo showing Obregón Santacilia's innovative use of volcanic stone and copper as building materials, relief sculptures depicting Mexican pottery, plants, and modern laboratory equipment on the facade, and stained-glass windows by Diego Rivera inside. Readers saw in Kahlo's images the ministry's crisp, clean lines and deep shadows, its unusual massing, and the lush patio at its center (figure 2.2). They learned of the architect's attempt to "produce a Mexican style of our times" that in some way "perpetuated" the architecture of the preconquest past.[2] Mexican observers cited the ministry as evidence of the country's capacity to construct buildings that were as good and up-to-date as any in the world, but were still distinctive. Writing in 1930, one remarked that the building proved Mexico capable of creating architecture that was "genuinely ours," and related to "our materials and climate," and rooted in "our customs and needs," but marked by "new and expressive forms."[3] He observed further the ministry's departure from formal precedents, and claimed that it was distinguished by a "simplicity of form and expression, by the force of its volumes, and the combination of masses that support sober ornamentation."[4] Obregón Santacilia and his client both claimed that the building expressed the progressive ambitions of the federal agency it housed to improve public health nationwide.

In the years immediately after the Mexican Revolution governmental patrons readily embraced historians' suggestion that buildings could convey some essential national quality, and they rhetorically linked new works to their own nationalistic agendas. By the late 1920s changes in social policy and politicians' frequent coupling of reform and nationalism sharpened the focus of many architects on the potential of architecture to help solve social problems, particularly ones that seemed to require new buildings in which progressive social policies would be shaped and executed. The intense focus on the reform of education, health care, and the living conditions of the working and peasant classes in the 1920s and 1930s led to a boom in public buildings and infrastructure projects dedicated in one way or another to those

FIGURE 2.2. Obregón Santacilia, Ministry of Health, corridor overlooking patio. Photograph by Guillermo Kahlo.

causes. In these decades the federal government—as eager to convince Mexicans and international audiences of its legitimacy as it was to institute real reform—became the foremost patron of art and architecture in Mexico.

In the 1920s Mexican architecture, along with the other arts, changed at a dizzying pace, invigorated by debates, discoveries, and innovations in literature and archaeology, and energized by the sincere efforts of people in many fields to reshape Mexican society to be more inclusive of and to better serve indigenous and mixed-race Mexicans.[5] Federico Mariscal and Jesús Acevedo had introduced the idea that Mexican architecture was closely keyed to social and cultural change during the colonial period, so when architects in the decades after the revolution received commissions that related to social reform they had a theoretical foundation on which to base new designs. Despite the apparent ideological clarity that certain images and events of the 1920–40 period suggest, the forms and politics of those decades were tremendously complex and varied.[6] There was no single or even dominant architectural style. After 1925, buildings that were later identified as examples of a colonial revival style, modern classicism, Art Deco, or functionalist modernism all coexisted in a rapidly growing metropolis. In many instances leading architects designed buildings in more than one of these languages in the span of a few years and did not favor a single idiom or articulate a unifying theoretical position.

Obregón Santacilia and the sculptors with whom he worked created a building that was not both "Mexican" and "modern," but was the first example of a brand-new Mexican architectural modernism defined, like colonial Mexican buildings, not by specific forms, but by the principle of formal fusion on the facade that made the building simultaneously legible from multiple perspectives. Their building, like those that followed it, relied on its viewers' ability to recognize an architectural language regarded internationally as up-to-date and to decipher representations of architectural elements and objects imagined to be particular to Mexico. Historians of Mexican colonial architecture had defined national architecture as that which bore a resemblance to European prototypes but was decidedly different from them because of the presence of forms, techniques, or patterns that were somehow related to indigenous Mexico. They claimed that national architecture had emerged in tandem with the new social and religious order of colonial Mexico. These buildings, created in the persistent awareness of connection to and difference from the European cultural and political centers that exerted so much influence in colonial Mexico, animated the imaginations of Obregón Santacilia and other intellectuals in the 1920s, when awareness of distance and difference from artistic and political centers was still acute. For them folk art, and images of or inspired by it, along with pictorial, sculptural, or material allusions to preconquest people and buildings provided a means of linking modern, cosmopolitan experience to a national architectural history that had been defined by its equally vital connections to European centers and indigenous art.

NEW PERSPECTIVES ON THE PAST AND POPULAR ART

In the 1920s colonial architecture and folk art became the subjects of extensive study in Mexico City; in publications and exhibitions and because of increasing tourism to provincial regions, they were more visible to metropolitan audiences than perhaps at any time since independence. In 1921 Montenegro, a major folk art collector, along with the painter Jorge Enciso (both of whom had recently returned from many years in Europe) and the artist Dr. Atl helped organize the Exhibition of Popular Art in Mexico City, the chief aim of which was to stimulate interest in folk art in the capital in the hope that high-quality works of this kind might replace what they regarded as kitschy Europeanate knickknacks as decorative objects in the homes of the affluent.[7] Numerous illustrated publications on folk art and colonial architecture, many of them funded by the federal government, appeared throughout the decade, and Dr. Atl wrote two of the most important. His *Las artes populares en México* followed the exhibition the next year, and was one of the first scholarly treatments of Mexican folk art and among the first texts to suggest that folk art expressed national character. Between 1924 and 1927 the Secretaría de Hacienda published the six volumes of *Iglesias de Mexico*, which cataloged Mexican colonial churches and in which many of Kahlo's photographs appeared. Dr. Atl supplied additional illustrations and wrote the text with the renowned historian of Mexican art, Manuel Toussaint. The book's organization was similar to Baxter's and each volume was dedicated to a single topic: cupolas, the cathedral of Mexico, "ultra-baroque types" in the Valley of Mexico, "Puebla types," and altars. The final volume was a survey of buildings from 1525 to 1925, but unlike the first five included references to contemporary social problems and discussed vernacular buildings, stressing their connections to the landscape. After summarizing discussions of sixteenth-century and ultra-baroque architecture in the first chapters, in the third chapter the authors analyzed "popular architecture," and

traced adaptations of the viceregal baroque in rural vernacular churches. Dr. Atl described the appearance of the churches far from Mexico
City, emphasizing their harmony with the surroundings: "With their
polychrome cupolas and soaring towers; with bare walls and multicolored facades, the churches of the countryside and of towns harmo-
nize well with the environment around them; it is as if they condense
the landscape, with blue flower-covered mountains or rounded hills
with yellow herbs behind which rises a volcano crowned with snow."[8]
Dr. Atl's specialty as a painter of landscapes explains in part his enthusiasm for the details of the churches' settings, but his connection of the
buildings with Mexico's physical splendor was consistent with efforts
by other Mexico City artists and the federal government to bring rural Mexican culture to the cosmopolitan readership of the capital. The
artist's vivid descriptions of the buildings' environments "naturalized"
the churches, and thus the work of rural people, within their settings
and within Mexican architectural traditions. By emphasizing their
sites, Dr. Atl further attached nationalistic meaning to them. Classi-
fying these churches as "ULTRA-BAROQUE popular constructions,"[9]
he noted that they were essentially simpler versions of the architect-
designed churches illustrated elsewhere in the series.

Dr. Atl lived in an apartment in the former convent of La Merced,
which had one of the most celebrated colonial patios in Mexico, and he
had highly developed perspectives on colonial buildings and their historiography. Insisting on nuance and accuracy, he referred to "Churrigueresque" as "that byword of the late Spanish baroque which so many,
whether students or not like to apply indiscriminately" to "almost all
of the seventeenth and early eighteenth century buildings in Mexico."
Echoing earlier scholars, Atl asserted that "the series of architectural
works of the seventeenth century have essentially Mexican characteristics and cannot possibly be confused with those of either Churriguera,
Tomé, Pedro de Ribera, Miguel de Figueroa, or any of the other Spanish
architects of those times. Nothing could be more absurd!"[10] Atl did not
explain which, if any, formal traits he believed differentiated Mexican
buildings from those by the Spanish architects he named.

Atl's comments on the historiography of the Churrigueresque
appeared in Spratling's essay on the "six figures of the Mexican Renaissance" and preceded the author's description of the Ministry of
Health, which he admired for its "sculptural quality and . . . primi-
tiveness of line that is almost Aztec," and because of the ways those
elements operated in a building that was "otherwise simply 'modernistic.'" Like historians of colonial architecture, Spratling sought and was

intrigued by the "native" elements in recent Mexican buildings, even as he recognized in them likenesses to architecture elsewhere: "While it cannot be denied that [Obregón Santacilia's] recent structures reflect in some measure ideals already advanced in contemporary French work . . . they are certainly far fresher and more vital forms of building than those to be found in the average State capital of the United States. Furthermore, it must be said that they do suggest a consciousness of what is native to Mexico, and that, after all, is the important thing back of all that is truly traditional."[11] For Spratling, because he was immersed in the visual and intellectual culture of 1920s Mexico, and because he had studied Mexican colonial architecture, "modernistic," "traditional," "native to Mexico," and "French" were not contradictory.[12] Like historians of colonial architecture, Spratling understood the combination of elements in apparently disparate categories—in the postrevolutionary period, "French," "modernistic," and "native," instead of "Aztec" and "Spanish," "fresh," and "vital," as in Baxter's time—as the source of a work's distinction. His characterization of Obregón Santacilia's architecture also alluded to the ambition he shared with other architects and some apologists of Mexico's modern buildings to place them in a national architectural history, which they often described in terms of "tradition." On the other hand, like many foreign observers who wrote about Mexican architecture in later decades, Spratling was also eager to emphasize Mexico City's comparably rapid acceptance of modern architecture, especially relative to the United States. In doing so he implicitly pointed to Mexican architects' unspoken ambition to create buildings that compared favorably with U.S. works and were admired by outsiders. This desire, inherited from late nineteenth-century Mexican architects and patrons, underlay twentieth-century architecture as well and helped fuel Mexican architects' interest in integrating elements and forms coded as "international" in buildings visibly linked to Mexican architectural history.

In the third and fourth decades of the century, architects continued to work out the problems that had been identified before the revolution. In September 1923 the Society of Mexican Architects (SAM) published the inaugural issue of its journal, *El arquitecto*, which took up many of the concerns Federico and Nicolás Mariscal had identified ten or even twenty years earlier. The journal was meant to further professionalize and elevate the practice of architecture, and to "foment the study and love of our National Monuments, of our artistic tradition" in order to foster the development of "a new and legitimate National Art."[13] To introduce its 1922 *Anuario*, which included articles on colonial archi-

FIGURE 2.3. *Study for a "Mexican Capital,"* published in *Anuario de la Sociedad de Arquitectos Mexicanos,* 1922.

tecture, archaeology, urbanism, and professional practice, the SAM included an ink drawing of a "Mexican Capital," in which the entwined snakes that formed the skirt of the Aztec goddess Coatlicue replaced the acanthus leaves of a Corinthian capital, an eagle with volute-like wings and perched on a cactus, and serpent head-like forms appeared where volutes might on a composite capital (figure 2.3). The drawing typified the complicated mixing of forms and historical allusions that characterized designs in the 1920s. From 1922 through 1931 Mexico City's leading paper, *El Excélsior*, regularly included a weekly section on architecture with essays by leading architects on a variety of topics including colonial and preconquest architecture, the regulation of the profession and discussion of its social role, and biographical accounts of Mexico's most important prerevolutionary architects including Eduardo Tresguerras, Manuel Tolsá, and Adamo Boari. During the same years, however, Mexican architectural education underwent dramatic transformations as progressive professors deemphasized mastery of historical styles in favor of greater attention to architectural program and the potential of architecture to affect social change.

FOLK ART AND FRANCE

Designs for several buildings created when he was a student and early in his career show that in the early 1920s Obregón Santacilia experimented freely with historical forms even as he absorbed information about the new architecture in Europe. As they would throughout his career, Beaux-Arts principles undergirded his work. Among his first projects were colonial revival–style houses and a library for workers (1920), and a school for deaf and blind students (1924–25), which, had it been built, would have been the most avant-garde building in Mexico. With its asymmetrical massing, planar composition, emphatic geometries, and the absence of ornament of any kind, the design was as up-to-date as any building in western Europe.[14] In a 1923 renovation he replaced the French Renaissance Revival–style decoration on Nicolás Mariscal's Ministry of Foreign Relations with more conventional Renaissance Revival forms.

Having been trained at the National School of Fine Arts in the late 1910s, Obregón Santacilia was steeped in an architectural culture that prized copying older buildings. Like architecture students in many countries in that period, he was expected to master historical architectural languages ranging from Renaissance and neoclassical to gothic and even Egyptianate.[15] Indeed, the attention to formal variety and multiple influences in the first architectural histories of Mexico was reinforced by the flexibility suggested by Beaux-Arts theoretical texts, particularly Julien Guadet's *Éléments et théorie de l'architecture* (1901), which was extremely influential in Mexico. While in European theory the problem of choice that the study of architectural history presented beginning in the eighteenth century animated debates about style and the moral or "truthful" use of materials and forms well into the twentieth century, in the Mexican context modern architects tended to be, as their predecessors apparently were, even more flexible and eclectic in their approach to form than their continental colleagues. In Mexico "style" rarely carried the charge that it often did in European debates. Ethical questions entered in rarely, and when they did it was nearly always in the context of whether a building was adequately "Mexican."[16]

In part because it was seen as a reaction against the "foreign" influences of Beaux-Arts training, during Obregón Santacilia's formative years, research on colonial buildings was considered as progressive in Mexico as the new developments in Europe were, and as a student he learned about both simultaneously from professors Manuel Ituarte and Eduardo Macedo y Arbeau. Ituarte was a masterful draftsman and painter, who, as a conservator in the Office of Colonial Monuments, oversaw the restorations of many major colonial buildings. Years after he studied with him, Obregón Santacilia referred to Ituarte as a "teacher of generations of architects."[17] Macedo y Arbeau, on the other hand, introduced him to *Moderne Bauformen*, the German journal of modern architecture, among other sources on new buildings outside of Mexico.[18] Dissimilar as Churrigueresque churches and International Style schools are, it is unlikely that they struck the young architect as inherently incompatible. Indeed, the formal diversity that early historians of colonial architecture identified in Mexico provided the intellectual framework on which buildings that looked quite different could be called "Mexican" and be understood as suitable to national conditions.

Invigorated by their studies and stimulated by the cultural and political changes all around them, the architects of Obregón Santacilia's generation became captivated by the problem of how to design modern buildings while acknowledging Mexico's architectural past. Writing of the early and mid-1920s decades later, Obregón Santacilia recalled that he and his colleagues

> sought to . . . devote ourselves to the search for abandoned traditions; I remember that we were almost obsessed as a group by the making of traditional architecture, we discussed it at length, we thought that the architects of America had the obligation to search for the roots of tradition for their architecture. We who had the blood of the indigenous and Spanish races . . . we had had an architectonic formation that participated strongly in the study and contemplation of the past, we worked many years with that end and realized some works.[19]

Mariscal's emphasis on mestizaje was clearly influential for Obregón Santacilia, who was among the very first of the next generation of architects to explicitly link notions of racial and cultural blending and architectural innovation, but he broke with Mariscal and Acevedo by abandoning historicism in favor of a more abstract relationship to architectural history. Like many young architects Obregón Santacilia keenly felt the impulse to innovate: "in trying to revive traditional forms or solutions we realized that they were completely dead and that it was impossible to use them in our architecture which we naturally wanted to be made for new needs for our time."[20]

He also shared with architects elsewhere aspirations to create a historically responsive "universal" architecture. In a 1927 issue of the arts journal *Forma* he declared that

> Mexican architecture, after many years of complete decadence, once again rises. It can have no more than one ambition: to be world architecture.
>
> The architect should work within tradition, but not be strictly subjected to it or limited by it, but instead, should make it evolve, listening to it, creating.
>
> Architecture will very soon follow the same tendency throughout the world. Means of communication will unify construction processes, and the needs of people and customs will be the same. The architect in Mexico should unite himself with the movement of international architecture.[21]

Just as his protégé Juan O'Gorman would in the early 1930s, Obregón Santacilia suggested that new technologies and the universality of human needs would ultimately give rise to a modern architecture that was basically similar in many places. Insofar as the "international architecture" to which he referred was indebted at least in part to industrialization, which was far more advanced in western Europe and the United States than it was in Mexico, in 1927 it was unlikely that his prediction about construction methods and universality would be realized. Mexico's abundant supply of labor and its technological conditions provided neither the incentive nor the opportunity for modern architecture to develop in the same ways that it had elsewhere. In Mexico then, the "international" architecture to which Obregón Santacilia referred and had learned about through photographs in foreign journals was ultimately received as yet another style from abroad. Working in a country where the issues of standardization and mass production exerted neither the practical nor psychological influence that they did in Europe and the United States, he and other Mexican architects necessarily understood the new "international" architecture primarily formally. Nevertheless, although he had neither resolved nor perhaps fully recognized the tensions in the task of creating a "universal" architecture, Obregón Santacilia, notably did not suggest that national and international tendencies were inherently opposed, and indeed was working on melding them in the Ministry of Health design at the time he made the remarks.

During the 1920s the architect also became fascinated by Mexican folk art, and with the period's leading painters and writers helped make it central to new definitions of Mexican visual culture. To an even greater extent than colonial buildings, the country's "popular" arts, which Mexico City intellectuals understood as manifestations of an authentic, rural Mexico that was rapidly slipping away, were imagined, despite their diversity, as distinctive manifestations of national culture. Like many important artists in the postrevolutionary era, Obregón Santacilia traveled within Mexico studying colonial buildings and folk art. Years later he recalled these experiences and the transformations he began to see in Mexico City: "the revolution brought songs that stimulated a return to what was ours, which had been neglected, and people who had commissioned their linens from Paris agreed that in Mexico serapes are made of magnificent wool, [and equally magnificent was] the china of Puebla, the bowls of Uruapan, and the pitchers of Tlaquepaque. In the city were seen jackets from the north and objects from other parts of the country, which had been completely unknown in the center, and national tastes came into vogue; in 1920 we began to discover Mexico."[22] The flood of objects from far parts of the republic provided architects and artists with a multitude of forms on which to base new visual languages that were dramatically different from those they encountered in their academic training. Like European modernists who prized "primitive" art for its abstract qualities and rejected academic realism as they revolutionized painting, Mexican painters and some architects found in folk art inspiration for new works that signaled a formal and even sociopolitical break with the recent past. Obregón Santacilia noted that for him and his colleagues folk art suggested the possibility of a "true renaissance."[23]

Although it began twenty years later, the "discovery" of folk art was analogous in nonarchitectural art and intellectual culture to the invention of national architectural history. Just as architects had begun to argue that Second Empire–style buildings were historically and culturally ill-fitted to Mexico, so too other aesthetically conscious residents of the capital began to exchange their Parisian textiles for those made in Mexico and leading painters and photographers began to depict the crafts of diverse Mexican groups. The critical difference was that folk art was imagined to give its owner some connection to indigenous Mexico, while colonial revival forms linked him or her to Spain. After the revolution, progressives in many fields recognized the importance of acknowledging more fully Mexico's indigenous cultures and its indigenous past—for cultural, economic, and political reasons—but none actually advocated returning to preconquest modes of governance and social order. The anthropologist Manuel Gamio suggested that part of integrating real, living indigenous Mexicans into mainstream society might involve affluent, white Mexico in becoming at least a little bit native.[24] The Ministry of Health's decorative program was part of a vibrant exchange about folk art, Mexican architectural history, and new ways of uniting them intellectually and artistically.

COLONIAL REVIVAL IN RIO DE JANEIRO

In two projects from the early 1920s, the Mexican Pavilion and Monument to Cuauhtémoc that he designed with Carlos Tarditi for the 1922 exhibition in Rio de Janeiro (figure 2.4), Obregón Santacilia began to experiment with ways of combining historicizing forms to shape buildings that recalled works from different periods of Mexican architectural history while retaining connections to classicism. Although they were built far from Mexico City, the Mexican contributions to the Rio fair helped elide architectural theory inherited from the early twentieth century with postrevolutionary political rhetoric and image-making strategies. Organized to celebrate the centennial of Brazilian independence, the fair showcased Brazilian progress since the end of colonialism and included a variety of exhibits intended to educate the public on health and hygiene. The legacy of colonialism and public health were also major concerns in Mexico, but for the Mexican delegation the fair was important primarily because it was the first major postrevolutionary opportunity to present Mexico to an international audience.

Among the Brazilian pavilions were some that recalled the era of Portuguese rule, but most of the visiting countries' buildings were neoclassical. In this landscape Obregón Santacilia and Tarditi's two-story colonial revival Mexican Pavilion stood out dramatically with its large, ornate frontispiece, arcuated second-story gallery, and mixtilinear parapet. Pairs of *estípites* framed the door, ornamental frames surrounded the ground-floor windows, and the main facade was framed by a prominent base and rusticated corners with upper-story niches. Although the entrance called to mind Churrigueresque buildings, the facade was composed of elements associated with both sixteenth- and

Exposição do Centenario - 1922

MEXICO

FIGURE 2.4. Obregón Santacilia and Carlos Tarditi, Mexican Pavilion, Centennial Exposition, Rio de Janeiro, 1922.

eighteenth-century palaces. The architects also combined elements from domestic and ecclesiastical buildings: whereas the massing and arcades evoked palaces, the arched doorway and retablo-facade-like center, with its modified Serlian door, were derived from colonial churches. In its integration of forms associated with two periods in Mexican colonial architecture, the design was fully consistent with the colonial revival buildings then transforming downtown Mexico City. But two details on the frontispiece linked the building to contemporary developments on the one hand, and explicitly nationalized the building using modern iconography, on the other. At the center, the national seal—an eagle perched on a cactus, with a serpent in its mouth rendered in profile—was depicted in relief. Versions of this allegory of Mexico appeared in paintings as least as early as the eighteenth century, but became far more common after Mexican independence in 1821.[25] Flanking the eagle were two pots from which sprang vine-like plants whose tendrils curled into scrolls. This detail united the decorative patterns of late eighteenth-century Mexico with the forms of early Art Deco to create an image that conveyed simultaneously conversance with up-to-date international decorative trends and Mexican architectural history.

The Rio de Janeiro Pavilion suggested that the architects had fully absorbed the arguments of the previous generation that combinations of diverse architectural elements—regardless of the periods in or building types on which they were used—and colonial forms themselves were authentically and distinctively particular to Mexico. The Rio Pavilion made the point particularly clearly; between the cornice and the frontispiece "MEXICO" was written in large letters. Although the colonial revival style waned in popularity in the late 1920s, Obregón Santacilia remained proud of his work in Rio many decades later, when he claimed that the pavilion was "the best neo-colonial building that was made" and recalled that he and Tarditi had studied colonial architecture "very well" and "had, above all, conserved the scale" of colonial works, unlike nearly all of their colleagues who had "imitated our past."[26]

The extent to which Obregón and Tarditi had adopted the theory of colonial architecture as national architecture that Acevedo and Mariscal had proposed is particularly evident when the Rio Pavilion is compared to the buildings the Mexican government commissioned for other international exhibitions before and after the Brazilian fair. As Mauricio Tenorio Trillo has demonstrated, the idea that aspects of national history might be used in international settings to convey Mexican distinctiveness and even modernity was nothing new in Mexican exhibition buildings.[27] Antonio Peñafiel, one of nineteenth-century Mexico's most important historians, designed the famous pavilion at the 1889 fair in Paris, known as the Aztec Palace, in a pre-Hispanic revival style. Just as architects would in later buildings, Peñafiel used the pavilion's facade to relate the building to older architecture. He decorated it with relief carvings and statues of Aztec gods, low relief patterns that evoked carvings on pre-Hispanic temples, and re-creations of iconic Aztec sculptures, including the famous calendar stone. Architects later used pre-Hispanic forms for the Mexican Pavilion at the 1929 Ibero-American Exhibition in Seville.

But in 1922 Mexican baroque architecture was prized, and it received special attention in the publication prepared by the Secretaría de Industria, Comercio y Trabajo to accompany the Mexican exhibits at the Rio fair. The book covered many aspects of modern Mexico and devoted special attention to the country's cultural and architectural resources. Like histories of Mexican architecture, the chapter on "Monumental and Artistic Mexico" explained the characteristics of colonial architecture at different periods between 1521 and 1821 and noted that the buildings constructed in this period were notable for their "perfect adaptation to the necessities of climate and for the varied influences that informed their style."[28] The publication described the "large stretches of wall carved with finely worked rocaille and falling leaves" and the "polychrome figures of animals, flowers and fruits" characteristic of Churrigueresque architecture. The text referred to the style repeatedly and noted that despite its having been first developed by a Spanish sculptor, it was energetically embraced in Mexico on account of its "creole character." Elsewhere in the volume, in the discussion of Mexico City churches, the authors noted that the Churrigueresque style "can almost be said to be the national style."[29]

Initial plans for the Mexican Pavilion had called for a neo-Aztec building, but the jury that ultimately awarded the commission specified that it be built in a colonial revival style. Composed of architects and engineers, the jury had been organized by Mexico's special diplomat to the fair, education minister José Vasconcelos who had been Jesús Acevedo's good friend and who, like him and the Mariscal brothers, had been a member of the Athenaeum of Youth.[30] Vasconcelos absorbed ideas from these architects about colonial architecture's relationship to the emergence of modern Mexico that informed his preferences as an architectural patron in the early 1920s. At the time of the Brazilian exposition Vasconcelos's own beliefs about architecture and culture were very much in flux. Shortly before the Rio fair opened he had inaugurated the renovated Ministry of Education building in downtown Mexico City in which engineer Federico Méndez Rivas used neoclassical elements on a colonial revival plan.[31] During his 1922 trip to South America for the fair Vasconcelos worked out many of his ideas about the development of a new culture, which he imagined as an ideal racial mix of people from Spain, preconquest America, India, and Greece, on which he expounded later, after he left the Ministry of Education, in the well-known book, *La raza cósmica* (1925).[32] Even before the book appeared, on the walls of one of the Ministry of Education's courtyards, the sculptor Manuel Centurión created relief carvings of allegorical figures of Mexican, Greek, Spanish, and Indian culture. The notion that a variety of influences combined to give rise to a modern Mexico that was fundamentally Hispanic in character echoed arguments about the nature of colonial Mexican architecture that had been advanced since Baxter's work at the turn of the century. Both Acevedo and Mariscal had critiqued pre-Hispanic revival buildings on a variety of grounds, and in the early 1920s their perspectives prevailed.

The Rio de Janeiro Pavilion was filled with folk art and painting that celebrated Mexico's folk traditions, especially as they were associated with colonial art. On the upper floor Roberto Montenegro and Jorge Fernández Ledesma created murals depicting fanciful scenes of colonial life and natural bounty. Although their works were less famous than those by Diego Rivera, like him, they painted large frescoes in the Ministry of Education beginning in 1921. These helped initiate the first phase of the Mexican mural movement that brought international acclaim to Mexico and shaped the course of painting in Mexico and throughout Latin America for decades to come. As early as 1923 a foreign critic identified Montenegro's work in Rio as being "distinctly national in character" and noted that he was "one of a group of artists who are developing a Mexican school of art."[33] In the Sala de Cerámica, one of Montenegro's murals showed "two men in native dress stretch[ing] their arms toward a pile of national products skillfully assembled with decorative effect."[34] On the opposite wall Montenegro depicted two women, one wearing the native dress of the Isthmus of Tehuantepec, the other that of Puebla; at the center was a stylized depiction of an urn, leaves, a flower, and butterflies. The pavilion's folk art exhibition included displays of serapes, painted lacquer trays and boxes, ceramics, and straw hats and was the second major assemblage of Mexican folk art in the 1920s.

Despite Vasconcelos's objections, pre-Hispanic history and its forms did not disappear altogether at the Rio fair. Again with Tarditi, Obregón Santacilia designed a tall pedestal for a reproduction of Miguel Noreña's bronze sculpture of the Aztec leader Cuauhtémoc (1886) that Mexico gave to Brazil during the fair. The original statue stood on the Paseo de la Reforma, Mexico City's great Beaux-Arts avenue, and copies of it had been sent to earlier fairs. Noreña had depicted Cuauhtémoc draped in a classical toga and wearing a helmet with tall feathers that evoked the helmets of Roman centurions. The Rio reproduction stood atop a classicizing granite pedestal with a base for which Hans Pillig sculpted giant serpent heads that resembled depictions of the animal in Mesoamerican art and architectural sculpture.

Together the colonial revival facade of the pavilion and the sculpture and its pedestal alluded to the pair of cultures imagined to have shaped Mexico, and both did so by representing elements from older buildings. At the exhibition the serpent heads and the colonial-style ornament on the pavilion were detached from their original contexts and repositioned on new works for the purpose of calling to mind historical ones. In Rio de Janeiro these representations of elements from colonial and preconquest architecture were imagined to convey Mexico's specialness and together and, perhaps unintentionally, pointed to the two strands of architectural research in Mexico since the mid-nineteenth century as well as to broader debates about the nature of Mexican society. Spatially the representations of preconquest and colonial architecture were kept separate; the forms did not adorn the same building, and it was clear that the pavilion—the reminder of colonial Mexican architecture—was the dominant structure.

Although Vasconcelos had hoped to keep the Cuauhtémoc replica from being sent to Brazil because he thought its implicit celebration of indigenous culture did not appropriately represent postrevolutionary Mexico, he gave folk art a prominent place inside the pavilion, where it was seen in carefully arranged museum- and shop-like displays, rather than in the hands of actual folk artists who were likely indigenous or mestizo. Whereas historicizing architectural elements could only represent architecture and awaken associations with other cultures or times, Mexican folk art suggested the possibility that (white) urban Mexicans could come into contact with the actual folk artists who had crafted and painted the objects, or at least be linked to them through the object. Contained within a Hispanic structure, or one that reminded viewers of one, folk art might enable elite viewers to come closer to "authentic" indigenous Mexico in the safety of the cultural and social norms to which they were accustomed and without having to confront the realities of poverty and discrimination with which many folk artists lived.

Obregón Santacilia's work in Rio de Janeiro paved the way for additional commissions from the federal government through his connection with Vasconcelos. His first major project in Mexico after the 1922 exhibition was the Benito Juárez School (1923–25), a large elementary school commissioned by the Ministry of Education in the Mexico City suburb of Roma (figure 2.5). Here the architect began to experiment with ways of evoking colonial buildings generally through abstractions of forms associated with them rather than using historicizing applied ornament copied from colonial facades. The two-story school occupied an entire city block and was organized on a centralized plan in which two large courtyards were separated by a large library. Although the design included elements that referred to colonial architecture, the building was far less ornate than the pavilion in Rio de Janeiro and much more obviously informed by Beaux-Arts principles. Other than its decorative detailing around the arched main entrance and on six windows, the mixtilinear base and parapet, and small finials, the build-

FIGURE 2.5. Obregón Santacilia, Benito Juárez School, 1925.

ing had relatively little exterior ornament. The form that most strongly recalled colonial precedents was the arch, which Obregón Santacilia used to form the ground-level arcades around the patios and to frame the windows on the upper story. Shaping voids in the smooth, sober walls, they more closely resembled the arches in buildings by Irving Gill in southern California than those in actual colonial cloisters. The barrel-vaulted, chapel-like library at the center of the plan in turn alluded to the federal government's attempts to replace religious devotion with secular education. Despite his increasingly distanced approach to historically evocative forms, Obregón Santacilia nevertheless created in Roma a school that read at first glance as a colonial revival–style building, but was governed by classical principles.

A MODERN MINISTRY

Classicism and colonial associations came together more powerfully and abstractly in the Ministry of Health, his next major project. Having been created in 1917, at the end of the Mexican Revolution, the Ministry of Health was the second-most important federal agency after the Ministry of Education and, like it, was charged with enacting wide-ranging reforms that bureaucrats hoped would improve the lives of individuals and Mexican society as a whole. Infant mortality, life expectancy, and a host of other indicators suggested that Mexican health was among the worst in the world, and Mexico's leaders recognized the consequences of that situation for the economic and political stability of the country.[35] The Constitution of 1917 had given the federal government broad powers to intervene in the lives of citizens in the name of public health, and in the 1920s an array of efforts were under way in Mexico City and in rural areas to improve access to and the quality of health care.[36] Because the vast majority of Mexicans deemed to need state-directed assistance were indigenous or of mixed race, and because these groups had been socially and politically marginalized since the conquest, public-health initiatives necessarily engaged an extraordinary array of social, political, and historical questions and assumptions.

The commission presented three challenges: organizing spaces that adequately housed a major federal agency and a laboratory; designing a building that suitably and simultaneously expressed governmental sobriety and commitment to social reform and modern science; and making the scheme fit on an irregularly shaped site along the country's most important boulevard. Ultimately, Obregón Santacilia arranged the building into three administrative pavilions and a laboratory around a courtyard with a driveway, relying on an essentially classical plan and disposition to convey institutional authority. On the facades, architectural elements associated with colonial buildings used representationally and materials evocative of preconquest buildings rooted the ministry historically, while relief carvings and projecting sculptures on the facades made the ministry's aspirations and tools legible. Over the course of three months in late 1925, the architect drew multiple perspectives, plans, and elevations that show how he worked to address the site, developed an increasingly abstract approach to massing, and gradually abandoned historicism. During the course of its evolution the scheme became tighter, more unified, and more elegant, although the parti did not change.

Two of the earliest drawings of the ministry were bird's-eye perspectives from October and December 1925 (figures 2.6 and 2.7).[37] The change from the October to December drawing shows the transformation of the plan and the emergence of a more steady command of architectural elements. Two months after he drew the first perspective

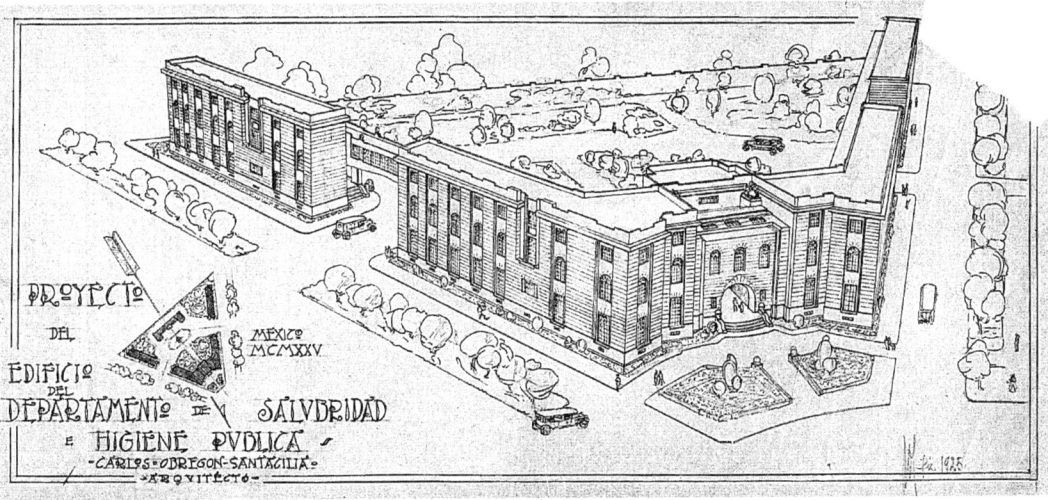

Figures 2.6 and 2.7. Obregón Santacilia, Ministry of Health, perspectives, October 1925 (*top*) and December 1925 (*bottom*).

Obregón Santacilia created a tighter composition defined by confident geometries and straight lines that shot through space and met at daring angles. The new design pushed the three administration buildings outward to the edge of the site, connected them with bridges, and added a third story to all three. The changes created a more clearly defined perimeter and a more monumental building that belonged not to the age of Cortés, but to the era of modern federal government.

In the span of three months the design also became taller and more

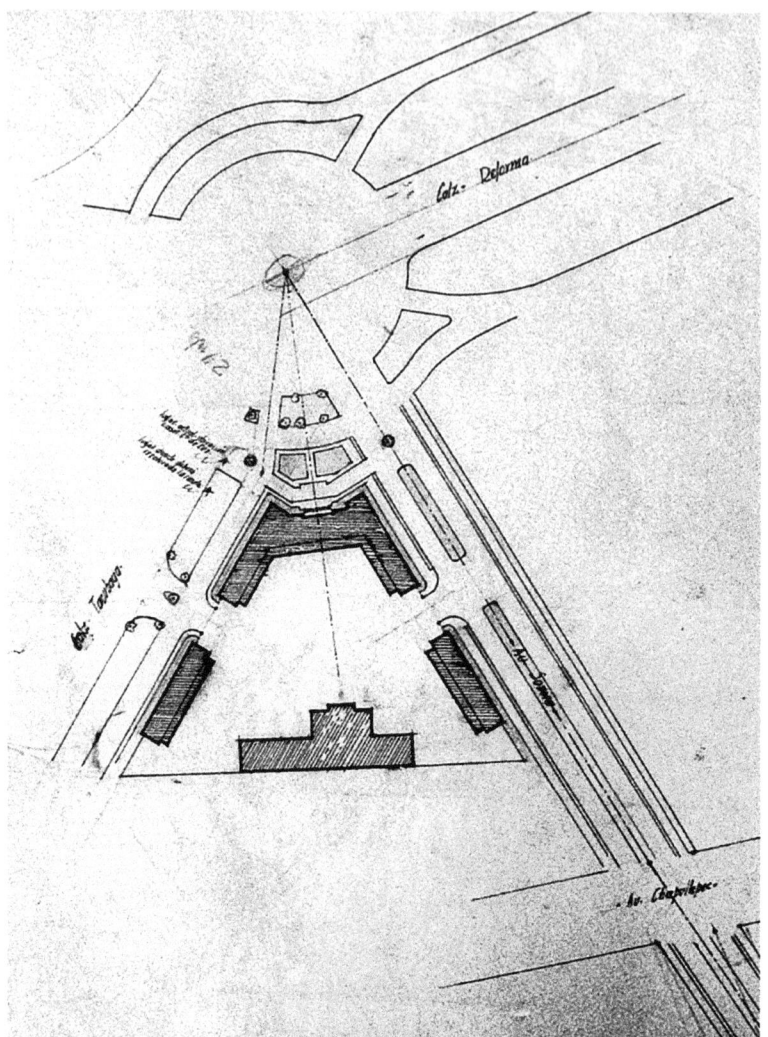

Figure 2.8. Obregón Santacilia, Ministry of Health, site plan, early 1926.

classical. Pilasters between the windows gave the building a greater visual verticality and emphasized its additional story. The ministry's distinctive W-shaped plan also came into view in the December drawing, as the gentle curve of the entrance in the October scheme was exchanged for a more artful arrangement. Obregón Santacilia now arranged the principal elevation, which faced the corner with Reforma, into a series of planes that met at angles like a folded piece of paper stood on its side. This change established in plan the powerful motif of recess and projection that animated the final design and it solved the problem of axial symmetry on the site with a bit of barely detectable visual manipulation. Obregón Santacilia clearly intended that the building appear regular and symmetrical. But in order to achieve the effect, he had to manipulate lines and planes, which created a series of modern "optical corrections" that would have delighted the architects of antiquity. In its built form, the main elevation appears to be a symmetrical arrangement of folded planes centered on an axis that runs from the main door of the laboratories to the spot where Reforma turns to go through the park (figure 2.8). In fact, the northwest and northeast blocks do not come into the central blocks at the same angles. The northwestern arm of the complex stretch out at a wider angle from the central mass than its complement on the other side, resulting in a more acute meeting on the main elevation. The discrepancy is identifiable from only a few points at ground level.

The building's classicism—which included on the administrative pavilions the tripartite facade composition, restrained pilasters, and a narrow cornice and dentils—resonated with broader currents in Mexican arts and letters in the 1920s. In that decade images of indigenous people, folk art objects, and interest in colonial buildings coexisted with a fascination with classical culture that often manifested as images in advertisements, magazines, and even government publications. Neoclassical buildings and monuments such as the Monument to Independence on Reforma and the unfinished Legislative Palace, which were imagined to convey the country's rightful place among modern republics, had been among the most important new projects at the time of the 1910 Centennial and stood alongside a variety of Porfirian references to indigenous cultures.[38] They belonged as well to the long historical arc typified by Noreña and Sigüenza y Góngora's monuments in which nativism and classicism entwined. Understood as an international visual language, classicism was used by Obregón Santacilia and his colleagues throughout the hemisphere to convey currency with European norms. At the Ministry of Health it conveyed effective governance in the Western tradition and, as it was filtered through the teaching of architecture at the National School of Fine Arts in Mexico, provided the intellectual framework for further experimentation in ways of organizing facades and associating buildings with architectural history.

An early 1926 elevation introduced the ministry's dramatic entrance, a mouthlike semi-octagonal arch that led visitors into a low, narrow vestibule evocative of the *zaguáns* of colonial palaces (figure 2.9). Just as he had in the Mexican Pavilion in Rio de Janeiro, Obregón Santacilia used the entrance to link the building to historical precedents, but at the Health Ministry the multilingual, semi-octagonal arch, instead of estípites and Churrigueresque ornament with their highly specific histories, carried meaning. Shaped in dark black volcanic rock

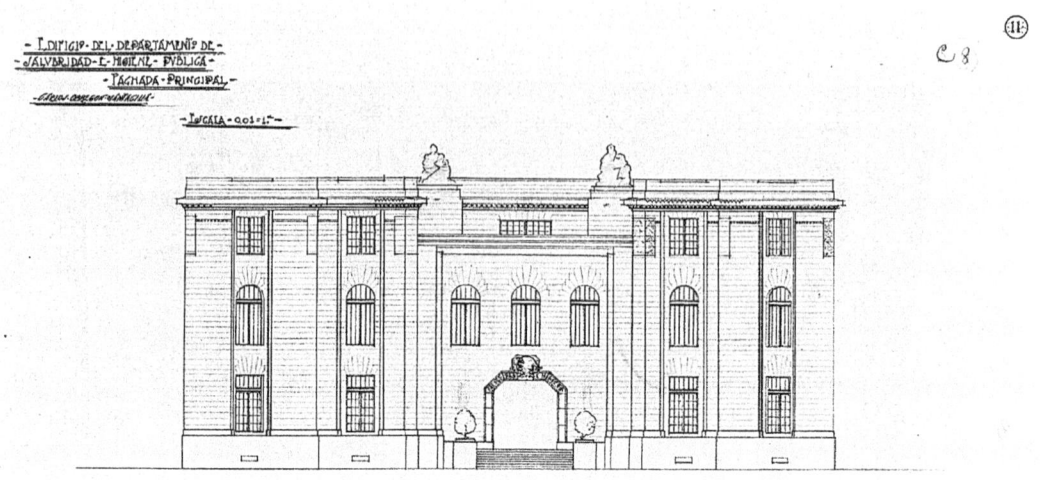

FIGURE 2.9. Obregón Santacilia, Ministry of Health, main facade, 1926.

and thereby differentiated from the gray mass of the building, the arch functioned as a representation of colonial semi-octagonal arches, which were well-known to students of Mexican colonial architecture, and resembled Art Deco forms elsewhere in the city (figure 2.10).

Strong polygonal, and especially octagonal and semi-octagonal forms appeared in churches throughout Mexico and in the 1910s had been documented extensively in photographs by Kahlo and others. The most famous such door frame was at Pedro de Arrieta's Basilica of Guadalupe, a 1695 building familiar not only to architects but also to the hundreds of thousands of Mexicans who passed under it on their way to see the mantle with the sacred image of the Virgin of Guadalupe. The basilica stood high on the hill of Tepeyac, north of downtown Mexico City. Much closer to the Ministry of Health, and institutionally related to it, was another building by Arrieta that stood at the northeast corner of the Plaza de Santo Domingo and also had an enormous semi-octagonal arch door frame, the form of which was repeated above as a window frame. Built on the site of the first Dominican mission in Mexico, and originally home to the Holy Office of the Inquisition, after 1820 the palace housed in the National School of Medicine, which was still operating there in 1925 (figure 2.11). The palace's dramatic corner frontispiece, with its pairs of columns and pilasters and prominent parapet, was one of the most exceptional in the capital, and its distinctive facade inspired Mexico City residents to nickname the building the Casa Chata, or flat-nosed house.[39] Opposite the colonial palace was

FIGURE 2.10. Obregón Santacilia, Ministry of Health, door. Photograph by Guillermo Kahlo.

FIGURE 2.11. Pedro de Arrieta, Palace of the Inquisition (later, National School of Medicine), Mexico City, 1695.

Arrieta's 1736 Church of Santo Domingo, which Baxter had called "the best example of baroque architecture in Mexico."[40] The plaza on which the two buildings fronted was one of three, including the Zócalo, that Federico Mariscal believed had "a very national character."[41]

The door that Obregón Santacilia designed for the Ministry of Health visually linked the new building to the School of Medicine, and to some of the most celebrated works of colonial architecture. Functioning as a representation of the eighteenth-century doorway at Plaza Santo Domingo, the entrance to the Ministry of Health conveyed to viewers familiar with the institutional link between the two buildings the continuity of a national tradition in a new building for a new agency, in a new and tenuous political order. By carefully integrating an allusion to an architectural history understood in national terms with the reliably assertive, institutional language of international classicism, Obregón Santacilia created a building that read not as an eclectic, confusing formal mishmash, but as a disciplined and nuanced composition that critics called "ultra-modern" and "worth visiting."[42] Standing far from the traditional centers of power, the ministry's colonial associations helped link it to the older parts of the capital and suggested historical and administrative continuity in the expanding city.

The Ministry of Health was not the only place where polygonal portals appeared in the 1920s and they were not only associated with Mexican colonial architecture. In his Pavilion of the City of Paris at the 1925 Art Deco exposition, Roger Bouvard had used identically shaped frames around the door and windows. Although Obregón Santacilia did not visit the exposition, images of it were published in 1925 and 1926 in the Mexican journal *Cemento*. The great number of Mexican buildings with Art Deco elements suggests that architects in the 1920s had considerable information about the new forms, and his 1926 interior renovation of the Bank of Mexico building showed that he had complete command of the idiom.[43] The semi-octagonal arch appeared on many building types, including office and apartment buildings, houses, and markets throughout the city, and by the late 1920s had become a signature element of international Art Deco architecture. In its evocation of buildings of the past and its conversance with the dynamic new rhythms of cosmopolitan buildings elsewhere, the polygonal frame typified the branch of 1920s modernism that sought to reinterpret historical, nationally specific forms in ways that resonated in a new age. Art Deco decorative details including metalwork, typeface, and even a jazzy interpretation of a maguey cactus in art glass appeared throughout the interior of the Ministry of Health.[44]

While Obregón Santacilia used forms, spaces, and architectural elements to represent colonial architecture at the Ministry of Health, he relied on materials to allude to pre-Columbian architecture and culture. The semi-octagonal entrance, the base of the building, and the steps were made of black volcanic rock, which provided a stark contrast to the smooth, light gray, cut stone that clad the pavilions. This organization of materials implied that modern Mexican bureaucracy and scientific progress were built on the foundations of Mexico's ancient past, through which the nation's modern leaders metaphorically passed on their way to work. Above the keystone, Centurión carved a Mexican eagle of the same stone, which recalled the Mexican Pavilion in Brazil and marked the building with the official imagery of modern nationalism. Obregón Santacilia boasted that his use of volcanic stone was the first since precolonial times, and noted that in the centuries after the Aztecs had ruled Mexico the stone had been used only for lowly projects like paving.[45] In reality blocks of volcanic rock had provided the foundations for many colonial palaces throughout Mexico City, but because volcanoes, like indigenous people, had existed in Mexico long before the arrival of Europeans, both were imagined by the urban elite to belong to the literal and metaphoric (rural) landscape of "timeless Mexico."[46]

In the ministry's verdant, sun-drenched patio was a large pool flanked by statues of healthy children with fruits and corn and the industrial-looking laboratories, where the ministry's scientists labored to make the promises of health and hygiene real for all Mexicans. Although the building had many links to historical architecture, Obregón Santacilia explained his work using terms from modern science. He suggested that the ministry literally embodied its purpose and, relying on anatomical analogies, explained that

> in the principal part (or cerebrum) are the offices of the directors and the conference room where they may meet with the chiefs of services. In the center are the laboratories where the ideas which the cerebrum has conceived [are studied and made applicable]. And on the sides, unifying the rest are four great wings [that function as] arms which are to carry to the people measures and practices for public betterment: as a symbol for each one of these wings there has been given the name of one of the elements of nature: Earth, Water, Air and Fire.[47]

The conception of the building as "headed" by bureaucrats reflected the way Mexican health was imagined to be best administered, and the ministry building mirrored the paternalistic approach to care in the postrevolution republic. But in Obregón Santacilia's hands the tedium of bureaucracy was exchanged for metaphor. The elements the architect referred to were allegorized in stained-glass windows designed by Rivera and placed in the building's ancillary staircases. The evocation of the ancient elements further linked the building to classical tradition, but like other parts of the ministry, Rivera's interpretation of the elements in terms of modern labor and technology—miners and airplanes stood for Earth and Air—and "Mexican" imagery—for example, by a sombrero-wearing peasant tilling fields—updated and localized them. Inside the ministry boardroom, above the main entrance to the building, Rivera painted female nude figures that allegorized health, life, strength, purity, continence, and science.

ARCHITECTURE, SCIENCE, AND SOCIETY

Analogues to Obregón Santacilia's efforts to unite nationally distinctive and recognizably international forms abounded in Mexican visual and intellectual culture in the 1920s as bureaucrats, artists, and scholars sought to develop a coherent theory of mestizaje and policies that would support the integration of indigenous Mexicans into modern society. Among the leaders of this broad cultural project was Obregón Santacilia's client, minister of health, and physician, Bernardo Gastélum. Although he is less famous today than Vasconcelos, Gastélum was one of the most important intellectuals to shape 1920s Mexico. He joined anthropologist Manuel Gamio, who linked archaeology, folk art, and the modern conditions of indigenous people, and educator J. M. Puig Casauranc, in bringing research about history and sociology to bear directly on the formation of government policies after the revolution. Indeed, despite the many changes that followed the war, Mexican politics in the 1920s was in many respects grounded in the prewar debates about positivism and the Western classical tradition in which questions about the roles of science and race in social progress were central.[48]

Establishing Mexico within a broad Western framework was central to the program of cultural regeneration that Gastélum and his colleagues advocated. In his writings in the journal *Contemporáneos* the minister repeatedly referenced ancient Greece, the Italian Renaissance, and a variety of Western philosophers in his calls for the emergence of a "mode of civilized thought" and a "public spirit" that valued history and culture.[49] The problem of cultural unity, he believed, was rooted in Mexico's mixed-race history. Referring to "the mystery of the structure of nationality" and the "difficulty of building it," he wrote, "some of these defects are not exclusively ours, but are common to various countries of America. Others are hereditary; they belong to the moral physiognomy of the conquest; blood played a fundamental role."[50]

As a leader of Mexico's reform efforts, Gastélum was keenly aware of the day-to-day effects on individuals and society of the tremendous disparities between poor indigenous and mestizo Mexicans and more affluent, (usually) whiter ones in health care, hygiene, and living conditions. For that reason he homed in on race as an issue central to transforming the country. Like Vasconcelos, he argued for the mixing of Spanish and indigenous Mexicans: "the decisive factor in spiritual unification—given the diverse ethnic groups that constitute the nation—is to locate [them in] the same landscape, give them the same tone, in order to sing the identical melody. To mix with the race other races of superior lineages. . . . The mental disintegration from which the country suffers is owed, in its essence, to the lack of a process of racial incorporation since independence."[51] Gastélum's reasoning was that of a physician and bureaucrat who was also trained in evolutionary theory, but the fundamental racism embedded in his thinking was shared by many intellectuals of the period. As Mary K. Coffey has shown, discussions of the so-called Indian problem underlay major works of art in this decade, particularly Rivera's cycle at the Ministry of Education, where the muralist attempted to create a unified "portrait" of a country whose diversity artists and intellectuals increasingly recognized.[52]

Gastélum used architectural metaphors repeatedly in his writings on cultural and political unity. In *La clase, arquitectura de la comunidad*, he argued that class integration under a coherent and consistent universalizing definition of nationality was essential to Mexican progress. Opening his discussion by evoking the cities of ancient Mesopotamia and Egypt, and calling the metropolis the fundamental building block of government, Gastélum claimed that civic ideals and values were particular to each culture and to each age and place.[53] This formulation created an opening in a general Western history for Mexico's particular historical and social conditions. Gastélum also argued that cultural values and social forces were most clearly visible in architecture and sculpture. Focusing on the house, the doctor argued that the history of architecture was indistinguishable from human history: "without the house history would not be possible, because civilization began when man learned how to build." He believed that houses reflected the professional or cultural identities of their inhabitants and claimed that "the house reveals the spirit of the person who lives there: artist, scholar, worker."[54] This idea closely paralleled Mariscal's definition of national architectonic art as "that which reveals the most general life and customs during the entire life of Mexico as a nation."[55] This coincidence of architectural and sociopolitical theory reflected the close ties between bureaucrats and intellectuals in the early twentieth century and anticipated the intensified relationship between architecture and politics in the second half of the century.

PICTURING INDIGENEITY

On the ministry building, materials and architectural elements intended to be read representationally carried allusions to Hispanic and indigenous Mexico, but architectural sculpture was also critical to shaping a recognizably "mestizo" building. Working with Centurión and Pillig, Obregón Santacilia continued a Beaux-Arts tradition that had thrived throughout the Porfiriato. With its colonial and indigenous allusions, and its incorporation of several arts, the ministry reestablished the intimate relationship between "European" architecture and "native" sculpture that historians of Churrigueresque architecture had identified. It also proposed a modern way of unifying the arts in

FIGURE 2.12. Manuel Centurión, Head of a Woman, Ministry of Health, 1929.

a seemingly nationally specific idiom. On each of the outside bays of the entrance pavilion Centurión carved large, masklike faces depicting indigenous people at different stages of life (figures 2.12 and 2.13). The sculptures functioned both as decoration on the main facade and as

FIGURE 2.13. Centurión, Head of a Man, Ministry of Health, 1929.

part of a sculptural sequence that continued on the short sides of each pavilion. Each head was different and expressive, and represented a man or woman in youth, middle age, or old age. Collectively the sculptures alluded to the cycle of human life, which was also the subject of the original murals painted by Fernando Leal inside the laboratory porch. Destroyed because of objections to Leal's representation of an amorous embrace by a dark-skinned couple in which a female breast was exposed, the murals were replaced by Rivera's decidedly nonerotic depictions of microscopic views of cells.[56]

As a group, the faces also suggested the enduring presence of a generalized indigenous population, but the sculptures were considerably more individuated than most 1920s images of native people. Unlike many artists, Centurión depicted his figures with distinct and believable facial features, rather than as warriors, historical figures, or generic typecasts. In this they were pointedly unlike Mexico's most famous recent indigenous references in architectural sculpture, the masklike renderings of Aztec eagle and jaguar knights—whose Euro-

FIGURE 2.14. Adamo Boari, Jaguar Knight keystone, Palacio de Bellas Artes, ca. 1910.

pean physiognomy was unmistakable—that decorated the keystones of the ground-floor arches at Adamo Boari's unfinished Palace of Fine Arts at the edge of the Centro (figure 2.14).

Boari's figures shared that facade with classical nymphs and Art Noveau masks of female faces, but in the arches beneath them slithered fanged serpents that were quite unlike fin-de-siècle European architectural sculpture. Although in the 1930s it was widely understood to epitomize the worst of Porfirian architectural excess and infatuation with "inappropriate" foreign models, the Palace of Fine Arts nevertheless probably suggested to Obregón Santacilia possibilities for integrating representations of forms drawn from a variety of contexts on the facade. Like the Ministry of Health, Boari's building was a classicizing modern palace. Although he later called it "a true white elephant" and implicitly critiqued the facade for conveying the "sense that each element was composed separately," Obregón Santacilia himself arranged the facade of the Ministry of Health similarly, but pulled the elements together in a subtler and more historically and culturally responsive way.[57]

Pillig's reliefs depicting plants and fruits also visually linked the building to "native" Mexico and to important national visual traditions and contemporary fashions. The representations of laboratory equipment, such as test tubes, microscopes, and even lab rats, alternated with those of American fruits and plants, departed markedly from the traditional subjects of Beaux-Arts architectural sculpture and pictorially annunciated the ministry's ambition to bring modern science to native Mexico (figures 2.15 and 2.16). Pillig's work also helped define a rapidly evolving and highly sophisticated system of depictions of folk art forms. Most of the carvings showed flora teaming out of a basket or a bowl (figures 2.17 and 2.18). Images of fresh produce called to mind public health reformers' growing concerns about food safety, their attempts to regulate Mexico City's markets, and evoked Mexico's rich gastronomic heritage. Many of Pillig's crops and flowers were central to the Mexican diet; among them were oranges, guavas, cacti, squashes of various kinds, jicama, peppers, corn, and grapes. With Centurión's heads, they alluded to Gastélum's arguments about health, society, and native people and linked the building to two national painting traditions—colonial *casta* paintings and *costumbrista* images, in which painters often included mixed race or native people with depictions of foodstuffs, crafts, and even settings regarded as typically Mexican. Pillig called folk art objects to mind by placing the fruits and vegetables in containers that resembled the woven and ceramic goods made by rural craftspeople.[58] Although they were carved high on the building, the reliefs could be seen easily from the street and, just as the exhibitions of the folk art had earlier in the decade, helped bring folk art into view in the capital.

The building's pair of enormous, shiny, copper-clad bridges, under which the cars of high-ranking bureaucrats passed as they entered the ministry, at once represented materially a dynamic industrial age of the kind European modern architects sought to convey with tubular steel and chrome, and the craft objects in one of Mexico's most important states for folk art and culture (plate 5). Hammered copper objects, such as bowls and plates, made by artisans in the town of Santa Clara del Cobre were among the many kinds of folk art objects from the state of Michoacán, which was one of the places most admired by Mexico City artists and intellectuals for its folk art. Shiny copper also clad the gates at the main entrance with playful curves that would have been at home nearly anywhere in the jazz-age world. Juxtaposed against the dark volcanic rock and its ponderous symbolic and visual weight, the gates advanced the building's overall argument that material and associative juxtapositions could shape decidedly cosmopolitan compositions.

FIGURES 2.15, 2.16, 2.17, AND 2.18 (*clockwise from top left*). Hans Pillig, relief showing laboratory equipment; relief showing cacti and squash; relief showing fruit in a basket; relief showing fruit in a ceramic bowl, Ministry of Health, 1929.

Pillig's reliefs were the first works in which pictorial representation on the facade of a modern building simultaneously conveyed internationalism and nativism and thereby helped begin a robust tradition to which many of twentieth-century Mexico's most important works of architecture belong. The panels resembled sculptural decoration, showing vessels overflowing with flowers, which was used widely on modern classical and Art Deco buildings and on decorative objects in many countries in the 1920s, but Pillig made the objects in the bowls and baskets function as Mexican artist Adolfo Best Maugard's conventionalization of Mexican folk art forms did in other contexts and likely drew inspiration from his ideas. Best Maugard's drawing manual, *Metódo de dibujo: Tradición, resurgimiento y evolución del arte mexicano* (Drawing Method: Tradition, Resurgence, and Evolution of Mexican Art), was first published in 1923 by the Ministry of Education, when Vasconcelos was still minister, and the book, which was illus-

CANASTAS.—Para hacer el motivo de la canasta, traza-remos dos líneas paralelas, una arriba de la otra, a regular distancia que uniremos por dos medios círculos hacia afuera, muy abiertos; así tendremos el cuerpo de la canasta. La línea de arriba que será más larga que la de abajo, la adornaremos con alguna *greca*, y el cuerpo de la canasta, con un *petatillo*, y dos espirales unidas en sentido contrario, como dos SS, nos darán las asas de la canasta. Sabiendo ya hacer las flores y las hojas, las emplearemos en adornar la canasta, e iremos colocándolas tra-tando de equilibrarlas, de manera que queden bien repartidas, que el peso sea igual de los dos lados, evitando hacer el lado izquierdo igual al lado derecho. Todo lo anterior lo podemos encerrar dentro de un círculo o dentro de un óvalo, adornado con una *greca*.

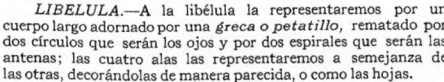

LIBELULA.—A la libélula la representaremos por un cuerpo largo adornado por una *greca o petatillo,* rematado por dos círculos que serán los ojos y por dos espirales que serán las antenas; las cuatro alas las representaremos a semejanza de las otras, decorándolas de manera parecida, o como las hojas.

FIGURE 2.19. Miguel Covarrubias, guide to drawing butterflies, dragonflies, and baskets, from Adolfo Best Maugard, *Metódo de dibujo: Tradición, resurgimiento y evolución del arte mexicano* (1923).

trated by Miguel Covarrubias, helped define the standardized visual vocabulary of folk art that was emerging in the 1920s (figures 2.19 and 2.20). Although it was officially suppressed in 1925, *Metódo de dibujo* was used widely to teach Mexican schoolchildren how to make "Mex-ican" art characterized by its abstraction and supposedly recognizable connections to indigenous art. The book was enormously influential for artists for a short but critical period in the development of twentieth-century Mexican art, and as Karen Cordero Reiman has explained, was "part of a pervasive trend in art education that sought to promote the expression of national essence."[59]

A student of preconquest and Mexican folk art, Best Maugard de-veloped a theory of art based on the manipulation and combination of seven basic elements—the straight line, the curved line, the spiral, the circle, the half circle, the S form, and the zigzag line—that he be-lieved were the basis of all art.[60] Arranged in certain combinations these elements, he argued, created distinctively Mexican patterns that could be the basis of drawings and paintings that were identifiably "Mexican." Like historians of colonial Mexican architecture, Best Maugard believed that it was during the colonial period that distinctive national forms—based on the melding of elements of indigenous and Spanish art, with influences from Asia (where Spain had colonies) began to appear. According to the artist, in the twentieth century, the most vital manifestation of this art was to be found in folk art. Like Best Maugard's imagery, Pillig's reliefs of plants in baskets and bowls helped create a conventionalized set of forms that were both derived from Mexican folk art and stood for it. Floral and fruit motifs had been used widely on colonial buildings, especially on frames of windows and doors, where they functioned quite obviously as ornament; but at the Ministry of Health Pillig and Obregón Santacilia pictorialized these motifs and treated the exterior surface of the building as a picture plane. In their hands, forms that had been used in colonial buildings as ornament became pictures, like Best Maugard's.

Conventionalized depictions of plants in architectural sculpture were neither new nor unique to Mexico. In the United States architects had used them since the mid-nineteenth century as they developed modern architectural languages for cities transformed by industrialization and new suburbs. Inspired largely by English theorists Owen Jones and Francis Bedford's *The Grammar of Ornament* (1856), beginning in the 1870s Frank Furness used Jones's principle of examining objects in nature to discover their underlying geometry and form to create architectural decoration that was recognizable as an abstraction from a plant. Shortly thereafter, Louis Sullivan followed Furness's precedent, and later and even more famously his student, Frank Lloyd Wright, developed it further.[61] Pillig's work was not as abstract as Wright's and by remaining representational, it retained its connections to the Best Maugard system. As part of a decorative and architectural program driven by an ambition to enter national architectural history and to express certain ideas associated with the agency it housed, Pillig's sculpture ultimately served ends very different from Wright's conventionalizations.

As scholars have long recognized, at the core of the development of many canonical modern buildings was the belief that one of the central tasks of the modern architect was to reveal in new designs the underlying geometries and principles that governed the great buildings of the past. Perhaps no text expressed this idea more clearly than Le Corbusier's passages on primary forms, which he claimed governed the best classical and Renaissance buildings, and which he illustrated and published in *Vers une architecture* the year after *Metódo de dibujo* appeared. While Best Maugard and others in Mexico like Pillig examined folk art, they too participated in an international tendency that was concerned with the problem of representation and abstraction in the development of new, up-to-date visual languages. Whereas European architects often discussed their investigations of geometric abstraction and conventionalization in terms of abstraction's "universalizing" qualities or potentials—a position that surely resonated widely in interwar Europe where modern architects and their supporters were, in many cases and with good reason, keen to distance themselves from nationalist rhetoric—in Mexico conventionalization served nationalist political and cultural aims. Far removed from the centers of the European avant-garde, where abstraction emerged as a response to long-standing debates internal to European painting and architecture and was also political, Mexican architects and their associates recognized the value of conventionalization and formal distillation not primarily as a means of responding to staid academic traditions (although it did that too), but as a way to reinvigorate the country's supposedly dormant native artistic culture. Like their colleagues across the Atlantic, however, they also believed that by revealing essences and originary forms, whether of folk art or of preconquest and colonial architecture, they were clearing away the visual debris of the recent past (embodied by the architecture built during the Díaz regime) in order to replace it with images and forms suited to their time and place.

The precedents for Pillig's translation into architectural decoration of conventionalized images with recognizable connections to folk art had been laid by Montenegro, who was good friends with Miguel Covarrubias, the illustrator of *Metódo de dibujo*, and who, like Best Maugard, helped create the image of "Mexican" art through stylized interpretations of folk art forms in paint. In 1921, the year before he worked with Obregón Santacilia in Rio de Janeiro, with Jorge Enciso, Montenegro painted one of modern Mexico's first important murals, *El árbol de la vida*, in the former Jesuit church of San Pedro y San Pablo, whose foundations dated to the sixteenth century. In addition to this Art Nouveau–esque painting, which was the single largest work in San Pedro y San Pablo, Montenegro oversaw the space's decorative program, which included sculpture, stained glass, and painted ceramic tile. To a greater degree than his mural, these works functioned architecturally and were among the very first in which folk art objects, images of indigenous Mexicans, and colonial architecture were united.

FIGURE 2.20. Covarrubias, figure with lacquerware bowl, fruit, and cacti, from Best Maugard, *Metódo de dibujo.*

On their own, Montenegro's two half-circle stained-glass windows, *Jarabe tapatío* and *Vendedora de pericos*, were the most impressive works in the building. Fabricated by Enrique Villaseñor, the stained-glass master who executed Rivera's designs in the Ministry of Health, the windows were installed in the transepts as clerestories. In the west transept, *Jarabe tapatío* depicted a couple wearing the traditional dress and dancing a traditional dance from the state of Jalisco as Mexican peasants played music and looked on (figure 2.21). Cactuses, corn, and

FIGURE 2.21. Roberto Montenegro, *Jarabe tapatío*, stained glass, detail, former Church of San Pedro y San Pablo, Mexico City, 1921.

the drooping branches of a tree framed the scene and earthenware pots, melons, and other fruits littered the ground. To the right of the couple in the background stood a Mexican church with a dome and single tower. In *Vendedora de pericos*, in the east transept, surrounded by similar foliage, a Mexican peasant woman sold parakeets from a platform balanced on her head. Elsewhere in the composition peasants wearing distinctive serapes and carrying earthenware vessels moved through the landscape. The windows were among the very first large-scale depictions in a public building of Mexican folk culture and although they were not nearly as large as *árbol de la vida*, in their material and location they acknowledged the architecture to a greater degree than the mural and alluded to the building's original use.

References to colonial architecture and folk art other than those in *Jarabe Tapatío* appeared in the tile mosaics Fernández Ledesma painted at the base of the east end of the building. In the central panel of one he depicted a Mexican peasant woman balancing a painted wooden

FIGURE 2.22. Jorge Fernández Ledesma, painted tile mosaic, former Church of San Pedro y San Pablo, 1921.

bowl on her head and standing outside of an atrial gate beyond which rose the blue-and-white tiled dome of a colonial church (figure 2.22). In another mosaic, against the backdrop of a yellow colonial church, he placed a Mexican male peasant wearing a sombrero and a serape with a Mexican eagle and the words, "viva Mex." Around both panels the artist painted intricate arabesque patterns reminiscent of the designs typical of polychrome Talavera pottery. Xavier Guerrero and Hermilio Jiménez also alluded to folk art in their painted decorations of the arches, door frames, and pilasters throughout the space. The artists' bands of intricate vine and floral patterns emphasized the structural elements of the building and, at the bases of the pilasters that supported arches of the crossing, appeared to grow from Talavera pots. Their painted bands of stylized baskets, leaves, petals, and peacocks, like images of vessels and fruits in Montenegro's windows and the parrots, pottery, and foliage Fernández Ledesma rendered in tile, resembled the illustrations of these objects in *Metódo de dibujo*. Like the images in the book, those in the building had clearly defined lines, depicted objects in profile and frontally, and read as conventionalized representations of plants and patterns that appeared in works of folk art.

In addition to the broad associations with indigenous Mexico awakened by the paintings and windows, positioned at the corners of the former church's crossing were four, freestanding bare-chested atlantes carved in stone with indigenous facial features (figure 2.23). Rather than supporting entablatures, the figures balanced large bowls decorated with floral patterns like that carried by the female figure in Fernández Ledesma's mosaic and reminiscent of the painted lacquerware of Michoacán. The sculptures were likely the work of Ignacio Asúnsolo or Manuel Centurión, both of whom created stone figural sculptures for the Ministry of Education building. Although the San Pedro y San Pablo sculptures were not structural, in the way that the torsos of the figures rose from inverted bases each decorated with a lambrequin, they called to mind estípites, an association heightened by their presence in the former colonial church. At the base of each sculpture small rounded forms evoking feet suggested that the indigenous figure melded completely into the architectural-sculptural form, as if to symbolize sculpturally the enmeshment of indigenous and colonial Mexico. By including the depiction of the folk art bowl, which viewers would have understood to have been painted, the sculptor implied not only that modern folk art rested on the shoulders of indigenous Mexico, but pulled together in a single work architecture, sculpture, and painting.

Except for Montenegro's mural and windows, the works in San Pedro y San Pablo have been accorded relatively little importance in the development of modern Mexican art. Nevertheless, the artistic program they comprised was the first modern attempt to unite architecture, painting, sculpture, and even stained glass and to visually link folk art, indigenous Mexico, and colonial architecture. The location of the building in the heart of Mexico City and of its artistic renaissance— just opposite the National Preparatory School where Rivera, Orozco, and others created the first major works of the muralist movement and just two blocks from the Ministry of Education—made it easy to visit for young students of art and architecture, such as Obregón Santacilia and his young mentee, Juan O'Gorman.[62]

FIGURE 2.23. Centurion or Ignacio Asúnsolo, atlante supporting a lacquered bowl, former Church of San Pedro y San Pablo, 1921.

Pillig did not use Best Maugard's system nor did his reliefs look exactly like the paintings at San Pedro y San Pablo, but he depicted many of the same kinds of objects and relied on the same principles of conventionalization and representation. At the Ministry of Health Pillig and Obregón Santacilia, more overtly than the Mexican painters, retained visual connections to European languages—Art Deco and modern classicism—while creating forms that read as nationally specific. In the process they shaped one of Mexico's first important modern buildings and laid the foundation for iconic works of later decades in which the kind of visual bilingualism they pioneered on Reforma would be updated and relied upon to carry increasingly complex messages about history and society. As a work patronized by the federal government for an agency charged with improving the lives of millions of Mexicans, the building was inherently political. By alluding to the complex context in which ministry bureaucrats took up their very modern task through their decorative program, Obregón Santacilia and his colleagues astutely knit together their art with the ambitions of their patrons. Their concerns were first and foremost architectural and artistic rather than political, but, more than any other, their building helped establish the links between public patronage, new understandings of architectural history, folk art, and the primacy of surface in Mexican modernism.

The ministry helped introduce an architecture that relied for its meaning on the viewer's capacity to identify and understand both "Mexican" representations and the languages of international modernism. By cultivating a mode of viewing buildings that depended on knowledge of local forms, the Ministry of Health began the process of constituting a viewership expert in "Mexican" iconography, thus further shoring up the idea that such a thing as "national" architecture did exist. The central tension between abstraction and representation at the Ministry of Health linked it to modern buildings outside of Mexico and, as its publication in international journals in the 1920s suggests, made it important not only in Mexico but also in the developments of a broader, international architectural modernism in which architects abroad, while coming to very different formal solutions, grappled with similar problems. As a response to the theoretical concerns raised implicitly, and in some cases explicitly, by accounts of colonial architecture from previous decades, and to the surge of interest in folk art and reform, the building embodied the first significant attempt to grapple simultaneously with the legacy that Mexican architectural history seemed to bequeath and the new social consciousness that the postrevolutionary period demanded.

CHAPTER THREE

FIT AND TRIM

PICTORIAL HISTORIES AT THE VENUSTIANO CARRANZA RECREATION AND ATHLETIC CENTER FOR WORKERS

> It has been nearly twenty years since Mexican artists began the movement of architectural introspection in an attempt to renew, or rather, recover the values created during the colonial period and deprecated completely between Independence and the end of the nineteenth century, fighting in that introspection to take from those colonial elements truly Mexican characteristics that could serve as a natural and logical base for an entire grand homogenous artistic movement that harmonizes most rationally with the premises of our culture and our artistic environment.
>
> —Alfonso Pallares, 1926

The highly charged relationship between historical forms, representation, and national specificity that the Ministry of Health embodied, and to which architect Alfonso Pallares referred in a Mexico City newspaper article, intensified in the late 1920s with the growth of governmental clients' reformist rhetoric, architects' understanding of the depth of the country's inequalities, and bureaucrats' concern with how Mexican culture was imagined by its citizens and perceived by foreigners. Colonial architectural history and folk art remained vitally important to architects, but continued archaeological research, and books and essays published abroad, suggested that by the end of the decade both the sources of historical references in modern buildings and the audiences for Mexican architectural history were expanding. At the beginning of the century scholars had indicated that flexibility and connection to cultural conditions were characteristic of colonial works, and by the end of the decade a substantial body of built and proposed projects in Mexico City made it clear that those qualities marked modern approaches to design as well. Among the large projects constructed in Mexico City in the late 1920s, Juan Segura's enormous workers' park, the Centro Social y Deportivo para Trabajadores "Venustiano Carranza" (Venustiano Carranza Recreation and Athletic Center for Workers) stood out for its size, reformist ambitions, and the

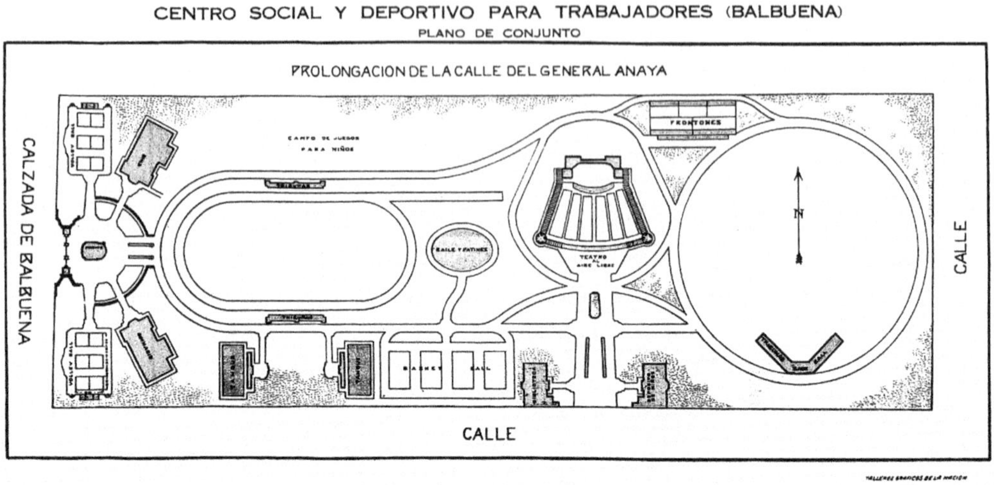

CENTRO SOCIAL Y DEPORTIVO PARA TRABAJADORES (BALBUENA)
PLANO DE CONJUNTO

FIGURE 3.1. Juan Segura, Venustiano Carranza Recreation and Athletic Center for Workers, site plan, 1929.

sophisticated ways it took up the questions of history and representation that had driven discussions of architecture since 1900.

As the most important building project undertaken by the newly created Federal District (Mexico City's administrative body) in 1929, it embodied the growing enmeshment of architecture and politics. Although little evidence exists regarding Segura's ideas about architectural history or this project, documentary photographs of the park's opening, reproductions of the architect's watercolors of the center, and new texts on Mexican architectural history published by the Mexican government suggest that the park existed at the intersection of increasingly complicated understandings of architectural history, indigenous culture, and social reform. With space for five thousand people to exercise and learn at once, the vast campus of the Carranza Center included a gymnasium, cinema, library, open-air theater, athletic fields, swimming pools, jai alai courts, and a child-care facility (figure 3.1) At the Ministry of Health, references to popular health and welfare were swaddled in complicated policies and rather abstract understandings of culture. By contrast, at the Carranza Center classicism and references to colonial architecture were deployed on a giant scale explicitly for the bodily, intellectual, and cultural improvement of a mass audience.

At the Carranza Center, Segura reworked motifs that he had first explored on buildings for private clients, reinterpreting baroque scroll patterns, using painted colonial-style tile and varied patterns of fenestration, but did so in a way that emphasized their character as representations of elements that belonged to another era. As a populist project with historical allusions, the Carranza Center echoed in built form early historians' claims about the entwining of colonial architecture and the emergence of a distinctive Mexican society, but seen in light of the architectural debates that unfolded at the time it was built, the park was also significant for the ways it revealed the absence of agreement on what "Mexican" architecture looked like. Indeed, in the same year that the Carranza Center was built the federal government commissioned José Villagrán García to create a very different building for the poor—a tuberculosis sanatorium at the edge of the capital—which he designed in a classicizing rationalist language.

Representation and allusion, on the buildings, in photographs, and in the performances staged to mark the Carranza Center's opening, were critical to the project's meaning. To a greater extent than any of his colleagues up until then, Segura recognized and exploited the representational potential of the wall surface and, in doing so, created buildings that implicitly pointed to the performative qualities of his client's approach to architecture and architects' increasingly fraught relationship to history. The enormous park was intended simultaneously to promote individual welfare and to serve as a vast stage on which local, national, and international audiences would see evidence of social progress. In choreographed images of mass exercise and patriotism viewers would identify a coherent, unified national culture embodied by brown-skinned workers and their children as they played on vast fields and performed in musical and theatrical numbers in a giant open-air theater.

Just as the athletic fields and stage were conspicuously empty and incomplete in the absence of bodies, so too the walls of Segura's buildings would have been austerely blank without the pictorialized historicist elements and associatively charged materials he pointedly applied so as to draw attention to their character as ornament. This was not so much a reworking of the principles of sixteenth-century planimetricism as it was an articulation of the tensions between historicism and abstraction recognizable in many places around 1930. More than Obregón Santacilia's, Segura's was an architecture of the surface and the wall, and as one of the first major projects in which stucco walls were painted, it helped establish the enduring association of "Mexican" architecture with smooth, colored surfaces. Through his manipulation of historical elements and materials, like Obregón Santacilia, Segura facilitated the establishment of a recognizably national visual system in which representations of historical architectural elements and materials associated with older buildings "Mexicanized" modern facades. The Carranza Center set overt populism against a cool, abstract historicism, while intense publicity and heavy-handed stagecraft on the part of the patron linked this new architecture to fitness in the broadest sense.

Segura's park was built at a watershed moment in Mexican architectural history. It helped define the modern civic center as a type, and the commission foreshadowed the increasingly important role the government would assume as an architectural patron in the 1930s, when bureaucrats further conflated government, the Mexican Revolution, and architecture. In the scale and breadth of services it housed, the Carranza Center also anticipated the dramatic lower- and middle-income housing and public education projects that transformed the capital in the 1940s and 1950s. The buildings prefigured the even more stripped-down public architecture of the decade ahead and expressed the increasingly strident rhetoric that accompanied ever more machinelike efforts to reform large numbers of people. By coupling large-scale modern planning with a program intended to convey progress to a broad audience, the Carranza Center also foreshadowed the major works of the mid-century in which architects would aggrandize public education and welfare spatially and more dramatically, and propose associations with a longer Mexican architectural history.

But the architect's restrained approach to historical forms, and his buildings' ultimate austerity against the spectacular riot of activity that occurred in front of and inside them also provided some of the first faint evidence of architects' doubt about the overall project of creating a modern, nationally specific architecture, even as doing so became more important to them and their patrons. Seen in light of his client's far-reaching ambitions for the park, the demographics of its users, and the growing chorus of critics and historians who identified links between architecture and social circumstances, Segura's restrained representations of and allusions to high style and colonial vernacular architecture and craft implied that modern workers were in some way descendant from the unnamed native and mestizo people who had built those works centuries before. And yet the buildings' austerity and their deeply intellectual, abstract relationships to history put them at odds with the rather obvious ritualistic displays of nationalism that took place in and around them. Indeed, the Carranza Center's similarities to private commissions from the same period that had little to do with reform or politics suggest that architecture and ideology remained

FIGURE 3.2. Workers arriving at the Carranza Center for the inauguration, November 20, 1929.

distinct for him. They reveal that through the end of the 1920s modern design was motivated by concerns internal to architecture, but embedded in a complex network of associations about society, race, and art.

THE CITY OF WORKERS AND TOURISTS

Between 1910 and 1930 the population of Mexico City grew from approximately 720,000 to 1.23 million people, largely because of internal migration from rural areas and small towns, and in the late 1920s the federal government began its extraordinary, multidecade campaign to attract foreign tourists to Mexico in large numbers. On the face of it these two events seem unrelated, but in fact both helped motivate far-reaching efforts to improve municipal and national infrastructure, continue social welfare programs, and to define a unified national culture clearly and compellingly, nearly always in reference to preconquest ruins, colonial churches, and folk art. The enormous population increase stressed existing infrastructure and inspired architects who were concerned about the future of historical buildings and, increasingly, about social problems, to devote close attention to urban planning. Throughout the 1920s they wrote about planning, urbanism, and "civic art," and published proposals for plans of Mexico City, improvements to the Alameda Central (the large garden just west of the historic center), preservation of pre-Hispanic sites, and colonial gardens.[1] Some designed new neighborhoods, including Condesa and Lomas de Chapultepec, for middle-class and wealthy residents. In these neighborhoods private developers marketed basic infrastructure, such as paving and lighting, along with houses and neighborhood amenities, but elsewhere in the city, in districts where there was little to attract private capital, infrastructure and planning lagged far behind. On the other hand, as the National Revolutionary Party was consolidated in 1929, in an effort to attract foreigners and their money, President Emilio Portes Gil relaxed restrictions on entering the country and created a national tourist commission.[2] It was in this context that the new Department of the Federal District hired Segura to design the Carranza Center and commissioned other architects to design housing, schools, and undertake planning.[3] The *Los Angeles Times* covered the grand opening of the center,[4] and Anita Brenner, one of Mexico's leading travel writers told tourists that it was "particularly worth visiting."[5] Just as the audience for Mexican architectural history was becoming international, so was the audience for modern architecture.

From its client's perspective, the Carranza Center was not only a palliative for social ills, but an anchor for the controlled development of the area near the Balbuena airfield at the eastern edge of the capital. Long the least desirable part of the metropolitan area, the land east of the ancient sacred precinct of Tenochtitlan had been symbolically rejected by the Aztecs who built causeways to the mainland from their island capital in each of the cardinal directions, except east. During the colonial and viceregal periods, Mexico City grew west and south and, to a lesser extent, north. The capital followed this growth pattern through the twentieth century, but as rural peasants teemed into the city after the revolution and became urban workers in need of housing and spaces to play, bureaucrats (many of them newly wealthy and able to move into new neighborhoods in the southwest) focused their attention on developing the eastern districts for these new residents who could afford to live only in less expensive parts of town.

With the development of Balbuena, the municipal government attempted to move faster than the city's eastward sprawl and prepared to meet it with sewage systems, paved roads, and lighting.[6] The engineer and architect, Guillermo Zárraga, who directed the Office of Public Works from 1925 to 1932, oversaw the planning of the area as a workers' district, commissioned the building of a hospital, and, in 1927 at the behest of the Ministry of Education, designed the Domingo Faustino Sarmiento Open Air School to serve the area.[7] In Balbuena in 1932, three years after the Carranza Center opened, the Federal District began constructing the first 120 workers' houses designed by Juan Legarreta. His modern housing designs for the area, some of which accommodated street-level storefronts, became prototypes for similar housing schemes in two other neighborhoods that were built in 1934.[8] Although Segura had no training in urban planning, in the Balbuena commission he created an orderly scheme for a vast empty plain that functioned as a neighborhood center and connected the old parts of the capital east of the Zócalo to the planned workers' districts.

JUAN SEGURA

Segura was born in 1898 and grew up in the very heart of the colonial center of Mexico City on a street that was later destroyed for the excavations of the Templo Mayor, at the heart of the Aztec city. Having been surrounded by colonial architecture from a very early age, he studied at the National School of Fine Arts as the curriculum expanded to include the study of Mexican architectural history and he was a contemporary of Obregón Santacilia and José Villagrán García. Here, in the late 1910s and early 1920s, Segura developed his disciplined, distanced approach to the currents of historicism and modernist style, and was shaped by the tenets of Beaux-Arts design. To a greater extent than his colleagues he embraced the aesthetics of turn-of-the-century French architecture and design, which manifested in his work as exquisite watercolor drawings and refined ornament and detailing. At first glance, his buildings registered stylistically somewhere between Art Nouveau and Art Deco, but with their pared surfaces and recollections of colonial forms, in many respects they typified the architecture of Mexico City in the late 1920s. Years after the Carranza Center was built, Segura refused to identify specific sources for his work or any particular theoretical positions, but insisted simply that artistic judgment had governed his choices. He noted, "I had influences, but one wanted to reject them and not be subject to old canons . . . the architect has to, should, have the creative faculty of an artist, each one has liberty because really what the architect develops is personal and it is exposed to the critiques of the world."[9] Reflecting on his training in painting, sculpture, and drawing as part of the architecture curriculum, Segura emphasized the importance of art in young architects' approach to their work in the 1920s: "we studied with the idea that we were not just architects, but artists" and stressed the importance of visual pleasure in architecture saying, "the architect has the obligation, in addition to constructing, to make agreeable houses that people like, that give satisfaction to live in."[10]

Although, like his colleagues, Segura rejected the classicizing language and imitative techniques that dominated their training, the principles of axial planning and the composition of architectural elements on the facade remained firmly imprinted on him. Antonio Toca has seen in Segura's work the influence of Jean-Nicolas-Louis Durand's system of composition in particular.[11] This understanding of architecture as a collection of parts to be arranged on an elevation, and the intense focus on architectural drawing that Segura and his classmates received, helps explain the strikingly graphic quality of the architect's use of detail in the late 1920s and early 1930s. His close attention to parti, evident in the plans of projects with complicated programs, such as the Carranza Center and the slightly later Ermita Building (which combined apartments, stores, and a cinema on a triangular urban site), also revealed the enduring influence of Julien Guadet's writings on program and Durand's emphasis on problem solving.

Segura's aestheticist approach to design was also shaped by his years of work with French architect Paul Dubois, who designed several important commercial buildings in downtown Mexico City. Most significant was his rebuilding of the famous department store, El Palacio de Hierro (1921), which stood on a large corner site on a major street south of Zócalo (figure 3.3). With its rounded, domed corner, colorful exterior mosaic decoration, rounded fourth-floor windows, and stylized lettering it read more as a late Art Nouveau Porfirian palace than as a postrevolutionary design. The building's implied frame and similarities to department stores in the United States (one thinks especially of Sullivan's Carson, Pirie, Scott store, now Sullivan Center in Chicago) located it firmly in the age of technological rationalism. Before his departure from Dubois's office in 1923, Segura worked on other commercial projects and on the French hospital. Between 1927 and 1929 he designed several apartment buildings in which he experimented with various ways of texturing and cladding facade surfaces to create pattern and developed a distinctive, but up-to-date, and rather moody synthesis of Art Deco and sparingly used colonial revival forms. In designs for apartment buildings, single-family houses, and institutional buildings for the Fundación de Mier y Pesado, a private philanthropic

FIGURE 3.3. Paul Dubois, El Palacio de Hierro, 1921.

organization to which he had familial ties, Segura created a distinctive formal language that, in its austerity and self-conscious use of ornament, provided a dramatic contrast with the ornate colonial revival buildings that were favored by wealthy private clients in new suburbs. Because of their conspicuous historicism, consumption of resources, and implicit glorification of colonial wealth in an era of growing attention to class inequality and the vilification of colonial power structures, such buildings were often viewed as ideologically suspect by the government and its supporters.[12]

Although it was one of the most important planning projects of the twenty years after the revolution, Latin America's first recreation center for workers, and in the 1920s clearly regarded as one of Mexico City's most significant works of architecture, Segura's project has appeared in few histories of twentieth-century Mexican architecture. His contributions have often been overshadowed by those of Obregón Santacilia, Villagrán García, Juan O'Gorman, and slightly younger architects. Unlike his better-known colleagues, Segura did not teach or write about architecture or participate in political and theoretical debates with his contemporaries.[13] His exclusion from early histories of Mexican modern architecture may also be explained by the fact that most of his work was for private clients, at a time when nearly all of Mexico's modern architects were employed by the federal or municipal government.[14] Segura's connection to Dubois, his engagement with colonial forms, and his client base may also have kept him out of early histories of modern Mexican architecture, which emphasized the buildings of the 1920s and 1930s that anticipated the dominance of International Style modernism at mid-century and public commissions, and often deprecated works by foreign architects.[15] The Carranza Center buildings, like much of the architect's work, seem, at best, to resist easy categorization, and in their classicism and restrained, abstract approach to ornament, in some respects resemble the modern buildings in the United States of the 1920s and early 1930s. The chromatic variety and tensions between austerity and ornament on the rather moody facades even occasionally call to mind Louis Sullivan's bank buildings. Having been destroyed, dramatically altered, or decayed, the buildings and plan of the Carranza Center in the twenty-first century further complicate interpretation. In September 2014, after an extensive renovation to modernize the sports facilities, the Carranza Center reopened as a "luxury" public space, where for a modest monthly fee, Mexico City residents could exercise once again.

Although the complexity of his approach and the dissimilarity of his career from those of twentieth-century Mexico's central figures led some historians to neglect his work, Segura's colleagues recognized his significance. In 1950 Villagrán García saw in Segura's reinterpretation of colonial motifs an architecture "of a totally new character,"[16] yet thirteen years later, observed that Segura was still "frequently ignored."[17] In the later twentieth century historians devoted more attention to him, but characterized Segura's style as "personal" and "unique."[18] Jorge Alberto Manrique provided the best characterization of Segura's work, noting that he incorporated colonial influences without copying them and integrated varied materials. He concluded that the "Segura style" was essentially modern and "enriched with elements that came from tradition, though very liberally interpreted."[19] Segura has appeared in every significant work on modern Mexican architecture since the mid-1970s, yet scholars have mentioned the Carranza Center only briefly, devoting most analysis to Segura's tall multiuse buildings, particularly the Ermita Building (1930–31) in the Mexico City neighborhood of Tacubaya.

HISTORY, SOCIETY, AND THE CRISIS OF REPRESENTATION

Segura matured professionally and designed the Carranza Center against the backdrop of debates about the role architectural history should play in modern design and how architects might intervene in social problems and urban growth. Having emerged from the early histories of colonial architecture, these conversations became increasingly contentious and highly charged in the mid- and late 1920s as attention to cultural expressions of national distinctiveness grew in many realms. Even before Obregón Santacilia had completed the design of the Ministry of Health critiques of revivalism had begun and centered on its seeming inadequacy to the problem of creating a modern national style. In a series of essays published in the Mexico City newspaper *El Universal* in 1924 and 1925, Luis Prieto y Souza, who was trained during the Mexican Revolution and president of the Society of Mexican Architects in 1927–28, called for an end to historicism, condemned the fixation on style he perceived in some architects' work, and urged his colleagues to help solve social and economic problems. Writing that "it is certain that the historical antecedents of a people are always the roots from which the life of the tree trunk and its branches emanate," he warned sternly of the "danger of servile and automatic imitation," and even more emphatically and in reference to colonial architects wrote, "IN ORDER TO BE CONSISTENT IN OUR ADMIRATION FOR THOSE WHO DID THEIR OWN WORK, WE SHOULD IMITATE THEM ONLY BY BEING ORIGINAL."[20]

In the late 1920s architects' increasingly emphatic rejections of historicism were coupled with growing awareness of the severe class inequalities that characterized the country. Prieto y Souza recalled his "sad odyssey though the poor districts of Mexico" and the "nightmare of the filthy cheap houses and dark tunnels of infected suburbs."[21] For six days he had walked alone through Mexico City's most impoverished neighborhoods where he was "surprised by some picturesque scenes," but saw mostly "dark and desolate" ones, and found them "all miserable." He wrote that "on my retina and in my heart were imprinted the impression of all possible human adversities."[22] The architect blamed the state, intellectuals, professionals, and capitalists for the conditions he saw, but praised the efforts of the Ministry of Health to ameliorate living conditions and recent attempts by some architects to draw attention to the living conditions of the poor. The aspirations to universalism that Prieto y Souza expressed elsewhere, and steady calls for a "national" architecture in the face of dramatic social differences (and therefore manifest challenges to conceptions of shared national experience) made revival styles seem both outmoded and irrelevant.

In the late 1920s the question of whether there should be an official national style and what it should be was debated in the three competitions held to decide the design of the Mexican Pavilion for the Ibero-American Exhibition held in Seville in 1929. As a fair about Spanish America held in the former colonial power while Mexico was reinventing itself in the postrevolutionary period, the event carried particular symbolic charge, and Mexican officials instructed that the pavilion be designed in a "national" style, which was understood to mean a pre-Hispanic or colonial revival style. Two abortive competitions were held before Manuel Amabilis's neo-Maya scheme was selected.[23] Changing design criteria and intense criticism of the jury's procedures contributed to the sense of chaos that accompanied discussions of how Mexico should represent itself and what Mexican architecture looked like. In a critique of the first competition written in 1926, Pallares identified three "trajectories" in the proposals—"archeological," "neocolonial," and "modern." He claimed that the stylistic differences in the proposals "reveal[ed] clearly . . . the lack of an architectural criterion on the part of the authors of the program, but also and especially the lack of ideological homogeneity in the conception of architecture on the part of our professionals . . . we have no style."[24]

Changes between the first and second competitions only added to the confusion as architects Ignacio Marquina, winner of the first competition, and Carlos Obregón Santacilia, who took second place, entered schemes that differed dramatically from their original entries. Marquina traded a pre-Columbian revival design with elements from buildings at Uxmal for a neocolonial one, while Obregón Santacilia exchanged a scheme reminiscent of the Benito Juárez School for a forceful stripped-down scheme with bare walls but large-scale replicas of iconic works of Aztec and Maya sculpture. With Vicente Urquiaga, Segura submitted to the first competition a proposal that had the jazzy rhythms of Art Deco architecture but included colonial references in a large window and corner fountain. The polygonal arch above the entrance in their design functioned as Obregón Santacilia's did at the Ministry of Health to convey simultaneously conversance with international cosmopolitan forms and colonial ones. Although the pavilion design was more highly ornamented and monumental than the buildings at the Carranza Center, in its essential restraint and rejection of historicisms it anticipated the workers' park.

As architects and patrons wrestled with stylistic choice, new histories of Mexican architecture appeared. Between 1924 and 1927 the Secretaría de Hacienda published the six volumes of *Iglesias de México*, the most important text of the decade on colonial buildings. With texts by Dr. Atl and distinguished scholar Manuel Toussaint, and photographs by Guillermo Kahlo, along with diagrams, maps, and colored plates, the book brought colonial architecture to life more vividly than any work since Baxter's. Its rather idiosyncratic themes dealt alternately with regional types, architectural elements, one major building, and continuities between the colonial and postcolonial periods. Volumes 1 and 5 were on cupolas and altars; volume 2 was dedicated to the Cathedral of Mexico, and volumes 3 and 4 were on "Ultra-baroque" types in the Valley of Mexico and the typical architecture of the state of Puebla. Volume 6 covered themes in four hundred years of Mexican architecture and was simply titled "1525–1925." In some respects *Iglesias de México* revisited works and borrowed approaches from histories written in previous decades, but its emphasis on the architecture of Puebla, its connection of rural vernacular works and metropolitan high-style ones, and the continuities it proposed across four centuries distinguished it from the earlier texts. Puebla was especially renowned for its brightly colored buildings, and in the late 1920s the state received special attention not only in architectural writings, but in the ever-larger number of travel guides and tourist literature by and for Mexicans and foreigners. Remarking on the view of Puebla from a distance, Anita Brenner wrote, "plenty of people have thrilled to verse at the sight of its blaze of majolica domes, massed like a great nestful of Easter eggs in dark green moss."[25] Dr. Atl claimed that Puebla's architecture was "essentially painterly . . . and fundamentally polychrome."[26] Stressing the importance of color to the state's architecture, the painter argued that although many ancient monuments, from the Parthenon to Toltec temples, were still of considerable interest despite the loss of their paint, poblano architecture "loses almost all of its interest when it is deprived of the coloration with which it was dressed."[27]

For Dr. Atl and other historians, most significant were the tile decorations on churches throughout the state. Puebla's famous Talavera tile, which was used to decorate buildings and to make decorative and household objects, was one of twentieth-century Mexico's most significant material links to colonial artistic practice. In the streets of the city, tourists could see extraordinary colonial palaces decorated in tile, visit workshops, and buy hand-painted ceramics to take home. Extraordinary patterns of red-orange brick and painted tile provided much of Puebla's color and distinguished it from other parts of Mexico. Among the churches in the city of Puebla that Dr. Atl illustrated was the Church of Nuestra Señora de Guadalupe (1694–1722), where zigzagging bands in blue, orange, green, yellow, and white tile stretched horizontally across the portal and painted tile pictures on the bases of the towers depicted the story of the Virgin of Guadalupe. Although Puebla was only ninety miles from Mexico City, and an easy trip from the city even in 1930, like the allusions in Obregón Santacilia and Montenegro's work to Michoacán and Jalisco, Segura's implicit evocation of a specific Mexican state helped shape an emerging metropolitan visual lexicon, which, although it was highly selective in its sources, metaphorically included "distant" regions and served to bring under a single "national" language controlled from Mexico City the places, people, and architecture and art of the large, diverse country.

Included in the survey of postconquest works were vernacular buildings and rural colonial churches—buildings that stood outside of the major cities and were not as easily classified stylistically in the terms that Baxter and Mariscal had outlined in discussions of their urban counterparts. Like the Carranza Center much later, Mexico's rural churches were defined by simplified interpretations of colonial baroque forms, and in the 1920s both were associated with the integration of heretofore-marginalized people into modern Mexico. In his analysis of untrained rural builders' adaptations of urban forms Dr. Atl celebrated vernacular architecture and its makers' rhetoric and tones that echoed Baxter's praise of indigenous artisans and paralleled statements by the government that attempted to bring all Mexicans into a shared national self-understanding. Dr. Atl wrote of the rural churches and their creators: "The humble and ignored overseers and builders who raised and decorated more than 8,000 churches worked according to the same . . . painterly concept which guided all the Baroque masters, and their workshops, although more humble, have that same sense of the . . . *bello pittorico*."[28] In using Italian to describe the work of rural Mexican builders and native painters Dr. Atl made an obvious attempt to link the nation's vernacular architecture to the Italian Renaissance, and reinforced the often-repeated idea that 1920s Mexico was comparable to the most widely revered period in Western art history. In the context of a work on Mexican colonial architecture, Atl's choice of words read almost as a response to Baxter's suggestion, nearly thirty years earlier, that such an efflorescence was possible.

Atl concluded his discussion of "Arquitectura Popular" with an allusion to Mexico's class inequalities arguing that twentieth-century builders were the descendants of the great architects of Mexican colonial buildings, but suggested that they had been limited in their creativity by professional influence:

> The contemporary master of works and the builder possess the qualities of their ancestors, the great builders of churches; but these qualities have not been able to be expressed in a personal form because of modern necessities and because the work executed under the direction of professional architects and engineers has disciplined the sentiment and manual ability of these workers. . . . But within that discipline can be seen the facility of those workers who have helped elevate the housing of inhabitants of the Mexico today, under empire (until relatively recently), from detestable taste and a dreadful concept of comfort and hygiene.[29]

The proclamation that these builders were instrumental in improving the conditions in which their unfortunate fellow citizens lived was offered in a patronizing tone similar to that of governmental reformist rhetoric and it anticipated the premise of self-improvement through contact with correct forms of culture that underlay the Carranza Center commission. Dr. Atl's implication that native or mestizo people were innately artistically talented also recalled a similar claim that Baxter had made, as well as the assertions of some 1920s intellectuals who oversaw Mexico's open-air schools of painting for peasants and

FIGURE 3.4. Ezequiel Negrete, *San Juan Chapel, Xochimilco*, illustrated in *Iglesias de México*.

workers.[30] *Iglesias de México* even included watercolors made by artists with little formal training, such as Ezequiel Negrete's *San Juan Chapel, Xochimilco*, which depicted provincial churches (figure 3.4).

Finally, the painter echoed architectural historians and cultural theorists when he suggested that modern Mexico was on the verge of a great reawakening that would be rooted in an engagement with its colonial forms: "It seems . . . that an architectural renaissance grows from the sources of Colonial Architecture, begun through the efforts of certain intelligent critics and the sensibilities of some young architects. We wait with faith. The positive force of a people initiated, like ours, in the art of building, invariably will be realized with eloquence, very often under the burden of the same difficulties [detestable taste and a dreadful concept of comfort and hygiene]. We hope—or, would it not be better to *act* . . . ?"[31] Dr. Atl concluded his discussion with a call to action, urging his readers to help stimulate

Mexico's latent artistic potential. His implication that the country's architectural vitality was dormant because of inadequate hygiene and the effects of empire echoed the federal government's claims about the effects of inadequate hygiene and political repression on culture more generally.

Nearly three decades after the first historians of colonial architecture had introduced the idea of national architecture, Dr. Atl announced at the very end of *Iglesias de México* that "our national style" is "ULTRA-BAROQUE."[32] Although there was abundant evidence that by 1929 federal officials and the architects they hired did not agree, the presence and prominence of the statement in a major work published by the government revealed the enduring centrality of colonial forms to the collective imagination of what constituted "Mexican" architecture. Equally significant was Dr. Atl's association of architectural style and postrevolutionary social reform. By introducing into 1920s discourse the notion that architectural form and social transformation might be linked directly, Atl's text, and Segura's buildings shortly thereafter, anticipated the even stronger connections ascribed to these things in the 1930s.

Even as Mexican understandings of colonial buildings became further nationalized, foreign scholarship and English-language publications on Mexican architecture increased. Among works published in Mexico that addressed international audiences were an illustrated 1925 history of the famous Casa de los Azulejos, the colonial palace covered in painted tile, and a thesis on this history of Mexican art and architecture written in a seminar at the University of California but published by the Ministry of Public Education in 1928.[33] *An Architectural Pilgrimage in Old Mexico*, by the English architect Alfred Bossom was published in New York in 1924, and Atlee Ayres, a Texas architect, wrote *Mexican Architecture: Domestic, Civil and Ecclesiastical* in 1926. Like Baxter's book, both were heavily illustrated with photographs. By 1931 Sacheverell Sitwell's *Southern Baroque Art*, which included Mexico alone among Latin American countries in its discussion of seventeenth- and eighteenth-century art and music, was in its third edition, having first been published in London in 1924.

Mexican Architecture of the Vice-Regal Period, a work by the U.S. architect Walter H. Kilham appeared in 1927. In contrast to Sitwell's rather romantic interpretation of Mexican buildings, Kilham's book resembled Baxter's by opening with a historical overview, affirming the distinctive excellence of colonial architecture, and included numerous photographs of major buildings throughout Mexico. Just as some artists and intellectuals claimed that indigenous Mexicans were naturally artistic, Kilham suggested that "love of beauty is a marked characteristic of the descendants of the Aztecs."[34] Although he emphasized works by architects, like Dr. Atl, Kilham was interested in vernacular forms and was one of the first writers to illustrate and describe a *pulquería*, a major popular type in 1920s Mexico. After explaining pulque (the highly alcoholic drink made from the juice of the maguey cactus) to his readers, the author noted that "many of the shops which dispense this beverage are provided with facades highly decorated by native artists in brilliant colors."[35] Interestingly, pulquerías were not strictly colonial types, but Kilham's inclusion of them suggests that the twentieth-century establishments were understood as descendants of much earlier ones. There is no evidence that Segura was particularly inspired by the many pulquerías he would have encountered in Mexico City, as Juan O'Gorman later was, but Kilham's text reveals that by the end of the 1920s, as Mexican reformers devoted increasing attention to "social diseases" like alcoholism among the working class, popular building types and aesthetics came to be included in a broadening definition of Mexican architecture—one that, as Atl's text did, fused colonial and popular forms.

Attempts to link art, history, indigenous Mexico, and working-class aesthetics were central to efforts by education minister José Manuel Puig Casauranc, who led the Department of the Federal District when the Carranza Center was built, to stimulate reform and shape a collective definition of national culture. Writing in the short-lived journal *Forma* (1926–28) that the ministry funded, Puig briefly sketched Mexican art history arguing that it revealed "the tremendous wealth of creative force which moves our race." Beginning with "the marvelous ruins of Uxmal and Teotihuacan, flower of the period of preconquest," Puig skipped the colonial era altogether and suggested that the "creative force" survived in the colonial era in "the light grace of the *tilma* . . . , in the decorated jar, in the bowl of perfect coloring and in the polychrome straw mat; which are, in the remote hovel, like a clear note of security and hope."[36] Damning "the bad taste for French things in the nineteenth century," he found promise of renewal in the art made by children in the open-air painting schools.[37] Although it seems unlikely that the workers who came to the Carranza Center found the allusions to folk art on the buildings comforting, as Puig imagined they would be for peasants, his suggestion that folk art might be emotionally resonant was revealing. If, as Benedict Anderson persuasively argued, nationalism begins in imaginative and emotional experience, it is no stretch to see how folk art—which was constructed throughout the 1920s as an anonymous but widespread, historical and nationally distinctive cultural product—could be converted into an agent capable of binding not only the preconquest and modern eras and the city and country, but of delivering to impoverished Mexicans the "security and hope" promised by postrevolutionary reformers.[38]

Documentation of the buildings and the events that took place at the Carranza Center's opening in newspapers and government publications in 1929 and 1930 swept the project almost instantly into Mexican architectural history on the one hand, and an emerging official postrevolutionary culture on the other. The newspaper *Excélsior* recorded that the Carranza Center opening was one of the major events on the day that saw "the most elaborate and widespread celebrations ever held in Mexico, both in the capital and throughout the country to commemorate the nineteenth anniversary of the revolutionary movement against Porfirio Díaz."[39] Beginning around 1929, the November 20 observance of the beginning of the revolution became one of the most important days of the year in Mexico. Revolution Day events typically included athletic displays, national music and dances, and, in some cases, military parades.[40] Fifty thousand people came to see the new center and participate in the festivities. In his remarks at the event Puig spoke of the need to forge a "homogeneous national life that is truly civilized and humane," and suggested that the Carranza Center and the institutionalized revolution would advance that goal by improving working-class Mexicans' access to health care, justice, and economic resources.[41]

Official representations of the center suggested that the Carranza Center was important artistically as well as politically. Among government publications, the 1930 *Atlas general del Distrito Federal* stood out in its lavish documentation of Segura's project and in the ways it implicitly equated it with other major spaces of the city, as if to enfold the new park into the historical city (plate 6). The two-volume atlas described the growth of Mexico City since before the conquest in prose, maps, drawings, and photographs. It was not a history in the usual sense, but its structure and images strongly suggested the existence of continuities between the preconquest, colonial, and modern cities. Aerial photographs probably taken by the new Compañía Mexicana Aerofoto (founded in 1930) appeared in both volumes and dramatically conveyed the size of the site and plan. The large-format, color second volume of the atlas was composed almost entirely of illustrations and included reproductions of Segura's watercolors of the site plan and of

FIGURE 3.5. View of the Zócalo, from *Atlas general del Distrito Federal* (1930).

the library, cinema, and open-air theater (plate 7). The volume opened with a map of Lake Texcoco based on the Franciscan priest Javier Clavijero's *Historia antiqua de México* and maps of the city in the sixteenth, eighteenth, and nineteenth centuries. These were followed by maps of the capital as it appeared in 1929 and images of the coats of arms of the delegations of the Federal District. Between aerial photographs of the cathedral and the north side of the Zócalo, and Chapultepec Park were the three images of the Carranza Center. Other new Federal District projects were illustrated elsewhere in the volume, but the extraordinary placement of three color images in the volume between these two most important centers in the capital that had deep historical roots marked the first time that a new building was so dramatically and instantly incorporated into an architectural and geographic history of Mexico City. Elsewhere in the book, aerial photographs of Zócalo (figure 3.5), the grid of the historic center, the National Palace, the Alameda Central, and the Basilica of Guadalupe all reinforced the idea that Segura's project belonged to an august architectural and urban tradition.

A PARK FOR THE PEOPLE

Reporters who covered the inauguration praised the buildings and the campus. They found "a gate with simple and majestic architectural motifs [that] serves as the entrance to the Recreation and Athletic Center, and a fountain with severe lines [and] gives the impression of strength and rectitude," marking the point where paths diverge, one to the cinema, the other to the gymnasium, which are "two beautiful pavilions of reinforced concrete and great capacity."[42] Segura pulled the various buildings together to create a vast campus governed by a major and minor axis set in a lush landscape that included native plants and materials. Interior paths were paved with reddish tepetate (blocks of volcanic rock) and lined with palm, ash, eucalyptus, and cypress trees, while tropical flowers and shrubs were planted elsewhere. Each of the two entrances to the park, on the narrow eastern side of the site and long southern side, were flanked by major buildings and led to important points inside the park. By careful arrangement of sightlines and walkways, which could be used for ceremonial processions, Segura brought into powerful relationships the track, soccer field, open-air theater, and the center of the baseball field. Just inside the east gate stood the large concrete cinema and gymnasium (figures 3.6 and 3.7). Segura painted the broad, unadorned concrete surfaces of both buildings light yellow and used a pinkish color to define the buttresses along the long sides of the buildings and to frame the windows and main entrance. In pinkish-red brick he expressed the buildings' bases and, near the top of the broad Dutch gables, on the main elevations represented baroque scrolls, clearly calling attention to them as ornamental and pictorial. The long narrow shape of the buildings, along with the expressed buttresses that divided the side elevations with few windows into bays, recalled single-nave sixteenth-century mission churches.

Chamfered corners and finials were balanced at the bases of these buildings by large buttresses that were framed by painted tiles that wrapped around the corners in a narrow band. With the tile bands and the base of the building, broad tile finials arranged in a zigzag pattern at four points on the gables of the main facades recalled Talavera ceramics, and continued the precedent Montenegro and Fernández Ledesma had set in San Pedro y San Pablo. Contemporary observers noted the color and tile on the buildings and remarked that "smooth planes and clear colors, with some notes of the painted tiles of Puebla" defined the facades.[43] By using tile and brick explicitly as architectural ornament, Segura called attention to the facade as a composition constructed of

FIGURE 3.6. Segura, Cinema, Carranza Center.

FIGURE 3.7. Segura, Gymnasium, Carranza Center.

both modern materials and elements associated with colonial craft and architectural history. Although the architect did not base his abstracted baroque on a specific building, downtown Mexico City and the recent books on colonial architecture provided abundant visual examples of colonial ecclesiastical and secular buildings. Like his predecessors who designed Churrigueresque buildings and turned the scroll in all directions and treated it as freestanding and engaged sculpture, Segura manipulated the scroll freely. His handling of the gables and use of brick and tile finials to "outline" them recalled very generally the forms of eighteenth century mixtilinear parapets—most famously that of Sagrario Metropolitano—in which stone trim defined the perimeter of smooth wall surfaces. On the long sides of the two large swimming pools he designed grandstands for two hundred spectators, while those flanking the track and soccer field accommodated four hundred. The stands were divided into regular bays by concrete columns that supported concrete vigas that were probably meant to be covered with vines or canvas awnings. Atop the columns the architect shaped abstracted ionic capitals reminiscent of the wooden capitals of provincial porticos and thus associated the otherwise plain construction with the historically evocative forms elsewhere in the workers' park.

In combining representations of sixteenth- and eighteenth-century colonial forms—the early mission church, baroque ornament, and rural types imagined as colonial—Segura used the same principles that had guided Obregón Santacilia's architecture. By drawing attention to the structural work of buttresses by expressing them clearly and straightforwardly on the cinema and gym, Segura emphasized the continuities in Mexican architecture over several centuries. Representing colonial scrolls plastically using painted tile as a surfacing material he further evoked historical buildings, but these self-conscious gestures also revealed the architect's awareness of international debates about historicizing ornament and abstraction, and the increasingly contentious ones within Mexico about which architectural history (if any) modern buildings should reference. In this way the Carranza Center, like the Ministry of Health, helped create a bilingual Mexican modernism reliant on sophisticated knowledge of the major forms and ideas of both colonial Mexican architecture and international modernism. The buildings were surely not legible in these ways to the workers who visited the Carranza Center, but they would have been to architects, and to savvy patrons and visitors.

The enormous pale pink concrete open-air theater at the end of the north–south axis was the most important single part of the campus, and it drew on classical and vernacular prototypes while alluding broadly to the forms of technological modernity (plate 7).[44] It survives in only a few images and descriptions, which record that

> above the end of a green grove the architecture of the stage rises, then descends naturally to meet the pergolas that enclose the space.
>
> At the front of the theater is an embankment with small staircases that lead into [the theater] and alternate with benches and small short decorative motifs. Across this terrace, which like the pergolas, is the true space of the theater, the terrain begins to descend creating the space of the orchestra, in the way required for clear visibility for all the spectators.
>
> The stage has the dimensions necessary to accommodate the large pro-

ductions to which theaters like these are dedicated. It is closed laterally by two large, heavy and sober motifs, through which there is access to the men and women's dressing rooms, which are equipped with all the necessary services.

The lateral pergolas retain the height of the entrance, and are built of reinforced concrete. Their lateral walls rise one meter above the level of the floor, and are covered . . . with climbing plants that cover the structure.[45]

"The architecture of the stage" was a huge arch supported by four piers that curved high into the air and were visible from all parts of the Carranza Center. As at the cinema and gymnasium, small bands of tile ornamented the structure. Segura's theater served both as the grand monument at the termination of the Carranza Center's wide entrance boulevard and as the backdrop to the performances meant to transport urban workers psychologically to the countryside and, like the architecture of the park, instill a sense of Mexico City's geographical and cultural connectedness to provincial parts of the country.

The arch at the back of the stage evoked the images and objects associated in general ways with modern industrial life: the grille on the front of an automobile, the grate form of the cow guard at the base of a locomotive, the shape and image of a radio and its speaker. This was an abstraction of the modern language of transportation and leisure like the architect's pictorial abstraction of the sculptural baroque but one that suggested the government's ambition to create a working class that would advance its industrializing aspirations. The associations awakened by Segura's theater were, even more than those provoked by the abstracted baroque, highly visual, almost impressionistic and seemingly operative at a deep psychological level. It was this quality that occasioned scholars to read in Segura's work the influences of the forms of the European architecture that are sometimes rather awkwardly categorized as expressionistic.[46] The theater's sober nonspecific recollections of the spaces and objects of modern life linked it to the strand of evocative twentieth-century modernism most familiar from architectural histories of northern Europe.[47]

SETTINGS FOR SPORTS AND SPECTACLE

On November 20, 1929, tens of thousands of brown-skinned, overall-clad workers and their children walked through the gates of the Carranza Center to participate in the grand opening of the park (see figure 3.2). Amid the crowd were also lighter-skinned, suit-wearing bureaucrats and dignitaries, including President Emilio Portes Gil and Puig,

FIGURE 3.8. Mass gymnastics performance during the inauguration on a playing field, November 1929.

who were eager to be associated with what the government billed as one of the "best [such parks] in the world" not only because of its capacity, but for the kind and quality of its amenities.[48] In the cinema 1,500 workers saw Mexican and foreign films,[49] which were intended to "promote knowledge and love . . . of the customs, traditions, yearnings, and the beauties of our country."[50] In the gymnasium, fitness classes, athletic exhibitions, and boxing and fencing matches took place, and in dressing rooms workers could store their belongings and use cold and hot showers.[51] Eager for worldwide recognition, the Mexican government invited international visitors to the inauguration, and the audience included representatives of nearly all the countries with whom Mexico had diplomatic relations.[52] They saw workers swimming, diving, doing rhythmic gymnastic exercises en masse on the soccer field, and rolling hoops (figure 3.8). They listened as workers and children sang songs celebrating Benito Juárez, Francisco Madero, Venustiano Carranza, and they rejoiced in the ousting of Díaz.[53]

Spectatorship and athleticism were central to the architectural and social programs of the Carranza Center. By making workers the athletes, performers, and audience, the Carranza Center made available an experience of inclusive civic participation unfamiliar to most members of the working class. However distanced the architectural forms of his buildings, and however outwardly apolitical Segura was, the plan of his park strongly reinforced the links between civic participation, physical fitness, and the inculcation of shared cultural values that his client proposed. The formal pairing of the cinema and gymnasium, the similarities of their elevations, and their prominent locations emphasized the Carranza Center's entwined agendas of physical and cultural renewal and underscored the importance of performance, image, and display. Similarly, Segura emphasized the open-air theater by placing it at the intersection of the axes. There giant sociopolitical performances were staged and mass spectatorship enacted. While Segura had already shaped his buildings with reference to nationally specific understandings of historical architecture, his patrons used images of them to bind architecture to nationalist political rhetoric.

Programmatically the Carranza Center was shaped by and served the impulse to aestheticize the indigenous or mestizo body and the belief that reforming those bodies—in every sense—was essential to broad national improvement. Since the early 1920s, in fresco Diego Rivera had painted romanticized images of workers and peasants, and by the end of the decade, photography and staged performances took up his project. In 1927 in *Forma*, Gabriel Fernández Ledesma, who had created the tiles in the former church of San Pedro y San Pablo, assisted Montenegro with the murals painted in the exhibition pavilion in Brazil, and researched folk art, published an article extolling the beauty of athletes' bodies as they competed, and the potential of sports competitions to awaken emotion in the viewer.[54] Such beauty, he suggested, was unintended, but nevertheless profound, a claim that echoed assertions about the "instinctive" artistry evident in Mexican crafts. Large-scale group athletic displays and performances of folk dances and songs—in the courtyards of the Ministry of Education and in the National Stadium Villagrán García had designed for Vasconcelos in 1924—had been taking place in Mexico City for several years before the German writer Sigfried Kracauer, who was trained as an architect, identified "mass ornament" as an international phenomenon in his 1927 critique of capitalism.[55]

Although Segura was surely unaware of Kracauer's work, the critic's architectural analogy in his description of ornament, which he declared "an *end in itself*," suggests a way of understanding the relationship between the activities at the Carranza Center and its buildings.[56] Kracauer's metaphor was concerned with structure, but could as easily have described facade composition: "The patterns seen in the stadiums and cabarets . . . are composed of elements that are mere building blocks and nothing more. The construction of the edifice depends on the size of the stones and their number. It is the mass that is employed here. Only as parts of a mass, not as individuals who believe themselves to be formed from within, do people become fractions of a figure."[57] So too in Segura's buildings were architectural elements—meaningless on their own—detached from their ancient theoretical and structural origins and positioned to serve as parts of a new whole whose aim was, like the displays that fascinated Kracauer, meant to be seen as a performance. In the case of Segura's architecture, they performed conversance with historical form and demonstrated understanding of its malleability. For Kracauer, the mass ornament made visible previously obscure aspects of the experience of modern industrialization in countries that industrialized far earlier than Mexico did.[58] In their way, Segura's highly detailed ornament exposed the essential facadism and increasingly vacuous approach to historicist styles that Pallares and others criticized in Mexican architecture in the late 1920s. Kracauer likened mass ornament to aerial photographs, which were so important in documenting and situating the Carranza Center as historically and politically significant, observing that neither "emerge[s] out of the interior of the given conditions, but rather appears above them. Actors likewise never grasp the stage setting in its totality, yet they consciously take part in its construction."[59] Like mass ornament and aerial photography, for Kracauer, inorganicism was arguably a characteristic of many 1920s Mexican buildings, which were so notable for their architects' disinterest in making facades express the structural or spatial arrangements of the interior.

Excélsior's dramatic headline of the story of the Carranza Center's opening announced, "the working classes will have a place that will combat ignorance, physical disability, atavistic sadness, and political disillusion."[60] At few points in the history of architecture had so much been expected of a single project. In addition to improving the minds, bodies, and political consciences of working-class Mexicans, the Carranza Center would, according to its promoters, dispel the essential melancholy that many people believed was inherent in the mestizo workers (and their indigenous relatives) for whom it was intended. By 1929 the work of government was widely understood to include the radical transformation of the bodies and minds of Mexican citizens and the molding of them into participants in a vast, remade social order. According to *Excélsior*, the Carranza Center was "a work with which the Revolution tries to improve and stimulate the social life of our people and with which it proposes to combat among other things . . . timidity, distrust, and the lack of general hygiene which are blights on our people and which must be corrected or at least reduced, in order to form a people that are more healthy, more virile, more conscientious, more optimistic, and more filled with faith about their individual destinies and the destinies of their country."[61] Many modern bureaucrats worried that the physical and intellectual inferiority they perceived in the mestizo worker population was traceable to a racially determined weakness of spirit.[62] The antidote to social ills, they imagined, was a modern space that facilitated fitness and helped integrate mestizo workers into modern civic life.

ENACTING HISTORY

The workers who attended performances at the theater during the park's opening festivities saw visually stunning dramas and plays. On November 23, 1929, *El laborillo*, a "great pantomime that trie[d] to reproduce a popular fiesta in the 'El Laborior' neighborhood in the City of Tehuantepec,"[63] premiered, complete with a backdrop painted with an image of a colonial church (figure 3.9). Young women from the Public Welfare Department's industrial school, the Women's Reformatory, and the Popular Music School of the Federal District, wearing the traditional dress of the Isthmus of Tehuantepec, performed regional dances against a backdrop painted to resemble a colonial church in a Mexican village. The Mexico City Police Band played music from Oaxaca,[64] the most important state in the Isthmus of Tehuantepec. Aurea Procel, the author of *El laborillo* also appeared at the Carranza Center wearing traditional Tehuantepec dress. The event visually brought rural indigenous culture into the heart of the workers' park and symbolically linked efforts to ameliorate conditions for urban workers with Mexico's rural heritage. *Liberación* (Liberation), a gigantic musical play that depicted the "historical and social evolution of the Mexican people," was performed the next day. Its author, Efren Orozco, dedicated the piece to the working class and wrote of the need to instill in workers a "social soul" so that they might seek their own "liberation."[65] Just as architects and artists had throughout the decade, Orozco sought to define Mexican history for a general audience using images and associations. His

FIGURE 3.9. Stage of the open-air theater, with a performance of *El laborillo*, November 1929.

play told the story of Mexico in six parts, from the founding of Mexico City to the Mexican Revolution, and cast the nation's history as a sequence of triumphs and defeats that ultimately "liberated" working-class and rural Mexicans. The 1,050 actors[66] were students at rural and urban cultural centers and schools.[67] Performances included elaborate costumes, the carrying of the Aztec chief on a chair high above the crowd, the arrival of Hernán Cortés on a real horse, and hundreds of soldiers carrying standards in one of Mexico's many military conflicts. *Liberación* and *El laborillo* made the workers for whom the Carranza Center was created direct participants in the telling of a national history in a new way that seemed to include them and their ancestors and connect them with their rural compatriots.

The Carranza Theater was the urban counterpart of the "Indian Theater" at Teotihuacan, which was built in the early 1920s and was Mexico's first open-air theater (figure 3.10). Like the one in Balbuena, it housed performances meant to help "build . . . the nation upon folklore."[68] In the 1920s rural and municipal governments promoted theatrical performances in villages and poor districts as a way of spreading

FIGURE 3.10. "Indian Theater" at Teotihuacan, ca. 1925.

knowledge of Mexican culture and to offer an approved form of enter-
tainment. At the end of the decade open-air theaters were built as part
of Cultural Missions in remote provinces, and some were painted by
prominent artists, such as the one at La Parilla, Durango, which muralist Pablo O'Higgins designed.[69] At Teotihuacan, in the shadows of
the pyramids, long benches for the audience were arranged in a semi-
circle on sloping ground, a configuration that linked the theater to the
classically inspired garden and forest amphitheaters in Europe and the
United States such as those at Pomona College and the Garden Theater
in Manheim, Germany.[70] Instead of the Carranza Theater's allusions to
modern technologies in reinforced concrete, the Teotihuacan Theater
"was decorated very simply by the Indians, very much in the manner
of the ruins. . . . The aisles are painted with symbolic designs. . . . The
actual stage itself [wa]s a wide grassy terrace, upon which can be built
native houses of adobe, corrals for animals, stables, mangers, shrines,
altars and all other structures needed in the daily life of religion. There
are no artificial aids nor effects."[71] The designers of the Teotihuacan

FIGURE 3.11. Performance at the "Indian Theater," Teotihuacan, ca. 1925.

Theater were likely well aware of current architectural languages. They planned a space that mixed "native" decorative patterns with neoclassical and modern ones. The fan-shaped space of the theater was enclosed by an organ-cactus fence—a type typical in rural areas—arranged so that the top formed a regular wavy line, but otherwise had much more in common with classical amphitheaters than did the one in Balbuena. The pylons at Teotihuacan framed a statue of a stern figure standing on a blocky pedestal that looked down toward the stage. Deep rows of curved stone benches were "carved and decorated very simply by the Indians." According to Brenner, Teotihuacanos painted the aisles with vegetal and geometric patterns and neoclassical motifs that evoked lutes.[72] On each side of the stage large pots with handles stood on pedestals. Such forms rarely appeared in pre-Columbian architecture and urban planning. Like the Carranza Theater, in its forms and the activities they housed, the theater at Teotihuacan sought to energize the present by evoking the past using an ancient medium and multiple, far-reaching cultural associations.

The resurgence of open-air theater in the 1910s and 1920s in Mexico and elsewhere was nearly always embedded in a complicated striving to reclaim or define local and national culture and often evoked premodern traditions as a starting point. In Mexico the open-air theater was the architectural type most purely and directly associated with modernizing programs rooted in cultural instruction. Funded by the Ministry of Education, the playwright and director of performances at Teotihuacan, Rafael M. Saavedra, had spent six years traveling in southern Mexico with a composer and painter documenting local traditions.[73] Like the artists who made similar journeys and interpreted their "discoveries" in new works of art, Saavedra returned to Mexico City eager to integrate the wares and customs of residents of remote villages in new plays and pageants that would help shape a modern national theater.[74] Central to his vision of modern drama was the establishment of regional theaters, of which there were eighteen in six states by 1929, and in which local people performed.[75]

Under the auspices of the Federal Department of Anthropology, at Teotihuacán Manuel Gamio choreographed performances based on modern suppositions about pre-Columbian ceremonies and contemporary ritualistic dances, which he shortened to a half or full hour (instead of eight to ten hours) and for which musicians used modern instruments in place of "primitive" ones.[76] Plays also included historically based dramas seen by audiences composed of peasants, city-dwellers, and tourists (figure 3.11).[77] The performances were social experiments in which the directors encouraged modern Teotihuacanos, whose humble lives and limited resources Gamio documented in his 1916 sociological survey, *La Población de la Valle de Teotihuacán*, to familiarize themselves with indigenous culture as it was imagined officially and to hone their talents as actors, artists, and musicians. The simple, natural setting seemed appropriate to the staging of performances that blurred the lines between real religious practice and a theatrical version. Gamio and his colleagues believed that this kind of contact with rituals identified by anthropologists would facilitate "regeneration" and "development." The Teotihuacan Theater was "not proposed to make a vast human museum. The psychological effect on actors and audience is the significant feature. The Indian of Mexico is ignorant and degraded, but he is not stupid and depraved. A sympathetic appreciation of him and of his things, from his own point of view, so far as possible, goes a tremendous way in establishing his self-confidence."[78] The same belief about the potential for self-transformation through performance and spectatorship underlay the creation of the Carranza Theater, only there the subjects were urban workers, many recently arrived from rural areas, and thus imagined to be closer to the native traditions evoked at Teotihuacan. Proucel and Orozco's arrangements for the Carranza Theater resembled performances at Teotihuacan, and in both great value was placed on creating "authentic" productions for large audiences. The images of the play that filled Mexico City newspapers closely resembled those shot at Teotihuacan as still images and in film.[79] But in both theaters, performances were intended not only to transform workers or Indians but also to display for a much wider audience approved Mexican customs and evidence of social progress, literally against the backdrop of works of Mexican architecture, whether they were actual ancient pyramids or evocations of colonial churches in modern materials.

MODERN ARCHITECTURE BEFORE AND AFTER THE CARRANZA CENTER

For a variety of reasons, 1929 was a turning point in Mexico City. That year the party that would be known as the Institutional Revolutionary Party, which would dominate politics and be the most important Mexican architectural client for the rest of the century, was formed. In architecture it was the year that rationalism—typified by the Huipulco tuberculosis sanatorium that Villagrán García began designing then—first seriously challenged the historically evocative modernism of Segura and Obregón Santacilia, and the year that the Seville Pavilion finally opened. With controversies about earlier designs now put to rest, that building anticipated the surge of interest in pre-Hispanic architecture that marked major works of the 1950s and 1960s. It is thus appropriate at this point to consider where the 1920s projects, and especially Obregón Santacilia's and Segura's, belong in a long history of modern architecture.

The Carranza Center's relationship to that history is best illuminated by its parallels with the intellectual genesis of architectural modernism in the first half of the nineteenth century in Germany and France, particularly as it manifest in the debates on style, history, and national expression. In the German context, the work of Heinrich Hübsch and Karl Friedrich Schinkel provide revealing, if surprising, comparisons and help situate Mexican concerns around 1930. Yet to be unified, in the first decades of the nineteenth century Germany existed as a group of markedly different states governed by rulers who were eager to use architecture to distinguish their regions and their regimes.

The writings and buildings of state architects—Hübsch in Baden and Schinkel in Prussia—responded to circumstances that in many ways were quite similar to those in which Segura and his colleagues worked in Mexico roughly a hundred years later. Just as Mexican architects debated whether colonial or pre-Hispanic references were more appropriate to a national architecture, in Prussia around 1810 a similar debate about classical and gothic forms raged. In 1811 Schinkel suggested that Greek and Gothic styles might be harmoniously synthesized and in 1828 Hübsch published his influential essay "In welchem Stil sollen wir bauen?" which captured European architects' disagreements about style that had emerged after archaeological and historical investigations in the mid-eighteenth century. Patrons too perceived a new flexibility. Eager to enrich Bavaria culturally and convey its modernity, after 1825 Ludwig I commissioned five new churches in five historical styles, built a new wing of his palace based on Renaissance models, and had a copy of the Arch of Constantine installed near a major road. Continental architects visited and studied ancient, Byzantine, and Gothic works, just as Mexican architects researched colonial buildings a century later. In another parallel to postrevolutionary Mexico, in the reform period in Prussia, when Schinkel worked, substantial government patronage supported an architecture undergirded in many instances by the insights of intellectuals who undertook far-reaching reassessments of Prussian culture, politics, and economics.[80]

Considering the ways that buildings by Hübsch and Schinkel anticipated Segura's and Obregón Santacilia's architecture helps clarify the substantial differences between the European and Mexican contexts. The Pump Room at Baden-Baden (1837–40) was Hübsch's most famous building and it exemplified his widespread use of the segmental arch as the signature element of the *Rundbogenstil* (round-arch style) that he advocated. Hübsch believed the form synthesized the Greek lintel and medieval pointed arch and therefore embodied the fusion of historical forms that the modern age called for. The result was a building that, like the Ministry of Health and those at the Carranza Center, looked historical but did not imitate older works, and was clearly new. Schinkel's most important work of the same decade was the Bauakademie in Berlin (1832–35), which drew from so many sources that contemporary observers struggled to pin it down stylistically, just as happened in discussions of Segura's and Obregón Santacilia's buildings (figure 3.12). Barry Bergdoll described the Bauakademie by posing a question: "Was it a variant on an Italian Renaissance palazzo or did the exposed brick piers tie it to the north German Gothic tradition, which Conrad Hase

FIGURE 3.12. Karl Friedrich Schinkel, Bauakademie, Berlin, 1832–36.

in Hanover and Alexis de Chateauneuf in Hamburg were promoting as the starting-point for a modern German architecture?"[81] Architectural history was present at the Bauakademie not only in its program and Schinkel's evocative facade, but in relief panels beneath the windows that depicted moments in the history of architecture. Like Segura's, and especially Obregón Santacilia's buildings much later, Schinkel's was a didactic work that relied on representation to convey meaning and assumed its audience to possess considerable knowledge of architectural history.

In Germany, France, and England the study of history and style quickly fused into debates about national architecture and character.[82] But vital differences marked European and Mexican investigations of these things. The innovations of both Hübsch and Schinkel were founded on close study of structure and the ways that form, and therefore style, seemed to result from it. The Bauakademie's distinctive patterns, textures, and rhythms were derived from the building's brick frame. Hübsch's approach was informed by deep skepticism of the historical explanation of style as imitation and focused on the structural qualities of the lintel and pointed arch. By contrast, Mexican architects' research into colonial architectural history was concerned almost entirely with form, visual effects, and cultural conditions, rather than with problems of structure. Unlike those by Hübsch, Schinkel, and many other nineteenth-century European architects, their buildings were neither intellectually buttressed by nor conversant with deep theoretical traditions. In France, Eugène-Emmanuel Viollet-le-Duc's work on the restoration and conservation of gothic cathedrals offered some parallels to Mexican concerns with the preservation and documentation of colonial architecture, but ultimately, Viollet's influential arguments about rationalism, building type, and the technological potential of iron and the significance for the conceptualization of space that his ideas implied, differentiated his work dramatically from that of Mexican architects, for whom interior space was of comparably little concern until later in the century.

The buildings of Segura and Obregón Santacilia were rooted in a broad history of architectural modernism, but they also anticipated aspects of architectural theory that emerged later in the twentieth century. The obviously applied ornament on the Carranza Center buildings, the general evocation of multiple historical moments in the Ministry of Health, and the primacy in both projects of complexly composed facades and surface details anticipated formally the historically informed "fragmented aesthetic,"[83] of buildings of the 1960s and 1970s by Robert Venturi and Denise Scott Brown. In this respect, one thinks especially of Venturi's house for his mother in Chestnut Hill, Pennsylvania, of 1963 (figure 3.13). Like Mexican architects thirty-five years before, Venturi and Scott Brown were motivated in their designs and writings in part by an ambition to create a nationally distinctive architecture—an impulse traceable at least back through Frank Lloyd Wright and Louis Sullivan. But, of course, critical differences between the Mexican buildings of the 1920s and those U.S. works sometimes called "postmodern" abound. Reviewing them helps keep an assessment of Mexico's place in twentieth-century architecture grounded in the particularities of the Mexican context. The most immediate and important difference was the place of irony—essential to Venturi and Scott Brown's built and written works, and lacking almost entirely in Mexican architecture throughout the century. Critiquing what they saw as the uninspired and watered-down interpretations of high international modernism at mid-century, particularly that patronized by corporations, Venturi and Scott Brown proposed that architecture be revitalized by engage-

FIGURE 3.13. Robert Venturi, Vanna Venturi House, Chestnut Hill, Pennsylvania, 1963.

ment with locally specific objects, and by an energetic formal variety, evidence of which Venturi had found throughout architectural history, and which together they identified in the commercial, vernacular forms of "ordinary" streets. For all of the playful aspects of their work, the groundbreaking Vanna Venturi house was rooted in serious and significant ways to the needs of its client and it participated in a highly sophisticated dialogue about social norms.[84]

Venturi based his defense of complexity as a formal and theoretical principle in evidence he found in centuries of European architectural history. In *Complexity and Contradiction in Architecture* (1966) he wrote of buildings in terms that could also have been used to describe Mexican works of the 1920s. The buildings exhibited "the phenomenon" of "both-and," some had "double-meanings."[85] Venturi observed that "most of the examples [of complex and contradictory architecture] will be difficult to 'read,' but abstruse architecture is valid when it reflects the complexities and contradictions of content and meaning." He identified these principles in buildings by architects from many periods, particularly in those he called "Mannerist," which included buildings of sixteenth-century Italy and Hellenistic Greece. The work of titans including Michelangelo, Borromini, British architect Nicolas Hawksmoore, French neoclassical architect and theorist Claude-Nicolas

Ledoux, Sullivan, Le Corbusier, Alvar Aalto, and Louis Kahn provided further evidence for his claim. Histories of Mexican colonial buildings had similarly identified multiplicity of form and association as characteristics of that architecture, which, although it did not give comparable attention to the interactions of plan and section with elevation, was similarly concerned with surface effects. Some of the most revealing points of connection between Mexican buildings and Venturi's architecture are centered on his concept of "inflection," which was "the way in which the whole is implied by exploiting the nature of the individual parts, rather than their position or number. By inflecting toward something outside themselves, the parts contain their own linkage. . . . Inflection is a means of distinguishing diverse parts while implying continuity. It involves the art of the fragment. The valid fragment is economical because it implies richness and meaning beyond itself."[86] The octagonal arch, the exaggerated base of volcanic stone, the detached scroll, the painted tile—these elements on the Ministry of Health and the Carranza Center buildings that read as fragmentary and representational made sense only when understood within the facade composition as a whole—and functioned just as Venturi described in that they referred to elements and ideas far beyond themselves.

Working in a country without the industrial capacities, wealth, and academic breadth and tradition that Venturi's had, Mexican architects had neither the theoretical depth nor the historical position to think about architecture in the detached way he did. But they shared a fascination with the communicative potential of surface, the richness of meaning that might be achieved through engagement with "popular" forms (however differently defined), and a distanced, critical position to both history and dominant fashions in architecture, which, from the vantages of the United States and Mexico, had been imported from Europe. Most profoundly, perhaps, like his colleagues in Mexico four decades before, Venturi believed that architecture was concerned with what he called "the difficult whole." Quoting from industrialist and philanthropist August Heckscher's *The Public Happiness* of 1962, Venturi wrote, "It is the taut composition which contains contrapuntal relationships, equal combinations, inflected fragments, and acknowledged dualities. It is the unity which 'maintains, but only just maintains, a control over the clashing elements which compose it. Chaos is very near; its nearness, but its avoidance, gives . . . force.' In the validly complex building or cityscape, the eye does not want to be too easily or too quickly satisfied in its search for unity within a whole."[87]

In Mexico City of the 1920s, staged performances by athletes and workers, new public health policies, and new buildings only just masked the social and political chaos that was both very recent and very near. The deep divides between the capital and the provinces, between reformers and conservatives, and within the architectural profession were bridged, just as the country itself was held together, by a tenuous new understanding of what Mexico was and what it looked like. Like Obregón Santacilia, and like the state in the postrevolutionary period, as architects debated which architectural history would best serve the future, Segura pulled together in taught compositions parts laden with multiple meanings to create unified facades. At the Carranza Center and in other works he created an idiom that acknowledged Mexico's colonial architecture but sought a new direction for architecture, not away from history, but from historicism. More than those by any of his contemporaries, Segura's facades emphatically affirmed the representational and visual qualities of modern architecture and its essential flexibility. In this respect his work anticipated some of the most important insights of later architects and historians.

PLATE 1. Juan O'Gorman, Gustavo M. Saavedra, and Juan Martinez de Velasco, Central Library, National Autonomous University of Mexico, 1951–53.

PLATE 2. Jerónimo de Balbás, Altar of the Kings, Metropolitan Cathedral of Our Lady of the Assumption (Mexico City Cathedral), 1718–37.

PLATE 3. Claudio Arciniega, José Damián Ortiz de Castro, Manuel Tolsá, et al., Metropolitan Cathedral of Our Lady of the Assumption, Mexico City, 1573–1817, and Lorenzo Rodríguez, Sagrario Metropolitano, 1749–68.

PLATE 4. San Francisco Acatepec, Puebla, eighteenth century.

PLATE 5. Carlos Obregón Santacilia, Ministry of Health, copper-clad bridge between pavilions, 1925–29.

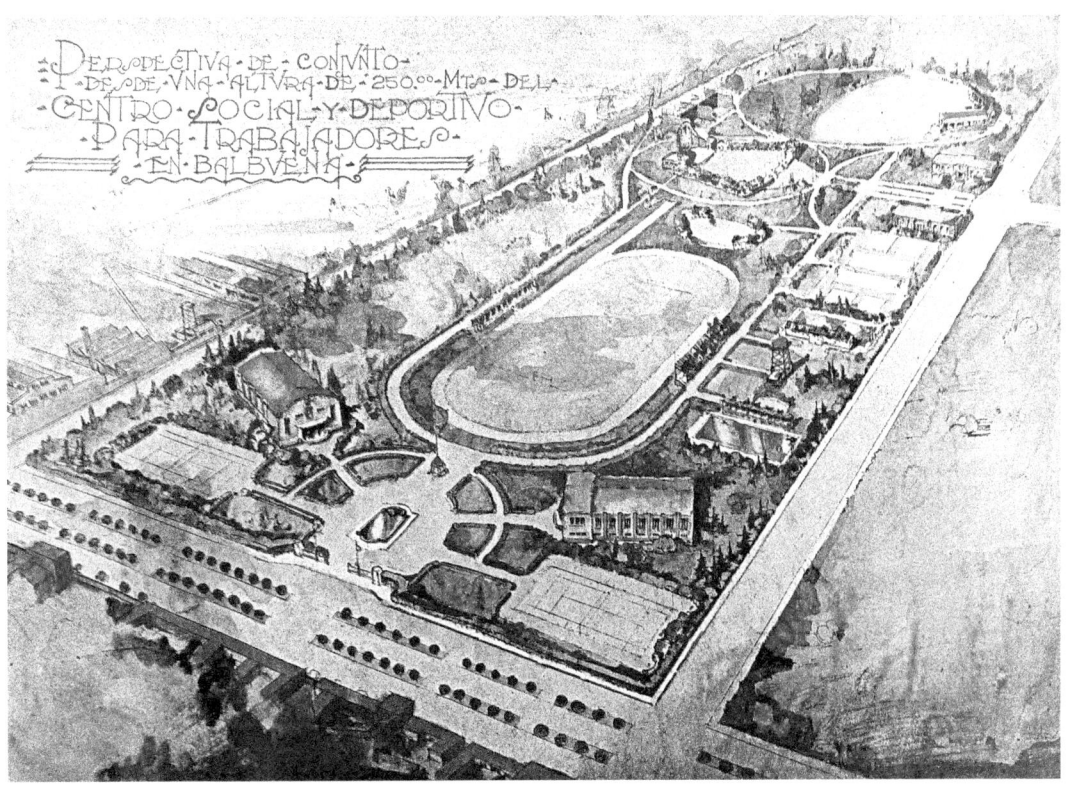

PLATE 6. Juan Segura, *Venustiano Carranza Recreation and Athletic Center for Workers*, 1929, aerial perspective.

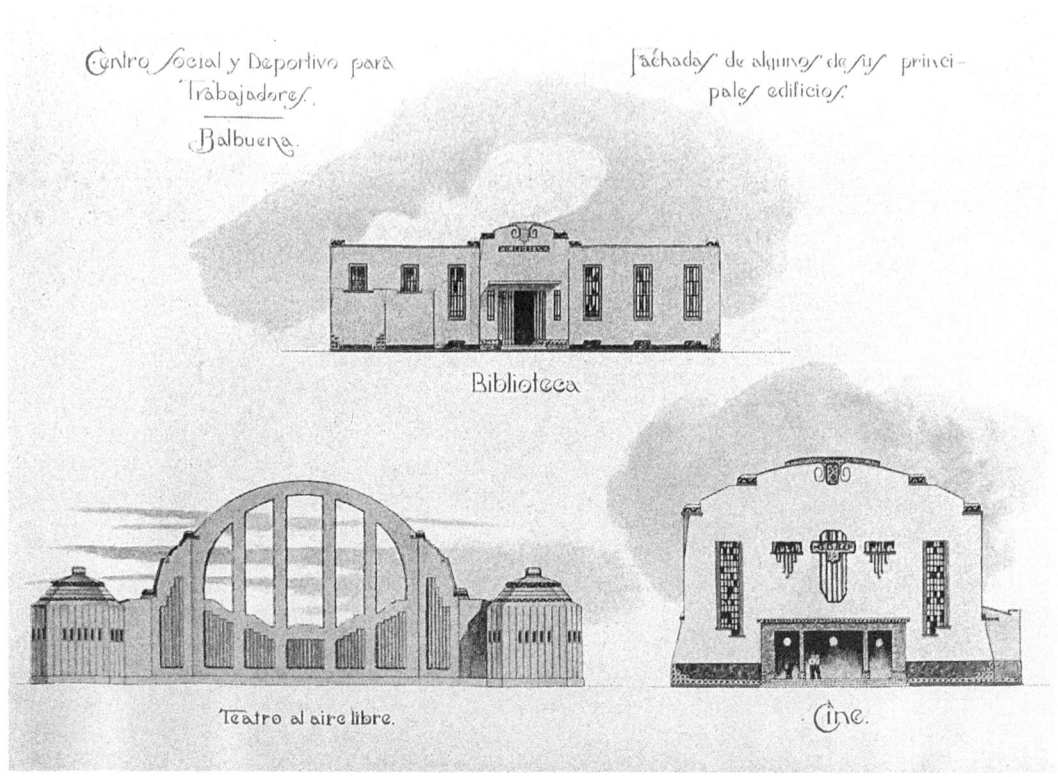

Centro Social y Deportivo para Trabajadores. Balbuena.

Fachadas de algunos de sus principales edificios.

Biblioteca

Teatro al aire libre.

Cine.

PLATE 7. Segura, *Façades of the Main Buildings*, Venustiano Carranza Recreation and Athletic Center for Workers showing the library, open-air theater, and cinema, 1929.

PLATE 8. Juan O'Gorman, *Plaza de las Carnicererías y antiguo Ayuntamiento de Tasco*, watercolor. Published in Tasco (1931).

CALLE DE LAS PALMAS #81 SAN ANGEL COL ALTAVISTA D.F. *Juan O'Gorman 1929.*

PLATE 9. O'Gorman, *Calle de las Palmas #81 San Angel, Col. Alta Vista, D.F.* (House for Cecil O'Gorman), watercolor, 1929.

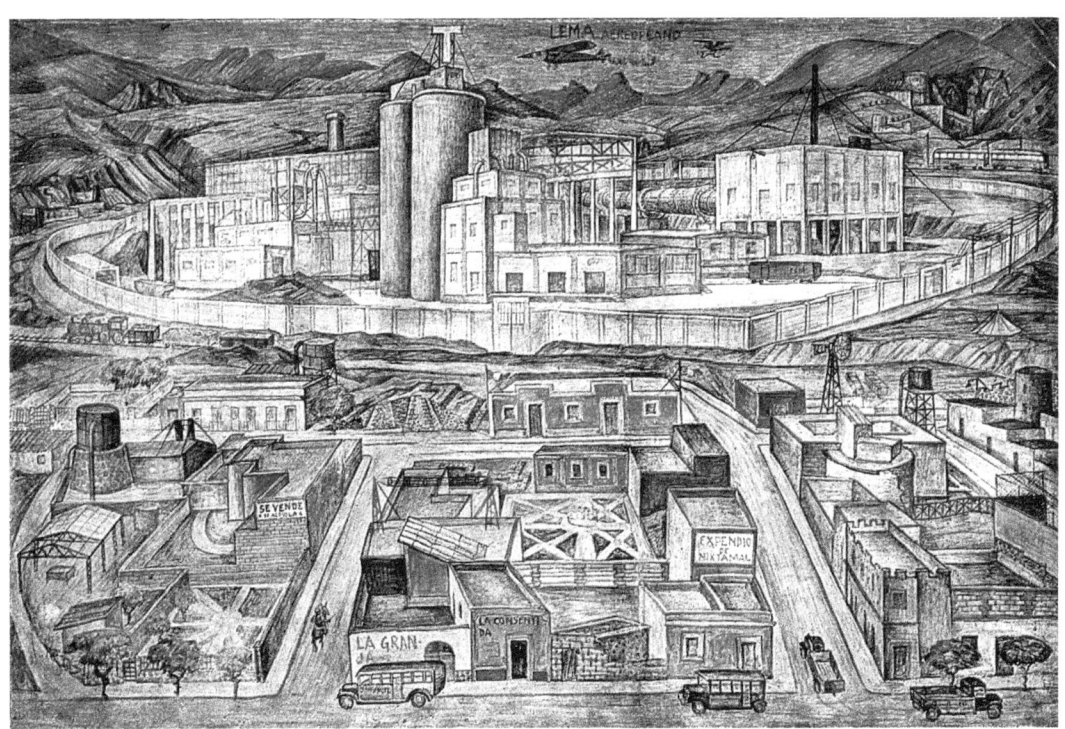

PLATE 10. O'Gorman, *Aeroplano*, 1931, fresco.

PLATE 11. José María Velasco, *Valley of Mexico Seen from Santa Isabel Hill*, 1877.

PLATE 12. Diego Rivera, *History of Mexico*, three central lunettes on west wall. National Palace, Mexico City, 1929.

PLATE 13. David Alfaro Siqueiros, *The People for the University, The University for the People: For a Neo-Humanist National Culture*, Rectory, National Autonomous University, 1952–56.

PLATE 14. Santa María Tonantzintla, Puebla, begun sixteenth century; decoration begun late seventeenth century.

PLATE 15. Ferdinand Bac, "The Red Gate," in *Jardins enchantés*, 1921.

Plate 16. Luis Barragán, Barragán House, hall and staircase, 1947–48, with Mathias Goeritz's, *Metachromatic Message* on wall at landing. Photograph by Rene Burri.

PLATE 17. Barragán, Barragán House, hall.

PLATE 18. Mark Rothko, Philip Johnson, Howard Barnstone, and Eugene Aubrey, Rothko Chapel, Houston, Texas, 1964–71.

PLATE 19. Ricardo Legorreta, San Antonio Central Library, San Antonio, Texas, 1991–95.

PART II

IMAGES, ABSENCE, AND OTHERNESS

CHAPTER FOUR

COMPOSITION AND CONFLICT

JUAN O'GORMAN AS PAINTER-ARCHITECT

Motivated by his deep sympathies for the working class, rather than taking a position in the debates of the late 1920s about which architectural historical references best suited modern Mexico, and unlike Carlos Obregón Santacilia and Juan Segura, who used architectural elements flexibly to connect their modern buildings to historical ones, in the 1930s Juan O'Gorman sought to banish history from modern architecture and to attach fixed meanings to forms whose representational character he denied. Yet his buildings, even more than theirs, were profoundly imagistic. Having begun his career in the 1920s as a protégé of Obregón Santacilia, he came to prominence with the house and studio he designed for Diego Rivera and the twenty-five elementary schools he created at the beginning of the next decade.[1] His concrete buildings' flat roofs, lack of historicizing ornament, and, in some cases, striking formal similarities to 1920s houses by Le Corbusier made them look and seem much more like the buildings that Philip Johnson and Henry-Russell Hitchcock grouped under the heading the "International Style," than the historically referential works of the 1920s. Yet even as they helped introduce the high modernist idiom that would dominate architecture at mid-century, O'Gorman's buildings revealed how thoroughly the framework established to describe Mexican architectural history decades earlier permeated approaches to new design. Selectively using elements borrowed from the vocabulary of 1920s Corbusian modernism, along with color, murals, and even plants in complex facade compositions, O'Gorman traded the image of architectural history for an image of economy inflected with vernacular references and cloaked in rhetoric, as earlier buildings had been, about social reform and national character.

Personally and professionally O'Gorman was steeped in Mexico's colonial architectural past, and his efforts to differentiate his work from earlier buildings, endow it with social and political ideals, and connect it with international developments revealed the anxieties and contradictions embedded in the project of creating a nationally distinctive modernism. Like Segura, he used vibrantly colored wall surfaces (and anticipated Luis Barragán's work), and like Obregón Santacilia, relied on buildings' exteriors to allude to indigenous culture, but did so much more abstractly than his predecessors had. References to vernacular architecture in colonial towns (which had had a prominent place in *Iglesias de México*) and rural landscapes now did the work that sculpted representations of indigenous figures, baroque scrolls, Talavera tile, and volcanic stone had at the Ministry of Health and the Carranza Center. Rhetorically, O'Gorman endeavored to situate his works outside of architectural history and its long tradition of representation, and yet wanted them to convey some essentially "Mexican" quality and to express values associated with urban industrialization, the working class, or rural life. This conflict appeared on buildings' facades, in photographs of the elementary schools, and in the murals that he arranged to have painted in them, and in his insistence that his work be understood ahistorically and in terms of a Marxist utilitarianism. Ironically, his attempts to attach to the buildings explicit, fixed political meanings in fact revealed the near impossibility of such a task and the very slippery definitions of "Mexican" architecture by the early 1930s. Two decades later, the tensions latent in O'Gorman's first important buildings manifested vividly in a host of new architectural histories and theoretical writings.

Reflecting in 1973 on architecture from the late 1920s O'Gorman wrote that in those years "it occurred to me that what was necessary [was] to make in Mexico a completely functional architecture, divorced from all academicism and devoid of anything that could be orthodox or aesthetically sectarian, and to create [instead] an exclusively functional architecture (engineering of buildings)."[2] O'Gorman did not define "academicism," "orthodoxy," or "aesthetic sectarianism," but we can assume that by these terms he meant classicism, historicism, and slavish copying of older or foreign forms in order to convey power or class status.[3] Throughout his life he referred to his early buildings as "functionalist" works and claimed that in this phase of his career he designed without concern for his buildings' artistic qualities. Of the house he created in 1929 for his father, which has often been called the "first . . . functional house in Mexico,"[4] the architect said, the "form was derived completely from utilitarian function. The installations, from the electrical outlets to the sanitation systems were apparent."[5] In that house, as in Rivera's and the elementary schools, O'Gorman aestheticized mechanical systems and wall surfaces, and, in the case of the schools, developed a visual language that seemed, in its austerity, to express the intensity and earnestness of his patron's commitment to making education available to as many children as possible. For these reasons, and because of his close associations with Rivera (a famous communist) and the minister of education Narciso Bassols, O'Gorman's buildings have long been understood as exemplars of the interdependence of modern architecture and left-wing politics in postrevolutionary Mexico. During his tenure as minister of education from 1931 to 1934, Bassols advocated a program of "socialist education," intended to remove all traces of religion from Mexican education in the service of agricultural reform and the shaping of a "rational" citizenry.[6] It is clear that social reform was important to O'Gorman and his clients, but his buildings were concerned not only with political values as they might be expressed by formal austerity and restricted budgets.[7]

Indeed, the formal similarities of O'Gorman's buildings to some by Le Corbusier suggested not that his architecture merely expressed mechanical systems, program, or ideology straightforwardly, but that he carefully selected and used elements familiar from the Swiss architect's 1920s work to create aesthetic effects.[8] Valerie Fraser identified the contradiction in O'Gorman's use of forms that supposedly proceeded from industrialized building techniques and materials in a country that had very little of either.[9] Despite claiming that Le Corbusier inspired his "functionalism," O'Gorman profoundly misunderstood the famous Swiss architect's arguments about the place of architectural history and art in new buildings, a fact critical to understanding how O'Gorman thought about these things in a Mexican context and to assessing the ways colleagues, critics, and historians responded to his work and positioned it historiographically. Understanding O'Gorman's early architecture in terms of the explicit and implicit presence of Le Corbusier through form and in photographs illuminates some of the most important, yet least understood differences between one of the foremost European modern architects and one of the foremost Mexican modern architects; the comparison serves as a case study of the differences between European and Mexican modernism at a critical moment in the history of modern architecture.

In the 1940s, as Mexico City rapidly industrialized and grew, landscape architecture and buildings' relationships to the topography and botany of their sites (which were often imagined as prehistoric) became increasingly important to the country's architects. O'Gorman and Rivera would help lead this shift in orientation, and its roots lay in part in O'Gorman's buildings and painting from the previous decade. His works included murals (many dealt with Mexican history) and portraits, but landscape was the genre to which he returned most often. He frequently depicted towns or buildings in moody, minutely detailed works, which became increasingly fantastical and strange later in his career. The interdependence of painting and architecture, particularly as they dealt with the themes of industry, history, landscape, and politics was one of the most pronounced qualities of his oeuvre. In buildings and canvases O'Gorman also revealed his acute consciousness of historical change and its unsettling psychological effects. One of his most interesting paintings embodied his overlapping interests and seemed to anticipate works by other architects. With a title that played with the conventions of a genre nearly always associated with rural or wilderness scenes, *Paisaje de la ciudad de México* (Mexico City Landscape; 1942–49), documented that decade's building boom and juxtaposed a map of colonial Mexico City with the rapidly changing skyline of the 1940s capital and the undeveloped area east of the city (figure 4.1).[10] To one side of the painting a dark-skinned young worker, probably a recent arrival from the countryside, held a trowel and plans, while the white hands of the painter-architect held the old map so that he and the viewer might understand new buildings in relation to historical ones and to the spectacular landscape beyond the capital. Created between the time O'Gorman designed his stripped-down buildings in the 1930s and his richly decorated Central Library in the early 1950s, the canvas was tinged with uncertainty about what progress meant in Mexico's historic center and for its people, and hinted at the ways urbanization challenged architects to reimagine themselves and the role of architecture in a city with an increasingly crowded and visually cacophonous skyline.

More than any other Mexican architect, O'Gorman registered in his buildings, paintings, and words a profound anxiety about the implications of industrial modernity for Mexican culture, customs, and the landscape. As strongly as the formal similarities between his buildings and those elsewhere, the intellectual tensions in his work linked him to problems in international modernism. They foreshadowed the deepening of doubt about modernism's relevance in the country's august architectural history and even about the idea of nationally distinctive forms that would become all the more clear in the great buildings

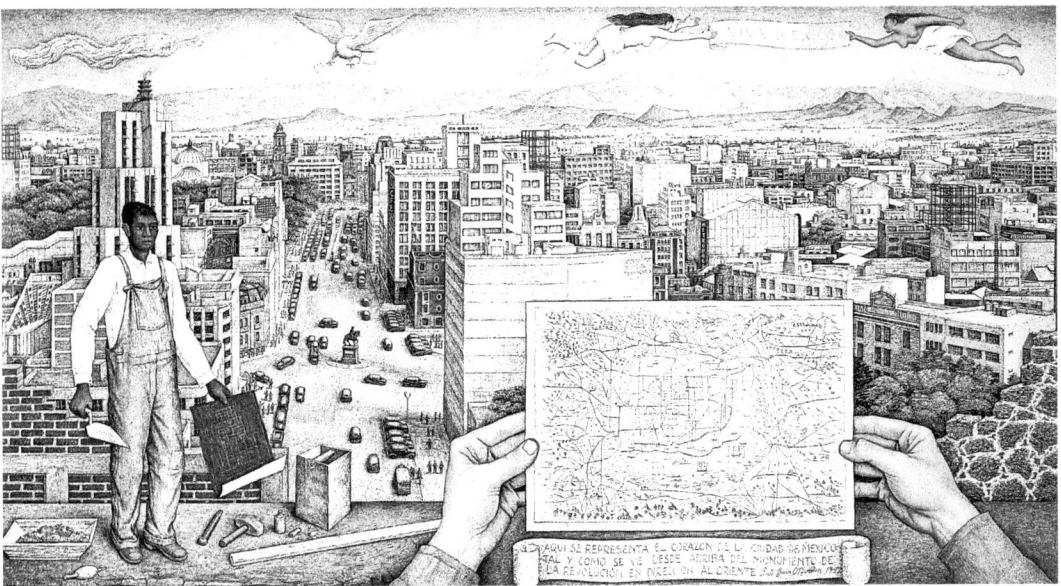

FIGURE 4.1. Juan O'Gorman, *Paisaje de la ciudad de México*, 1942–49.

and architectural texts of mid-century. As it manifested in O'Gorman's work, uncertainty about how to meld a rural past that was increasingly imagined as the locus of national character with an industrial urban future was particularly significant because it appeared at the very moment that an official image of national culture was being shaped. His buildings contributed in vital ways to that image, even as they pointed implicitly to its fragility and its contingency.

COLONIAL ARCHITECTURE AND
THE MEXICAN LANDSCAPE

Although historicism lost favor in the late 1920s, federally funded research and documentation of colonial architecture continued at a robust pace during the next decade, during which the Mexican government became the foremost patron of modern architecture. While some of the new research was used to promote tourism, it nevertheless contributed to architects' knowledge of Mexican architectural history and to the growth of an academic field with increasingly distinct outlines. At the same time that the Ministry of Education commissioned O'Gorman to design its elementary schools, it published *Tres siglos de arquitectura colonial*, a book composed almost entirely of photographs of colonial buildings with a brief introduction and captions in Spanish and English. The next year the ministry issued an illustrated translation of the text of Baxter's *Spanish-Colonial Architecture in Mexico* with a long introduction in which Manuel Toussaint summarized the historiography of Mexican colonial architecture. By the end of the decade, surveys and narrowly focused treatments of colonial architecture—from analyses of building types to urbanism—by Mexican architects and historians abounded.[11] In the early 1930s, the Secretaría de Hacienda undertook a project to record colonial Mexican religious buildings, parceling the country into zones and hiring architects, including Federico Mariscal and Vicente Mendiola, to make detailed drawings and descriptions of the buildings. This work was followed by studies of architecture in several major colonial cities, which resulted in publications (by various federal entities) on Huejotzingo (1934), San Miguel de Allende (1939), Morelia (1936), Oaxaca (1933, 1938), Guanajuato (1933), and Guadalajara (1937).

O'Gorman not only was aware of the surge of interest in colonial architecture that paralleled his introduction of a seemingly ahistorical and international architectural vocabulary in the 1930s, he participated in it. In 1931, with the urban planner Carlos Contreras and the art historian Justino Fernández, he coordinated the writing of *Taxco*, a book that explored the town's "history, monuments, current characteristics, and touristic possibilities," for which Toussaint wrote the text. O'Gorman helped render the plan of *Taxco*'s former convent of San Bernardino, and an elevation of the grand doorway of the Humboldt House. In watercolor he depicted the Plaza de la Carnicerías and the colonial city hall, capturing the hill town's rolling topography and the distinctive siting of its buildings (plate 8). At the center of the image was the large town hall in pink, blue, and red (the same colors that he used in the watercolors of his new buildings of the period) with a prominent, abstract cylindrical buttress at one corner.

The tensions that characterized O'Gorman's famous works of the 1930s reflected rapidly shifting approaches to design and history in architectural training during the formative years of his career and were rooted in his own experiences. As the example of the Mexican Pavilion showed, in the late 1920s, when O'Gorman was in architecture school, modern national architecture was still associated with historicist forms, even as new understandings of what constituted modernity and "Mexican" were coming into being. As a young architect, O'Gorman coupled his absorption of these developments with his strong personal responses to colonial buildings and landscapes. He was deeply immersed in colonial architecture until 1929, and analysis of his work and influences up to that point reveals how profound his break with his colleagues was in his designs for the Rivera house and the schools. As the example of the Carranza Center demonstrated vividly, in the late 1920s progressive social aims and programs were understood to be fully consistent with historically evocative designs. By rejecting colonial allusions early in the next decade, O'Gorman not only helped establish a new vocabulary that linked unadorned, flat-roofed buildings to progressive social values but also symbolically rejected his teachers, his parents, and the tendency to couple historical representation and social progress—a tendency to which he would later return and help foster.

O'Gorman grew up surrounded by Mexican colonial buildings and furniture, first in the town of Guanajuato in central Mexico, and then in the affluent suburb of San Angel, eight miles southwest of downtown Mexico City, which in the 1910s and 1920s retained its character as a colonial town to a far greater degree than it does today. The child of an Irish immigrant father and Mexican mother, and brother of one of twentieth-century Mexico's foremost historians (Edmundo O'Gorman), throughout his life he lived with an awareness of history and cultural distinctiveness. O'Gorman believed that the few years he spent as a child in Guanajuato profoundly shaped his development as a painter and his interest in color. Speaking of the city in nostalgic, almost folkloric words, he reminisced, "Guanajuato, quite a city with its popular architecture, filled with enchantment, color, and mystery owing to the location of its houses, built among gorges, while the great aggressivity of its landscape accentuates the topography and gives to this region of the Republic an especially interesting aspect, from a plastic point of view."[12] The architect's recollection emphasized his visual, rather than spatial, experience of the town. Recalling Guanajuato he noted that "the influence of geography on the mind of a painter is, perhaps, more important than the influence of history, given that geography is that which the eyes see in the surroundings." O'Gorman responded deeply to architecture and to the landscape and recalled: "the houses painted in diverse and vibrant colors and the bald hills, red, filled with green cactus and dry vegetation."[13] Years later, he used native plants and color, instead of historicizing elements, to nationalize buildings. Applied in various shades and intensities, color, because of its association with colonial towns and folk art, made it possible to create visually sophisticated buildings and allude to the architecture of a general, preindustrial past without imitating or representing historical forms.

In San Angel the young O'Gorman lived in a setting reminiscent of the one he left. Still separated from downtown by undeveloped stretch-

FIGURE 4.2. Cecil Crawford O'Gorman House, San Angel, ca. 1920.

es of land in which cactuses grew and from which the mountains of the Central Valley were easily visible, San Angel had cobblestoned streets, colonial churches and plazas, some colonial houses, and others that imitated them. One of the area's landmarks was the San Angel Inn, an elegant restaurant that occupied an eighteenth-century building that, until the early twentieth century, had been at the heart of a hacienda that dated to the seventeenth century. Near the Inn stood "a number of charming bungalows set among a host of lovely flowers. From the roof and balconies of the Inn . . . extensive views of the Valley of Mexico and the surrounding mountains [could] be had. Behind the Inn [was] a charmingly restful garden with many splendid trees and flowers."[14]

O'Gorman spent much of his youth in a nineteenth-century house "with a large patio and an enormous garden," which, despite having been built after independence, had a colonial character.[15] In the early 1910s O'Gorman's father filled the house with an eclectic combination of colonial art and other objects from the period as he, like architectural historians and preservationists at the same time, attempted to save such works from destruction. Years later O'Gorman's colleague, architect Enrique del Moral, recalled seeing "numerous mural paintings [that] decorated the house, which had a marked colonial flavor, and in[to] which Don Cecil, Juan's father, had incorporated sculptures, low reliefs and architectural details appropriate to the style, achieving a quite attractive result with a great personality." Del Moral remembered Cecil explaining "the way he had acquired the large number of diverse kinds of colonial objects that we saw and how, at the beginning of the century, this art was totally disappearing, to the point that many of the pieces he rescued practically from the trash, and others had to be patiently restored owing to their poor condition."[16] In the dining room, Cecil O'Gorman (who was also a painter) arranged his objects in a way that both gave the space a generally colonial character and revealed its quality as an eclectic composition (figure 4.2). The room had high ceilings with heavy wooden beams, wood paneling that came about two-thirds of the way up the walls, and a large fireplace decorated in painted tiles with different patterns. Vine-wrapped twisting columns with ornate capitals, oil paintings (from the colonial era or nineteenth-century copies that resembled styles popular before independence) in carved wooden frames, and large carved wooden doors that were either from the eighteenth century or inspired by originals from it, were integrated into wall surfaces or attached to them. The room could hardly have looked more different from those that his son would design in the 1930s.

OBREGÓN SANTACILIA'S STUDENT

O'Gorman's professional introduction to colonial architecture began in the mid-1920s when he was a student and worked as a draftsman in Obregón Santacilia's office. Having entered architecture school when the colonial revival style was at its height, and at the same time that Obregón Santacilia and Villagrán helped lead the transformation of architectural education away from rote copying of classical forms, O'Gorman knew well the centrality of colonial architectural history to new conceptions of modern Mexican architecture as well as the arguments against slavish imitation of historical forms. Embracing Obregón Santacilia as a mentor, under his direction O'Gorman worked on the Ministry of Health project throughout its design and through the conclusion of construction in 1929.[17] He resigned from the office only in 1932, after he had accepted the Ministry of Education's offer to lead the team that designed the elementary schools.[18] O'Gorman's

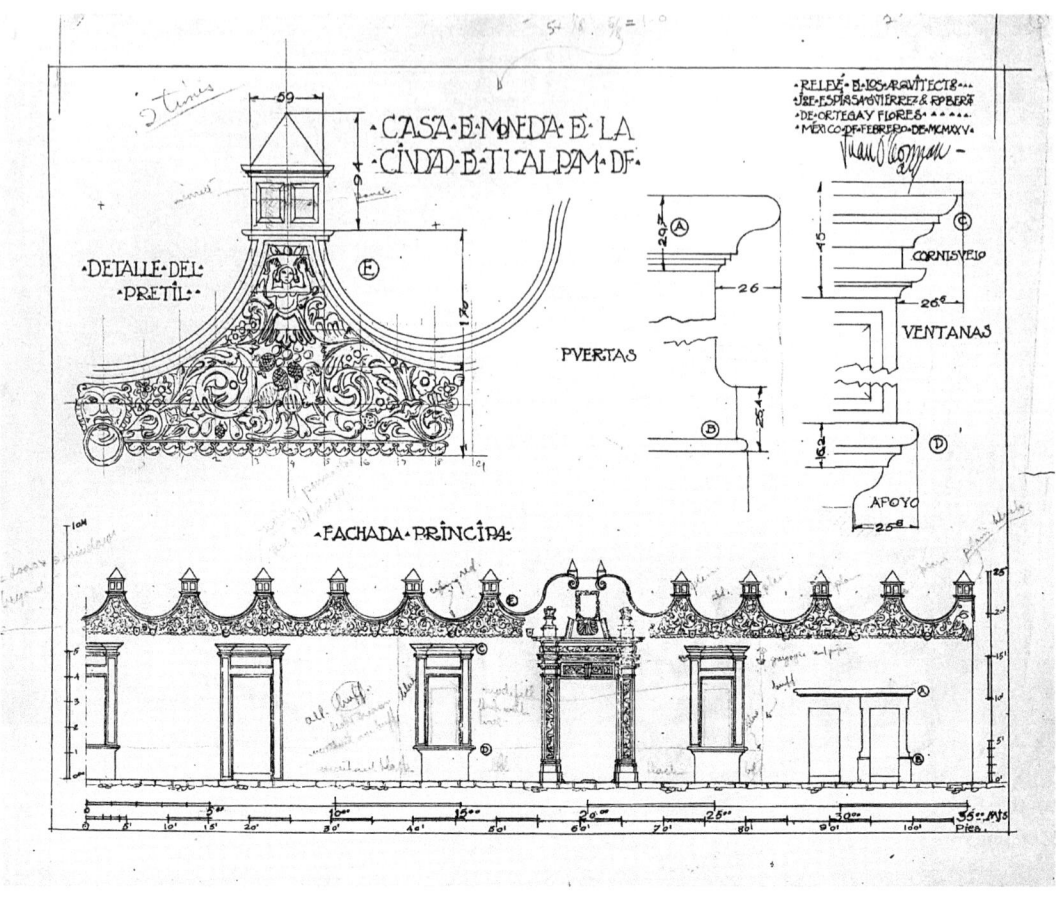

FIGURE 4.3. O'Gorman, *Casa de Moneda, Ciudad de Tlalpan, D.F.*, main facade and details, 1925.

work as a draftsman on the project taught him to view, for modern purposes, colonial architecture as a series of elements to be alluded to representationally and reinforced the principles of facade composition that he learned in architecture school. Drawings from the mid-1920s that O'Gorman made when he worked in Obregón Santacilia's office reveal that in addition to his role designing new buildings, the young architect carefully studied the colonial buildings of central Mexico. From 1925 to 1927 he drew at least seven colonial buildings in downtown Mexico City, San Angel, Tlalpan, and Taxco in which he perfected his skills copying colonial forms (figure 4.3).[19] While some of the studies were plans or sections, most were elevations in which the architect emphasized colonial architectural ornament and sculptural detail, and several were stamped as belonging to Obregón Santacilia's office. The senior architect and his student presumably used such drawings

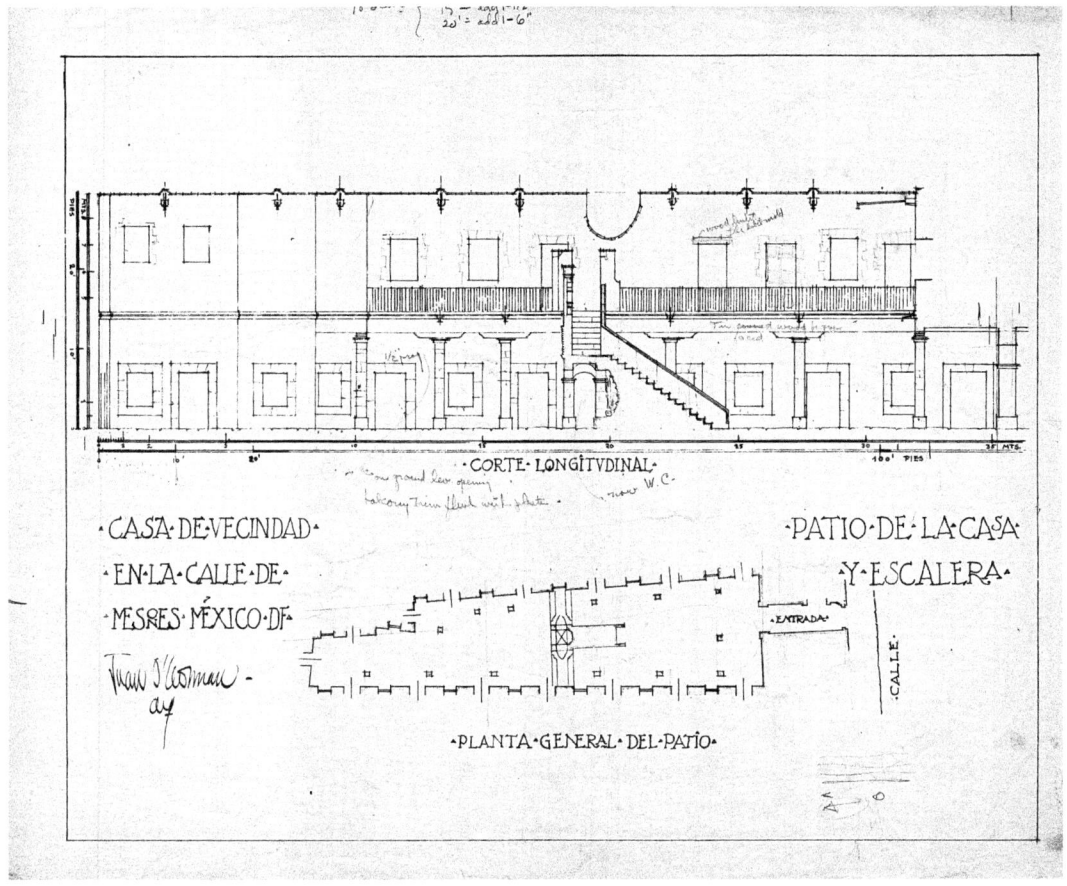

FIGURE 4.4. O'Gorman, *Casa de Vecindad en la Calle Mesones, México, D.F.*, longitudinal section and plan of the patio, 1925.

as references as they shaped the Ministry of Health and other projects that included representations of historical forms.

Among the least known of the projects on which Obregón Santacilia and O'Gorman worked was a 1925 design for a small housing development, known as a *casa de vecindad* (sometimes translated as tenement house), in central Mexico City (figure I.2; figure 4.4) The casa de vecindad was a colonial building type in which apartments were arranged in two- or three-story buildings around a narrow central courtyard. Most common in the densely populated districts of the capital, by the twentieth century these buildings usually housed the working class. The project was one of O'Gorman's first to address the needs of the urban workers, but, as in the Ministry of Health, the design integrated elements evocative of colonial forms. Drawings acquired by the U.S. architect Lionel Pries and dated February 1925, signed by O'Gorman and stamped as belonging to Obregón Santacilia's office, suggest that the Casa de Vecindad project either underwent considerable transformation in the course of design as the architects traded colonial revival–style elements for less ornamental forms, as happened at the Ministry of Health at the same time, or that they closely studied an actual colonial casa de vecindad on Mesones Street, very near the site, before completing the design of a new building. Either way, O'Gorman would have participated firsthand in the process of transforming historicist forms into abstract, historically evocative ones. Also participating in this process, twenty-five years before he became one of the lead architects of the University City, was the young Enrique del Moral, whose name appears on two drawings of the Casa de Vecindad on Mesones. With the dome of the ca. 1700 Church of San Miguel, designed by Pedro de Arrieta, who had also created the Palace of the Inquisition (later the National School of Medicine; ch. 2), visible from completed building, the site must have been particularly suggestive as a place to explore the legacies of colonial architecture.

Completed by mid-1926, the project was hailed as architecturally and socially progressive by the most important leftist in 1920s Mexico City, O'Gorman's friend and future client, Diego Rivera, who considered it an example of "the new Mexican architecture."[20] Few images of the completed building exist, but it is possible to get a fairly good sense of it from those that do, and from a 1926 description (figures 4.5 and 4.6). Built of stone and covered in stucco, the complex included one- and two-story blocks arranged around a narrow central courtyard and a secondary passage paved with large, irregularly shaped stones. Obregón Santacilia arranged on the wall surface slightly recessed windows and doors, without frames or other ornaments, and opened them onto the exterior spaces in a composition reminiscent of French socialist architect Tony Garnier's housing schemes for an industrial city published in 1917. He divided the courtyard using single-story arched openings and defined the space further with a large exterior staircase with a slight curve. He lined the upper edges of arched partitions and the roof with brick in a way that called attention to the smoothness of the wall surfaces. The central courtyard opened onto the street through a large trebeated opening lined with narrow multicolor tiles arranged in a zigzag pattern. On the main facade, between the opening and an arched window above, Obregón Santacilia installed an ornate relief consisting of a framed panel of a figure apparently holding a staff flanked by a pair of urns from which vines rose. Although it lacked

FIGURE 4.5. Carlos
Obregón Santacilia,
Casa de Vecindad,
main door, 1926.

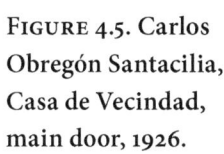

the pair of columns typical of the type, Obregón Santacilia's arrangement of the doorway and the relief recalled the doorways of sixteenth-
century Mexican palaces, very few of which survived by the 1920s.[21]
The relief contrasted dramatically with the unadorned surfaces within
the building, but symbolically linked the modern working class with
the colonial aristocracy.

FIGURE 4.6. Obregón Santacilia, Casa de Vecindad, roof, 1926.

Understood with Rivera's responses to it, the Casa de Vecindad project illuminated just how entwined Mexican modern architecture was with colonial forms and international modernism as embodied in Le Corbusier's work, and how social concerns and leftist politics became associated with all three. It also revealed the importance placed by leading twentieth-century artists and architects on integrating different media in a single architectural project—just as colonial architects had—as early as the mid-1920s. Writing in *Mexican Folkways* Rivera summarized Mexican architectural history in terms strikingly similar to those architectural historians had used for twenty-five years. He said that "Mexican" architecture came into being during the colonial era and argued that buildings should respond to climate and social conditions, and be built of local materials. Unsurprisingly, Rivera found the architecture of the nineteenth century and the Porfiriato offensive culturally and ideologically, and was among the first to politicize that architecture so specifically. The muralist, however, praised the Casa de Vecindad's "cheap apartments, hygienic and beautiful," as well as the relief, in which he saw "the harmonious collaboration of the worker and the architect, when the latter is really one; that is if he has at least the necessary combination of sculptor and painter to be authorized to manage usefully and logically forms, volumes and colors; in other words, to make architecture." Rivera described the design using language very similar to that which O'Gorman and others would soon use in discussions of very different looking buildings: "in this work Carlos Obregón followed the tendency of truth in his profession with undeniably happy results. He avoided all 'camouflage,' all waste of material, employing factors of beauty, the economy of materials and their maximum utility."[22] The muralist drew attention further to the building's exposed mechanical and utility fixtures, which he linked to the idea of architectural honesty and economic efficiency, just as O'Gorman did later in his designs for the Rivera and Cecil O'Gorman houses in San Angel.

In 1926 Rivera admired the exposed fixtures not only as expressions of budgetary efficiency appropriate for a nation endeavoring to redress deeply entrenched social and economic equalities, but for their forms, and the ways they made neighboring colonial buildings more visible:

> In one of the most prominent corners of the house, novel and harmonious contrasts play: the fastenings of the pipes and statics, cylinders of the tubes with the pure and simple cubes and parallelograms of the rooms. Beyond this, as a background, are the cupola and the walls of a small and beautiful colonial church, . . . whose beauty the new architecture has left apparent, and given a decorative role even to the electric light meters. The new architecture harmonizes perfectly with that which preceded [it] and demonstrates the extent to which [it is possible to achieve] architectural harmony given present need, without destroying either the vital beauty nor the proper aspect of a city.[23]

Rivera's description located the building simultaneously in the rhetoric of international modernism and in debates about Mexican colonial architecture while affirming its ideological correctness in terms of leftist national politics. His definition of architecture, his evocation of "pure and simple cubes and parallelograms," his claim that the building exemplified architectural "harmony," and assertion that architecture was the practical and "logical" arrangement of "forms, volumes, and colors," rhetorically linked the Casa de Vecindad to Le Corbusier's descriptions and drawings in *Vers une architecture* and to European abstract painting, and firmly placed it in the realm of art. Rivera had spent most of the 1910s in Europe, where he was an accomplished cubist, and had a lifelong interest in architecture. By 1926 he had become skillful in bringing international attention to Mexican art and surely recognized the advantages of linking new buildings in Mexico to European modernism.

DIEGO RIVERA AS CLIENT AND THEORIST
OF MODERN ARCHITECTURE

Even before he left Obregón Santacilia's office, O'Gorman attracted national and international attention with the pair of buildings he designed for Rivera in 1931 opposite the San Angel Inn and next to the house for his father (plate 9). In both projects O'Gorman used exposed mechanical systems and fixtures and strong, simple geometric volumes like those Rivera had praised at the Casa de Vecindad. Because of their formal differences from and proximity to the San Angel Inn, the buildings read as pointed rejections of the colonial character of neighborhood. Describing Cecil's house, O'Gorman said, "The contrast between its appearance and the architecture that was made in the Federal District was notable. Located in front of a colonial building, the Goicoechea Hacienda, which is now the San Angel Inn, [it] caused many people who passed by to turn their heads away so as not to see that 'horror' built in front of the San Angel Inn by an individual whose professional title should be revoked so that he does not continue making houses as horrible as that."[24] Backed by a client more likely than most to be forgiving, O'Gorman used his father's house as an opportunity to define himself in opposition to his mentors and to the profession as a whole. He apparently relished shocking the neighborhood, and his iconoclastic instincts and willingness to conform to a tight budget surely appealed to Rivera, the self-styled leftist who, by 1931, when he hired O'Gorman, was famous for his satirical images of the rich and powerful.

Years later, O'Gorman claimed that he embraced "functional" architecture after reading Le Corbusier's *Vers une architecture* in 1924, saying, "I bought and read this book several times with the greatest interest."[25] In 1924 O'Gorman was nineteen years old, and like many who read that work for the first time at about that age, he was undoubtedly taken with Le Corbusier's sweeping rhetoric and the book's dramatic images of automobiles, airplanes, and ocean liners. Energized by progressive political and architectural reform in 1920s Mexico City and inspired by dynamic professors barely older than he, O'Gorman found many similarities between the world of *Vers une architecture* and the Mexican capital, despite the very great differences in the extent of industrialization in western Europe and Mexico. He was apparently either unfamiliar with or uninterested in Adolf Behne's *Der moderne Zweckbau* (The Modern Functional Building; 1926) or Louis Sullivan's understanding of form as a "function" or result of interior structure, although he did use it to describe expressed construction systems. For O'Gorman "functional" meant the "engineering of buildings," which implied that the architect was unconcerned with aesthetic qualities, the visual (or spatial) experience of the viewer, and that the building had only the most basic elements required to satisfy the program. In this respect O'Gorman's position resembled that of Swiss architect Hannes Meyer, who argued in the late 1920s that architecture was little more than building and also emphasized mechanical systems formally.[26]

In his collaboration with O'Gorman, Rivera supplied the young architect with a platform for his work and a way of talking about it that acknowledged its aesthetic content. O'Gorman professed surprise when Rivera announced that he found the Cecil O'Gorman house beautiful. Recognizing that the young architect had clearly not intended it to be regarded in this way, the muralist justified formally successful compositions in terms of a theoretical utilitarianism that associated beauty with economic austerity, so that cash-strapped Mexico could build more buildings for the poor and thus advance the cause of class equality. Tortured though it was, and although Rivera surely recognized the obviously expressive gestures and manipulation of avant-garde forms such as the sweeping curve of the exterior staircase and curtain wall, Rivera's logic was so compelling for O'Gorman that the architect believed that the muralist had, on the spot, "invented the theory that architecture realized according to strict procedures of the most scientific functionalism is also a work of art."[27]

As O'Gorman remembered it, Rivera was so impressed with his work that he hired him immediately to design a house on the front portion of the lot on which Cecil's house stood, an even more prominent site on the corner across from the San Angel Inn. There O'Gorman built two buildings that are usually interpreted as separate houses for Rivera and his wife, Frida Kahlo (figure 4.7), and a small, one-story building that Guillermo Kahlo used as a photography studio.[28] The

FIGURE 4.7. O'Gorman, House and Studio for Diego Rivera, south elevation, San Angel, 1931. Photograph by Guillermo Kahlo.

buildings' low cost enabled Rivera to live in one of the more expensive, bourgeois parts of town, and their unusual appearances and the way they were explained allowed him to assert his ideological differences from his neighbors and link himself to the international avant-garde. O'Gorman connected the buildings by a bridge that led from the roof of the smaller house—usually understood as "Frida's"—to the uppermost floor of the larger one, typically imagined as "Diego's." Since the rise of scholarly interest in Kahlo in the 1980s, the separate but linked buildings have occasionally been read as stages on which the couple enacted their tumultuous relationship, which was notable for the partners' independence and enmeshment with one another.[29] In his account of the commission decades later, O'Gorman did not suggest that Kahlo was involved in the commission and alternately recalled that he "began to construct the house of Diego Rivera" and that he designed Rivera's "studio, applying the principles of functional architecture" and "a small house" for Kahlo.[30]

FIGURE 4.8. O'Gorman, House and Studio for Diego Rivera, north elevation. Photograph by Guillermo Kahlo.

Because of their travels in the United States in the early 1930s and, later, their separation and divorce, Kahlo lived in the buildings only briefly, and early plans suggest not that the buildings functioned as separate dwellings supporting independent households, but that they operated as public and private zones and were arranged according to conventionally gendered divisions of labor and space. The larger, four-story building contained a sculpture gallery and a spacious, double-height studio where Rivera worked and met visitors. Other rooms were for painting supplies and books; there was also a kitchenette and, on the uppermost floor, a very small bedroom. The smaller, three-story building included a considerably smaller studio, a much larger bedroom, and on one floor, a kitchen, dining room, and large living room, and laundry facilities on the ground floor. A 1933 account, written before the couple lived there, noted that the program included separate workspaces for each artist, but presented the buildings as "the house of Diego Rivera,"[31] which was composed of a single household with two roofs and functioned as a single unit. Rather than viewing the buildings as two separate houses, the muralist understood the spatial organization more as we might a home office today. He noted that in relation to program the plan "is entirely practical. . . . Dentists who have offices at home—families with lively and noisy children—people who like game rooms, and many others are helped by its advantages. And also, unless a house is skillfully arranged the odors from the kitchen permeate the entire house. This way it is impossible."[32] Rivera's statement about cooking odors confirms that most domestic activities were fully separated from his workspace, and as a whole his assessment of the parti helped lend credence to the idea that the buildings were somehow simply "logical" responses to programmatic or "functional" necessities and without particular aesthetic preoccupations.

Like those at the Carranza Center, the buildings had striking colors. O'Gorman surfaced them in plaster mixed with pigments. Although since restorations in the 1990s the larger building has been bright pink and white, it was originally entirely terracotta, with vermillion ironwork and "blue bands on the stairway." The smaller one was pink, with its large cylindrical stair barrel painted "clear light blue." The interior of the larger building had white walls and yellow floors, with ironwork painted blue, while inside the smaller one the staircase was pink and "a wide blue border" covered the lower portion of the walls of the main room.[33] As if anticipating the exterior mural-mosaics created at the National University twenty years later, in 1933 Rivera contemplated adding autobiographical frescoes to the buildings' exterior walls, saying, "someday the house will probably be completely covered with my paintings." Proposing a theory of the relationship between muralism and modern architecture, Rivera suggested that "frescoes should be functional too. . . . They should either carry out the architectural intent or bring further understanding of the purposes of the building."[34]

THE SHADOWS OF PRIMARY FORMS

As striking as the bright colors were in 1933, the buildings' forms and composition were equally dramatic, and have been of greater enduring interest to historians. The formal similarities between O'Gorman's buildings and photographs that appeared in publications by Le Corbusier suggest that O'Gorman not only interpreted *Vers une architecture* as a prescription for architectural utilitarianism as he claimed, but borrowed from it specific forms. Consciously or not, by reproducing and rearranging facade elements from images in a European

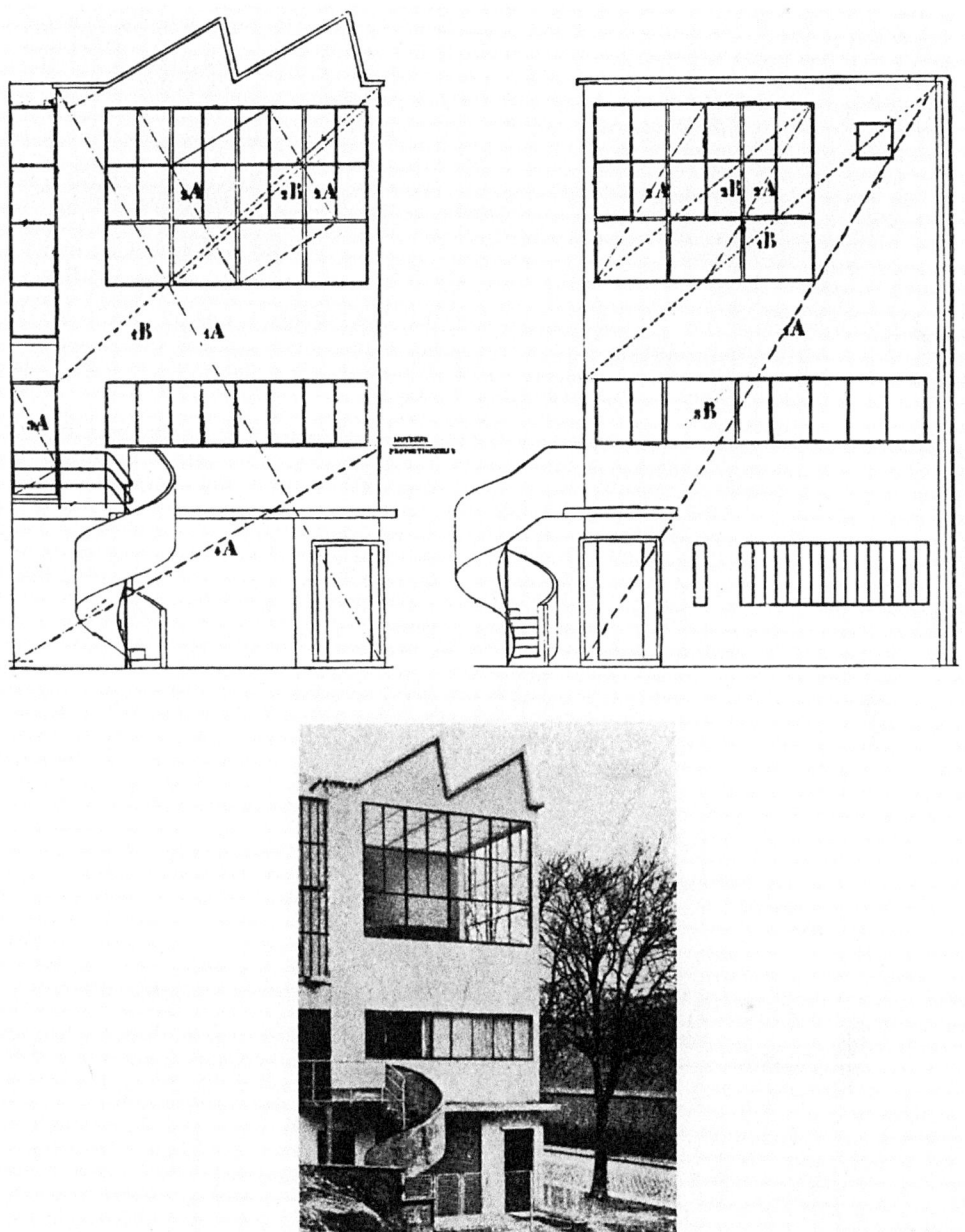

FIGURE 4.9. Le Corbusier, Ozenfant Studio and "Regulating Lines," in *Vers une architecture*, 1927.

text, O'Gorman did exactly what Mexican architects had done since the sixteenth century. In this way, although he never acknowledged it, O'Gorman's early buildings belonged firmly in a national tradition of flexibly reworking elements from foreign architectural treatises to

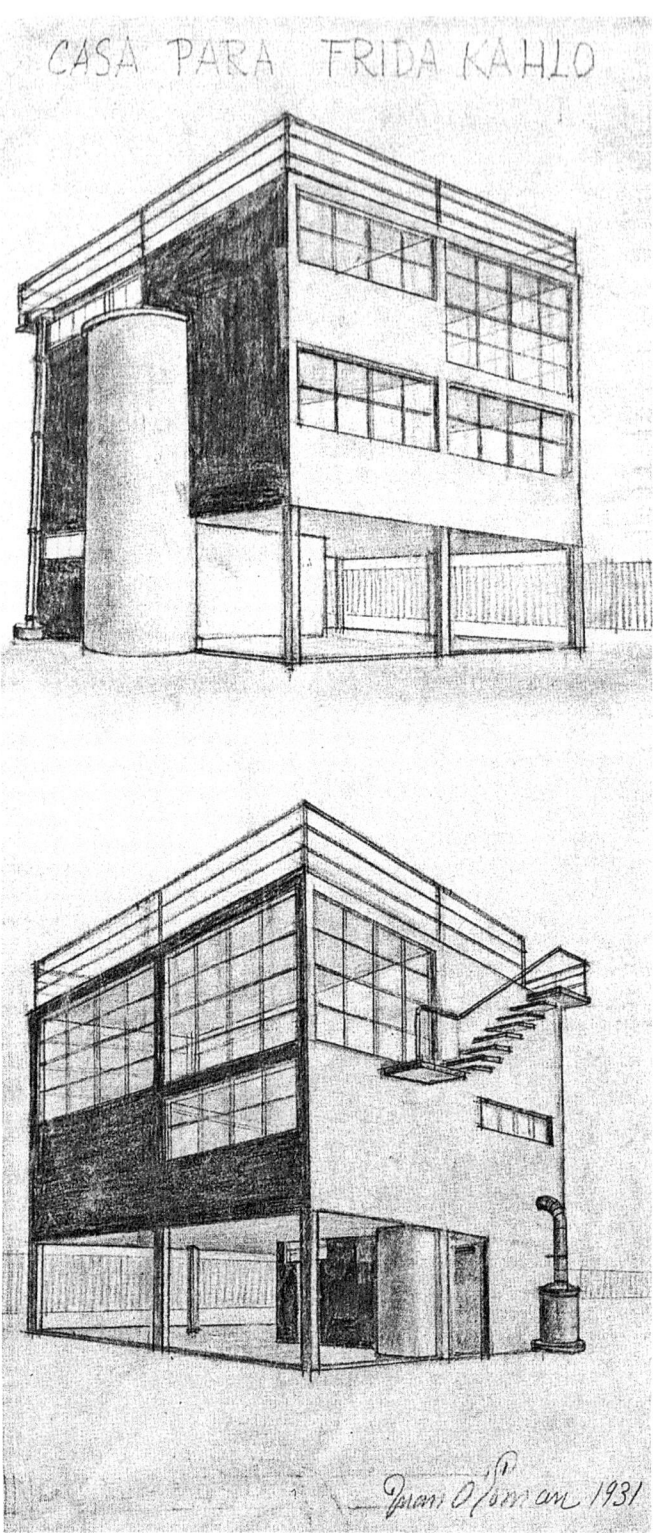

FIGURE 4.10. O'Gorman, House for Frida Kahlo, 1931.

serve new purposes. In San Angel, the disposition of elements on Rivera's studio provided the most vivid example. With its multistory wall of windows, sawtooth roofline, and exterior spiral concrete staircase, the building resembled the studio that Le Corbusier designed for the painter Amadee Ozenfant in Paris in 1923 (figure 4.9). The programmatic and personal similarities—a painter-architect designing a studio for his painter friend—between the projects must have made the Ozenfant studio seem a particularly appropriate model. Knowledgeable observers in the early 1930s would have been unlikely to miss the similarities between the Ozenfant and Rivera studios, and although she did not remark on the likenesses in her text, Esther Born included in her 1937 survey of Mexico's "new architecture," only two photographs of the Rivera studio, both of the facades that resembled the Paris building most closely.[35]

O'Gorman recalled reading *Vers une architecture* first in 1924, meaning that he had read the 1923 edition of the book, which did not include images of the Ozenfant Studio, but a photograph of the building did appear in the 1927 edition published in London and showed its roof, spiral staircase, glazing on the double-height upper story, and strip window below (figure 4.9).[36] Above it were two elevation drawings that illustrated clearly the fenestration, staircase, and roofline. Although the north and west facades of the Rivera studio were the parts of the complex most obviously indebted to one of Le Corbusier's buildings, O'Gorman drew from images elsewhere in the Swiss architect's oeuvre as he composed the San Angel buildings. A large barrel-like form that enclosed the stairs bulged from the west facade of the smaller house and recalled the grain silos that appeared in seven images in the first chapter, on volume (later translated as mass), of the 1923 edition of *Vers une architecture* (figures 4.10 and 4.11). Here Le Corbusier dismissed architectural "styles," and argued that the architecture of all great civilizations had been based on "cubes, cones, spheres, cylinders, or pyramids." These forms were not merely utilitarian building blocks, but *"beautiful forms, the most beautiful forms."*[37] Primary forms, when used properly, advanced the cause of order, and in Le Corbusier's view it was engineers who employed them best thus far in the modern age. Although they did not *"pursu[e] an architectural idea,"* engineers used primary elements in ways that *"provoke in us architectural emotions and thus make the work of man ring in unison with universal order."*[38]

O'Gorman explained his buildings without mentioning "beautiful forms," "architectural emotion," or "universal order," and apparently missed or dismissed the central arguments of the text. Le Corbusier made clear throughout the book that the ultimate purpose of architecture was to provoke emotion aesthetically. He believed that the architect learned how to do this not just by understanding geometry and modern engineering, but by studying the principles at work in the great buildings of the past. In rejecting "academicism," O'Gorman, like Le Corbusier, rejected slavish copying of Renaissance and baroque revival styles, but seemingly also dismissed a great many lessons of architectural history. By embracing the idea that architectural beauty resulted when an architect took a utilitarian approach to design in order to serve social goals, O'Gorman not only lost sight of the many metaphors in *Vers une architecture* but also metaphorically mutilated the Vitruvian triad. When he rejected the interdependence of program, structure, and beauty (and thus of plan, section, and elevation) that had been regarded as the foundation of western architecture at least since the Roman period, O'Gorman left himself with very few choices when designing important buildings, such as those for Rivera. Ever the painter, yet strangely uninterested in Le Corbusier's claims about the plastic arts, ultimately O'Gorman composed pictorially. Rather than creating an architecture rooted in plan and primary geometries, he borrowed literally and imagistically for his own buildings the expressions of those geometries that Le Corbusier identified and illustrated, such as the semicircular barrel and spiral staircase. In San Angel such elements were ultimately representations of the "originals" in Le Corbusier's work, just as Segura's scrolls at the Carranza Center had represented "real" scrolls on Mexican baroque churches and palaces.

Central to O'Gorman's explanation of his buildings as "functional" were their exposed metal pipes, electrical fixtures, water tanks placed prominently on the roof, and simple metal railings. Clearly these things "functioned" primarily as representations of mechanical and plumbing systems and were intended to convey economy and to associatively link the buildings with industrial modernity. They also functioned as representations of primary forms and of elements associated with the ocean liners that Le Corbusier illustrated in *Vers une architecture* and adapted in many of his 1920s houses. The Swiss architect used photographs of giant ships, with huge smokestacks that reappeared as water barrels at the Rivera buildings, and hooters that later took shape as the large pipe at the northeast corner of the smaller building in San Angel, to illustrate his argument about how a style appropriate to the current age might be recognized. O'Gorman's rooftop railings and gangplank-like bridge between the two buildings recalled unmistakably Le Corbusier's

FIGURE 4.11. Le Corbusier, "Tres Rappels I, Le Volume," in *Vers une architecture*, 1924.

interpretations of ships' railings and decks, first at the widely published Villa at Garches (now usually called the Villa Stein-de Monzie) of 1927, and later at the Villa Savoye. In San Angel, O'Gorman reinterpreted the spiral staircase composed only of cantilevered concrete slabs and a single metal railing on the Garches roof as an elegant upper-story exterior staircase on the north facade of the smaller building that led to the roof. Alighting was an act of bravery for even the most confident climber, and the arrangement would have been anything but functional for Kahlo, who had walked with difficulty since having had polio as a child.

Finally, O'Gorman seized on Le Corbusier's emphasis on standardization, but understood it not as a way of talking about the process of refining "types" that the Swiss architect argued had occurred throughout architectural history and was present in modern automobile manufacturing, but instead as a call for the use of modular units in organizing space. The dimensions of the rooms in the San Angel buildings were dictated by readily available lengths of steel, and in the elementary schools O'Gorman pursued modularity even more doggedly, attempting to organize every aspect of the buildings according to a three-meter unit. His focus on modularity and efficiency blinded the architect to two of Le Corbusier's most important contributions to modern architecture: innovation in plan and section. At the core of Le Corbusier's conception of architecture was the belief—closer to Louis Sullivan's functionalism than O'Gorman's—that the appearance of the facade was a result of the plan and section. In discussing surface he wrote that "the task of the architect is to vitalize the surfaces which clothe . . . masses, but in such a way that these surfaces do not become parasitical."[39] Expressions of mass and treatments of surface—primary in O'Gorman's work and in many works of Mexican modernism— were secondary, at least rhetorically, in Le Corbusier's. The plan (not fixed dimensions) organized space and dictated form. Implicit in Le Corbusier's argument was the idea that departing from axial planning as it was taught at the École des Beaux-Arts was necessary if architects were to shape buildings that were well-suited to modern needs and were as aesthetically affecting as great works of the past. O'Gorman apparently missed this point almost entirely. Although less so than the elementary schools, with the exceptions of a few large open interior spaces, the buildings he designed in San Angel largely obeyed conventional modes of divisive planning.

At the heart of *Vers une architecture* was a powerful statement about the nature of art and the emotional work of architecture that could hardly have been more different from what O'Gorman argued. Le Corbusier wrote of the difference between construction and architecture:

> You employ stone, wood and concrete, and with these materials you build houses and palaces. That is construction. Ingenuity is at work.
>
> But suddenly you touch my heart, you do me good, I am happy and I say: "This is beautiful." That is Architecture. Art enters in.
>
> . . . By the use of raw materials and *starting from* conditions more or less utilitarian, you have established certain relationships which have aroused my emotions. This is Architecture.[40]

For Le Corbusier the capacity of architecture to provoke emotion and to awaken in the viewer an awareness of beauty distinguished architecture from construction and from engineering. Unlike O'Gorman, Le Corbusier imagined a single subject—the modern (European) man—perceiving and dwelling in his buildings, and believed that by transforming individuals' experience of housing architects might transform society. Certain that the gap between well-designed machines, tools, and workplaces and poorly designed houses and apartments was responsible for the psychological stress that modern individuals experienced, and for their perception that they lived "in an old and hostile environment," Le Corbusier identified the roots of a contemporary social crisis. He argued that by failing to support the psychological well-being of the individual by helping advance a new and better architecture, societies risked self-destruction. It was a matter, he believed, of "Architecture or Revolution. Revolution can be avoided."[41] While Le Corbusier was concerned with architecture's capacity to transform society through its renovation of individuals' experience of form and space, O'Gorman and his patrons believed the opposite—that collective experience could be transformed if individuals, notably those in positions of political and cultural authority, used materials efficiently. To the extent that emotion entered into O'Gorman's view at all, it was political, not aesthetic emotion excited by an experience of class difference and perhaps stirred by the paintings about the Mexican Revolution by Rivera and others. An unapologetic elitist, in the 1920s Le Corbusier sought to diminish the likelihood of class revolt by improving housing and urban planning; a member of the elite who embraced the mantle of socialism, O'Gorman sought to advance the aims of the class revolt, as he understood them, that had already occurred. Ironically enough, and despite his claims to the contrary, O'Gorman designed some of the most highly formalist buildings in Mexico.

CONCRETE AND THE COUNTRY

As imagistic buildings, the San Angel houses, and later the elementary schools, were aspirational expressions of a long-standing desire for Mexico to be up-to-date industrially, a yearning that for postrevolutionary leftists was freighted with the hope that industrial progress might engender far-reaching social transformation, like what had already been under way in western Europe for almost two hundred years. Few events in Mexico encapsulated the entwining of images, Le Corbusian modernism, industrial progress, and modern concrete construction, or the tense coexistence of these things with rural landscapes and indigenous people as the 1931 painting and photography competitions sponsored by the Tolteca cement company. By taking the name of one of Mexico's most ancient native groups, the company implied that it belonged to the "timeless" Mexico of the great preconquest builders. Unlike its predecessor trade publication, *Cemento*, which promoted cement without advocating any particular architectural language, *Tolteca*, a new company organ begun in 1931, advocated International Style modernism and reprinted parts of Le Corbusier's writings and published images of his buildings.[42]

The year that O'Gorman began designing Rivera's house, *Tolteca*, promising cash prizes, invited artists to depict its new cement factory in Mixcoac on the edge of Mexico City in ways that celebrated architectural and engineering modernity.[43] In the photography competition Manuel Álvarez Bravo's famous *Cement Triptych-2*, a dramatic abstract composition that emphasized texture and form, won first place (figure 4.12). O'Gorman took the top prize in the painting contest with a portable fresco panel, *Aeroplano* (approximately 23 × 39 inches; now in a private collection), a landscape painting in which the enormous factory in the middle distance loomed over the town's brightly painted one- and two-story popular shops clustered in the foreground (plate 10). A pair of large concrete cylinders, like the one he designed on the smaller building at San Angel dominated the factory and also captured the attention of several important competitors in the photography contest, including second-prize winner Agustín Jiménez, perhaps, as James Oles suggested, because of their likeness to Le Corbusier's grain silos.[44] In its January 1932 issue, *Tolteca* published the winning entries, which, with other images of modern concrete buildings elsewhere in the journal, helped link concrete with industrial forms and progress, and unintentionally alluded to one of the central conflicts emerging in Mexican photography and painting: the tension between representation and abstraction.

The images Álvarez Bravo and Jiménez made of the factory helped establish them as leaders of the photographic vanguard, while O'Gorman's entry connected him to older traditions. Tightly cropped compositions that emphasized form, pattern, the play of light, and primary geometries, the photographs were arguably more like Le Corbusier's 1920s buildings than were O'Gorman's paintings of the plant, which were more conventionally representational, had strong ties to Renaissance landscape traditions, and had narrative implications. In his paintings O'Gorman organized buildings in the same way that

FIGURE 4.12. Manuel Álvarez Bravo, *Cement Triptych-2*, 1931.

he organized architectural elements on facades: as representations of forms that stood for something else. Enrique de Anda has suggested that in his paintings, O'Gorman "used landscape not as a visual support, but rather as a depository of cultural symbols."[45] The landscape in *Aeroplano* did function in that way: the painter arranged the picture plane in layers, creating space for an unmistakable symbol of industrial modernity, and for equally unmistakable (in Mexican eyes) symbols of preindustrial, folk Mexico, such as the vernacular buildings with their commercial signage painted directly onto the wall surface and the allusion to indigenous foodstuffs in the *nixtamal* shop.[46] By placing the factory and town against a mountainous landscape, O'Gorman located both in a long tradition of Mexican landscape painting, linked industrial vernacular buildings to nature understood as distinctively Mexican, and alluded to the transformations of real Mexican landscapes and towns. Unlike the energetic compositions by Álvarez Bravo and Jiménez, however, the mood of *Aeroplano* was tense, even somber. O'Gorman neither celebrated industrialization nor critiqued it. The painting's subdued hues and airlessness suggested a profound ambivalence about the implications of industrialization, an ambivalence that was also discernible in his elementary schools. In postrevolutionary Mexico the cultural and social projects of integrating rural people and vernacular or popular forms into a single, shared understanding of modern nationhood and shaping a society capable of realizing the benefits of industrial modernity ran parallel.

Surrounding Rivera's studio and house was a fence formed by closely spaced green column-like organ cactuses, a species native to Mexico that was often used as fencing in rural areas. Seen from the street, with the buildings' great sculptural forms in concrete and metal, and the brightly colored planes rising behind the cactuses, the architectural ensemble read as a series of allusions to rural landscapes, international industrial modernity, and popular and vernacular forms. The fence consisted of real cactuses but it, like the other elements of the suburban residence, also functioned representationally, and to viewers able to interpret the rapidly evolving visual lexicon of local and foreign elements it would have been as unmistakably coded as Obregón Santacilia's representations of colonial architectural forms. Against the buildings behind it, the fence, with its contrasting texture, color, and rhythm, gave the ensemble an arresting compositional balance akin to formal arrangements in abstract painting and, like the main door of the Ministry of Health, which was legible simultaneously in terms of Mexican colonial and international Art Deco architecture, operated simultaneously in international and nationally specific visual systems.

SCHOOLS FOR THE WORKING CLASS

To an even greater extent than the Rivera commission and *Aeroplano*, O'Gorman's work for the Ministry of Education, begun in 1932, suggested that he, like modernists in many countries, regarded industrial modernization as simultaneously exciting and anxiety-inducing, if not on a personal level, than because of its implications for historical and rural Mexican landscapes. As equally strident rejections of architectural history as the Rivera houses, O'Gorman's urban schools revealed yet

FIGURE 4.13. O'Gorman, School in Colonia Pro-Hogar, main facade, 1933, in *Escuelas primarias*.

more vividly the ways his work as a painter animated his architecture. They also reflected his desire to situate his work in a nationalist framework that, like Rivera's murals, celebrated the urban working class and tried to honor vernacular types and forms. Although the best-known schools O'Gorman worked on for the ministry were the rationalist buildings in urban areas that some observers compared to factories, he also oversaw the building or restoration of very different-looking schools in parts of the capital that retained a rural character.

Most of O'Gorman's elementary schools were designed for the poorest children in Mexico City, and built in some of the capital's most economically depressed areas under the joint patronage of the Ministry of Education and the Department of the Federal District. The buildings are famous for helping spread an austere rationalist language throughout the capital and for linking it with social reform. But like other aspects of O'Gorman's oeuvre, the buildings were equally notable for their formal and intellectual tensions. In them the architect united three strands of Mexican visual modernism: rationalism—adapted from its French academic context in Mexico first by José Villagrán García; forms borrowed from and allusions to Le Corbusier's 1920s houses and *Vers une architecture*; and the painting of Mexico City's working class, particularly popular murals and commercial sign painting. In referring to all three, whether on the buildings' facades, fixtures, or interior murals, O'Gorman continued the practice established by Obregón Santacilia of uniting in single works references to multiple idioms and, like Segura, shaped settings for linking "national" art, popular customs, and the working class.

All the schools were built, O'Gorman claimed, according to strict principles of economy and efficiency and designed to minimize maintenance costs.[47] The urban schools usually had two stories, were supported by reinforced concrete piers, and had flat roofs, metal windows and doors, and cement and asphalt floors. As at the Rivera house, water tanks were often visible on the roofs and balconies had thin metal railings. The buildings were constructed according to a three-meter module system; their walls were surfaced in lime, and in most cases the exteriors were painted in three colors. Exterior play spaces and patios were surfaced with volcanic rock. Although socially progressive impulses underlay the ministry's commission, like many rationalist buildings of the era, its urban schools conveyed hierarchy and authority. Most plans were axially symmetrical and shaped like short-Ts. O'Gorman positioned administrative offices at the crossing, arranged classrooms in the long wings, and grouped bathrooms and water systems in the short wing that extended perpendicularly from the crossing. In their rigidity and formality the plans conveyed the stridency of the ministry's ambitions to rationalize and regularize education as well as architecture. In most urban schools a platform over the bathroom wings that overlooked the outdoor exercise areas was intended to "be improvised as a tribune or as a place to put a radio with a loudspeaker so that it can be heard in the play patios," or a place to install a movie projector for the showing of films.[48] At the Carranza Center, films and performances were intended to instruct the working class in the ways of modern Mexico and its culture; the radio programs and films shown to school children were undoubtedly meant to be similarly edifying.

On the principal facades simple trebeated forms framed factory-like windows, while tiny porthole windows, placed near the top of a smooth wall were the only openings on the opposite end (figure 4.14), The porthole windows, along with the long balconies and railings recalled the ocean liners associated with Le Corbusier, while the regular rhythm of the trebeation elsewhere evoked his images of factories and called to mind the work of José Villagrán García, whose design, begun in 1929, for a large tuberculosis sanatorium for indigent consumptives embodied the connections between architectural rationalism, social control, and underclass reform perhaps more than any other building in Mexico.[49] Although the facade elements represented forms associated with international industrial modernity, the ministry attempted to "nationalize" the buildings rhetorically. The patron believed they were suited to the "economic and social reality" of Mexico, and that "this school architecture is simple, bare, strong, lasting," its "beauty consist[ing] only in the harmony" of "its technical conditions."[50] This description of the buildings, "as simple, bare, strong, and lasting"

FIGURE 4.14. O'Gorman, School in Colonia Pro-Hogar, balconies, 1933, in *Escuelas primarias.*

echoed idealized depictions of the bodies of indigenous and mestizo workers whose children might attend the schools, and whose physical conditions had been of particular concern to the patrons of the Ministry of Health and the Carranza Center. As in other projects concerned with social reform, making available adequate light, air, and sanitary facilities was a priority in the elementary school project. O'Gorman positioned windows to maximize ventilation and calculated the dimensions of the exercise patios so that, in most cases, each student was allotted five square meters of space.

Designed for a government eager to demonstrate its commitment to social reform, by an architect ideologically committed to the nationalist impulses of his client, almost as soon as they were finished O'Gorman's urban schools were caught in the rhetorical tangle of "Mexican" architecture, and they were highly controversial. As early as 1933 the buildings were critiqued as being "imported," "German," inappropriate for "our country," and "lacking style, or having a very strange or surprising style."[51] Such comments revealed the extent to which

FIGURE 4.15. O'Gorman, School in Colonia Pro-Hogar, view of short wing, with open-air walkways and rooftop water tanks, 1933, in *Escuelas primarias*.

"Mexican" had become synonymous with historical representation or allusion. As apologists for rationalism in the 1930s quickly discovered, it was essential that their buildings be regarded as nationally specific in some way. The imperative that the schools be recognizably "Mexican" was undoubtedly especially strong because they were intended to help inculcate in poor, mostly brown-skinned children a shared sense of national belonging. To make the buildings legitimately "Mexican" required complicated rhetorical twists that nationalized them based on their capacity to fulfill programmatic and budgetary requirements, as these were imagined to reflect the clients' progressive social commitments. Such an argument undermined the principles of formal representation and association with Mexican architectural history, upon which "national" architecture had been understood to be based since the turn of the century.

O'Gorman acknowledged that the "facades" and the "appearance or form" surprised audiences, but then proceeded to explain the buildings with reference to program, historical buildings, nationally specific ones, and construction: "we all agree that if human needs are similar or equal in one country and the next, then the building that satisfies these needs could be similar or equal in one country and the next. I believe . . . that no one would opine that in Mexico efficient construction systems are employed that are not used in other countries; or is it that to be nationalists we have to return to colonial or Aztec construction systems? Science is universal, and reinforced concrete can be used in our country without our ceasing to be good Mexicans."[52] The architect's inclination to link his buildings to problems he imagined were "universal" was nothing new of course, and it belonged to a multidisciplinary attempt to reconcile a belief in Mexican exceptionalism and yearning to be "universal" that reached its apex at mid-century. Like his predecessors, O'Gorman believed that architectural modernity in Mexico should be recognizably like architectural modernity elsewhere, but his emphasis on construction and his connection of it to "science" rather than history differentiated him from Segura and Obregón Santacilia. By referring to colonial and Aztec architecture O'Gorman himself recentralized Mexican architectural history in the debate and alluded to the fractious disagreements within the profession about its place in modern design. O'Gorman pled not for modernism, but for modernization, a goal that was ultimately less threatening to the nascent shared understanding of "Mexico" that had historical, popular, and rural visual culture at its core.

ESCUELAS PRIMARIAS

Despite O'Gorman's claims that he was indifferent to aesthetic questions in designing the elementary schools, the differences in form, materials, and construction systems between his urban and rural schools suggest that he did believe that different vocabularies better suited different circumstances. In general, there was more formal variety in the schools in rural areas than in those in Mexico City, but as a group they were recognizably different from their urban counterparts. Nearly all were only one story and had inclined roofs; piers were rarely visible and beams were often expressed as vigas. In many the lower one-third of the facade was painted a single color. The rural buildings also differed dramatically in their fenestration patterns. In some, such as the school in Tláhuac, classrooms were partially open to the air and others had narrow, vertical windows rather than the horizontal, industrial-frame and porthole windows that defined those in Mexico City (figure 4.16).

FIGURE 4.16. O'Gorman, School in Tláhuac, 1933, in *Escuelas primarias*.

Although O'Gorman placed water tanks on the roofs of the rural schools, none had the distinctive metal railings or open-air walkways of their urban counterparts. The rural schools had load-bearing brick walls covered in lime, and some had vaulted brick roofs. Floors were surfaced with stone tiles rather than concrete and asphalt; doors and windows were framed in wood rather than metal.

The schools' formal and material differences embodied one of the central tensions in Mexican modernity and revealed how much importance O'Gorman and his clients ascribed to facades as surfaces on which to convey beliefs about conditions specific to Mexico, even at the same time that they proclaimed the universality of their architectural and educational programs. By looking decidedly different from one another, the groups of schools reinforced the very real differences between urban and rural Mexico and underscored the conflict in Mexican visual modernity, as it was constructed by Mexico City artists and intellectuals, between these two places. Nothing revealed the divide more vividly than the Ministry of Education's 1933 publication on the schools, *Escuelas primarias*, in which it outlined the architectural and philosophical program of its patronage of a "new economical and simple architecture" for one million pesos. Eighty-nine pages of photographs—primarily of the buildings' exteriors, but also of some of the murals, and a few interiors—taken by three of Mexico's foremost photographers followed an unsigned, sixteen-page introductory text that was likely written by O'Gorman and included assessments of the schools by architects Juan Legarreta and Manuel Ortiz Monasterio.

The photographers were Manuel Álvarez Bravo, Agustín Jiménez, and Luis Márquez. While Márquez's works were decidedly picturesque, those of Álvarez Bravo and Jiménez typified the opposite tendency. Winners of the Tolteca photography competition of 1931, Álvarez Bravo and Jiménez had firmly established credentials as shapers of the image of Mexican industrial modernity. John Mraz characterized them as "experimenters who broke with painterly notions of art and sought to establish photography as a medium in its own right. . . . They rejected the picturesque and focused on modern urban life as found in telegraph lines, typewriters, and toilets."[53] Márquez, however, did the opposite. Mraz located him among the "traditionalists who constructed a romantic vision of a bucolic rural Eden absorbed in its nature and peopled by *charros* and *chinas pobladas*, regional figures that were transformed into national archetypes."[54] *Escuelas primarias* did not credit the photographers for specific photographs,[55] and although many of the images do not bear particular formal "signatures," it is possible to venture some suppositions about authorship.

Shot at raking angles, cropped to emphasize the "industrial" details like the metal railings and porthole windows, and often captured at times of the day when the long lines of the roofs and balconies cast dramatic, diagonal shadows, the most notable images of the urban schools, such as those of the schools in Colonia Pro-Hogar and Xocotitla likely belonged to Álvarez Bravo or Jiménez (figures 4.13–4.15; 4.17). These images recalled *Estridentista* compositions of the 1920s, which were informed by Italian Futurism and sought to express the dynamism of industrial modernity and radical social change by arranging vigorous diagonal lines in shallow picture planes and collages. *Estridentista* prints often depicted skyscrapers and factories in a forceful graphic style echoed in the stylized typeface that appeared in *Estridentista* publications. On the front cover of *Escuelas primarias*, Julio I. Prieto and Angel Chápero created a collage of the photographs of urban schools overlaid with boldly stylized off-white letters accented in orange to spell out the title, subtitle, and key figures (figure

FIGURE 4.17. O'Gorman, School in Xocotitla, 1933, in *Escuelas primarias.*

4.18). Atop the composition, "$1 000 000 00" appeared, a reference to the one million pesos that the Ministry of Education allotted for the schools. Wrapping around the bottom of the cover and up the right side the reader saw, in white, "nueva arquitectura economica y sencilla." Providing the eye few places to rest, the cover suggested that the building program was vigorous, almost frantic in its pace, and far-reaching. The back cover was also a collage of the photographs, but it was a more visually restful composition of horizontals instead of diagonals.

The photographs in *Escuelas primarias* almost never included students or teachers and instead drew attention to formal expressions of order, rationality, and a dynamic, if abstract, progress related broadly to industry. Many images emphasized the repetition of bays and piers on facades, often in contrast to distant mountains; others captured the exterior lettering or the most politically charged or violent imagery

FIGURE 4.18. Julio I. Prieto and Angel Chápero, *Escuelas primarias* cover.

in the interior murals. Other images recalled specific photographs by important modernist photographers in 1920s Mexico City. An image of three metal water fountains, with their pipes exposed below, and another of a row of toilet stalls shot at an angle in which the door of the one in the lower right corner swung open to reveal a single white porcelain toilet, all in the school in Colonia Portales, not only illustrated the schools' modern facilities, but evoked Edward Weston's *Excusado* (1925) and his *Washbowl* (1926) (figures 4.19–4.21). Álvarez Bravo in particular was influenced by Weston, and the *Escuelas primarias* photographs linked the urban schools to a widespread modernist interest in hygiene, plumbing, and the mechanical systems that revolutionized daily life.

In contrast, the photographs of the rural schools, likely made by Márquez, often included objects that by the early 1930s were firmly codified as rural and were associated with "vanishing" and "ancient" Mexican landscapes and ways of life. Some alluded to a broader conflict between industrial modernity and rural landscapes, such as the

FIGURE 4.19. Water fountains, School in Colonia Portales, in *Escuelas primarias.*

one of a school in Tláhuac (figure 4.16), In this image, presumably taken from the rooftop of a nearby building, the regularity and order of the four school buildings, organized in a pattern reminiscent of the arrangement of pavilions in modern hospitals and factories, was juxtaposed with the irregular heights of the perimeter cactus fence that surrounded the campus, the more sharply inclined thatch roofs of houses outside of it, and, in the far distance, a giant mountain. In its perspective and allusions to industrial and rural Mexico this photograph had more in common with O'Gorman's *Aeroplano,* than with many of the photographs of urban schools in *Escuelas primarias.* Even more pointed in its use of rural imagery was the photograph of a school in Tilhuaca (figure 4.22) The most prominent object in the composition was a giant maguey cactus in the foreground to the right; beyond it to the left, three sheep grazed and a young peasant stood in the shade of a tree. Classroom pavilions appeared in the middle ground and distance, and between the two, an adult peasant wearing a large a straw hat and a child holding a baby were just visible.

FIGURE 4.20. Toilet stalls, School in Colonia Portales, in *Escuelas primarias*.

With such prominent emblems of Mexican rural culture, the photograph could hardly have been more different from those of the urban schools in which the photographers seemed to make explicit comparisons with the architecture of Le Corbusier. Instead of cactuses, Álvarez Bravo or Jiménez used automobiles, carefully positioned in several compositions made at the school in Colonia Pro-Hogar, to associate the building with international, industrial modernity, and particularly the 1920s buildings of the Swiss architect. In a distant shot of the facade an automobile is parked in the right foreground, and in another the same car is seen from inside the school looking through the gate whose metal letters spelling "ESCUELA PRIMARIA" are inexplicably legible, suggesting that the photographer manipulated the image to heighten its associative power (figures 4.13 and 4.23). The photographs called to mind the many images of cars in *Vers une architecture* and, even more immediately, the widely circulated pictures of the Villa Stein-de

FIGURE 4.21. *Washbowl,* 1925. Photograph by Edward Weston.

Monzie in which the building was shown with an automobile, such as Charles Gérard's of 1927 (figure 4.24).[56] Images of the French house in which a touring car, more like the one in *Escuelas primarias* than the sports car in *Vers une architecture,* was positioned as a prop appeared in Le Corbusier's 1928 *Une maison–un palais* and in a 1929 issue of the German journal *Die Bauwelt.*[57] In both the metal railings, rounded volumes, and cantilevered steps on the roof—the elements that reappeared in O'Gorman's designs for the Rivera house and the urban schools— were clearly visible. Although O'Gorman's name did not appear in the credits of *Escuelas primarias,* his imprint is detectable in the contrasts throughout it—in the images that linked the schools to Le Corbusier, and those that almost nostalgically framed the Mexican landscape; in the frenzied rhythm of the cover collage appropriate to a manifesto, and the subdued, dry recitation of facts and figures in its text.

FIGURE 4.22. O'Gorman, School in Tilhuaca, in *Escuelas primarias*.

No contrast in *Escuelas primarias* was more striking than that captured in two photographs near the end of the book that showed a new school in Xochimilco that was built in the forecourt, or atrio, of a sixteenth-century church. The siting of the building, which radically altered the character of the atrio, was an extraordinarily aggressive symbolic gesture that seemed to foreshadow the Ministry of Education's assertion in the introduction of *Escuelas primarias* that the colonial revival style should be criminalized. The new school obscured views of the main facade of one of metropolitan Mexico City's rare surviving early colonial churches, and O'Gorman aligned the long wing of the new building with the single nave of the old one, as if to suggest the replacement of religion with secular education. The photographs in *Escuelas primarias* dramatically juxtaposed the two buildings and made visible the dilemma modern architects faced in designing new buildings literally in the shadows of extraordinary historical works (figure 4.25). In one, three bays of the school nearly filled the frame, while the main facade of the church was visible in the middle ground on the right. The rhythm of straight lines of the school's cantilevered roof and balcony, the industrial glazing, and smooth concrete surfac-

FIGURE 4.23. O'Gorman, School in Colonia Pro-Hogar, gate and touring car, 1933, in *Escuelas primarias.*

es contrasted dramatically with the jagged pattern of merlons, nearly windowless facade, rough, dirty wall surfaces, and rounded arched opening of the church. A low, uneven wall of rocks between the church and the schoolyard read as a pile of rubble, strengthening the implication that the new school embodied modern progress and even the triumph of the present over history. In another photograph, taken at a greater distance from the church, in the left foreground the edge of the short wing of the school and its balcony framed the view of the long wing and appeared higher than the tower and cupola of the church in the background. This image also implied the dominance of modern architecture over historical buildings, even its eradication of them. At the same time, by drawing attention to the dome and tower looming in the distance, intentionally or not, the composition pointed to the sometimes uncomfortable relationship between colonial and modern buildings, and even to O'Gorman's own irresolution about how to approach seemingly contradictory aspects of Mexican architecture and visual culture.

FIGURE 4.24. Le Corbusier, Villa Stein-de Monzie, Garches, France, 1927.

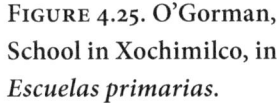

FIGURE 4.25. O'Gorman,
School in Xochimilco, in
Escuelas primarias.

PAINT, *PATRIA*, AND *PULQUERÍAS*

Throughout his career O'Gorman used color and painting as means of bridging the intellectual and ideological gaps he wrestled with in architecture. In black-and-white photographs, the urban schools appear monotonously uniform, but large planes of color on their exteriors distinguished them from one another, and interior murals enlivened their walls. The Carlos A. Carrillo School, in Colonia Portales, for example, was the largest of the new schools and it was painted green, gray, and blue and, as in the San Angel buildings, the window frames and railings were "a brilliant red vermillion."[58] The facade of the new, twenty-four-classroom school in Colonia Ex-Hipódromo de Peralvillo was painted rose, gray, and orange, and the walls of the smaller Melchor Ocampo school in Coyoacán were blue and brown (figure 4.26). Painted on the exterior walls of all the urban schools, usually in two colors and capital letters rendered in a dynamic, highly graphic style, were the words "Escuela Primaria." The stylized letters helpfully announced the buildings' purpose and resembled commercial sign painting. Throughout Mexico City proprietors of middle- and lower-end shops and eateries often painted the names, services, and products of their establishments in bright colors on exterior walls using bold, graphic styles. O'Gorman's use of a similar iconographical style visually linked the schools to commercial spaces familiar to members of the working class whose children might attend the school, and to a vibrant vernacular urban tradition.

Similar-looking lettering also often appeared on the exterior walls of Mexico City's pulquerías, working-class establishments where workers consumed pulque, a low-grade, high-alcohol beverage distilled from cactus sap. Because of their association with drunkenness, and morally suspicious behaviors that might follow it, pulquerías were the targets of a variety of reform efforts in the 1920s by Mexican public health officials. But the establishments fascinated 1920s artists and intellectuals who were interested in folk culture. Centers of popular revelry that were associated with a beverage derived from a quintessentially "Mexican" plant, the pulquerías attracted special attention because of their painted decorations. In addition to stylized lettering and small decorative motifs, many had murals, most of which were painted by unknown artists, on interior and exterior walls.

Anita Brenner codified pulquería painting as a major urban type and metropolitan folk art in her 1929 account of Mexican popular art and customs, *Idols behind Altars*. Photographs of pulquería murals and

FIGURE 4.26. Melchor Ocampo School, in *Escuelas primari*as.

FIGURE 4.27. O'Gorman, School in Colonia Alvaro Obregón, 1933, in *Escuelas primarias*.

lettering taken by the U.S. photographer Edward Weston (who was so fascinated by the establishments that he chronicled their unusual names in the daybooks he kept in Mexico City) illustrated the book (figure 4.28). In her description of the pulquerías and their decoration, Brenner, like historians of colonial art, identified in the paintings the intermingling of Spanish and preconquest influences and drew attention to the wall surface as the site where painting and architectural structure worked interdependently:

> The streets of Mexico are painted galleries. . . . In every block there is at least one pulquería. . . . It is the focus of the block, focus of the eye, the ear, the nose, the memory. An insistent place, with an air of ritual about it, and a genial waywardness.
>
> Outside and in, the walls are broken into scenic panel and doors (startled, one sometimes in a glimpse mistakes which is the door) framed in scarlet, indigo, sulphur, cubes and spirals and blocks and scrolls which make the surfaces advance, retreat, bow; dance under lettered fantasy. The doors are curtained by tissue-paper fringes, chains, rosettes, little flags. . . . Polychrome Aztec sculpture is translated literally in these solid walls of cubes, squares, scrolls, moving by color geometry around each other, into and out of the wall, preserving unity. The fusion, the Spanish-Indian image, is in the scenic panel which sometimes dethrones abstract art and uses it as a frame.[59]

Positioning the decoration and murals in relation to both Mexican historical types and international abstraction, Brenner argued that the paintings, which were usually rendered in "cheap, brilliant oils which quickly fade and peel" constituted a vital and distinctive national art. The murals' transience and frequent repainting was part of their charm for patrons and painters alike. As urban vernacular works they helped establish a tradition of making and remaking Mexico City walls with color and linked high, low, and historical art. Because they appeared on buildings associated with the working class, they seemed to join ancient indigenous Mexicans, who had also painted murals, and the modern urban working class in an imagined narrative of historical-cultural continuity that appealed to progressive intellectuals and bureaucrats alike. Brenner explained that the murals "are always the national landscape in the present, which includes beloved and amusing things of the past."[60]

She claimed as well that pulquerías played crucial roles in the lives of individuals and in the visual and psychological mediation of Mexican historical forces. Brenner believed that in the murals, urban

FIGURE 4.28. *Pulquería, Mexico City,* 1926. Photograph by Edward Weston. Published in *Mexican Folkways,* 1926.

and rural Mexico came together and influenced one another: "As a place of emotional escape . . . the pulquería is post-Spanish. . . . As a place of catharsis, a solution of problems, of emotional and mental gymnastics, it is native. . . . It corresponds in painting, to the ballad-publisher. . . . Paintings and ballads pass from city to country and ranch and village, and back again. The small-town pulquería artist copies his metropolitan fellow-craftsman; but the metropolitan takes his theme and his imagery from the peasant."[61] In the mid-1920s, as part of the Ministry of Health's efforts to regulate and "sanitize" the pulquerías, officials demanded the whitewashing of many interior murals, but occasionally approved the painting of new ones by trained artists, including O'Gorman. Painted in 1926 and 1927, O'Gorman's murals in three pulquerías—two in the historic center, and one farther south at Chapultepec and Insurgentes avenues—were several of his very first works of public art.[62] Antonio Luna Arroyo, O'Gorman's biographer, characterized the paintings "as his first productions of a very Mexican, typical, vernacular flavor."[63]

O'Gorman's evolution as a painter—notably of architecturally scaled works—coincided exactly with his development as an architect, and his muralist-client Rivera strongly influenced his ideas about both. Throughout the 1920s Rivera was the foremost exponent of pulquería art. As early as 1923 he stylized himself as a "pulquería painter" and said that he had admired the murals since childhood.[64] Writing in *Mexican Folkways* in 1926, in essays illustrated with Weston's photographs, Rivera claimed that pulquería paintings were a truly proletarian and Mexican art form.[65] He found in them evidence that the defining characteristic of Mexican art was color and wrote that, "the Mexican is eminently and above everything else, a colorist."[66] Elsewhere he extolled the establishments' quirky names, and claimed that they "constitute[d] the best synthetic Mexican poems."[67] Listing them, he argued that they were distinctively Mexican linguistic expressions and remarked on "their untranslatable quality" and the necessity of "penetrat[ing] into the language" to understand folk culture.[68] Rivera's association of color, politics, wall painting, and national exceptionalism rooted in indigenous culture, and his emphasis on the pulquería's names, which were written on their exterior walls, provided a framework that O'Gorman could adapt to particularize the elementary schools ideologically and culturally. Recalling having learned of "pulquería artists, of retablos, of the Judases of Holy Week, of Hermenegildo Bustos, the greatest portraitist of Mexico, of José María Estrada and of the anonymous painters of the 18th and 19th centuries, of his teacher José María Velasco, the greatest landscape painter in the world"[69] from Rivera, O'Gorman located the genre in a Mexican art history that did not distinguish "high" and "low" works. O'Gorman's history implicitly culminated with Rivera, who painted the papier-mâché Judas figures burned during popular celebrations of Holy Week on the walls of the Ministry of Education, and echoed countless efforts in the twentieth century to shape a narrative of Mexican artistic and cultural history unified across class lines and time. In his designs for the elementary schools he similarly sought to integrate diverse elements of modern visual culture.

While the exterior decoration of the urban schools alluded to commercial wall surfaces in the capital, the murals painted inside six of them linked the schools to the "mural Renaissance" that Rivera had helped initiate in the 1920s and to the official spaces of postrevolutionary Mexico, where many of the famous murals were painted. At O'Gorman's urging, the Ministry of Education hired muralists to paint fres-

Figure 4.29. Pablo O'Higgins, *Exploitation of Children in the Factories*, Emiliano Zapata School, Colonia Industrial, 1933.

coes in entryways and on staircase landings in the new urban schools. Some of Mexico's leading painters, including Julio Castellanos, Pablo O'Higgins, Jesús Guerrero Galván, Máximo Pacheco, Raúl Anguiano, and Alfredo Zalce worked in the schools.[70] Most of the murals depicted children learning or playing, or treated contemporary political themes related to children and childhood. Among the most notable were Castellanos's images of children's games in the Melchor Ocampo school, and U.S.-born O'Higgins's five frescoes in the Emiliano Zapata School in Colonia Industrial.

In the Emiliano Zapata School, O'Higgins created two grisailles panels in the entry, and at the head of the main staircase *Exploitation of Children in the Factories*, which showed small children with grown workers in a glass-blowing plant (figure 4.29). Frances Toor noted of the mural that "the theme . . . is not of a character that a child can readily understand. The painting is along the traditional constructive lines of a great decoration and the fresco technique is perfect. The blues, violets and earth colors are very well blended and the drawing, angular, firm and definite, is peculiar to this young artist." Two smaller panels, *The Exploited against the Exploiters* and *The Rebellion against the Domination of Catholic Clergy*, to the left and right of another staircase continued the political theme begun in the main work, and in them O'Higgins linked contemporary labor struggles to indigenous resistance to the Spanish conquest. In the panel dealing with the clergy, the painter included an inscription from the Maya book Chailam Balam de Chayamel, which, according to Toor, "literally describe[ed] the scene" O'Higgins painted: "Scarcely art thou born and thou art already bowed under the weight of Tribute."[71] O'Higgins was a committed leftist and his imagery undoubtedly seemed appropriate for a building where the principles of socialist education were practiced. Like Rivera and other leading muralists, O'Higgins related modern themes to national history, and like the pulquería murals, his work linked ancient indigenous Mexicans to modern workers.

The approach O'Gorman and his colleagues took in the murals inside the schools and the painted walls outside suggest that they understood wall surfaces essentially in the same ways that Segura and Obregón Santacilia did: as representational planes. Unlike countless predecessors in western architectural history who used paint to emphasize structure, O'Gorman and his Mexican colleagues used it to draw attention to facades and surfaces, and embraced it for its representational and narrative potentials. Unlike Le Corbusier, Gerrit Rietveld, and the artists and architects of the Bauhaus, O'Gorman and the elementary school painters appear to have had no interest in using color on the wall planes to experiment with spatial perception or as a means of differentiating spaces of differing characters.

EDUCATION IN PLEIN AIR

As important as they were in helping advance the language of rationalism and in giving painting an important place in schools, O'Gorman's buildings introduced neither the ideal of airy classrooms with clearly expressed structural systems nor murals to Mexico City's elementary schools; both were already present in a series of little-known elementary schools designed by Vicente Mendiola in 1927 and sponsored by the Ministry of Education and the municipal government (figure 4.30).[72] Although only eight were built, like O'Gorman's works, these buildings also served working-class students, in whom teachers sought to instill the habits of modern hygiene and shared national values. Conceptually rooted in research on ways of schooling sick children who were imagined to benefit from exposure to light and air, the 1927 buildings had classrooms with only three walls or windows that were "always open."[73] Mendiola combined expressed piers, beams, and in some cases large concrete buttresses, with applied ornament and decoration, which usually consisted of brick and tile arranged in a way that evoked colonial

FIGURE 4.30. Vicente Mendiola, *Tipo de una de las clases para la Escuela al Aire Libre*, 1927.

architecture generally. The regular rhythm of the beams and visible modularity of the classrooms made the buildings some of the earliest examples of an emerging rationalist architecture associated with social reform, while their tiled fountains, pergolas covered in viga-like beams, and decorative brickwork firmly situated them in the very brief but distinctive late-1920s moment when several leading Mexico City architects (Segura foremost among them) experimented with integrating brick and tile into concrete constructions to express historical continuity representationally and materially.[74] As with other projects from this era, the schools were understood to belong to a "modern tendency" because they did not rely on historicist forms and because of the social orientation of their programs.

As at the Carranza Center, in these schools physical well-being and the forging of the correct kinds of reciprocal social relationships went together. Classrooms opened out onto gardens, courtyards, and passages where students were instructed in physical education and participated in synchronized exercise. Like O'Gorman's later buildings, the Open Air Schools were built at "minimum cost and greatest . . . capacity," and designed so that "all children . . . had the same advantages of [access to]

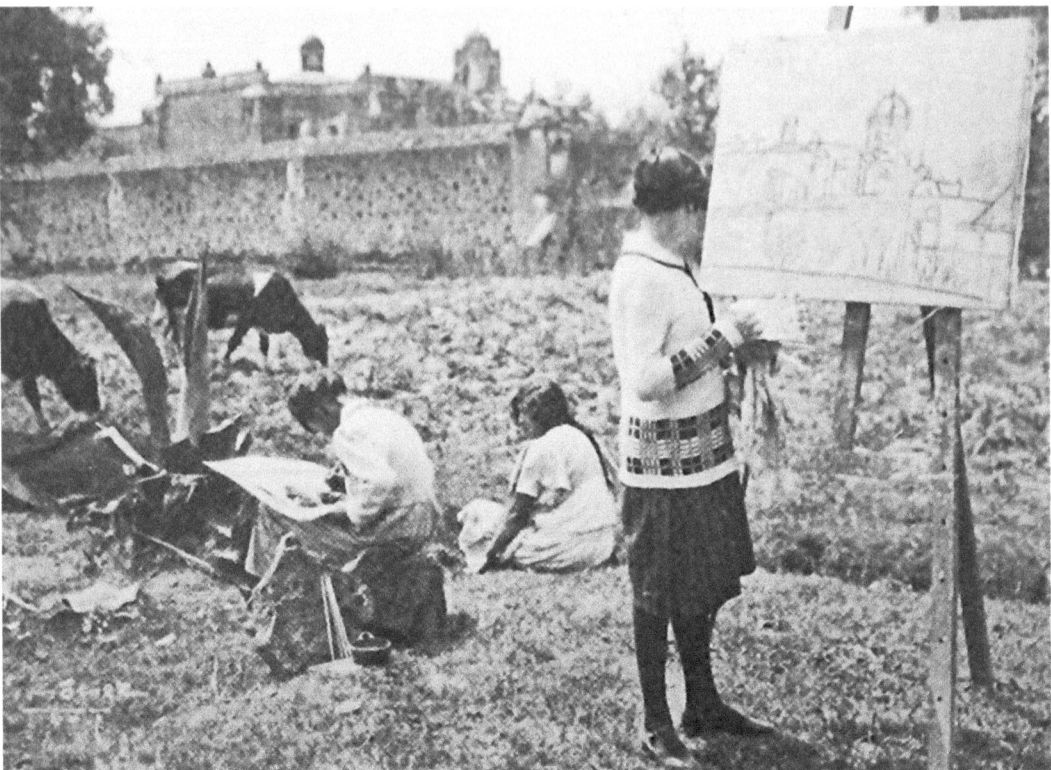

FIGURE 4.31. Students at the Open Air School of Painting in Churubusco, 1926.

air and sun."[75] By being visible to members of the public, the classrooms were imagined to "augment society's interest in the schools, to establish or affirm bonds of solidarity between the work of the school and civic life outside," and thereby to extend the educational work of the school beyond the physical spaces of the buildings, ultimately functioning, their patrons hoped, as small civic centers.[76]

Like those of the buildings at the workers' park and O'Gorman's schools, the facades of the Open Air Schools were brightly painted. Murals or low reliefs decorated the exteriors of some buildings and the insides of others, often appearing alongside chalkboards in classrooms. Since 1913, when Alfredo Ramos Martínez founded the first Open Air School of Painting at Santa Anita, just outside of Mexico City, art and outdoor education had been linked in Mexico. Inspired by the plein-air principles of French Impressionism, Ramos Martínez's school embodied the rejection of methods and subjects taught at the Academy of San Carlos, which many students increasingly viewed as antiquated. In the late 1920s they were understood as popular extensions of the muralist movement and students' success was cited, along with folk art, as yet more evidence of the innate artistic talent of indigenous people.[77] The binding of art, indigeneity, history, and nationalism also took place in the less well-known Open Air School of Sculpture, where colonial forms were important references. Classes met in the patio of the colonial Convent of La Merced, in 1927 and 1928, under the direction of sculptor Guillermo Ruiz. There students learned to carve stone- and woodworks that resembled preconquest sculpture and created an ornate pair of wooden doors in the style of colonial carving (figure 4.32). Relief panels depicted workers sculpting as well as stylized representations of animals native to the Americas that resembled the forms in Best Maugard's drawing manual.[78] Into the late 1930s, numerous open air painting schools were founded and closed, and, especially after the revolution, they were associated with efforts to document vernacular buildings and landscapes and revitalize indigenous aesthetic traditions. By the late 1920s, in urban areas, the schools became known as People's Painting Centers and, being open to people of all ages and free of charge, in their social aims were increasingly like the open air schools Mendiola designed.

Mendiola was the professional partner of Guillermo Zárraga, from whom he surely received the Open Air School commissions (although Zárraga designed the Domingo Faustino Saramiento School), and with whom, in the late 1920s, he produced some of Mexico City's most sophisticated Art Deco buildings. As head of Mexico City's Public Works office from 1925 to 1932 Zárraga oversaw not only the building of the Open Air Schools and the Carranza Center, but at least the first phase of O'Gorman's work for the Ministry of Education, with whom the Federal District collaborated to build both groups of schools. Before he helped shepherd the adoption of architectural modernism in public buildings, Zárraga taught architectural theory in the National School of Fine Arts, where he had a profound influence on O'Gorman during his first year of architecture school. The younger architect credited Zárraga with helping him identify alternatives to Beaux-Arts classicism, recognize the need for an architecture suited to contemporary conditions, and sharpen his focus on structural expression and materiality.[79] Zárraga also helped lay the foundation for O'Gorman's conception of functionalism and directed him to a number European theoretical writings, including, presumably, *Vers une architecture*.[80] It is likely as well that O'Gorman absorbed at least some of his beliefs about the relationship between architecture and politics from his teacher, who was closely connected with President Plutarco Elías Calles's po-

FIGURE 4.32. *Door Made by Pupils of the 'Escuela de Talla Directa' at the Ex Convent of the Merced,* ca. 1926. Photograph by Tina Modotti.

litical regime, which provided more support for public architecture and infrastructure and sought to link these things to its own political program and legitimacy than did any other postrevolutionary administration until the 1940s.

Far more dramatically than Mendiola's buildings, O'Gorman's urban schools expressed governmental ambitions to rationalize and even "industrialize" education by making it available to working-class children on an unprecedented scale. They established a new vocabulary for educational buildings in Mexico and set the precedent for linking rationalist forms to muralism and populism. Under O'Gorman's direction, walls became even more important surfaces than they had been in the 1920s for conveying through representation and association the links between social ideals, international architectural modernism, and increasingly codified expressions of national and native culture. In dialogue with their rural counterparts, the urban schools helped set the terms of an investigation into the relationships among history, landscape, indigeneity, and modern architecture that would deepen on the campus of the National University, to which O'Gorman would contribute a signature work. That building confirmed what his earlier buildings already suggested: that whatever the claims he and others made about the virtues of ahistoricism and economy in the 1930s, Mexican architectural history, painting, folk art, and vernacular forms remained powerful, vital forces in modern design. The contradictory aspects of his 1930s work underscored not only his own complicated relationship with representation, architectural history, and notions of national specificity but also the ways in which these tensions continued to animate Mexican architecture as mid-century approached.

FIGURE 5.1. Juan O'Gorman, Gustavo M. Saavedra, and Juan Martinez de Velasco, Central Library, National Autonomous University of Mexico, with the statue of Miguel Alemán by Ignacio Asúnsolo, 1952.

CHAPTER FIVE

LANDSCAPE AND SUBJECTIVITY AT THE CIUDAD UNIVERSITARIA

We drove to . . . University City, past the statue of [President Miguel] Alemán, carved out of sandstone and larger than life, dressed as a rector. We got lost in the labyrinth of roads which are marked with hundreds of big arrows without any clues as to what they are pointing *at*. O'Gorman couldn't find the way to his own Library, though it loomed above us at various angles as we circled aimlessly for ten minutes. Finally we took a chance on a sign reading "COMMERCE-HUMANITIES" and got close enough to park the car.

—Selden Rodman, 1958

In his elementary school designs Juan O'Gorman rejected canonical architectural history in favor of abstract allusions to industrial modernity, vernacular types, and popular culture, but in his next major project, and on the campus where it stood, architectural history came roaring back—this time with an emphasis on preconquest architecture and the now-historical modern buildings of the 1920s and 1930s. As architects began to write the history of those early works, the campus of the National Autonomous University of Mexico (UNAM), also known as University City (Ciudad Universitaria; CU), marked the country's definitive embrace of ahistoricist modernism as the language of official architecture even as it laid bare—at enormous scale—the questions about the proper relationship between historical forms, representation, and the articulation of national architectural character that had occupied Mexican architects for decades.[1] The fascination with Mexico's native landscapes that had also influenced O'Gorman's work in the 1930s surged in the next decade and shaped a project that was fueled as none other was by its architects' ambition to create a design that would stand with the greatest works of Mexican architecture. Organized into distinct zones for academic, athletic, and residential uses across a rugged, two-square-kilometer site on an ancient lava bed at the southwestern edge of the capital far from the historic center, with its multistory glassy slabs, walls, steps, and terraces clad in volcanic rock, and native plantings, the campus alluded to pre-Columbian architecture spatially and materially, seemed geologically and ecologically linked to the an-

FIGURE 5.2. View of University City looking southeast from the Olympic Stadium, ca. 1952. Bridge and road design by Santiago Greenham and Samuel Ruiz García.

cient past, and reflected the influence of modernist planning principles associated with the International Congress on Modern Architecture (CIAM) (figure 5.2).[2] Because of the centrality of landscape architecture and use of building materials to evoke preconquest associations, UNAM represented a major shift in "Mexican" design, toward an earthier, more overtly nativist approach to architecture than any that had preceded it.[3] Giant mosaics on the exteriors of several buildings reinvigorated debates about modern architecture's relationship to the other arts, particularly muralism and folk art.

Even before it was completed in 1953, critics in Mexico and abroad heralded the campus as an innovative, ambitious, collaborative ensemble. Mario Pani and Enrique del Moral, two of the leading lights of the second generation of Mexican modernists, planned it, designed its central administration building, the Rectory, and organized approximately 150 architects into teams of two or three, each with a senior and junior architect, to design individual buildings. Planner, architect, and bureaucrat Carlos Lazo served as the director and general administrator of the entire project, which he hoped would be regarded as hemispherically significant, tied to Mexico's ancient cultures, and embodying "universal" values. Among the architects who designed buildings at UNAM were pioneers of 1920s modernism, including Carlos Obregón Santacilia (the main auditorium, with Mauricio Gómez Mayorga) and José Villagrán García (the Museum, Art Institute, and School of Architecture, with Alfonso Liceaga and Xavier García Lascurain), and a great many of their students. Shaped by the debates and techniques that defined early modernism, these architects revisited old problems and found new ways of addressing them in robust, forward-looking designs. To a greater extent than any public architectural commission that had preceded it, the campus was meant for an international audience, and workers raced to have it presentable when architects from throughout the hemisphere converged on Mexico City for the Pan-American Congress of Architects in October 1952. The setting for the training of a new national professional and bureaucratic class for the atomic age, the university was freighted with the modernizing aspirations and nationalistic rhetoric of a country still negotiating its indigenous and rural inheritance and acutely aware of its lag in scientific innovation and industrialization relative to its increasingly powerful northern neighbor.

As innovative as it was in many ways, in its tenuous cohesion the campus embodied the culmination of fifty years of research and debate. It crystallized architects' decades of attempts to create modern buildings that belonged to Mexican architectural history and revealed their profound uncertainty about the likelihood of the success of that project and about architecture's status relative to those arts, especially painting, in which national character could be expressed less ambiguously.[4] In the early 1950s, texts and photographs suggested that with the university Mexican modernism had finally come of age. Indeed, the CU existed at the center of an increasingly complex debate grounded in deepening study of architectural history and carried out in books, journals, conferences, and exhibitions about the status and direction of the country's architecture. UNAM's architects worked in the shadow of national architectural history even as they participated in the writing of it and designed buildings intended to be seen as its apogee. Cognizant of early architectural modernism as historical and motivated by the deepening sense that the "functionalism" O'Gorman and others had championed in the 1930s might be only another in a succession of styles incapable of conveying national distinctiveness, these architects designed buildings and wrote texts that affirmed modern architecture's significance in a long national architectural history and suggested new means of revealing and reconciling Mexico's cultural differences, rural heritage, and modernizing ambitions.

In the ways that the CU presented Mexicans with a radical new kind of spatial experience, in which both volcanoes and modernist buildings dwarfed them, vastly scaled plazas opened out before them, rugged, mostly undeveloped, land beyond the campus's edge surrounded them, and in its simultaneous, at times jarring, allusions to ancient history and modern technology, the campus materialized its architects' interests in the intersections of history, subjectivity, and perception. Representing or rejecting architectural history now seemed not only a means of distinguishing facades and defining shared national culture, but of probing the discomfiting nature of individual experience in twentieth-century Mexico City. In this regard, UNAM marked a dramatic shift in Mexican modernism's relationship to the architectural past.

Around the time the campus was built, Alberto Arai, architect of its celebrated fronton (handball) courts, examined the psychological, and even bodily, experience of contact with historical buildings, which he imagined in relation to national culture. His essays, along with Enrique del Moral's, anchored the growth of architectural theory writing in Mexico, which, like some new buildings, reflected new understandings of the problems of geographic and historical distance and similarity that had defined Mexican architecture since the sixteenth century. The elision of historical time and beliefs about national character that often marked discussions of artistic integration and modern architecture in Mexico, and the widespread belief that architects might be losing their way, inspired del Moral and Arai to suggest to their colleagues in essays and exhibitions ways that Mexican architectural history might inform approaches to new works. At mid-century del Moral emerged as one of the profession's most astute theoretical minds. In separate texts written as the CU was being planned and built, he and Arai transformed the discussions of national architectural history into rich theoretical considerations of the problems of otherness and the status of the pre-Hispanic past that had underlain Mexican architecture since the conquest.

Viewed in the context of Mexican architectural history, the legacies of the two major camps of 1920s Mexican modernism were legible on the campus. The historically evocative approach associated with Federico Mariscal and Carlos Obregón Santacilia manifested, for example, in the domes of the engineering studio and in Alberto Arai's celebrated fronton courts, while works like Enrique Yañez's School of Chemistry and Raul Cacho's tower for the sciences belonged to the more abstract, rationalist branch associated with Guillermo Zárraga and José Villa-grán García. As a whole, the campus continued the Mexican tradition of selectively choosing and combining recognizable forms. On a taut, formalist plan indebted to Pani's training at the École des Beaux-Arts, he and del Moral positioned towers and slabs of glass and concrete to convey Mexico's technological modernity and commitment to international capitalism. Throughout the campus the juxtapositions of bold orthogonal forms and the volcanic rock expressed the long-standing ambition to merge expressions of internationalism and nativism, and reflected modern architecture's enduring preoccupation with the relationships among industry, abstraction, and nature. They also revealed Mexican architects' increasing appreciation of the depth and variety of modernism elsewhere and placed the campus among the major works of the twentieth century notable for their architects' attention to site and materiality.[5]

Representation was more obviously important to the meaning of the campus than it had been in any single architectural project. A renewed interest in landscape painting in the 1940s that centered on the canvases of the nineteenth-century painter José María Velasco informed investigations into the relationships among history, landscape, and subjective experience at UNAM. Discussions of alienation and the unknowable, ineffable qualities of landscape echoed throughout new assessments of Velasco and new theories of art and architecture. The campus's even more obvious association with painting, however, came through the giant, figurative mural-like mosaics. They reaffirmed the importance of the facade in Mexican architecture and betrayed a collective doubt about the efficacy of mid-century International Style modernism as a language capable of signifying Mexican distinctiveness.[6] The mosaics also advanced the transubstantiation of Mexican muralism from a revolutionary experiment to official art, even as other kinds of painting gained prominence.[7] Criticized for being formally *retardataire* and for failing to truly embody the ideal of artistic integration so highly prized at mid-century, some mosaics rehashed once-revolutionary themes that now appeared tired, and thereby seemed to support arguments made by younger artists, such as José Luis Cuevas and Mathias Goeritz, that Mexican muralism, and perhaps even figuration, had run their courses. The attempt to fuse this version of late muralism with Mexican modern architecture's most ambitious project represented an attempt to reclaim from muralism the central place in national art that architecture had occupied in preconquest and colonial times.[8] But the unsuccessful aspects of some of the mosaics in fact underscored the overwhelmingly architectural character of the campus and the facadism that continued to dominate approaches to Mexican architecture. Furthermore, the formal differences between the university buildings that were clad in volcanic rock or to which mosaics were affixed and those that lacked these things, helped solidify the ideas that "modern" and "Mexican" were mutually exclusive categories and that there was such a thing as national architecture. As the clearest expression to date of the classically modern dilemmas of the relationships between the present and the past, representation and abstraction, and self and other, UNAM also signaled Mexican architecture's full entry into an international intellectual modernity.

The CU has long been regarded as a signature example of "Mexicanized" modernism,[9] and, calling attention to its function as a political symbol, some scholars have interpreted it as an embodiment of utopian modernist visions of the city.[10] Its relationships to earlier projects have been less fully considered, in part because, regardless of their materials or vocabulary and even before they were complete, UNAM's buildings and plan were subsumed within the rhetoric of social progress and modern nationalism, both of which were firmly entwined and often confused by mid-century with notions of national architectural distinctiveness inherited from earlier buildings and histories.

Begun on the heels of the so-called Mexican Miracle of the 1940s, when the economy industrialized rapidly and internal migration made the capital home to more people than at any point in its six-hundred-year history, UNAM was intended to convey Mexico's capacity to educate its citizenry for full participation in the new postwar global order and its preparedness to contribute new research, especially in science. Although politicians had long sought to link their agendas to modern architecture—whether in the service of public health reforms or working-class access to recreational facilities and education—as the signature project of President Miguel Alemán's administration and because of its size, program, and cost, the Ciudad Universitaria even more firmly established the close ties between politics and architecture than the works of the 1920s and 1930s had. It was also one of several major Latin American projects that marked the beginning of a new era in architectural and urban growth throughout the region characterized by its close connections to developmentalist programs.[11] As UNAM's architects grappled with how to respond to and build upon Mexico's architectural history, the symbolic weight of the project linked the university with nationalistic rhetoric about the Mexican Revolution that masked mounting political corruption and rapidly growing distance between the Alemán administration and any truly socially progressive agenda.[12]

Apart from the campus as a whole, when they were built the fronton courts, the Central Library, the Olympic Stadium, and the plan of the campus as a whole received the greatest critical and scholarly attention. Their richness as individual works, their differences from one another, the ways they revealed their architects' efforts to grapple with old problems in innovative ways make them enduringly interesting. A complete study of the Ciudad Universitaria would fill a volume much longer than this one, thus the Central Library and fronton courts, the meanings attributed to landscape, the debates on artistic integration, and new architectural histories have been selected to anchor this discussion of the new campus and the architectural context and culture out of which it grew, and that it in turn affected.[13]

MAKING HISTORY

Around 1950 the writing and research of Mexican architectural history again boomed, coinciding with the rise to preeminence of modernist forms in new buildings. Books, articles, and exhibitions—nearly all of them written or curated by practicing architects—advanced research on national architectural history, canonized the first generation of Mexican modernists and their buildings (often against the architecture of Porfiriato, which was increasingly demonized), and sought to either discover new directions for contemporary design or position new buildings in a historical narrative that stretched back to the pre-Columbian era. At the core of many texts was a sense that the "functionalist" buildings of the 1930s were inadequate to the task of creating an expressive and suitable architecture for Mexico. At the same time, archaeological investigations, such as that at Bonampak (where exquisite murals were uncovered deep in the Yucatán jungle), and their reconstitution as tourist destinations continued, and ongoing restorations (and retouchings) of colonial buildings for an ever-growing number of visitors made architectural history more accessible and attractive than ever.[14] The idea that modern architecture was worth documenting and that it was closely tied to the other arts was suggested in 1937 with the publication of Esther Born's *The New Architecture in Mexico*, the first survey of modern architecture in Mexico. The product of extensive research and collaboration with Mexican architects, Born illustrated the book with her own photographs and gave particular attention to

O'Gorman, José Villagrán García, and the works of architects whose buildings were similarly unornamented. The text emphasized architecture's role in social reform and included discussions of vernacular buildings, modern Mexican painting and sculpture, and brief biographies of major artists.

By mid-century the Mexican government had created an institutional and educational infrastructure for researching architectural history so large and sophisticated that it impressed leading foreign scholars. Approximately two thousand photographs and an extensive library supported the study of colonial buildings in the architecture school of the National University. Students there participated in research trips where they measured and drew historic buildings.[15] As early as 1943, Kenneth Conant, professor of architecture at Harvard, observed that the "Mexicans actually have a better governmental set-up for the preservation and study of historic monuments than we have here in the U.S.A." In addition to the architecture school at the National University, he admired the archives and publications of the Institute of Aesthetic Investigations and its "brilliant staff historians," as well as the resources and research of the National Institute of Archeology and History.[16]

Architects and critics noted and promoted the entwining of history and design that went on in the academy. In 1952, Richard Grove, one of the authors of the *Guide to Contemporary Mexican Architecture* published in association with *Espacios*, a new journal that published photographs and descriptions of recent buildings and on whose editorial board many UNAM architects sat, observed that

> there is a lengthy and incalculably rich architectural tradition and I have not yet met a Mexican architect of any standing who was not well versed in it. I do not think that the University City, for example, can really be understood by anyone who has not experienced the sense of space, the organization of masses, of Teotihuacan or Monte Alban. The same is true of the churches at Acatepec and Tonantzintla, to mention only two of . . . the masterpieces of the Mexican baroque. They are anonymous and native, they remain close to the hearts of Mexicans today.[17]

As the author's references to the colonial vernacular churches at Acatepec and Tonantzintla suggested, at the same time that the CU canonized a modernist vocabulary as "national," interest in provincial Mexican vernacular architecture surged (plates 4 and 14).[18] But at the moment when international political and technological supremacy had shifted so decisively to Mexico's northern neighbor, history could sometimes seem burdensome. Elsewhere in his guidebook Grove noted that "the immediate presence of the past . . . seems here to provoke an atmosphere in the city in which contemporaneity is worn like a badge."[19] As works like O'Gorman's schools became part of new national architectural histories, modern skyscrapers transformed Mexico City, and as planners including Pani and Lazo mapped out radically new visions of Mexican towns and cities, the anxieties about the disappearance of rural landscapes and vernacular architecture latent in O'Gorman's work of the 1930s, and implied in the photographs of *Escuelas primarias*, manifested even more clearly in exhibitions, books, and the architectural press.

Teaching and research on Mexican architectural history were also entwined in the work of Jose Villagrán García, who wrote one of the first histories of twentieth-century Mexican architecture around 1950, taught architectural theory, designed the architecture building at the CU, and was Pani's close personal friend.[20] Villagrán's *Panorama de 50 años de arquitectura mexicana*, an extended essay written in conjunction with a conference of the same title that he organized, followed the 1950 exhibition of Contemporary Mexican Architecture at the Palacio de Bellas Artes curated by architects Raúl Cacho, Alejandro Prieto, and Enrique Guerrero. Both were supported by the architecture department of the National Institute of Fine Arts, which Enrique Yañez led. In his essay Villagrán classified Mexican buildings from the past fifty years, located the origins of Mexican modernism in 1925, and published for the first time in a single place the theory of architecture that he had been expounding as a professor for nearly twenty-five years.[21] As the most important academic theoretician of modern architecture in Mexico, Villagrán was widely admired and highly influential for at least two generations of architects. In *Panorama de 50 años* he grouped buildings designed since the late nineteenth century in four categories: Those built before about 1915 exemplified "exotic anachronism," and included works with neoclassical vocabularies. "Anachronistic national" buildings appeared from then until about 1923 and had colonial revival vocabularies. The "Individualist" stage followed. It was typified by the works of Segura and characterized by a seemingly greater consciousness of history and contemporary developments abroad than was evident earlier. Villagrán believed these buildings were also more "original" than older ones. The "modern" period, he said, began in 1925, the year that he designed the National Hygiene Institute at Popotla. This era was defined by works that were usually called "functionalist" and more or less followed the principles of International Style modernism. By locating the beginning of Mexican architectural modernism with a work that eschewed all historical references, but was firmly rooted in a Beaux-Arts tradition of composition, Villagrán made himself Mexico's first "modern" architect. In doing so he denied the possibility that history and modernity were two parts of the same phenomenon and reinforced the centrality of composition and formalism to Mexican modernism. By semantically linking history and national expression in two of his periodizations, Villagrán affirmed the long-standing association of the two in the historiography of Mexican architecture. Like his predecessors, he used photographs of buildings' exteriors to make his points; with illustrations of neither plans nor sections, the book reinforced the idea that facades mattered most.

Also in 1925, Obregón Santacilia had begun drafting the Ministry of Health building, and less than two years after Villagrán's history appeared, he published his account of architecture from the same period. His *50 años de arquitectura mexicana (1900–1950)* was a longer and more detailed discussion of Mexico's early modern architecture, and in it, starting with works designed in the mid-nineteenth century, he too classified buildings stylistically and chronologically. Like others writing then, Obregón Santacilia worried that a "new academicism" marked by the reworking of the forms of International Style modernism was taking over Mexican architecture. He concluded his text with a plea for architects to give greater attention to the country's distant and recent pasts, to its rural areas, the landscape, and climate.[22] Evoking Le Corbusier in the title of the final section of the book, "Toward a Mexican Architecture," Obregón Santacilia warned against historicism as a localizing tool, but as the Swiss architect had in the 1920s, encouraged architects to find in history an "essence" that was particular to place. Like his fellow architects at UNAM, Obregón Santacilia hoped to shape an architecture that was, while still nationally specific, "universally" legible and relevant.[23]

Like Lazo's ambition for the Ciudad Universitaria project as a whole, the tensions in this position echoed concerns in architecture in many countries, as architects elsewhere grappled with the consequences of the Second World War, the associations of classicism and monumentality with fascism that it engendered, and the historicity of the avant-garde. Whether they were fully aware of it or not, by wrestling with these problems and privileging associations with ancient people and native landscapes in new designs, Obregón Santacilia and his Mexican colleagues brought their profession closer to developments

in modern architecture in the United States and Europe than it perhaps had ever been. The decisive turn toward landscape and tradition
broadly defined, whether in Le Corbusier's earthy, grounded works,
Alvar Aalto's ongoing development of sensual, site-specific buildings,
or the mid-century architecture of "regionalism" being theorized by
architects such as Harwell Hamilton Harris and William Wurster, to
mention only a few examples, marked a profound shift away from the
historicist and machinist vocabularies that had seemed to dominate
in previous decades. What distinguished the Mexican situation from
most others, however, was its architects' persistent inclination to interpret these concepts in national terms above all others. They did so
not out of a sense of postcolonial inferiority, but because, as architects
and historians, they encountered architecture in national frameworks
repeatedly and continuously in professional practice and research.
Because the history of architecture in Mexico had always been written relative to ideas about what "Mexico" was, and because almost all
major architectural commissions came from the government and were
created in dialogue with the explicitly nationalizing goals of realist art
and the celebration of folk art, modern architectural theory, when it
finally began to be written methodically at mid-century—often in tandem with history—by Villagrán, del Moral, Obregón Santacilia, and
Arai, was almost inevitably connected by its authors with ideas about
Mexican culture and history.

The connections between beliefs about history and national distinctiveness, and anxiety about the status and direction of contemporary design, were particularly evident in several major exhibitions
and books on twentieth-century Mexican architecture that appeared
around 1950.[24] As director of architecture at the National Institute of
Fine Arts, Arai proposed links between Mexican architectural history
and contemporary design. In November 1953, his exhibition, *Arquitectura contemporánea y sus antecedentes históricos*, which opened at
the Palace of Fine Arts helped cement the idea that modern buildings
belonged to a long national traditional that stretched back through the
colonial era to Teotihuacan. Mounted near the repainted version of Diego Rivera's 1933 mural *Man at the Crossroads*, with its giant atom-like
form at the center, the show quietly nodded to Mexican architecture's
long-standing connection to the other arts, and to the modernizing
aspirations that lay behind many of the country's important twentieth-
century works.

Often bilingual and well-illustrated, new books, most notably I. E.
Myers' *Mexico's Modern Architecture* (1952), brought modern Mexican

architecture to a much wider audience than the one that Villagrán and Obregón Santacilia reached through their slim volumes. The narrative of Mexican modernism that emerged in these venues reinforced the idea that UNAM embodied the maturation of modernism, the origins of which lay in Villagrán's work of the 1920s. His anointing as the founder of modern Mexican architecture unfolded as well in articles by Arai, del Moral, and others.[25] Collectively the publications and exhibitions shaped a history of Mexican architecture that privileged rationalist vocabularies, implicitly denied their representational qualities, and deemphasized the other, equally significant strand of Mexican modernism embodied by Obregón Santacilia that was concerned with history.

Pani and del Moral each contributed significantly to the deepening inquiry into architectural history. After his return to Mexico from years of study at the École des Beaux-Arts in the late 1930s, Pani had played perhaps the single greatest role introducing modernist planning and high-rise construction to the capital. As a member of a highly influential family and the nephew of Alberto Pani, who had held several major political appointments before and after the revolution, he obtained plum commissions almost as soon as he returned.[26] Yet he also did more than anyone else to keep older buildings in current conversations about architecture. In the pages of Mexico's leading architectural journal, *Arquitectura/México*, a monthly publication that he founded and edited, architects learned of new and historical buildings in Mexico and abroad.[27] Pani read widely and was extremely knowledgeable about colonial architecture, which he discussed with enthusiasm.[28] Even as his works transformed parts of the capital into a modern metropolis, he and del Moral shared with architects a generation older concern about the demolition of historic buildings in downtown Mexico City, which del Moral compared to a beautiful mouth with missing teeth.[29]

More even than Pani, del Moral probed Mexican architectural history for lessons about new design. Like O'Gorman and Rivera, del Moral grew up partly in Guanajuato, and like them, brought to Mexico City a deep interest in colonial and vernacular architecture and townscapes.[30] Also like O'Gorman, as a young architect he worked for Obregón Santacilia and assisted in the design of the Ministry of Health and the Casa de Vecindad. After a year in Europe, del Moral returned to Mexico and to Obregón Santacilia's office where he assisted in designing the Monument to the Revolution and the Hotel del Prado. Later, in his own practice, del Moral's deepening interest in Mexican history led him to participate in a seminar at the National University on the intellectual and cultural history of eighteenth-century Mexico. Other participants in the seminar included several of twentieth-century Mexico's leading intellectuals: Edmundo O'Gorman (Juan's brother), Leopoldo Zea, and Justino Fernández, a renowned historian of Mexican art. This experience formed the basis of his many writings on Mexican architecture. Most of del Moral's built works before he began collaborating with Pani were private houses in Mexico City, but in the 1930s and 1940s he designed workers' housing and schools in the state of Guanajuato, where he explored vernacular typologies and forms. His own house in Mexico City of 1948, as William J. R. Curtis has argued, represented a sophisticated engagement with the traditional Mexican patio house and principles of Miesian composition (figure 6.13).[31] The school in Cosacuarán, Guanajuato, one of fifteen federal primary schools he designed in that state between 1944 and 1946, combined material rusticity with the geometric clarity of high modernism. Although he used rough stone, unglazed terracotta, ordinary bricks, and tree trunks rather than travertine and polished chrome, the architect's use of different materials for distinct surfaces and volumes enriched the building visually and tactilely in the manner of Ludwig Mies van der Rohe's elegant houses. Del Moral had met Mies and Walter Gropius in the United States when, in 1947 as director of the National School of Architecture, he visited the Illinois Institute of Technology and Harvard Graduate School of Design to learn about their programs. Del Moral thus followed closely in the footsteps of Mexican architects from the early twentieth century who were also students of eighteenth-century architecture and were committed to strengthening the profession through improved architectural education, knowledge of international developments, and historically informed modern design.

Beginning in the 1940s he wrote widely on Mexican architectural history, especially of the eighteenth century, and explained Mexican architecture's distinctive development with reference to national culture, internationalism, and locality. His ideas about these things appear to have evolved through his work in a seminar on the history of philosophy, in which he wrote an extended essay on the baroque style in France and Spain.[32] Like the first historians of colonial architecture, del Moral believed that specific cultural and historical circumstances had shaped Mexican architecture and he related the "historical-social-ethnographic" characteristics of Mexico since the conquest to formal innovation. Like Baxter, Mariscal, and Acevedo, he concluded that the eighteenth century "marked the cultural and economic apogee of the colony and . . . in that epoch Mexico began to elaborate, assimilating in itself a formal expression authentic and appropriative to its experience," ultimately creating the Churrigueresque style.[33] Entering decades-old debates about the proper place of folk art in modern culture, del Moral zeroed in on the "divorce of the 'cultured' and the 'popular'" that he said began at the dawn of the modern era in the Renaissance and had reached new heights in the atomic age.[34] In the twentieth century, technological advances exacerbated class differences and now, he believed, the "cultured classes" lived with the implications of modern science "without understanding them" and as "dogmas of faith." The result was that the "'modern world'" took on a "magical, ultra-sensorial character," as physics revealed that it was possible to "capture only an inexact illusory reality." Formally the gap between the cultured and the popular classes was wider than ever, he believed, as popular art, made by people relatively untouched by technological modernization remained largely as it had been, while new machines introduced new forms to the industrialized classes.[35] With these observations, the architect attempted to explain the modern experiences of disorientation, consciousness of race and class differences, and artistic debates with reference to history—themes that the campus embodied.

SPRAWL, SPACE, AND SKYSCRAPERS

Geographically and psychologically removed from the historic center of Mexico City, where university offices and departments had been scattered in various colonial and late nineteenth-century buildings, the campus consolidated the university spatially. On its new site it symbolized the expanding reach of both an increasingly powerful state and rapidly growing city, much as the Ministry of Health had on the Paseo de la Reforma in the mid-1920s. Just to the west, Luis Barragán, acting as a private developer, simultaneously shaped a new suburb for the rich. The campus's location and vocabulary made it read as a resounding rejection of Mexico's colonial and Porfirian pasts, as those eras were constructed as retrograde and "anti-Mexican" in political rhetoric and some histories. At first glance the new buildings did seem unrelated to the historical, historicizing, and historically evocative works in and closer to the city center, and certainly to the buildings of Porfiriato.

Pani and del Moral organized the plan according to the cardinal directions and used the extension of Insurgentes Avenue, one of Mexico City's longest and most important north–south arteries, to divide the campus into east and west sectors (figure 5.3). A smaller road near the center of the site ran east from Insurgentes and divided the eastern

FIGURE 5.3. Aerial View of University City, 1952. Photo is oriented with north at the bottom.

sector into two parts, with the academic zone placed north of the road and athletic and residential facilities positioned south of it. At the center of the academic zone was an enormous grassy field around which buildings were arranged as if to evoke a colonial plaza programmatically, but at a scale that recalled the monumentality of pre-Hispanic plazas.

A sixteen-story glass and concrete slab of one of the main science buildings visually framed the giant plaza at the east end. At its base architects tightly grouped smaller science buildings and beyond it were other, smaller plazas onto which the schools of medicine, dentistry, and veterinary medicine faced, and on one of which stood Felix Candela's small, thin-shelled concrete Cosmic Ray Pavilion. On the eastern side of the great central field and immediately adjacent to Insurgentes, was the most architecturally and symbolically significant part of the academic sector. Up a flight of broad, low steps made of volcanic rock was the terrace on which stood del Moral and Pani's sixteen-story Rectory Building, the glazed tower that housed administrative offices and

FIGURE 5.4. Mario Pani, Enrique del Moral, and Salvador Ortega Flores, Rectory.

whose base, on its east facade, recalled constructivist compositions (figure 5.4). On the north, east, and south facades of the building were David Alfaro Siqueiros's "sculptural paintings" in mosaic. Across from it was O'Gorman and Gustavo Saavedra's famous Central Library clad in square panels that formed a giant mosaic that wrapped around the four sides of the ten-story slab housing the stacks. Originally a large rectangular pool at the north end of the plaza and a giant statue of Miguel Aleman on a pyramid-shaped pedestal towered over pedestrians in the plaza between the rectory and the library (figure 5.1).

Opposite the academic quadrant, across Insurgentes and occupying its own sector stood the giant bowl-like Olympic Stadium, which primarily hosted public sporting events (figure 5.5). Scooped out of the earth, the stadium accommodated 110,000 spectators around an oval playing field and resembled a giant crater. Embanked walls made of the dark rock dug out to form the building bulged out east and west from the center, and the stadium was surrounded on all sides by parking lots and connected to the academic zone only by a passage for pedestrians

FIGURE 5.5. Augusto Pérez Palacios, Jorge Bravo, and Raúl Salinas, Olympic Stadium, with Diego Rivera's partially completed mosaic on the east facade.

that ran under Insurgentes (along which cars raced at high speeds) and came out on the terrace near the Rectory. Mosaics designed by Diego Rivera that depicted ancient and modern athletes as well as a double-headed eagle and serpent were installed on the west facade of the stadium and were part of a larger mosaic scheme that the muralist designed for the building, but it was never completely installed (figure 5.5). University athletics were accommodated in the southeastern quadrant of the campus, where playing fields and swimming pools were arranged. The most significant works of architecture in this zone were Arai's massive, sculptural fronton courts that seemed to rise out of the earth. The fourth sector of the campus, to the southwest, was designated for faculty housing, but was never developed. The only residential buildings that were constructed were student dormitories built as a tight cluster of slabs northwest of the athletic fields, in the southeastern quadrant. Arterial roads ringed the entire campus and, for the most part, kept vehicular traffic far from the centers of university life (students used university buses to travel large distances). In all directions, but especially to the south, east, and west, the great mountains that ringed the Valley of Mexico were visible.

DISCIPLINING THE VOLCANOES

Fusing history with geology and ecology, architects and campus promoters, especially Lazo, argued that the campus's suitability to the problem of shaping a modern, educated citizenry prepared to realize a bold new future lay in its association with Mexico's ancient, deep roots as embodied by the site. In composing the campus Pani and del Moral took great care to retain the site's rocks and craggy vegetation and, as if to further bind the university to the earth and the Mexican landscape, set aside four kilometers as an ecological preserve (figure 5.6). This attention to site had roots in modern urban planning principles that dated to turn-of-the-century proposals for garden cities that sought to rationalize circulation and use while facilitating residents' contact with nature.[36] But it also emerged from a new celebration of the Mexican landscape, and particularly the Valley of Mexico and its magnificent mountains and volcanoes.[37] Since their first discussions of a new campus in 1928, architects had envisioned a location in far southwest Mexico City, but it was not until 1946 when President Avila Camacho appropriated six kilometers of land in the Pedregal de San Angel that the location was finally fixed.[38] The barren volcanic landscape was suited to the project practically and symbolically.[39] Because indigenous peasants who lacked the resources to meaningfully resist its expropriation were the only people who inhabited it, the land was comparably easy for the government to acquire. Untainted by associations with the Spanish or the conquest, and visually and geologically so unlike European cities and landscapes, and especially the colonial core of the capital, the site provided an ideal backdrop for a campus whose patrons wanted the university to be grounded in tradition and embody the forward-looking aspirations of a nation that was increasingly less dependent on European (and U.S.) resources. The link to preconquest culture was heightened by the proximity of the only temple that remained from the ancient city of Cuicuilco, which stood just beyond the southwestern perimeter. Home to twenty thousand residents at its apogee, Cuicuilco had been occupied since about 900 BCE, but was abandoned around 1 CE during the eruption of the nearby volcano, Xitle, which covered the site in eight meters of lava. Excavations of the site took place in the 1950s, but had begun in 1922, when archaeologists

FIGURE 5.6. Architects included rock walls and native plants throughout the campus.

revealed an unusual four-tiered circular pyramid. The building captured the attention of architects and gained greater fame after Born gave it a prominent place in *The New Architecture in Mexico*. Pairing her introduction with an image of the pyramid, she related it to Corbusian geometries and claimed that it was "probably the oldest structure on the North American continent."[40]

The association of indigenous people, volcanoes, and strong sentiment ran deep in Mexican visual culture. In 1910 the painter Saturnino Herrán created a lusty, vibrant triptych depicting the legend of the creation of Popocatépetl and Iztaccíhuatl, the two volcanoes east of Mexico City, from two lovers. Converting the figures into an indigenous man and white woman, Herrán linked the volcanoes to racial mestizaje and the landscape to human isolation. The final panel showed the man alone and heartbroken because his lover, a princess, had been turned into a volcano. The image joined indigeneity, a volcanic landscape, and isolation to illustrate a story that fused human and geological time. In 1911, the painter Dr. Atl had suggested in expressionist canvases that mountains and volcanoes might have mystical, mysterious qualities.

The Pedregal in particular was imagined to have such characteristics, and throughout the twentieth century it attracted artists interested in exploring these concepts and the landscape itself.[41] In the 1930s Dr. Atl painted it repeatedly and contributed to the popularization of vulcanology in two books on the topic, *Volcanes de México* (1939) and *Como nace y crece un volcán, el Paricutín* (1950), published before and during the construction of the CU. The subject of the latter was the emergence and eruption of the Paricutín volcano in a Michoacán farm field starting in 1943, which astonished locals and scientists alike and refocused the country on its at times volatile geology. Over the course of a year, Paricutín rose more than 1,400 feet, spewed lava on a nearby village (covering everything except the top of the early seventeenth-century church of San Juan), and continued to erupt through March 1952. The volcano's spontaneous emergence and eruption added a sense of disorientation, dislocation, and fear to anxieties awakened by the uncertain dynamics of dormancy and activity, and its appearance seemed to elide geologic and human time, as if collapsing the distance between the present and the ancient past. Although the CU was built far from Paricutín, Mexico City's great ring of mountains, including Popocatépetl and Ixtaccíhuatl—upon which the Aztecs had oriented their greatest temple at the center of Tenochtitlan—formed the campus's backdrop.

ROCK AND RHETORIC

The university's new site lent itself to bold planning and inspired nearly hyperbolic rhetoric. Since the 1920s Mexican politicians had talked about the modern buildings they patronized in terms of national destiny and political values, but the promises and proclamations about architecture, history, and the future uttered at the groundbreaking of the Ciudad Universitaria (and well after it) rhetorically exceeded claims made about any project to date. Unlike the Ministry of Health, the Carranza Center, and the elementary schools, the CU had an architect as one of its chief public spokesmen. As the coordinator of the entire Ciudad Universitaria project, Lazo oversaw logistics and played a central role in crafting the image of the new university and its campus. In soaring tones he linked architecture, preconquest cultures, hemispheric cooperation, and Mexico's destiny and reiterated the themes of racial mestizaje and the making of a new, modern, Mexican subject that had been interwoven in the great public projects of the 1920s and 1930s. Like O'Gorman's elementary schools, most of the buildings of the CU bore little resemblance to Mexican buildings of the past, but the imperative of rhetorically positioning the new campus of the four-hundred-year-old university (which was the first in the hemisphere) historically and nationally was far greater. Speaking at the laying of the first stone in June 1950, he proclaimed:

> Mexico, a geographical cross-roads, has been historically possible thanks to the collaboration of diverse forces and cultures . . . Mexico has been built stone by stone, and this is one of those. . . .
>
> On this very terrain, when Nahua and Olmec immigrants met in the Valley of Mexico, at the pyramid of Cuicuilco, the most ancient indigenous culture of the continent arose from the contemplation of this landscape and this sky.[42]

Linking national modernization, architecture, and planning, he proclaimed that "building Mexico is a work of integrated planning" that included "the physical," "the human," "the economic," and "the political," and promised that Mexico, through its new university campus would "form the new man of America; the Mexican, conscious of his destiny and the destiny of his *Patria* and his continent." Concluding, he said, "we are not placing the first stone in the first building of University City, we are placing the first stone in the most fervent construction of our Mexico."[43] At the CU stone-laying ceremony, Lazo rehearsed tradition and foregrounded the material—whether it was used for paving or cladding, or left in place to define the landscape—that distinguished the site so dramatically from Mexico City's colonial center, with its reddish *tezontle*, and newer suburbs, with their concrete. The architect's reference to the Cuicuilco pyramid cemented the association of the material, the site, and the landscape with pre-Hispanic Mexico. Pani, del Moral, and Obregón Santacilia had all explored modern uses for volcanic rock in earlier projects, and colonial buildings had, of course, been constructed using native stone, but it was at UNAM that allusions to indigenous materials, people, and architecture first dominated a major commission, rhetorically marking a decisive shift away from the many preceding decades in which colonial references had signified the national in architecture.

The combination of high international modernism and nativism at the Ciudad Universitaria was also traceable to a growing appreciation in Mexico of the complexities, nuances, and differences in modern architecture elsewhere. In addition to del Moral's contact with Gropius and Mies, by mid-century Barragán and O'Gorman had came into contact with Richard Neutra and Frank Lloyd Wright and were clearly influenced by their work.[44] Despite architects' widening understanding of the diversity of modernism abroad, largely because of Pani, on the campus the greatest foreign influence was Le Corbusier's. By now, Mexican appreciation of the variety of Le Corbusier's oeuvre had grown as well, in part due to the presence of Russian architect Vladimir Kaspé, who had emigrated to Mexico in 1942 and designed the School of Economics building at UNAM. Having been encouraged to come by Pani, whom he met at the École des Beaux-Arts, Kaspé took up an important editorial position in *Arquitectura/México*, which he held from 1942 to 1950, and, on Villagrán's invitation, began teaching compositional theory in 1943.[45] With his command of Corbusian theory and knowledge of the Swiss architect's post-1930 work, Kaspé helped bridge the gap between seemingly acontextual International Style formalism and the emphasis on rugged, local materials emerging in Mexico in the 1940s.[46] In a 1946 essay he summarized the Swiss architect's arguments in *Vers une architecture*, illustrated his buildings, and most significantly, drew attention to aspects of Le Corbusier's work that Mexican architects had missed or dismissed, particularly the centrality of history to his theory, and his innovative plans. Kaspé wrote, "many believe, for their own convenience, that Le Corbusier rejected knowledge of the past. In reality the past is for him a source of inspiration, and . . . is a school, but not a school of styles, of details, but a school of a way of seeing."[47] Kaspé liked Le Corbusier's plans and admired him as a "poet, polemicist . . . and as an architect," and revered him most as a planner. The Russian architect here used urbanism "in its broadest sense," which went far beyond the satisfaction of the programmatic and practical requirements of city planning, to include planning for all aspects of human activity.[48] His reading of Le Corbusier in this way closely resembled Lazo's views on planning.

As if in response to a vague, but apparently widely held belief that all of Le Corbusier's buildings looked more or less like the Ozenfant Studio or that they all stood on spindly piloti, Kaspé drew special attention to Le Corbusier's use of rock and brick, and illustrated several of his earthy, earthbound works of the 1930s, which departed radically from the iconic buildings of the previous decade. Calling the Swiss Pavilion at the University City in Paris of 1930–33 "one of Le Corbusier's greatest works" and emphasizing his "use of natural and prefabricated materials," Kaspé proclaimed that the building "signaled the path for architecture today and tomorrow" (figure 5.7).[49] As if to reinforce the point about history, native materials, and modernity, Kaspé placed a photograph of the large stone wall of the pavilion, with the dormitory block rising behind it, on a page with Le Corbusier's sketches of the Hagia Sophia and Hadrian's Villa, a photograph of the portico of Parthenon, and the famous image of a 1921 Delage sports car from *Vers une architecture*.

FIGURE 5.7. Le Corbusier, Swiss Pavilion, Paris, 1929–31.

Elsewhere he illustrated two works of the mid-1930s: the House in Les Mathes, with its great stone wall, and the interior of the Petite Maison de Week-end at La Celle-Saint-Cloud, with its brick hearth and low barrel vaults. After explaining the interrelation of exterior and interior space in Le Corbusier's work, Kaspé praised the buildings' "economy, simplicity, sincerity of contrasts and play of distinct materials, and, above all . . . [their] naturalism."[50] The essay repositioned Le Corbusier in Mexico, and refuted many of the claims about his work, implicit and otherwise, made by architects who had conflated Corbusian modernism with utilitarian functionalism. Intentionally or not, Kaspé's essay suggested that Pani was now the bearer of Corbusianism in Mexico and made room for native rock in a narrative of modern architecture centered on Europe.

NATURE AND THE VIEW FROM ABOVE

In his discussions of UNAM, rhetorically Lazo reached forward and backward in time and his lofty language had corollaries in the scale of

FIGURE 5.8. Le Corbusier, *New urban structure for Rio de Janeiro*. Pencil on paper, 1929.

the campus, the images of it, and those that it called to mind. Aerial photographs, bird's-eye views, and elevated perspectives of the campus appeared repeatedly in influential sources on architecture, including the national and international architectural press and the Sociedad de Arquitectos Mexicanos monumental 1956 history of Mexican architecture, *4000 años de arquitectura mexicana* (4,000 Years of Mexican Architecture).[51] Such depictions were arguably the most efficient means of conveying the form and scale of the new campus, but they linked it to Lazo's ideal of integrated planning, and to international, hemispheric modern urbanism, as well as to Mexican art history, and the landscape. Even before the campus was finished, Pani published two renderings of the campus—a detailed overhead map showing the locations of buildings, and a map showing its location in the Pedregal and its relationship to the rest of Mexico City. A third image was a photograph of del Moral and Pani looking like consummate planners as they leaned over a plan of the campus. An iconic 1952 photograph taken from an airplane showed the campus at an angle (figure 5.3). Turning the camera southeast, the photographer captured the two main roads—gleaming under the bright sun—that intersected to form the major sectors of the plan. The extension of Insurgentes Avenue narrowed and disappeared near the upper-right corner of the photograph, trailing off into the undeveloped wilds of the Pedregal. With its great raking lines and angled composition against the landscape, the photograph suggested the plan's formal dynamism, Lazo's rhetoric about destiny, and the bold incursion into nature by its architects.

Such images also situated the campus firmly in the realm of high modernist urban planning, especially in the Americas.[52] The bird's-eye perspectives and aerial views called to mind Le Corbusier's famous 1929 sketches of slab high-rises and giant roads set into the mountainous landscapes of Rio de Janeiro, São Paulo, and Montevideo that he published in *Precisions*, as well as his 1935 book, *Aircraft* (figure 5.8). While such allusions were recognizable only to well-read architects, and certainly to Lazo (who likely orchestrated some of them), they powerfully conveyed the idea that Mexican architecture and planning had come of age. The association with urbanism elsewhere in Latin America echoed Lazo's attempts to position the CU in terms of hemispheric cultural development and unity.

JOSÉ MARÍA VELASCO AND THE REDISCOVERY OF LANDSCAPE

The aerial views of the campus helped make it, like many of its predecessors, legible simultaneously as a work of international modern architecture and as one deeply embedded in Mexican art history, particularly landscape painting. At the heart of Mexicans' newfound appreciation of their landscape was the rebirth of interest in the 1940s in the paintings of José María Velasco, whose career spanned the 1860s to the early 1900s. Although today Velasco is one of Mexico's best-known painters and his work was admired internationally in the nineteenth century, his art received relatively little attention in the twentieth century until it was shown in a large exhibition at the Palacio de Bellas Artes in Mexico City in the fall of 1942.[53] Among UNAM architects, O'Gorman was instrumental in popularizing Velasco's works, and Pani had probably known the painter's work from an early age, and admired it.[54]

Velasco began painting nearly a century before the CU was built, but in his technically excellent representations of the Valley of Mexico, its colonial ruins, and distant parts of the country newly accessible by train, Velasco treated many of the same themes that engaged the campus's architects, especially the ambiguous legacy of colonial architecture and the relationship between technology and nature. Velasco's canvases fascinated his student Rivera and in particular O'Gorman (who, by the 1940s, made landscapes and townscapes the main subjects of his paintings), and the revalorization of his work centered on claims by curators, critics, and intellectuals that it uniquely revealed the Mexican landscape's distinctive, ancient, national, and even mystical qualities. The Ministry of Education had organized the show and at its end president Avila Camacho declared Velasco's work a national monument, thereby anointing it as especially "Mexican" in a way that the work of few other artists had been. Two conferences about Velasco, one of which Rivera organized, followed the show, and with traveling exhibitions to the United States and several essays on his oeuvre, helped canonize the painter and the Mexican landscape yet further.

Velasco's transformation into a "national" painter with hemispheric significance was complete when a smaller version of the Bellas Artes show traveled to the Philadelphia Museum of Art (PMA) and, later, to the Brooklyn Museum in 1944 and 1945. Muralism's hegemony since 1921 as *the* "national" art, and the demonization of paintings and buildings from the Díaz years by postrevolutionary artists, architects, and critics had largely obscured important works in other media that dealt with topics besides history and class struggle. By sending the exhibition to the United States, the Mexican government gave to Velasco a place that had been occupied heretofore only by Rivera, the only Mexican to whom a major U.S. museum had devoted an entire show. In doing so it suggested that "Mexican" art now meant muralism *and* landscape painting. U.S. historians eagerly embraced a new master of the genre and suggested that there was something almost metaphysical about his work. Writing in 1942, Alfred Barr compared Velasco to Frederick Edwin Church and Thomas Moran, and observed, "in Velazco's [sic] painting this awareness of the sublime is never obvious, never approaches sentimentality or sunset melodrama so frequent in the romantic panoramas of Church and Moran. Velazco's mysticism is deeper just as his structure is more convincing, his knowledge profounder and more calm."[55] Discussing Velasco's works in relation to those by Church, Moran, and Albert Bierstadt, the PMA curator Henry Clifford reiterated references to the painter's "mysticism" and elevated him beyond merely national significance, commenting that Velasco was now, finally, being given "his rightful place in the history of American art."[56]

While foreigners interpreted Velasco first in relation to a tradition of landscape painting, Mexicans focused on how he revealed the natural splendor and architectural heritage of their country and captured something ineffable and even emotional about them. O'Gorman's long article on Velasco (to which Barr wrote the introduction), appeared shortly after the 1942 exhibition in the U.S. publication, *Magazine of Art*. The essay helped define Velasco for twentieth-century English-speaking audiences, and both O'Gorman and Barr drew particular attention to the ways the painter's precise, almost photographic depictions of geological formations and plants and his careful use of geometry to compose his pictures awakened emotion and created distinct moods. For his part, O'Gorman read Velasco's paintings as personal and highly expressive, and admired the way he captured the feeling of ancientness evoked by encounters with raw geological landscapes. Comparing his canvases to architecture, O'Gorman wrote:

> He . . . express[ed] in paint . . . what one can feel if one knows about the formation of the clouds in sky, the volcanic or sedimentary rocks on the earth, the growth of the different species of plants, and also the action of light and air that is continually transforming all of these. . . .
>
> [Velasco] made use of the materials which he took from nature in a very pure, perfect and subtle way to give us his most personal convictions. This is comparable to the work of an architect who builds a wonderful house with the materials of the very soil on which he works, and allows the building to become part of the landscape to such a degree that one would never notice it unless invited to go in to admire from the inside its comforts, structure and beauty. . . .
>
> In the longest period of his life he expressed in his paintings a feeling of the geologic greatness of the formation of the earth and a cosmic poetic sense that seems to be derived from an imaginative impression of our planet as it might have been millions of years ago.[57]

O'Gorman deemphasized Velasco's calculated formal manipulations and the relative detachment evident in many of his canvases, and anticipated the new earthier, massive architecture of the 1940s that he helped shape and that Anahuacalli, the museum of pre-Columbian art he designed with Rivera (1944–46), and his house in the Pedregal (1953–56) typified. O'Gorman's emphasis on imaginative contact with prehistory also anticipated Arai's focus on imagination, disorientation, and subjective experience of landscape, pre-Columbian architecture, and indigenous culture on the part of modern people.

The most famous painting illustrated in O'Gorman's essay was the 1877 *Valley of Mexico Seen from Santa Isabel Hill* (plate 11). In this canvas the viewer, seemingly suspended above a hill north of Mexico

City, surveyed a vast valley that unfolded below. In the foreground, a large bird swept toward rough rocks and cactuses beyond it and subtly evoked the Aztec story of the founding of Tenochtitlan on the site where, in the midst of a lake, an eagle landed on a cactus. Beyond this and barely visible at the base of the hill stood the village and church dedicated to Our Lady of Guadalupe, Mexico's most important religious figure. From there the straight lines of the road to Mexico City raced diagonally into the distance, leading the eye past Lake Texcoco and Popocatépetl and Iztaccíhuatl on the left, and on to the city and mountains to its south. For twentieth-century viewers, compositionally, *Valley of Mexico Seen from Santa Isabel Hill* recalled the aerial perspectives associated with modern city planning and seemed to anticipate the many widely reproduced aerial photographs of the UNAM campus. In such images the crater-like Olympic Stadium replaced Velasco's rocky mountain and the straight lines of Insurgentes took the place of the road to the Villa de Guadalupe, while Mexico's mountains rose in the distance of both. By coupling exquisitely detailed depictions of geologic formations and plants with references to iconic events in Mexican history—the founding of Tenochtitlan and the apparition of the Virgin of Guadalupe—Velasco powerfully linked national history to nature.

In a brief essay in the catalog for the U.S. version of the show, the Mexican poet and high-ranking official in the Ministry of Education, Carlos Pellicer, rhapsodized about the Valley of Mexico, linking the landscape, and especially its geology, to the great buildings of the pre-Hispanic and colonial eras. Pellicer began in a tone as lofty as Lazo's and proclaimed that, "the Valley of Mexico is one of the major phenomena in the history of our planet."[58] Looking north from the valley's southern reaches he proposed a geography of geology, architecture, and history: "a lesser valley, an arm of the Valley of Mexico . . . wears, like a jewel on its breast, one of the most impressive archeological groups in the world—the holy buildings of Teotihuacan, mysteriously linked to the serpentine cones of Cuicuilco, built many thousands of years ago, and now half-covered by the latest lava flow from Ajusco. The Cathedral of Mexico, the masterpiece of Colonial art on this continent, is built on the axis—a religious axis—of such illustrious pre-Hispanic monuments."[59] By rhetorically aligning Teotihuacan, Cuicuilco, and the Cathedral with the mountains beyond them, Pellicer obliterated the division between preconquest and colonial architecture (and the extraordinary differences among the cultures that built them) and subsumed Mexican architectural history before 1821 in a national geography. The proposed site of the new university lay directly on Pellicer's axis and, according to his vision, its construction—between Cuicuilco and the Cathedral—would make it the most important work of modern Mexico, a symbol of the state and of the triumph of education and modernity.

In his 1943 essay O'Gorman had repeatedly emphasized Velasco's expression of subjective experience of the Mexican landscape. In his discussion of the Valley of Mexico, Pellicer also moved from geology and topography to the personal, fusing landscape, architecture, the human body, and even the psyche. He wrote that the valley was "an enviable dwelling, where the walls are built of the hearts of men and light streams clearly through the windows. . . . The least movement leaves a mark in space, and any deep pause increases and solidifies its volume. It has a clarity made of grays, paling to blue and deepening to black. A monumental solitude follows us, and, in the diaphanous projection of its shadow, we would—if we could—say things full of spaciousness and elegance."[60] In Pellicer's painterly description the landscape itself became architectural—a "dwelling"—where space, light, color, and form gave rise to an experience of "solitude." The poet claimed that Velasco captured this experience in his paintings, and thereby developed the association between the Mexican landscape and individual, subjective experience that O'Gorman had claimed could be identified in the nineteenth-century artist's work. Indeed, like the photographs of the campus at mid-century, human figures rarely appeared in Velasco's paintings, and when they did they were nearly always dwarfed in scale by the landscape, and were often alone (figure 5.9).

Although both Lazo and the Alemán government hoped the CU would be seen as a symbol of economic progress and cultural achievement, as splendorous an embodiment of national greatness as Velasco's landscapes appeared at first glance, like his paintings, the campus was tinged with ambiguities and disquietudes of the kinds that haunted some new architectural histories and about which Arai would write explicitly. While in some respects the university's great modernist buildings, like the Rectory, were familiar, reliable emblems of modernity, positioned far from one another, across vast planes, and set against the dramatic mountains, the skyscrapers and slabs seemed eerily out of place. Visually more at home on the bustling, dense, urbane Paseo de la Reforma, Mexico City's spine of corporate capitalism, where Pani and del Moral also designed tall, modernist office buildings, than on the lava beds of the Pedregal, such buildings dwarfed students and on their own did nothing to suggest a four-hundred-year-old institutional his-

FIGURE 5.9. Faculty of Philosophy and Letters (Enrique de la Mora, Enrique Landa, and Manuel de la Colina) and Law buildings (Alonso Mariscal and Ernesto G. Gallardo) on the right. The Central Library can be seen in the distance.

tory. Similarly, the neo-pre-Hispanic works, like the fronton courts and the Olympic Stadium, although they were more topographically and geologically contextual than their International Style neighbors, stood, like them, apart from other buildings and separated from them by vast distances and busy roadways. The dramatic formal differences between the Rectory and the Stadium, for example—buildings that could easily be seen from one another—and the considerable distance between them (it took about fifteen minutes on foot to reach one from the other) gave the pedestrian-viewer the uneasy sense of simultaneously experiencing proximity and great distance. When moving between buildings, the pedestrian had to cross large plazas and navigate changing elevations, at the same time that he or she processed a visual landscape in which isolated architectural and painterly allusions to an ancient Mexican past and a technological international present appeared and receded. Far removed from the sites, sounds, smells, and bodies that went along with the informal street markets that had choked the colonial city for centuries (vendors were and still are tightly regulated at the CU), the pedestrian-viewer experienced the campus as both isolated and isolating. Here, the vast scale—of the automobile and pre-Hispanic monumental center—created for modern Mexicans a new way of interacting with architecture, one in which they were made more aware of their physical and psychological conditions than ever before. Moving through the campus often entailed braving hot, beating sunshine or chilly, driving rain on foot, or meant being ferried at high speeds in a bus or car on perimeter roads through the craggy, desolate Pedregal with its ancient-seeming trees and ominous-looking rock formations.

The experience could hardly have been more different from being packed shoulder to shoulder with the unpredictable multitudes on the crowded, narrow sidewalks of the capital's center, where cars passed at close range and the giant colonial and Porfirian palaces shaded the streets and even occasionally provided shelter from the rain. It was different also from the places UNAM students were likely to live, or at least visit their grandparents—the pleasant, quiet colonial suburbs, like San Angel and Coyoacán, or the leafy, genteel neighborhoods from the late nineteenth and early twentieth centuries such as Roma and Condesa. In this context, the CU was both strange and estranging. Its buildings' forms and materials, and the images in the mosaics were certainly familiar as components of a visual code for antiquity, modernity, and nationality that had been developed over several decades, but the mode of perceiving these references, and the physical and psychological experience of landscape and space were not. In bringing these images, associations, and experiences together, Pani and del Moral's plan functioned as an intermediary between the familiar and the new and, symbolically, between the past and the future, as well as the indigenous and foreign as they were coded in architecture. At once eloquently and uncomfortably, the campus embodied the push–pull of Mexico's cultural history as it was contained in and revealed by architecture.

PICTURING HISTORY

Perhaps the single most recognizable building at UNAM, the Central Library embodied more vividly than any other work Mexican architecture's characteristic facadism and the fusion of International Style architecture and nationally specific pictorialism at mid-century. O'Gorman clad the main block of the building, a ten-story slab containing the closed stacks, in a giant mosaic on the theme of Mexican history.

This mass was set back and atop a large platform-like volume surfaced in glass and yellow onyx that housed library services, open stacks, and a reading room. At the ground level, on the southeast side of the building a tall wall of black volcanic rock and carved with masks, serpents and glyph-forms enclosed a small garden (figure 5.1 and plate 1).

Despite having left architectural practice in the late 1930s renouncing International Style modernism and Le Corbusier, a decade later O'Gorman returned to architecture, this time using a very different vocabulary and materials, but with the same beliefs in architecture's potential to promote social change and the importance of its being suited to national conditions. He entered the running conversation on architectural history in 1952 declaring that Mexico is a "country with a profound love of color and a deep rooted tradition in the architecture of its past history, in which painting and sculpture have been used profusely."[61] As he had when he designed the elementary schools, O'Gorman treated the facade of the library as a representational surface and used building materials to associate architecture with notions of progress or national specificity. In the schools, concrete and glass conveyed the Ministry of Education's aspirations to modernize, rationalize, and efficiently deliver primary education, and their painted lettering and murals linked them to Mexico City's *pulquerías* and their working-class patrons. At UNAM mosaic made of colored stones gathered throughout Mexico depicted images, figures, and buildings recognizable to an audience trained in an increasingly well-established iconography of national history, and symbolically linked the building to the land. By using these stones O'Gorman pointedly differentiated the library from his earlier buildings and implicitly referenced one of the most potent aspects of Mexican architectural history. Many of Mexico City's colonial buildings had been built using the stones of Aztec temples, which were, of course, made of local stone. Built on and faced with volcanic rocks, the Central Library reworked the material and symbolic layering evident in colonial architecture and, like the Ministry of Health, suggested that the modern institution rested on deep, indigenous foundations.

The building's pictorialism also tied it to Obregón Santacilia's work, but for O'Gorman the Marxist painter-architect, the political and social histories of Mexico were inseparable from the country's architectural history. He anchored the lower corners of the composition on the south facade with pale green and mauve stepped pyramids that wrapped around the corners of the building. The organization of the mosaic on this facade echoed the argument of the building as a whole

FIGURE 5.10. Central Library, north facade.

that modern architecture descended from a long architectural history that began before the Spanish arrived.[62] In the lower left- and right-hand corners, scenes of the religious and military conquest of Mexico appeared and small figures enacted this historical drama against the backdrop of indigenous temples that were topped, on the left with a colonial church, and on the right, a baroque palace. Two buildings appeared in the center of the composition—a blue colonial church, also built on a pre-Hispanic building, and, at the very center of the mosaic, a Greek temple. To the left and right of it were giant blue orbs, one dedicated to Ptolemy, the other to Copernicus. References to preconquest culture appeared throughout the composition and were embodied in the orbs, which seemed to resolve at a distance into the giant eyes of the pre-Columbian deity, Tlaloc, the most famous sculptural depiction of which was on the temple of the Plumed Serpent at Teotihuacan. On the north facade O'Gorman illustrated preconquest people in a composition that recalled early colonial illuminated codices (figure 5.10).[63]

References to science, modern industry, sports, and the National

FIGURE 5.11. Central Library, east facade.

FIGURE 5.12. Central Library, west facade.

University itself dominated the short ends of the building, where the links between cultural and political progress and architecture are perhaps most vivid (figures 5.11 and 5.12). On the east end, the Mexican Revolution was referenced in banners that read, "Viva la Revolución" and "Tierra y Libertad." On the left side, workers appeared in front of and atop the pyramid, on which stood a factory with a sawtoothed roofline, which, in this context, recalled O'Gorman's house for Rivera. Two other references to modern architecture appeared on the west facade, where O'Gorman depicted, again atop a pyramid, two buildings raised on piloti. One was a tall slab that towered over a shorter, flat-roofed two-story building, the facade of which was defined by three strip windows on each floor, organized in a way that called to mind the facades of the elementary schools. Even as he rejected the modernist forms of the earlier part of his career, O'Gorman gave modern architecture a prominent place in the history of Mexico. Indeed, when the mosaic is read as a continuous composition, the modernist buildings on the minor facades occupy the same plane as the colonial church and palace on the library's most important surface, but their positions clearly signaled modernism's lesser status relative to colonial works. Relegated to the sides, the images betrayed the anxiety detectable in recent architectural histories that modern architecture had yet to match colonial buildings in quality or importance. The east facade was also notable for what appeared on its right side. There, folkloric images of peasants and revolutionaries, surrounding a depiction of an eagle and cactus, stood opposite workers and a globe, on the other side. Atop the pyramid, above the peasants, O'Gorman depicted vernacular dwellings and mixed-use colonial buildings of the kind found in small Mexican towns. Like the figures, the buildings were easily legible to an audience that had been trained to read images more or less according to the typological system that Rivera had developed in his 1920s murals and of the kind that Best Maugard had promoted in his drawing manual. Relying on this system, on the facade of one of Mexico's most important twentieth-century buildings, O'Gorman pictorialized Mexican architectural history and now linked it not only to the nation's social and cultural history (as historians of colonial architecture had) but also to its political history. The consequences of this, and the parallel developments in texts and exhibitions, for the writing of Mexican architectural history would be born out in the decades to come, as political readings of Mexican architectural history came to dominate scholarship.[64]

Thematically and iconographically, the mosaic linked the building to early Mexican muralism, state authority, and the colonial city center.

In 1929 Rivera began painting his monumental fresco, *History of Mexico*, in the staircase of the National Palace, on the east side of Mexico City's main plaza (figures 5.13, 5.14, and plate 12) The striking similarities between Rivera's work and O'Gorman's twenty years later underscored the extent to which by 1950, Rivera's iconography was regarded as widely legible and capable of conveying something nationally specific. Like O'Gorman, Rivera had stretched national history over several walls. His fresco cycle began on the north wall of the staircase, where he depicted preconquest civilization. On the largest wall, the west, he represented Mexican history from the conquest to the twentieth century as an astounding ensemble of portraits and types. The south wall was dedicated to the future, in which Rivera imagined the proletariat and rural revolutionaries taking control from a debauched right wing made up of the rich and the Catholic establishment. Although unlike Rivera, O'Gorman pictorially entwined Mexican political and social history with the country's architectural history, several of the forms that he used on the library's facade came directly from Rivera's fresco, and, like the more famous muralist, O'Gorman made Mexico City central to his version of national history. On the lower left of the south facade, O'Gorman depicted the burning of Aztec codices, as Rivera had; his rendering of a canon firing on the right side of the composition strongly resembled Rivera's and was placed in the same position relative to the depiction of the burning books. The "Tierra y Libertad" banner on the east facade had also appeared in the National Palace frescoes (in the central lunette) as had factory imagery (in the panel depicting the future). O'Gorman's rendering of an enormous atom on the east facade both alluded to the university's ambition to improve research in atomic science and recalled Rivera's atomic imagery at the center of another fresco, the repainted version of *Man at the Crossroads*, in the Palace of Fine Arts, on the edge of downtown Mexico City.

By associating his mosaic with Rivera's mural, O'Gorman grounded his work in the cannon of Mexican art and could be reasonably confident that his design would be accepted. Indeed, he had had significant differences of opinion with Lazo, who tightly controlled the mosaic artists and their work, and surely did not wish to risk losing the commission.[65] The similarities to Rivera's mural also linked the library and the campus symbolically to the heart of Mexico City, which the university pointedly rejected by moving to its new site. Rivera had affirmed the centrality of Mexico City in national history by making Aztec history—symbolized by the eagle on the cactus—the center of his National Palace murals. O'Gorman too affirmed the city's special

FIGURE 5.13. Rivera, *History of Mexico*, National Palace, north wall, 1929.

status and the enduring connection of the university to national government. Beneath the "Copernicus" orb O'Gorman represented the famous 1524 map of Tenochtitlan made for Cortés and sent to Charles V. This cartographic reference to the city on which modern Mexico City was built further associated national and urban/architectural history and reminded viewers in distant Pedregal of central, federal authority.

THE PROBLEM OF PLASTIC INTEGRATION

O'Gorman's library mosaic has long been cited as an example of "plastic integration," which was a major topic of debate among artists and architects in Mexico at mid-century, and was related to the growing sense that modern buildings of the 1930s did not adequately express what was distinctive about Mexico. Modernist ideals of integration and unification—of the arts, society, past and present, city and country, and ultimately, the Western Hemisphere—that were distilled and understood in nationally specific ways appeared repeatedly in discussions of

FIGURE 5.14. Rivera, *History of Mexico*, National Palace, south wall, 1929.

CU and in many of its buildings. This yearning for totality was nothing
new in Mexican art and architecture, but at UNAM, a project of unpar-
alleled scale and ambition in the Americas, the contradictions, imper-
fections, anxieties, and the stakes of the attempt to achieve it were laid
bare.[66] Architects and artists discussed aesthetic unification in terms
of "plastic integration," which O'Gorman, Siqueiros (who created three
sculpture-murals on the exterior of the administration building) and
del Moral, three of the more thoughtful contributors to the campus's
program, all understood as a historical problem.[67] The very mixing of
forms, media, and materials in and on the buildings seemed to make
them Mexican in the sense that "Mexican" in mid-century architectural discourse meant having recognizably "European" and "indigenous"
elements and being essentially eclectic, an idea that was supported by
histories of national architecture and several decades of discussion. In
this sense the campus embodied architectural mestizaje in the most
far-reaching respect. Where UNAM differed from earlier projects
whose architects had also sought to merge the foreign and the native,

was in its simplified, scaled-up symbolism and representations, which could be relied on to convey Mexicanness because their iconography and associations had been firmly established by 1920s muralists and architects. The unambiguous, and even at times clumsy pictorial expressions of national culture on university buildings made those on the works by Obregón Santacilia, Segura, and O'Gorman earlier appear subtle.

O'Gorman himself was one of the most strident critics of the architecture he had championed only twenty years earlier.[68] Objecting to the International Style on political and nationalistic grounds, he wrote in 1955 that such buildings in Mexico reflected "the imposition of the anti-Mexican taste that expresses the ideas of the wealthy and powerful class."[69] Elsewhere he critiqued his colleagues for having created "a new Academy of modern architecture as obtuse and closed as was the old Academy of San Carlos"[70] and for designing buildings that were disconnected from their landscapes, "regional conditions," and the "tradition of a place."[71] Analogous, and equally bad, was abstract art. The solution to modernism's shortcomings, he believed, was to strengthen the study of culture and art history (emphasizing its social aspects) in architectural education, return to realism in art, and give greater consideration to the lessons of vernacular architecture, all of which might support plastic integration. For O'Gorman this meant the integration of architecture and landscape, with particular attention to form and color and the use of painting and sculpture as "architectonic elements" to create "an element that architecture lacks by its own nature," which was also to be the "theme of painting and sculpture."[72] This melding of media and content mirrored university planners' ambitions to unify the campus, the institution, and the country through the university and with reference to history.

O'Gorman now argued that history proved the importance of the other arts to Mexican architecture saying, "in Mexico there is no case, either pre-Hispanic or Colonial, in which sculpture and painting were not an integral part of the architectural composition."[73] Modern architects were of course well aware of this from their study of history. The first works of the muralist movement had been painted in actual colonial buildings, and many of the major new buildings of the 1920s and 1930s had included them. In the 1940s, following the precedent Obregón Santacilia had established at the Ministry of Health, Pani designed two important schools that followed the norms of Beaux-Arts design with their hierarchical plans and use of sculptures and paintings, and included references to pre-Columbian architecture and art.

FIGURE 5.15. Pani, National Normal School, 1945–47.

In his National Conservatory of Music of 1946 and the monumental National Normal School of 1945–47 (figure 5.15), he began to explore ways of using painting to activate space visually. It was in these projects that his close collaboration began with José Clemente Orozco, whom he had wanted to do the mosaics at the Rectory.[74] At the National Conservatory, on walls on either side of a circular stage, Orozco painted two murals on concrete that, according to an article on the building published in Pani's own journal, appeared to have been painted "on different planes," and together constituted "a very important essay on liberating painting from a single plane." On walls at the back of the stage in the school's giant open-air auditorium were two drawings made by architect Roberto Engelking that depicted music abstractly. Exterior walls faced in native rock appeared throughout the building. They contrasted dramatically with the concrete, brick, and glass Pani used elsewhere, and anticipated similar wall treatments at the Ciudad Universitaria.

On the back of the outdoor stage of the Normal School, and on axis with the reproduction of the colossal Olmec head that the architect had placed in front of the entrance, Orozco created one of his most

FIGURE 5.16. José Clemente Orozco, *National Allegory*, National Normal School, 1947–48.

innovative works. Six stories tall, seventy-two feet wide, and painted in ethyl silicate on a curving wall, the nearly abstract *National Allegory* (1947–48; figure 5.16) looked much more like Siqueiros's paintings of the late 1940s than the highly figurative frescoes most typical of Orozco. National history was the theme of the mural, and historical Mexican architecture was literally in it. At the center of the wall and at the bottom center of the composition was an enormous eighteenth century doorway that Pani had installed—this too, of course, was on axis with the Olmec head. Orozco explained that the painting, which is somewhat difficult to read, depicted "stone and metal," "the Eagle and the Serpent, a representation of life and death, of the Mexican earth. At the left, a man with his head in the clouds moves up a gigantic staircase; at the right, a hand puts a block into place. . . . The forms of the composition are organized so as to acknowledge and preserve the par-

FIGURE 5.17. José Chávez Morado, *Conquest of Energy*, Faculty of Sciences.

abolic form of the wall to be seen at a distance." References to ancient
and modern building materials, national history, a modern (perhaps
transcendent) subject, and evidence of a new engagement with space
surrounded a piece of architectural spolia that itself functioned representationally in Pani's colossal new building. Although it differed from
nearly all the mosaics at the UNAM stylistically and in its response to
real space, *National Allegory*, by being set in a building that expressed
the ambitions to modernize, monumentalize, and institutionalize education with reference to the ancient and colonial pasts, was perhaps
the single most important intellectual precursor to plastic integration
at UNAM, and a critical link back to the modernism of the Ministry
of Health and the Carranza Center. It also suggested that at least one
important approach to plastic integration, like much of Mexican modern architecture itself, was informed by Beaux-Arts principles and local
concerns, and provided a hint of what muralism might have looked like
on the campus had Pani and del Moral had more control over the process of selecting and including artists in the project.[75]

Pani, like O'Gorman and many others, complained bitterly about Lazo's interference in decisions about art and design,[76] and it seems likely that the somewhat tepid quality of many of the mosaics may be attributed to Lazo's attempts to ensure that the works were not too challenging aesthetically or politically, and that they conformed to his vision of the university as unified and unifying. That ambition was revealed most vividly in the three mosaic murals that Chávez Morado created for the Faculty of Sciences. *Return of Quetzalcoatl*, *Conquest of Energy* (figure 5.17), and *Science and Work*, which related the Spanish conquest, scientific progress, and the building of the Ciudad Universitaria in a realist style, and echoed themes that Lazo articulated and that O'Gorman treated in the library mosaics.[77] Of the three, *Science and Work* was most notable. In it the muralist alluded to Mexico's uneven modernization and class differences by showing the peasant workers (likely former tenants of the Pedregal) who constructed the buildings of the new campus, the architects and bureaucrats who planned the campus, and the engineers, with the university's prized Van de Graaff accelerator, the purchase of which Lazo had championed.[78]

Progress and history as well as hemispheric unity were also topics of Siqueiros's sculpture-mural mosaics at the Rectory, two of which were meant to be seen at high speeds from a car zooming down Insurgentes Avenue. On the south facade he created *The People for the University, The University for the People: For a Neo-Humanist National Culture* (plate 13). The muralist rendered this rather abstract and far-reaching theme using five figures that reached toward the road and held tools used in architectural design—a pencil, a model of a steel-framed building, and a compass. The figure on the upper left extended his arms as if to reach from the direction of the road back toward the central library and the core of the academic zone. Beyond him, in the upper left corner, tiny figures, presumably international workers, carried flags as if in a march. Although it was somewhat difficult to read, and lacked the dynamism of Siqueiros's strongest works, *The People for the University* vividly expressed the links between architecture, the university, and aspirations to internationalism that Lazo voiced. On the north facade of the Rectory, Siqueiros dealt with Mexican history. In *Right to Learning*, a long arm with an enormous pencil-bearing hand reached across the narrow, rectangular composition leading the eye to an image suggestive of hands in motion and to four dates, 1520, 1810, 1857, and 1910, which referred to the Spanish conquest, the beginning of the war for independence, the passage of the reform laws, and the start of the Mexican Revolution. Beneath "1910," in paler paint, Siqueiros wrote,

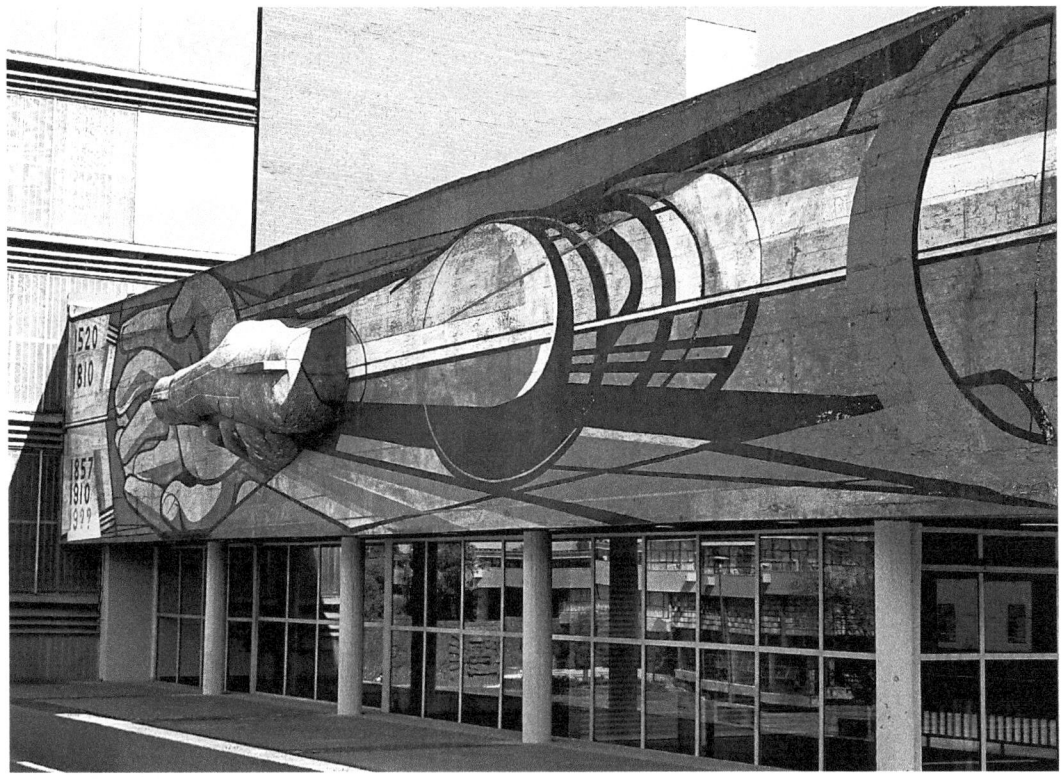

FIGURE 5.18. David Alfaro Siqueiros, *Right to Learning*, Rectory.

"19??" (figure 5.18). Potentially provocative, the final, unfinished date, reflected the muralist's Marxism and, perhaps, his dissatisfaction with the commission and statist aspects of the Ciudad Universitaria project.

Unlike the mosaics by O'Gorman, Chávez Morado, and Francisco Eppens (who created an enormous composition of conventionalized pre-Columbian imagery on the east facade of the School of Medicine), Siqueiros's sculpture-mosaics broke the plane of the wall. By extending his work beyond the facade, Siqueiros called attention to it as a surface and attempted to engage space dynamically. He had experimented with anamorphic projection as a means of uniting the arts and creating an avant-garde Marxist art since the 1930s,[79] but the spatial sophistication of his compositions grew beginning in the 1940s as he explored national historical themes, such as in *Cuauhtémoc against the Myth* (1944), originally painted on the interior and exterior walls of the stairwell at his Center for Realist Art, and the more abstract *Patriots and Parricides* (1945) in the staircase of the former Santo Domingo customs house, one of Mexico City's great seventeenth-century buildings. Siqueiros's space in the UNAM mosaic murals was, of course, radically different from the campus's vast plazas and vistas, but both proposed a new kind of relationship between the viewer and the work in which he or she might grow increasingly conscious of his or her position in space and history. Although it was undoubtedly informed by the muralist's political views, the association in his works of national history with new approaches to space in painting and architecture, and the implicit suggestion that history itself might be fluid and dynamic, paralleled similar investigations in the work of Orozco and Arai.

The mosaic murals at UNAM received widespread attention and critique, and Siqueiros himself was one of their most vociferous critics. He chastised Lazo for failing to bring painters into the design process from the very beginning and for attempting to disrupt work on the murals. He rebuked O'Gorman and Rivera for their indigenism and condemned all his colleagues for failing to truly adapt muralism, which had been fundamentally an art of the interior, to the very different requirements the CU commission presented.[80] The muralist hated the "scenographic" qualities of the campus—its terraces and plazas—and the "dressing up" of "Corbusian" buildings in "*huipiles* and Mexican shirts" in order to "Mexicanize" them.[81] O'Gorman's library was a particular target and Siqueiros repeated architect Raul Cacho's critique of it as "a little Olinalá box," in a reference to the painted lacquerware from the town of Olinalá, Guerrero. The reference to folk art underscored the library's continuities with earlier works, such as the Ministry of Health, the Carranza Center, and even O'Gorman's schools, in which such allusions also appeared. Siqueiros's slight intimated that the mosaics were, like made-for-the-market folk art, decorative—one of the worst things they could be from the perspectives of international modernism and Marxism. Although the mosaics were very different from the representations of colonial elements on the facades of the ministry and Carranza Center buildings, their function as ornament was similar, as contemporary observers quickly recognized. Describing the mosaics in 1952, after admiring the use of varied materials at the CU, the U.S. magazine *Interiors* noted that "the Mexicans have dared to partake of the forbidden fruit of ornament, which is still such a tempting taboo for less warm-blooded architects. It is not the all-enveloping ornament of Baroque indulgence, but art which has a life of its own and yet becomes vital in the form of buildings. Sparkling mosaic murals are being applied lavishly."[82] That the mosaics, like Segura's scrolls, were obviously applied to the surface did not bother the essay's author in the least, and he even implied, in an echo of early twentieth-century Viennese architect Adolf Loos, that ornament might actually be appropriate for darker-skinned architects in a country that was imagined to be less rational than the United States or those of western Europe.[83] Although he shared with O'Gorman, Rivera, and Chávez Morado a commitment to realism, largely for ideological reasons and in opposition to the growing prominence of abstraction as embodied by the work of Mathias Goeritz, Siqueiros felt strongly that his art differed from theirs on the basis of technique and materials, and therefore in its capacity to be truly integrated with architecture, its environment, and society.[84]

ART (AND) HISTORY

O'Gorman and Siqueiros, despite differing significantly in aspects of their positions, both understood plastic integration historically.[85] According to Siqueiros it had existed in Western art until the Renaissance, when works of art began to be made for private consumption and possession.[86] O'Gorman too drew from pre-Renaissance examples to argue for the historicity of thematic and material integration claiming that in Byzantine and gothic churches "the form and color of the paintings and sculptures, besides being organized fragments with the architecture, served to express in a direct and emotive way and to all who contemplated them (from the monarch to the last servant) the religious ideas contained in the theme, and at the same time were the highest synthesis of the cultural forms of the time."[87] Integration in architectural history also fascinated Enrique del Moral, who was the most intellectually disciplined of the three to enter the mid-century debate on plastic integration.

In December 1953 del Moral gave a talk titled, "Tradition vs. Modernity: Integration?"[88] in which he challenged his colleagues' interpretations of integration and offered his own, grounded in a historical reading of major works of western architecture. Del Moral particularly faulted Cacho for suggesting that plastic integration was a new and uniquely Mexican phenomenon, and O'Gorman, for his claim that the separation of the arts occurred only with capitalism. (Del Moral disputed this using the example of an apartment building designed by Moisei Ginzburg in the Soviet Union.) The architect identified plastic integration in the nunneries at Chichen Itza and Uxmal, in the main portal of the Chapel of San Gregorio in Valladolid, Spain, in Romanesque and baroque architecture and in Venetian gothic works. He saw it as well in Hindu temples, the Great Mosque at Córdoba, and in

Egypt, at the temple of Abu Simbel. Claiming that the "study of the history of art leads us to the conclusion that integration . . . has only been achieved in certain times and places,"[89] and not by a single economic system or style, del Moral argued that integration came about through quite abstract conditions.

Although in his writings del Moral revisited the relationships between folk art and modernity that had animated Mexican artistic culture throughout the century, and examined plastic integration as a theoretical problem in detail, he did not believe that he and Pani, as the head architects of the Ciudad Universitaria, had shaped a campus that was particularly well integrated. The mosaics at the Olympic Stadium and the Central Library were the product of collaboration, not expressions of integration because, he argued, from the very beginning architects had conceived of the buildings as complete in themselves without the mosaics.[90] Del Moral buttressed his argument using photographs of the stadium and library taken before and after the mosaics were installed. The comparisons vividly illustrated the facadism of this kind of "Mexicanization" of architecture and recalled histories from earlier in the century whose authors also relied on photography to bolster arguments about the nationally specific qualities of the buildings they discussed. According to del Moral, real integration was something like what Frank Lloyd Wright called organicism: an expression of some quality or characteristic that defined the whole work. It occurred "naturally," and was inherent in the work.[91] Focusing primarily on the differences between painting and architecture, del Moral implied that modern architecture, in contrast to some historical examples he cited, retained its "autonomy" and "self-sufficiency," even as contemporary architects attempted to design buildings with "greater expressive force" than functionalist ones seemed to provide. Nevertheless, he described this new architecture using painterly terms, suggesting that it was characterized by "the play of contrast, texture, color, and the dramatization of forms."[92]

For del Moral, integration and its absence lay in the nature of the society and its relative cohesion, and in the gap between high and popular culture. Linking plastic integration and the notion of style as an expression of an age, which he derived from the art historical writings of Heinrich Wölfflin and Wilhelm Worringer, del Moral suggested that the formal similarities in some Mexican high-style and "popular" colonial churches, such as the Rosary Chapel in Santo Domingo, Puebla, and the vernacular church of Santa Maria Tonantzintla (plate 14) in the state of Puebla, were the result of artist and architects' success in assimilating different forms to shape a cohesive, recognizable language that seemed to belong to its time.[93] He suggested that such formal consistency derived from a variety of social, historical, and demographic conditions and it emerged from a "special way of sensing form" that was particular to each society.[94] Integration, furthermore, was a "way of being of certain peoples, in certain times," and it "had no country," was not exclusively western or limited to certain periods.[95] Somewhat unexpectedly, perhaps, del Moral found at the core of cultures where artistic integration flourished a "metaphysical conception that has God at its center."[96] This theory of integration had much less in common with notions of the *Gusamtkunstwerk* or Walter Gropius's vision of the Bauhaus as the site where craft, industry, and all the arts would be united in the service of social transformation, and instead was much closer to other mid-century explorations of plentitude, religiosity, and emotion in the work of abstract expressionist painters in the United States, particularly Mark Rothko and Barnett Newman. Although they unequivocally affirmed the singularity of painting, by working at large scale and often with intense colors and elemental forms, these painters created works that invited the viewer into totalizing visual experiences not unlike those that del Moral identified in the Rosary Chapel and in Santa Maria Tonantzintla. In all these cases, and in the other examples of integration the architect described, the handling of surface was paramount. Del Moral also offered an image of the integrated subject, who was, of course, male. He was a "harmonious man without great shocks or anxieties" who lived in a "centripetal, magic and transcendent, metaphysical world," and was "submerged in the world of faith, not reason."[97] Del Moral's attention to subjectivity, wholeness, and metaphysical and spiritual experience paralleled the exploration of these ideas by Arai and Barragán, whose built work at mid-century expressed them far more vividly than most parts of the UNAM campus did. The architect's assessment also echoed discussions by O'Gorman and Pellicer of these themes in Velasco's paintings.

Del Moral's interest in the relationship between popular and high art, and his engagement with Mexican architectural history manifested in written form the attention these things had received in built work since the 1920s. Their reappearance in his theory of plastic integration, with its parallels to developments in international modernism, underscored once again not only their centrality to modern architectural discourse in Mexico but also the extraordinary flexibility with which Mexican architects used popular art and architectural history to shape buildings and theory. The explicit and implicit facadism in del

Moral's approach furthermore reinforced the attention to surface that had characterized Mexican architecture, and paralleled in Arai and Barragán's built work a renewed emphasis on the wall as an expressive architectural element.

TEMPLES, TORTILLAS, AND TIME

The entwining of historically informed theory and design was nowhere more evident than in the work of Alberto Arai, whose widely photographed fronton courts appeared in Mexican and foreign publications on the Ciudad Universitaria more often than other buildings there, except the national library. Arai's work at UNAM consisted of four pairs of courts, with each court formed by three very high concrete walls faced on the exterior with volcanic stone set in mortar in a pattern reminiscent of pre-Columbian masonry (figure 5.19). The slope of the walls, their scale, their formal dialogue with the distant mountains, and the ways they shaped space to monumental effect further recalled preconquest architecture. Between the concrete and stone walls Arai included dressing rooms and showers for the athletes. A fifth building, a large enclosed court that could accommodate four thousand spectators stood at the west end of the group; its talud-like walls were clad in the same stone. The courts were widely admired in Mexico and abroad and they were the first twentieth-century buildings readers saw in the catalog of the landmark exhibition, *Latin American Architecture since 1945*, held at the Museum of Modern Art in 1955. The catalog's author, Henry-Russell Hitchcock, paired two photographs of the courts with an image of the Pyramid of the Sun at Teotihuacan and the Altar Room at Machu Picchu (the next image in the book was of the nave of the eighteenth-century church of San Martín at Tepozotlán) and later in the text noted that "architecture . . . is much affected by psychological . . . factors. . . . Only in Mexico is there a conscious preoccupation with retaining continuity in modern national culture."[98] Some found the intersection of history and psychology that the courts embodied disquieting, even as they were attracted by the buildings' exoticism. Writing of the reaction of a U.S. architect to the buildings, Villagrán recalled that the visitor "waited, horrified, half expecting to see warm human blood trickling down the walls."[99]

As the example of the Ibero-American Exposition pavilion (discussed in chapters 2 and 3) showed, allusions to preconquest architecture were nothing new in Mexican or international architecture, and, somewhat superficially, Arai's work belonged to this tradition. In the

FIGURE 5.19. Alberto T. Arai, Fronton Courts, 1952.

1920s and 1930s pre-Columbian forms inspired Art Deco designs internationally and some architects and critics argued that new skyscrapers were fundamentally like Mesoamerican pyramids because they were tall, sometimes had stepped crowns, and were a typological invention of the Americas.[100] However, as abstractions of ancient works, and because their formal and symbolic charge came from materials, their relationship to the site, and the ways they repositioned the viewer in relation to the landscape and history, the courts differed dramatically from revivalist and Art Deco buildings. More than any other single project at the CU, the buildings made space and the subjective response to architecture central to the experience of viewing buildings. Like so many architects before him, Arai used architectural history imagined as Mexican to shape new works, but rather than using it in the service of statist, institutional, or political projects of modernization, he focused on defining individual experience and awakening consciousness of the past.

Arai had been an early champion of "functionalist" architecture and also one of a relatively small group of left-leaning architects who, influenced by Villagrán, led the charge to create socially responsive, politically engaged buildings. In 1939, with Cacho and Enrique Guerrero, Arai designed the headquarters for the Confederation of Mexican Workers, which typified the strident, class-conscious modernism of 1930s Mexico. More important, he inherited from Villagrán the ambition to theorize architecture in national terms. Unlike most of his colleagues, Arai was highly trained in history and philosophy and, having grown up in Brazil, Chile, Argentina, Peru, and Spain as the child of a Japanese diplomat father and Mexican mother, he had a distinctive perspective on matters of nationality and locality. In the 1940s he became fascinated by Maya architecture, which he encountered through his work as the regional head of the Administrative Committee on Federal School Building in Chiapas, and when he participated in a government-led expedition to Bonampak in 1949. Like many of Mexico's cultural leaders in the first half of the twentieth century, Arai believed that Mexico should create a distinctive, recognizable national culture and that doing so required moving beyond simplistic formal and theoretical oppositions. Although modern architects had responded in nuanced ways to colonial and preconquest buildings since the beginning of the century, by 1950, as disenchantment with functionalism grew and the federal government more consistently patronized buildings that used International Style and historicist vocabularies for developmentalist and touristic agendas, Arai sought a way out of the apparent formal, rhetorical, and symbolic impasses of modernism and historicism. Rather than offering formal or technical prescriptions, he proposed a way of approaching pre-Hispanic architecture that might stimulate in architects a richer, deeper approach to problems of form, technique, site, and national specificity.

In 1952 Arai wrote a dense two-part essay, "Caminos para una arquitectura mexicana" (Paths toward a Mexican Architecture), part of which was published in *Espacios*, in which he outlined why it was essential to have a national "architectural doctrine." He examined ways of using "indigenous tradition" not only to create a "Mexican" architecture but also to move past the seemingly intractable oppositions of pre-Hispanic buildings and works that looked like the Confederation of Workers building. Arai's essay refined and synthesized ideas he had explored in two earlier writings: a 1937 extended work on film theory, and a book from 1949 about the Maya ruins at Bonampak. Like the handball courts, "Paths toward a Mexican Architecture" (hereafter "Paths") entered a dialogue begun at the turn of the century about the modern uses of Mexican architectural history and architecture's role in defining national culture. In its discussions of landscape and history, in some respects the essay echoed themes that O'Gorman and Pellicer had introduced in their descriptions of Velasco's canvases.

Arai discussed history and geography at length, endeavoring to fuse historical consciousness and geographic specificity at the same time that he examined the categories of "self" and "other" in individual and collective experience. Working with acute consciousness of the psychological distance between "here" and "there"—of Mexico as indebted to Europe culturally but profoundly different from it—he responded to long-standing Mexican debates about the dangers and inevitability of "importing" foreign forms. The architect distinguished copyism from learning from the principles of great works of the past or those of other countries. Using the metaphor of a compass, he urged architects to locate themselves in historical and cultural time in order to identify the "coincidence of the present with the here."[101] Like architects outside of Mexico at mid-century who questioned European modernism's claims to universality, he argued that architecture should "be firmly settled in the definition of that region it inhabits . . . in relation to other regions of the globe."[102] A new architecture would emerge when the architect was correctly oriented in time and space and could select forms or principles from the past that were well-suited for modern uses and the specific needs of place.

Arai's focus on time and place paralleled del Moral's examination of these things. In his 1948 essay, "Lo General y lo Local" (The General and the Local), in which he dealt with the question of what a nationally specific architecture might be, like Arai he sought to clarify the difference between expressions of temporality and geography as they manifest stylistically. Del Moral suggested that the "general" in architecture was a result of an architect's consciousness of existing in a particular epoch and could be used to explain the "international" qualities of some buildings. Locality, on the other hand, had to do with culture and the relative progress of mestizaje. The most "local" expressions were found in works created by people in places where "the process of the integration of both cultures is the least advanced."[103] The "general" referred to the seemingly international forms of cosmopolitan places like Mexico City (which he believed did not represent the country as a whole), while the "local" was to be found in the provinces, and "certain regions" in particular. The general and the local could be modified by expressions of the other.

In "Paths," Arai's overarching concern—indeed, the point of Mexican architecture—was to "enrich contemporary culture" and to "continu[e] to build Mexico." Orientation in history, awareness of place, and attention to social concerns were critical to the task, but so too was understanding of tradition, which Arai said was "dynamic" and "relative,"[104] and constituted by Mexico's preconquest and colonial pasts. Knowledge of these periods might shape modern psychological experience just as they had historically played roles in defining what he called Mexico's "psycho-historical process." Fascinated, as countless Mexican thinkers had been before him, by the historical, social, and racial phenomenon of mestizaje, Arai seized on its psychological implications, first for indigenous Mexicans after the conquest. Their bodies, minds, and interior worlds, he said, coexisted with the material manifestations of New Spain to give rise to a complex and uneasy psychological existence. Equally complicated was the twentieth-century viewer's relationship to preconquest buildings. Mexico's indigenous architecture was "the most ancient and elemental, the most distant, the most healthy, and most spontaneous tradition of our nationality." But it also contained the germs of something profoundly unsettling for modern people.

Seizing on the experience of viewing ancient buildings, Arai suggested that at the core of a truly distinctive national architectural theory was the modern viewer's perception of the unfamiliar in pre-Columbian architecture and awareness of his or her own distance from the culture that created it. That viewer's encounter with "the rare, the strange, and the foreign" and the resulting "psychological states" of surprise, disorientation, and confusion was born from the confusing experience of being in close physical proximity to the buildings, but not apprehending them fully. He described ancient works as "ignored or unknown objects," and was fascinated by the moments in which a viewer became aware of the gap between the proximate and the past—in the relationship between place and history. For Arai the critical moment came when, looking at an ancient building, the viewer perceived the "collision" of preexisting beliefs about Mesoamerican architecture and the new understanding awakened by actually seeing a preconquest building. The architect honed in on the ways that such an experience might change modern people's perceptions of themselves as they discovered "that which we were and are [is] in evident contrast with that which we want to be." Confident that the transformation of pre-Columbian culture from the incomprehensible into the familiar had been happening gradually for some time thanks to developments in archaeology, Arai outlined the potentially productive possibilities of a more complete modern cannibalization of preconquest culture that was at the same time a kind of reconquest of Mexico by its indigenous inhabitants. He wrote: "To accustom oneself to a thing is to forgive the defect or vice of its exoticism, place it alongside familiar objects that we manipulate daily. In this way the archeological cultures of Mexico return to re-conquer the place that they occupied before the . . . conquest. Once this position is recuperated, it is possible to study with complete calm those products of the past in order to assimilate and take advantage of them according to our present need."[105] Arai was not the first to suggest that modern, urban Mexicans might benefit from adjusting their approach to indigenous culture, nor the first to cast it in terms of retaking and rebirth. As early as 1916 the anthropologist and archaeologist Manuel Gamio called for a "new conquest" and pushed the federal government to adjust its policies to acknowledge the demographic realities of a country that was overwhelmingly mixed-race or indigenous.[106] Valorization of indigeneity was a dominant theme in the murals of the 1920s, when cosmopolitan artists and the intelligentsia raced to display, collect, and institutionalize folk art. But Arai's reconquest was fundamentally about psychological accommodation and it denied the modern viewer the pleasures of spectatorship, shopping, self-fashioning, and travel that the 1920s had provided, instead asking him to probe his own interior experience and to confront the "rare, strange, and foreign, that which is not replaceable in the soul itself."[107]

Arai's argument that a truly innovative Mexican architecture for the twentieth century required modern people to make space in themselves and to engage visually and psychologically with works of architecture calls to mind art historical and architectural theory from very different contexts from the early twentieth century: notions of empathy in the work of Heinrich Wölfflin and others, Alois Rigel's concept of attentiveness, and, perhaps most closely resonated with Hector Guimard's idea of "sympathy," with its implications not only for the viewing subject, but for society and politics.[108] The parallels of Arai's ideas to these were likely the result of his close study of art history and theory, but they also echoed contemporary investigations into psychological and mystical experience in painting and letters in Mexico and abroad. By seeking to shape a theory of modern national architecture with reference to pre-Columbian architectural history, Arai brought together two dominant strands of twentieth-century Mexican visual culture and proposed new ways of approaching both. Against Arai's vision, Villagrán's celebrated modification of the Vitruvian triad to become quatrapodal—with the addition of the category of the "social" as a means of localizing and modernizing rationalism—and the

FIGURE 5.20. Reproduction of a Maya fresco at Bonampak, 1949.

government's staging of traditional dances and promotion of folk art seemed somewhat tepid interventions into the question of modernizing indigenous forms. But it was nevertheless descended from both of these projects of the 1920s and related to more recent developments in art and archaeology, as well as to Arai's own, very personal experience of seeing Maya buildings.

In 1949 Arai participated in an expedition to the recently uncovered Maya temples at Bonampak, deep in the Yucatán jungle, where he made drawings of the buildings and site and wrote an essay in which he interpreted Maya architecture and explored many of the ideas that he refined and published in "Paths" three years later.[109] Although other

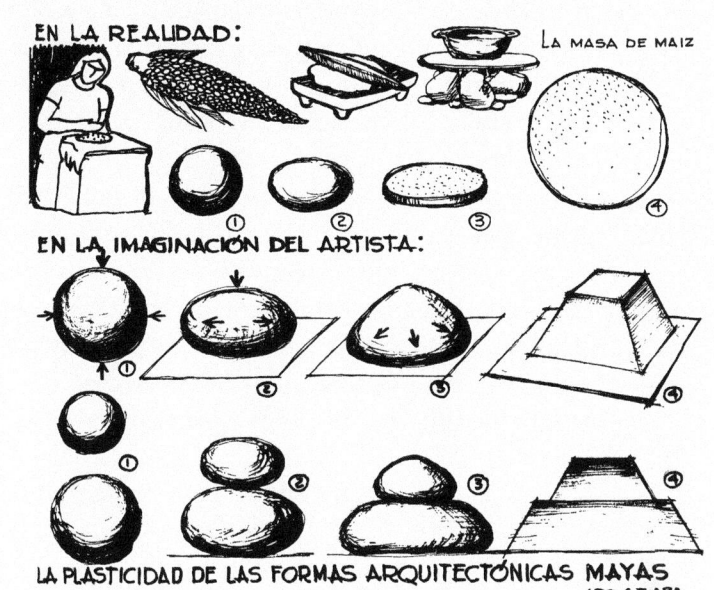

FIGURE 5.21. Arai, *La plasticidad de las formas arquitectónicas Mayas*, 1949.

Maya sites were more impressive architecturally and urbanistically, Bonampak had the best-preserved and most extraordinary murals in all of preconquest Mexico (figure 5.20). Like others then and since, Arai marveled at the realism of the figures, and the murals' "dynamism, composition, drawing, color, vitality and fluidity."[110] The Bonampak figures' activities were easy for modern outsiders to identify, but they were rooted in a cultural experience and region very different from those of the cities from which those viewers came; they brought the Maya—as individuals and a culture—vividly to life.

At Bonampak, Arai also found evidence that, like modern architects, the Maya prized formal rigor, linear clarity, and plasticity, and were concerned with the relationship of the figure to space. He suggested that these characteristics were also found in ancient temples, the most "Mexican" buildings. First in his Bonampak essay and then in "Paths," he proposed a theory of the origin of those temples that related them to perhaps the preeminent symbol of Mexican culture and to the modernist emphasis on geometry and pure form. According to Arai, the pre-Columbian pyramid, with its platforms and sloped walls, began with the tortilla and with the architect's experience as a child of watching his mother shape masa into spheres and then flatten them into circular forms to be cooked. The transformation of masa into architecture was not literal, of course, but imaginative. Arai claimed that the making of tortillas was "represented mentally in the conscience of the artist, reproduced and revived,"[111] and made it possible for him to conceive the form of the pyramid abstractly, picturing the formal transformation of a sphere into a trapezoid. Smaller spheres might be stacked atop larger ones to create the successively smaller forms in stepped pyramids. Arai illustrated this process in a diagram titled *La plasticidad de las formas arquitectónicas Mayas*, which he published in his own book on Bonampak (figure 5.21). The architect's creation myth centered on materiality, seeing, and subjective experience and he wrote that the "artistic will of the adult sculptor came to have its roots in . . . retrospective sentiment" and that "the seed of this primary emotion took shape in a material, became fixed, truly impressed on the infant soul when the eyes of the child saw the daily making of tortillas."[112]

URBANISM AND ALIENATION

For Arai Maya temples were defined by materiality, mass, and, especially by the sloping walls that gave ancient pyramids and ball courts their distinctive profiles, and he traced all these characteristics to the ephemeral form created during the flattening of the masa. Although it began in the kitchen, the ultimate work of these talud walls, Arai argued in "Paths," was to shape urban form and "soften the contrast between the work of architecture and the landscape."[113] For him the inclined plane embodied the fusion of the utilitarian and the artistic and it served to shape civic space. It supplied the rudimentary form from which were carved the stairs that connected the earth and elevated platforms, and which could be used as grandstands. The sloping wall could "differentiate" and "separate spaces at the same time that it unite[d] and connect[ed] them, establishing distinctions between constructive masses of different dimensions at the same time including them in a total conception."[114] Arai imagined the talud wall doing no less than unifying the many opposites that he identified throughout "Paths." The description of its work echoed his desire to dissolve the distinctions between "functionalism" and "historicism" and the gap between preconquest and western architecture. Rooted in the making of the tortilla, the inclined plane in Arai's interpretation also contained the Vitruvian triad with Villagrán's addition: utility, structure, and art, for the shaping of civic life. In his ambition to write a unified theory of architecture that preserved a place for Mexican exceptionalism Arai was like the other architects and the patrons of the Ciudad Universitaria who hoped it would embody universal values and national achievement.

FIGURE 5.22. Way of the Dead, looking toward the Pyramid of the Sun, Teotihuacan.

If the campus materialized these things, like the courts, it also presented modern Mexicans with a wholly new spatial and, potentially, psychological experience. The giant plazas and buildings dwarfed human beings and left them exposed to the elements—not in the ruins of a preconquest city, but in the midst of a very modern university. Countless photographs of the campus taken after the university opened showed tiny human figures often isolated in the university's vast spaces and against its enormous buildings, and captured the potentially disorienting and uneasy encounter with modernist space for a lone subject who beholds architecture and landscape in isolation. In "Paths" Arai grafted a similar kind of psychological experience onto preconquest people when he imagined what occupying pre-Columbian space was like for them (figure 5.22). He wrote of an early city in which

all is empty and the nudity of the mountains purified by geometric lines dwarfs the human being . . . the inhabitant becomes agitated . . . and . . . his thoughts become confused and complicated. Internal experiences are born bubbling out of control, as if overflowing a dark, deep well of conscience, trying to fill in, to overpoweringly inundate with their capricious images and confusing sentiments the large arid, bare surfaces. A fear of solitude overcomes the indigenous soul to situate the man in those interminable amphitheaters, making him unconsciously obligated to become saturated with himself first, his psychological content, in order to saturate later, to the furthest corner of the plazas and terraces with his unreal, fantastic visions. . . . The house of man is based upon humanized volcanoes, hills, abysses, and canyons, each after the other replicating nature.[115]

Arai's vision closely paralleled 1940s interpretations of Velasco's canvases. Perhaps perceiving from afar that students might have experiences in their new university like that which Arai imagined, in 1958 the editor of *Architectural Forum* sent photographer Wallace Litwin to the CU just to "find out how students were adjusting to their monumental surroundings,"[116] and to record images of the living, breathing embodiments of the state and the architects' experiment with forging new national subjects (figure 5.23). The students in Litwin's images appeared, the journal noted, "ant-sized" against the buildings and plazas, and in contrast to the colossal statue of Alemán.[117] Forging a new national architecture seemed to require identifying imaginatively with the experience of alienation and disorientation that Arai assumed indigenous viewers must have had when they contemplated vast spaces and tried to understand monumental natural forms beyond the buildings immediately in front of them. This was a far more nuanced, psychologically complicated way of nationalizing historical forms than his predecessors who had championed revival styles had proposed, and conceptually it differed considerably from the ways figurative imagery was used in mosaics on some of UNAM's most prominent buildings to "Mexicanize" International Style modernism.

In 1950, at the same time that Arai was developing his architectural theory and designing the ball courts, and just after Pani and del Moral had finalized the campus plan, Octavio Paz wrote his groundbreaking essay, "The Labyrinth of Solitude," in which he linked Mexican culture, alienation, and history and suggested that the experiences of difference and isolation, inflected though they may be by culture, were ultimately universal. Paz's equation of the individual and history,[118] his juxtaposition of Mexico and the United States, and his abiding interest in Mexican indigenous and folk traditions paralleled closely Arai's examination of these things. His famous discussion of the "Mexican mask" and the implication that the "real" Mexican lay concealed behind it echoed

FIGURE 5.23. Wallace Litwin, from "Mexico's Mammoth Campus," *Architectural Forum* (March 1958).

Arai's calls for viewers of ruins to search inside themselves to realize a more complete subjectivity and understand more profoundly their own culture. For both, although national character remained paramount, transcending it was a vital part of the project. Like Paz, Arai sought the universal through the particular and concluded "Paths" with a vision of a world made "unified and organic by its heterogeneity and mestizaje." This would be an "interregional world capable of transcending undifferentiated and monotone cosmopolitanism."[119] Paz too explored issues of subjectivity, space, form, and representation in relation to Mexican culture.[120] The parallel contributions of the writer and the architect to multidisciplinary debates about the nation, the individual, and the role of the arts suggest the continuity of the tradition of Acevedo and the

Mariscal brothers who, through their membership in the Ateneo de Juventud and their association with early twentieth-century thinkers in that group helped make architecture an important topic in larger debates about Mexican arts, letters, and culture. Formally and theoretically Arai bridged a widening gap in Mexican art as abstraction and other conventionally international vocabularies began to challenge the hegemony of figuration and the canonically "Mexican" subjects and idioms of muralism. By recasting pre-Columbian forms in modern terms and experiences, Arai participated in a broader mid-century re-presentation of the titanic legacy of national art and cultural history in response to a strengthening imperative to resist reprovincializing Mexican art and architecture, as muralism and the International Style ran their courses.[121]

By theorizing Mexican architecture in relation to private experience—even as he worked for the government—and affirming the importance of history abstractly, Arai expanded the bounds of what Mexican architecture might be and do. Representation and history for him were far more abstract than they were for O'Gorman and Rivera, and despite sharing the ambition to resuscitate the pre-Columbian past as a source of architectural inspiration, the UNAM fronton courts, lacking the figuration that the Central Library and National Stadium had, differed dramatically from them. In their abstraction they were uniquely capable of standing with the most cutting-edge experiments in Latin American abstract art *and* were profoundly grounded historically. Arai's texts, the campus's monumental and potentially alienating exterior spaces, and major new interpretations of Velasco's landscapes centralized the bodily, psychological, and even metaphysical experiences of the viewer in new ways in twentieth-century Mexico.

Unexpectedly perhaps, Arai's turn toward abstraction and the realm of the private and personal in dialogue with history had its most important parallel in the new work of the man who was to become more strongly associated with Mexican modern architecture than anyone else. Less than a mile from the new campus, but invisible from it, the first residents had moved into Luis Barragán's Gardens of El Pedregal, the extraordinary work of landscape architecture and private development that made his career and fortune. But it was ultimately the houses he designed, and especially his own, far from the campus, that defined a new direction in Mexican architecture, and seemed, with UNAM, to confirm the maturation of a modern national architecture, even as they revealed the fragility and tenuousness of the concept.

CHAPTER SIX

ALONE IN HISTORY

LUIS BARRAGÁN'S "MEXICAN" HOUSE

While Mario Pani and Enrique del Moral drafted the initial plan for the Ciudad Universitaria and Alberto Arai began to contemplate the modern experience of encountering pre-Hispanic buildings, Luis Barragán designed a house for himself that, at first glance, seemed to have little in common with UNAM and nothing at all to do with Arai's work. Yet both the campus and the Barragán house became icons of twentieth-century architecture and, for all their differences, showed the enduring importance of Mexican architectural history to the country's foremost architects, and their deepening investigations of the relationships among landscape, the self, and national character.

Today, outside of Mexico, and to a lesser extent within it, the buildings of Luis Barragán are nearly synonymous with "Mexican" architecture. He is the only Mexican and one of four Latin Americans to have won the Pritzker Prize (1980), although he designed relatively little. He is the only Mexican architect whose work has been the exclusive subject of an exhibition at the Museum of Modern Art in New York (MoMA), and as recently as 2014, the *New York Times* practically equated him with Mexico City itself.[1] The house he built for himself in 1947 is a UNESCO World Heritage Site, and countless photographs and discussions of his famously colorful houses with their red, pink, blue, and yellow walls appear on tourists' blogs and in glossy popular books. Little more than passing familiarity with Barragán is required to know that his modern buildings, like the others in this study, were shaped by their architect's interests in Mexican architectural history and popular art. They were also, like the other works in this book, informed by

knowledge of modern design in Europe. But whereas his colleagues designed buildings for public purposes with the ambition that they enter
an impressive national canon, Barragán used abstractions of historical
and vernacular architectures and folk art to create spaces for private
life and to shield himself from what he experienced as the invasive eyes
of others and the disquieting changes to urban life that accompanied
Mexico's mid-century economic and industrial expansion.

In many ways Barragán is perfect for an international canon of
modern architecture: Like Le Corbusier, Ludwig Mies der Rohe, and
Frank Lloyd Wright, many of his important works were houses or
religious buildings. His roof terraces, attention to materials, clear geometries, avoidance of ornament, and asymmetrical facades made his
architecture easy to place in a narrative that even today often treats
"modern architecture" and "International Style" as synonyms. Indeed,
Barragán's architecture has proved considerably more attractive to
canonizers than, for example, the glamorous boxy, glassy houses designed by his less appreciated contemporary Francisco Artigas for other wealthy Mexico City residents in the 1950s and 1960s. Lacking large
expanses of bright color, these buildings were perhaps not Mexican
enough for international audiences. Time and again critics and historians have praised Barragán for integrating elements of modernism
with forms that awaken associations with haciendas, rural vernacular
houses, and colonial churches, and the architect himself repeatedly
cited his recollections and admiration of these things in explaining
his architecture.[2] His use of "Mexican" materials like volcanic stone in
flooring, his regularized vigas, and large brightly painted stucco walls
have been interpreted widely as evidence of yet another, and perhaps
the quintessential, "Mexicanization" of architectural modernism.

Like the other architects examined here, Barragán was deeply interested in and influenced by painting, and he was obsessed with wall surfaces. In his later works, most significantly his own house in the Mexico
City neighborhood of Tacubaya, he used painted interior walls to create
the illusion of spatial expansion or contraction, provoke emotion, and
stimulate feelings of liberation or encourage certain behaviors. The
ways facades could be made to disappear and make those who dwelt
behind them disappear as well captivated him. Writing of the Tacubaya
house in 1955, Henry-Russell Hitchcock observed that it "has, in effect,
no exterior. The almost blank street façade is hardly distinguishable
from its older neighbors" (figure 6.1).[3] Indeed, the studied nonchalance
of exteriors that disappeared into historical (and sometimes only seemingly historical) streets made Barragán at least as fully a facadist as

FIGURE 6.1. Luis Barragán, Barragán House (at Calle Francisco Ramírez 14), Tacubaya, Mexico City, 1947.

any of his colleagues. Easy to miss, and seemingly easy to ignore, his facades concealed the rooms that were his most lasting contributions to Mexican architecture. Barragán defined "room" broadly—it included conventional kinds of rooms, like living rooms and bedrooms, but also terraces and gardens hidden behind high walls. In the same years that Arai formulated theories of history, space, and subjectivity that were predicated on meditative engagement with the unknown and the other, Barragán created an architecture of the interior concerned with what could not be seen and therefore not known. Although he has often been portrayed as a singular figure who was largely unconnected to the currents of Mexican architectural modernism, in his most important works Barragán investigated the themes of alienation and distance that underpinned the Ciudad Universitaria and, like his colleagues, selectively abstracted and reinterpreted images and forms from a variety of sources to shape buildings that—despite his own statements to the contrary—many have read as nationally specific.[4]

Whether he intended it or not, his profoundly visual architecture, in its persistent engagement with occlusion and revelation, his representation of himself and his work, and the extraordinary reception he had as quintessentially "Mexican"—particularly outside of Mexico—laid bare the essential paradox of the project of creating a modern, nationally distinctive architecture that had consumed architects since the beginning of the century. In 1975, near the end of his career, and at the moment of his canonization internationally in the MoMA exhibition, in response to the Mexican poet and critic Elena Poniatowska's question, "Is there an essentially Mexican architecture?" he replied: "No. Definitively no; I do not believe there is."[5] Emphatically rejecting the assumption that had guided most of his colleagues' work, Barragán distanced himself from them and resisted having his buildings classified according to a term that was potentially confining and often vague. In doing so, he created rhetorical space to reconsider the relationship between national distinctiveness and architectural history and challenged the intellectual structure that had defined architectural practice in Mexico since the beginning of the century.

Analyzing Barragán's buildings demands a somewhat different approach than the one I have taken throughout this book. Writing about houses almost always means writing about private lives, and in Barragán's case doing so is particularly tempting. He was his own client in his most important design (and quite selective in his choice of clients in other commissions), and he claimed that his architecture was autobiographical.[6] Throughout his career he skillfully promoted his buildings, carefully crafted his image, and had his work widely published abroad.[7] The textual documentation of Barragán's architecture and approach—articles in the mainstream and architectural presses, interviews, his notes and letters, and the brief speech he gave when he accepted the Pritzker Prize—constitutes one of his most important engagements with representation, one of the themes I have argued is central to Mexican modernism.[8] In these venues, and for much of his life, Barragán wove the tensions between the interior and the exterior, between what is actually seen and what is not revealed, that his own house embodied. Thus, to understand his architecture these materials must be read critically, as one would a building, and in tandem with his designs.[9]

The houses and the texts—with their many references to "mystery," "silence," and "magic," words that imply absence, the unknown, the unseen, or the unspoken—tantalize and distance the viewer/reader at once. Although they superficially recall statements by other architects, such as Enrique del Moral's in his interpretation of plastic integration in eighteenth-century vernacular churches, or Juan O'Gorman's in his assessment of Velasco's canvases, when used in reference to the interiors of houses, they suggest different meanings altogether. Barragán's "silence," "mystery," and "magic" were intensely private and personal, and in that sense dramatically different from when they were describing works of "national" art. His usages conjured the idea of the uncanny that was so strongly associated with surrealism, which he greatly admired, and conveyed a desire to manipulate the visible and the known that was rooted, it seems, in some deep underlying discomfort. The architect, Barragán believed, should be "an artist who attempts to remove anxiety and create illusions."[10]

Many scholars have documented and interpreted Barragán's buildings and life.[11] They have drawn attention to themes of solitude, surrealism, religion, and equestrianism in his work, and the importance to his architecture of representation and the other arts, as well as its scenographic qualities.[12] They have also helped locate it in broader histories of modernism, particularly his connections to Richard Neutra and Louis Kahn, his buildings' similarities to some by Adolf Loos, and to work by architects concerned with regional expression and landscape architecture.[13] Antonio Riggen Martínez has interpreted Barragán's consciously distancing statements in terms of Mexican culture. He observed that "as a good Mexican, Barragán knew the art of disguise; behind his cautious expressions was a meticulous, astute, calculating man. He rarely spoke, not because of false modesty or modest academic preparation."[14] My reading of Barragán builds and relies on much of this research. It also demonstrates, by illuminating some of the less closely studied aspects of the historical context in which Barragán worked, both how many continuities his work had with the history of Mexican modern architecture and how distinctive his designs were.

OUTSIDE AND IN

Like his built work, Barragán's position in the architectural profession in Mexico City, relative to his colleagues', was characterized by ambiguity. Unlike most of them, he grew up entirely in provincial Mexico and divided his time mostly between his family's hacienda in Mazamitla, Jalisco, and Guadalajara, Mexico's second city. As a young man he was neither steeped in the rhetoric of revolutionary social reform nor trained in the National School of Fine Arts, and instead studied to be an engineer in Guadalajara. For twenty months he lived in Europe, before he ever spent significant time in Mexico City. A devout Catholic in an era of cultural anticlericalism and reform, he made no apologies for his faith or his social views. He was the architect primarily of houses for the rich, and became wealthy himself through real estate development while nearly all the other protagonists of twentieth-century Mexican architecture depended for their livelihoods on major public commissions that served public health, housing, education needs, or the expanding federal bureaucracy.

As early as 1951 colleagues and critics remarked on Barragán's insider/outsider status in the profession, and, perhaps unintentionally, frequently differentiated him from an unspecified norm.[15] Often laced with critique, the assessments by architects most strongly associated with Mexican "functionalism" often implied that Barragán's work was neither sufficiently architectural nor political. In its tone and content José Villagrán García's was one of the harshest:

> The architecture of our good friend Barragán has a decorative value. It has a high value, though its basic intention is not completely contemporary. In other words, it disintegrates the architectonic, which explains why, when plastic artists (and not architects) evaluate his work, they recognize it as being highly artistic and do not understand why it is considered not completely architectonic. They should bear in mind that architecture is impure art, that among its values are the useful, hierarchically inferior to the aesthetic, and the social, which is superior, and that when someone sacrifices one or the other or both of those values partially or totally, the work's plastic value is that of scenery or decoration and not authentic architecture.[16]

Written as the UNAM was being built, and at the moment that "true" modernism was being defined in Mexico as the structurally and formally rationalist, socially engaged kind that Villagrán pioneered, his words about Barragán narrowed more decisively what Mexican modernism could be than did any of the new essays and exhibitions on Mexican contemporary architecture, and denied the flexibility that had characterized definitions of Mexican architecture since 1900. His categorization of Barragán's architecture as "decorative" and scenic was particularly searing because it rhetorically positioned Barragán outside the parameters of international and Villagránian modernism. "Decorative" conjured excess and femininity, while the numerous references to scenography (Villagrán's was one of many) and drama were suggestive of artifice and concealment. Villagrán's description also implicitly brushed aside the important place long accorded to the other arts and to Churrigueresque architecture, which had also been called "decorative," in histories of Mexican architecture. With his parallel implication that artists could not evaluate architecture, and the claim that Barragán's work was not entirely up-to-date, Villagrán, the most esteemed architect in Mexico at that time, relegated both Barragán and the other arts to second-class status.

The next year, Enrique Yañez, then the head of the Architecture Department of the National Institute of Fine Arts, echoed Villagrán's assessment, although in somewhat gentler and more magnanimous terms, in his introduction to I. E. Myers's book, *Mexico's Modern Architecture*: "Because of his ever-widening influence on contemporary works, especially [the] middle class residence, Luis Barragán must be cited. Through his own singular path, with great sensitivity and a profound recollection of provincial images, he has carried out unusual work, restrained, sound and austere, although perhaps at times bordering on scenic decorativism through a preoccupation with landscape design."[17]

"Singular," "sensitive," "provincial" buildings could hardly have been less like the collaboratively designed, assertive, "national" campus of the university, just as "unusual" architecture inspired by "recollection" seemed wholly unlike rationalist slabs clad in images drawn from a codified cultural iconography. Yañez's assessment distanced Barragán from mainstream Mexican architectural culture yet, unlike Villagrán's, acknowledged that he was contributing something lasting and worthwhile to the profession. Barragán's insider/outsider status within mid-century Mexican architectural culture was something that he himself remarked on, as Emilio Ambasz noted when he wrote that for Barragán architecture was "a lonely road, but as he confesses, it is only among architects that he feels himself to be a stranger."[18] The spatial and visual parallels to his professional experience manifest in his house, where he presented the dynamics of estrangement—of connection implied and denied—repeatedly in its rooms, using elements that invited and distanced the viewer.

Yañez's mention of Barragán's "own singular path" was both accurate and misleading. In some ways Barragán's career had followed the general outlines of Mexican architecture since the 1920s, and at times read as a magnified version of it. His earliest works were houses for members of the Guadalajara elite, most notably Efraín González Luna, that evoked, but did not copy, colonial buildings in their use of roof tile, pronounced arches, patios, and turned wooden balustrades. In the 1930s Barragán moved to Mexico City and designed speculative International Style apartment buildings. And, beginning in the 1940s, he created Mexico's most important new residential subdivision near the

Ciudad Universitaria, the Gardens of El Pedregal, where he and other architects designed freestanding modern houses set in private gardens and helped introduce the Anglo-American typology of the detached suburban house to Mexico. Barragán, like many others, was captivated by the rugged beauty of the volcanic landscape and influenced by Dr. Atl's paintings of and writings about it.[19]

On the other hand, his influences and the processes by which he arrived at his designs were very different from those of most of his colleagues. Like O'Gorman and del Moral, Barragán had considerable firsthand knowledge of provincial colonial and vernacular architecture from his youth. But some of his most significant contact with it was at his family's hacienda in rural Jalisco, rather than in an urban center like Guanajuato. From the perspective of most of his Mexico City colleagues, the value of whatever special knowledge he had of the particularities of hacienda architecture would have been eclipsed by the symbolic weight this type carried in many Mexicans' imaginations of the colonial past. For ideologically committed leftists like O'Gorman, Yañez, and Villagrán, no building type so thoroughly represented unqualified colonial oppression and the continued abuses of indigenous Mexicans before the revolution. Other differences concerned his training. Having studied engineering, Barragán lacked in his formal education an exposure to the principles and methods of Beaux-Arts design that shaped the work of almost all other architects in Mexico City. This probably explains his comparatively minimal interest in plan and the few references to classicism in his buildings. However, whether instinctively or through training, like architects steeped in Beaux-Arts principles, Barragán often pieced together designs using elements that were borrowed or abstracted from other works. In the 1920s and 1930s, while most of his colleagues learned about European developments only or primarily through the relatively few foreign journals that made it to Mexico and the somewhat haphazard reporting on new architecture in Mexican sources, Barragán saw many buildings firsthand. Indeed, his first two trips to Europe, the first from mid-1924 to late 1925, when he visited France, Spain, Greece, and Italy, and a much shorter one during the summer of 1931, decisively influenced the course of his career.

THE LESSONS OF FRANCE

Barragán's most significant discovery on the first trip was the work of French landscape designer and writer Ferdinand Bac, who designed the Gardens of Les Colombières in Menton, France, in 1925. Color plates dated 1921 that illustrated Bac's book, *Jardins enchantés* (1925), helped awaken Barragán's lifelong passion for garden design, likely informed his approach to architectural drawing, and supplied some of the forms and elements that appeared in major works throughout his career.[20] Bac's idealized, romantic vignettes of secluded courtyards composed of generalized Mediterranean forms appealed to Barragán tremendously. The French designer tempered the severity of his blocky, stucco masses with broad arches that opened onto patios with hanging and potted plants, fountains, painted tile, wrought iron, and gridded wooden gates and fences with turned balusters. Bac's walls were sometimes pink; his fences were red; and the ceiling of one of his rooms was blue. Traces of Renaissance and Islamic architecture were legible in capitals, screened lookouts, and fenestration patterns, and strong central axes defined many of his gardens. Traveling in the Mediterranean around the same time that he read the book, Barragán surely appreciated Bac's abstractions of regional forms, but looking with Mexican eyes he would also have seen in the drawings much that reminded him of colonial Mexican architecture, indebted as it was to some of the same sources that Bac quoted. In the patio adjacent to the "Tower of the Caliph" (figure 6.2), he would have seen a space like that of so many colonial Mexican cloisters. The "Red Gate" (plate 15) combined a simple arched gateway, vivid colors, strong geometries, and restrained classical elements in an arrangement that may have suggested colonial atrios, and informed some of the architect's iconic compositions years later.

Bac designed his gardens at exactly the same time that Carlos Obregón Santacilia was developing his spare abstractions of Mexican colonial buildings and Roberto Montenegro had begun to transform the colonial church into a pictorial type in the painted tiles in the former convent of San Pedro y Pablo. Striking formal similarities existed between many of the illustrations in *Jardins enchantés* and Obregón Santacilia's Benito Juarez School. Barragán may have been entirely unaware of his Mexican colleague's work when he encountered Bac's, but both architects' early oeuvres were defined by their painterly manipulations of architectural elements arranged to create facades that evoked but did not copy generalized historical types. Unlike other young Mexicans, in his study of Bac's designs, Barragán encountered such forms removed entirely from the political and social concerns of the postrevolutionary period. Not charged with the reformist, nationalist ambitions that swirled around Mexican architecture, this architecture would not have read to the young Barragán as nationally particular, and he would have seen in it much that was familiar and relevant to the

FIGURE 6.2. Ferdinand Bac, "Tower of the Caliph," from *Jardins enchantés*, 1921.

creation of a modern architecture informed by historical precedents with Mediterranean antecedents.

The influence of the drawings first appeared vividly in Barragán's design for the González Luna House in Guadalajara of 1929–30 (figure 6.3). Here he used a broad arch, tile roof, and an elevated garden lookout to define the main mass that opened onto a patio. Elsewhere, in an arrangement that called to mind Bac's drawing of the Caliph's Court, a blocky tower rose behind a one-story arcade that was supported by a pair of large arches and opened onto a patio with a rectangular

FIGURE 6.3. Barragán, Efraín González Luna House, Guadalajara, Mexico, 1929–30.

pool. For a gate that framed five, rail-less steps he reworked elements from the "Red Gate." Inside were turned wooden balusters of the kind that framed Bac's fountains on the railings of balconies and stairs and carved wooden doors that recalled Mexican colonial precedents and resembled one in Bac's "Sultan's Bath." In later buildings, Barragán used broad, low, rail-less stairs very similar to the ones in the "Court of the Spanish Romances," and the heavy, wooden grids in his Capuchin Monastery of 1953–60 first appeared in the "Red Gate," "The Port des Ibis Blancs," and other plates. Although he consistently cited the influence of Mexican antiquarian Chucho Reyes in the development of his use of color, Barragán certainly saw examples of brightly painted walls used with white ones in *Jardins enchantés*. His facility with color was already evident in the Park of the Revolution in Guadalajara, designed in 1934, before he met Reyes sometime around 1940. Commenting on his "clever use of color" in this playground, Esther Born characterized Barragán and his work in terms that foreshadowed Yañez's when she noted that he, "of all the younger group, has been most successful in his imaginative use of color in modern architecture. His naturally sensitive aesthetic perceptions have never found satisfaction in restriction to the palette popularly associated with the 'international style.'"[21]

That Barragán's buildings, seemingly so indebted to Mexican precedents, resembled illustrations by an ultimately rather minor French designer underscores not only the similarly selective approach to design that Barragán shared with Mexican architects who had more exposure to Beaux-Arts methods but also demonstrates just how tenuous claims to national specificity in architecture were in Mexico. The architect may well have had Bac's influence in mind when he declared that there was no Mexican architecture. Indeed, in that conversation he went on to say that "popular architecture, which I so love, came to us from the Mediterranean; the colonial came to us definitively from Spain, and we remain outside of the pre-Columbian [because] we are not pre-Columbians."[22] Barragán's explanation of influences revealed his deep appreciation of the historical transmission and modification of architectural forms, something of which historians of the Churrigueresque were keenly aware. But in denying the possibility of a connection to pre-Columbian cultures and that pre-Columbian architecture was "Mexican," he pointedly rejected long-standing claims about the centrality of indigenous influence in postconquest architecture and the revival of interest in it as a source for mid-century design.

The other major discovery of his European travels came in 1931, when his understanding of Le Corbusier's work deepened. In 1925 the young architect had seen the Esprit Nouveau Pavilion at the Art Deco Exposition. Most significant for him in it was surely the double-height section, with the loft-like space above the living level. In 1931, however, he met Le Corbusier, saw the Villa Savoye, and visited the recently completed Paris apartment of Charles de Beistegui, which he had made a special effort to see.[23] De Beistegui was one of Europe's most famous bons vivants, who was known for his extraordinary art collection, the lavish, sumptuously decorated interiors of his houses, and his extravagant parties. He also had close connections to Mexico. Although de Beistegui grew up in Europe, his family had made its fortune in Mexican mining, agriculture, and real estate after immigrating to Mexico from the Basque region in the eighteenth century. The de Beisteguis left Mexico after the execution of Maximilian von Habsburg in 1867, but Barragán nevertheless referred to Charles de Beistegui as a "fellow countryman in Paris."[24] Le Corbusier's main contribution to de Beistegui's apartment on the Champs-Élysées was the "surrealist" roof terrace, with its high walls that cut off the view to all but the top of the Arc de Triomphe, and the small lookout reached through a narrow opening at the top of a "floating" staircase. Here Barragán first saw an example of the sophisticated play of occlusion and revelation he would later develop. On de Beistegui's roof Le Corbusier wittily manipulated the principles of the *promenade architecturale* to create uncanny effects (figure 6.7). But fifteen years passed before specific elements from the de Beistegui roof appeared in Barragán's work. The more immediate effect of his contact with Le Corbusier and international modernism was evident in the apartment buildings he designed in Mexico City shortly after he moved there in 1935, and in his proclamation in 1932, after having spent time in the capital, that the "marrow of the modern is science and industry" and that "the lessons of our ancients" should be studied.[25]

The limitations of Bac's historicism and of axial symmetry apparently also became clear to Barragán at this point, but most important, being in Mexico City awakened a new interest in the dynamics of public and private life, and the possibility of disappearing from view that the de Beistegui roof must have suggested. Reflecting on the inappropriateness of Bac's work for the modern age, Barragán wrote, "when I chatted with Bac I understood his fear of our times and why he sought refuge in the lap of the beauty of yesterday. . . . Bac made things that are very beautiful, but not in harmony with the spirit of today."[26] These reflections came in the middle of notes written in 1932 on Mexico City, which he found entirely unlike Guadalajara, and extremely liberating. He wrote:

> I have traveled to the capital. . . . In the center is the future of this country. Guadalajara continues to be a little girl that doesn't want to grow up.
>
> The vigor of the center seduces me. The speed at which things happen, the smell of the new, the sensation of being "truly" alive. There I am a don nobody, but nobody asks and nobody wants to know about the life of everyone else. That is protection, being nobody makes me free to be. There, there are very smart, capable and hardworking people who offer me the air that I lack.[27]

In Mexico City Barragán began to equate modernity, anonymity, security, and liberation. He found in the city's pace and its people a world that offered possibilities far greater than any he had in Jalisco and that

FIGURE 6.4. Barragán, Duplex on Avenida México, Mexico City, 1934.

seemed to provide "breathing room." For ten years he too worked hard in the capital, developing real estate and designing buildings, like the duplex on Avenida México in the new Hipódromo neighborhood (figure 6.4) and the apartment buildings in Colonia Cuauhtémoc (designed with José Criexell), that were as modern as anything else in Mexico City, and that, in their similarities to other new buildings by O'Gorman, Yañez, and Villagrán, allowed him to disappear into the capital's architectural culture. In 1937, when Born came to survey the new architecture, Barragán's Speculation House and Avenida México buildings were just two of the many works she photographed. They merited little discussion and she placed them between José Villagrán García's own house and Juan Legarreta's workers' housing—buildings by architects who, in their belief in architecture's political and social duties, could not have been less like Barragán or more central to the narrative of Mexican modernism from which he was soon cast out.[28]

DWELLING ALONE

In 1947 Barragán designed the "exterior-less" house at 14 Francisco Ramírez Street in the neighborhood of Tacubaya that set the tone for the rest of his work and ultimately transformed Mexican architecture. The house was the second he designed on Francisco Ramírez. The first, created in 1940–43, included some of the elements he used in the 1947 house, and one of the first four significant gardens he designed.[29] The house at number 14 was originally intended for Luz Escandón de R. Valenzuela, but after the commission collapsed, and before any construction began, Barragán modified the design for his own use and acquired the property next door at number 12, where he built his studio. He then sold the first house. Unlike the houses that Barragán and Max Cetto proposed for the Gardens of El Pedregal in 1948–49, which were set in their own large lots in a model that resembled suburban houses in the United States, Barragán's buildings in Tacubaya were more like townhouses. Here, lots were deep and relatively narrow, the buildings came directly to the sidewalk, and shared walls with the adjacent structures.

He modified the house at number 14 repeatedly after he moved in, but most of the main elements were in place in a presentation drawing from 1947 or 1948 (figure 6.5). Barragán's design called for a three-story house with roof terraces on the second and third floors, and a large garden behind the building on the ground floor. In it the plane of the facade was interrupted only by two garage doors, a narrow main door, and three square windows—a very large one that allowed light into the library and two tiny ones, for the small bathroom on the ground floor and the upper-level loft. In the fenestration pattern of the facade somewhat recalled Bac's schemes, but in its greater austerity it called to mind Adolf Loos's early houses. Inside he projected a large, double-height living room and library that ran the entire depth of the building. A large, square window at the back of the living room provided views of the garden. On the ground floor was a dining room that looked onto the back garden, as well as a kitchen. He placed two bedrooms on the second floor at the back of the house, and designed a high-walled terrace with a square fountain and a mezzanine space

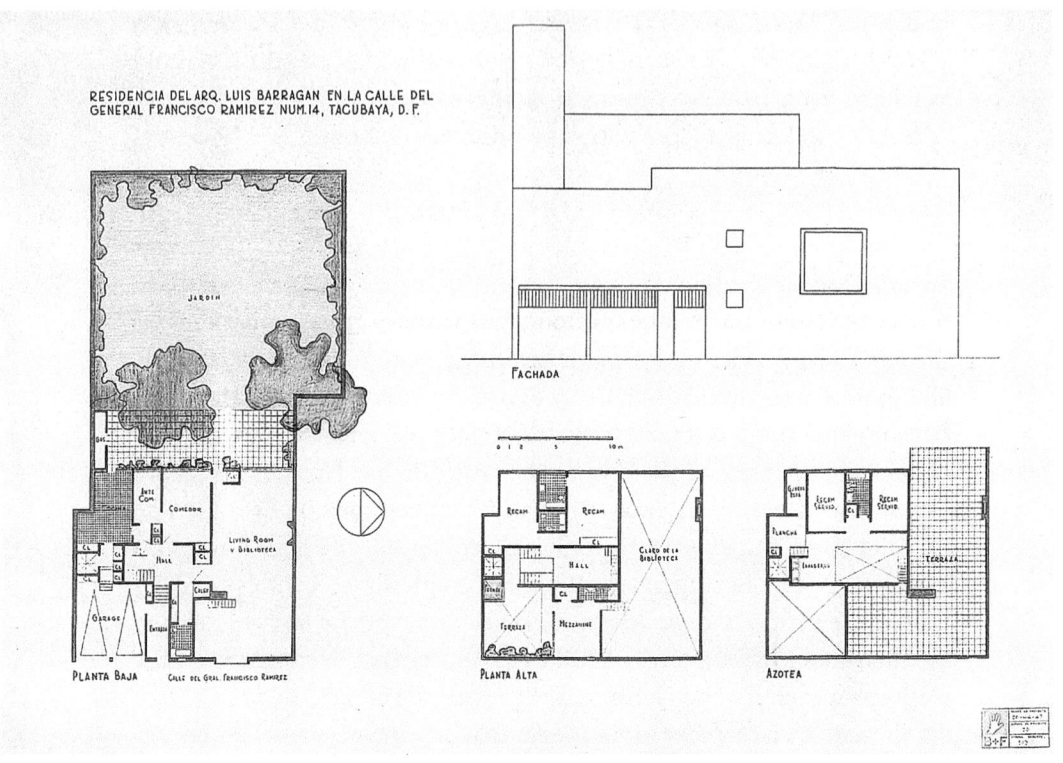

FIGURE 6.5. Barragán, Barragán House, early presentation drawing, 1947–48.

with unspecified use at the front. Servants were amply provided for—a smaller dining room separated the main one from the kitchen, and two small bedrooms on the upper floor were designated for household help. A large L-shaped terrace, with very high walls was the main space of the third floor. In plan it echoed the living room–library and mezzanine spaces below. A hall at the core of the house that contained the main staircase acted as a buffer between public and private spaces. Although the large, open-plan living room–library, the spacious terrace, and enormous window onto the back garden suggest parallels with the great free-plan houses of high modernism, Barragán's house was in fact quite unlike, for example, Miesian designs in which spaces flowed into one another, or Le Corbusier's houses with smooth promenades intended to move viewers through space. Rather than creating a sequence of interconnected spaces, Barragán designed a collection of rooms, each with distinct characters, between which passage was carefully controlled.

The house was therefore perhaps best understood from the vantage of the visitor, whose movement the architect sought to regulate carefully. From the front door, he or she stepped into a narrow, windowless corridor, at the end of which were six steps that led to another door. Passing through the door at the end, the visitor entered the hall, in a sequence that vaguely recalled the passage in colonial palaces from the street through the *zaguán* into the arcade, which gave access to a central patio and the rest of the house. In Barragán's hall the eye was immediately caught by two bright pink walls—distillations and abstractions of the color of Mexican folk art—a rail-less staircase like that of Bac, and, rather unexpectedly positioned against one corner of the landing, Mathias Goertiz's shimmering, nearly reflective, yet actually deflecting, gold-leaf painting, *Metachromatic Message*, seemingly floating beneath a clerestory window (plate 16). Reading the space as one would a painting, the viewer looked to the lower right, opposite the Goeritz, and noted the cantilevered wooden telephone table, the simple chair of straw and wood (originally an equipal chair stood there),[30] and then, turning, discovered a profusion of closed doors. Standing in the middle of this second room of the house, on a floor paved with the volcanic, nearly black rock associated with indigenous Mexico and used by colonial architects to form the bases of eighteenth-century palaces, the visitor saw six doors, each with a small aluminum knob, no threshold, a narrow frame painted to blend visually with the wall surface, and, seemingly, no hinges (plate 17). Having been directed, even beckoned, down the narrow corridor from the front door, the visitor now stopped. He or she had no idea that the doors opened onto a bathroom, the dining room, another smaller dining space, the living room, onto the mezzanine on the landing, and a closet—the first of eighteen in the house, according to the 1947 plan. (Most other closets were themselves somewhat concealed in servant and private or semi-private spaces.) Seemingly designed to disappear into the wall and become part of its surface, the doors here embodied, in exaggerated and magnified form, the modernist interest in built-in furniture and storage, but the arrangement also deemphasized and discouraged passage and discovery. In addition, visitors were visually arrested by the painting on the landing. Having perceived the contrast between depth and flatness embodied in the *Metaphysical Message* and in the juxtaposition of saturated color and stark white on the walls, the viewer waited, having been let in, but now being emphatically kept out. Here began the house's dynamic of opening and closing, and of attraction and repulsion.

Having materialized in the vestibule, the potential tension inherent in the first moments of a new visitor's arrival, Barragán relieved it

FIGURE 6.6. Barragán, Barragán House, stairs from reading room to study, looking toward living room and garden. Photograph by Rene Burri.

momentarily in the transition to the large living room, entered through the door on the short wall of the hall. With its high ceiling, wood floors, and large picture window, this room seemed to open up and out. But the urge to control conveyed in the vestibule was also perceptible in this space, and is particularly evident in the history of the changes Barragán made to it. The living room was originally, and briefly, more spacious and light-filled. After living with it as a relatively open-plan space, the rather agoraphobic Barragán began to find its openness stifling. He put up the five-foot wall that now divides the living room from the library. Eventually he used screens and bookcases to further divide the space (figure 6.6).

More barriers went up elsewhere. He transformed the roof from a deck to an outdoor room, replacing a rather low wooden barrier with high, emphatically solid walls of the kind he loved, and that permitted views only of the sky. But from the beginning, Barragán experimented with walls and their absences to explore the play of revelation and

FIGURE 6.7. Le Corbusier, de Beistegui Apartment roof terrace, Paris, 1929–31. Photograph by Lucien Hervé.

occlusion, relationships between the inside and the outside, and to control the view and even the viewer. One of the house's most photographed elements was the rather precarious cantilevered stairs from

FIGURE 6.8. Barragán, Barragán House garden, looking toward living room. Photograph by Armando Salas Portugal.

the reading room to the loft-like study above. The study's character as neither fully public nor private was suggested by the wall that did not quite reach the ceiling, but was not low enough to permit seeing between the spaces. Here the architectural ensemble materialized the difficulty of moving between public and private space and echoed the play of solid and void created in the space between the living room and reading room. These rail-less stairs were steeper and narrower, and thus potentially more treacherous, than the ones in the vestibule. As recitations of the outdoor staircases on the roof terraces of the Barragán/Ortega house and the de Beistegui apartment that did not lead to rooms, they metaphorically likened ascent toward the un-

FIGURE 6.9. Barragán, Barragán House, guest bedroom.

known to ascent into the recesses of private residential life. The very narrow door at the top of these stairs and at the one that led to the roof terrace further suggested the difficulty, or even discomfort, of passing between different kinds of spaces.

Just as he built new and higher walls in his living space and on the roof, Barragán closed out the world in other ways as he lived in the house. Over time his hatred of glass and the direct view seems to have increased, and he partially covered the large window at the front of his house. In the main living space he placed long curtains not only on the inside but also on the outside of the giant picture window, and in the mid-1950s built walls on either side of it that prevented lateral viewing in or out (figure 6.8).[31] He also turned what had been a second-story terrace into a bedroom. Here, and in other bedrooms and his studio next door, were shutters to match the doors—planes of wood that could disappear into the wall or open entirely, or only from the top, emphatically closing out, or in, but expressing and assuring privacy far more emphatically than the louvered kind (figure 6.9).

PRIVACY, PUBLICITY, AND THE MEXICAN HOUSE

Barragán's desire for people to see his house was nearly as great as his desire for them not to see it. He repeatedly made the building publicly available through photography, first in architecture journals and books in Mexico, and ultimately in the MoMA show. The house attracted considerably more international attention than did residences by his Mexican colleagues.[32] In 1956 *Harper's Bazaar* hyperbolically proclaimed that Barragán was widely viewed as "the most important man in Mexico City" and inaccurately announced that "he has built just two houses in his life—and influenced thousands."[33] The magazine's feature was one of two it published on his house. The building also appeared in the *New York Times Magazine* in 1964, *Look* magazine, London *Vogue*, and *House Beautiful* in 1966. One of the main attractions, especially for foreign audiences, was the house's "Mexicanness," which they found primarily in its material, furnishings, decoration, and contradictions. One critic found the house "haughty . . . but provocative, warm, enticing."[34] Another claimed that it "wed up-to-the-minute comfort and luxury with ideas gleaned from typical Spanish design, executed in the simplest indigenous materials and brilliant interior color."[35] Many noted the influence of and references to provincial buildings and techniques. In the 1950s Hitchcock, remarking on Barragán's "highly personal talent," was impressed by the "visual drama" he created with "rudimentary means."[36] Calling the house "one of the outstanding examples of residence architecture in Mexico," I. E. Myers emphasized its "popular Mexican characteristics": color, pine beams on the ceilings of the living room and studio, indigenous textiles, and its "simplest furnishings" of wood and leather.[37] The architect's use of what Clive Bamford Smith called "primary and rustic" materials placed the house firmly in the tradition of using references to folk culture and through them implicitly suggesting a connection to the past. But as impressive as this apparently was, especially in a house that without historicist references seemed so modern, it was not particularly unusual.

Barragán's house was part of a building boom in modern private houses around 1950 (largely made possible by the economic growth associated with the "Mexican Miracle"), which he helped foment in the Gardens of El Pedregal. There and elsewhere in the city, modern architects created fully up-to-date buildings, many of which incorporated native rock and included folk art and wooden furniture. New houses were cataloged in the 1952 *Guide to Contemporary Architecture* and illustrated extensively in Myers's survey. The August 1951 issue of the

FIGURE 6.10. Enrique Yañez, Yañez House and Studio, 1941.

U.S. journal *Arts and Architecture* was devoted to new houses in Mexico and, in addition to Barragán's Tacubaya house, included a feature on the Gardens of El Pedregal and buildings by O'Gorman, del Moral, Cetto, and four other architects.

Many of the notable new works were designed by architects for themselves and some included materials and furnishings like those in Barragán's. Yañez decorated his own house (1941), which, from the outside, would have seemed at home in the Weissenhofsiedlung, with serapes, wooden chairs with woven leather seats and backs, and Mexican glass (figure 6.10). Architects' designs for themselves were considered so significant that in 1951 the National Institute of Fine Arts published a book on architects' own houses built between 1930 and 1950. Yañez introduced the volume raising the questions about national specificity and the durability of functionalism that attended so many discussions of architecture at the time. Differentiating "national" and "modern" architecture, he said, in the past twenty years, "there seems . . . to have evolved a truly Mexican architecture, modern and at the same time national."[38] Yañez also emphasized the importance of folk art and allusions to Mexican craft traditions, and his summation of the houses suggested that Barragán's was not so exceptional. Distinguishing 1930s "functionalist" buildings from more recent ones, Yañez identified "a more recent trend to incorporate a Mexican tradition whose essential characteristic is concern with the inner life of the building and a consequent lack of interest in the exterior."[39] Yañez went on to note that

> a new decorative sense is being applied to the use of our native materials, volcanic rocks, wood and brick rich in architectural qualities, texture, and color. . . .
>
> It is perhaps a sign of dissatisfaction with the national expression achieved in architecture alone that furniture, statues, clay figures, and other archeological pieces are often placed in the living rooms in an attempt to give them a Mexican character. In the same way folk art masks, textiles, and toys are brought together with modern furnishing in a logical and happy desire to unite tradition with the dictates of the new architecture. These are manifestations of a nostalgia that feels the need to combine with present-day conditions to form an artistic unity.[40]

In its seeming disinterest in the facade and the use of materials—volcanic rock used to pave the vestibule and main stairs, and wood for floors, ceiling beams, and some furniture, Barragán's house fit Yañez's description. The leather and wood frame equipal chair that originally stood at the telephone table in the vestibule, woven floor mats, and the leather-covered chairs that Barragán designed and used in the living room were additional allusions to provincial rusticity. Yañez characterized the decorative use of folk art and "archeological" objects and attention to the symbolic significance of materials in terms of "nostalgia," a word Barragán used repeatedly in descriptions of his own work. He implied that modern architecture needed to be "softened" with objects that may or may not have actually been old, but that, by virtue of being handmade, called the past to mind generally.

The impulse to bring the crisp lines and (seemingly) industrial materials of modernism together with folk art was well established by 1951 and represented long-standing attempts by artists, architects, and intellectuals to somehow unite provincial Mexico and the capital and reconcile the idea of the past with modern changes. One of the first examples of this kind of mixing was the house Juan O'Gorman designed for Frances Toor in the mid-1930s (figure 6.11). Toor was one of the most important chroniclers of Mexican folk art and customs, and she decorated her living room with textiles, a painted wooden chest, ce-

FIGURE 6.11. Juan O'Gorman, Frances Toor House, 1934. Photograph by Esther Born.

ramic figurines, bowls, and candelabra, and painted wooden furniture of the kind she documented in the journal she edited, *Mexican Folkways*. From the outside, the house resembled Le Corbusier's Maison Cook (1924), except that it was painted "deep blue" and "Venetian red," with metal railings and window frames painted vermilion. Barragán himself embodied the unification of Mexico City and the provinces, and by designing works most notable for their interiors and their rustic references he was able to, in yet another way, stand both inside and outside of Mexican architectural culture. Whether Yañez recognized it or not, the new attention to the interior connected modern buildings back to the major Mexican colonial types—cloisters and palaces that were centered on courtyards and emphatically closed to the street—potentially heightening their "Mexican" qualities, and to concerns of international modernism.[41] More specifically, an interior-focused architecture, however, made possible the use in buildings of more varied objects, such as textiles, papier-mâché, and lacquered wood—relatively fragile works of folk art or rare archaeological objects—that could not have been integrated into facades.

DISTILLATION AND DISCRIMINATION

Barragán's use of color and the references in the house to provincial culture were thus neither particularly new nor unusual. In 1943 *Arquitectura/México* even published an illustrated article on rebozos, the shawls woven and worn by Mexican women throughout the country. What distinguished Barragán's approach, however, was its abstraction, and the avoidance of much actual folk art. There were no toys, figurines, masks, draped serapes, candelabra, or chests. The textiles Myers noted were apparently limited to the simple off-white bedspreads that covered twin beds upstairs, and perhaps to table linens neatly stored in wooden furniture. Any ceramic dishware was put away in cabinets in the kitchen or dining room. Unlike Toor, Yañez, and countless others in Mexico, and despite his friendship with Reyes, who apparently loved such things, Barragán seems not to have collected or displayed objects associated with children, fantasy, or culinary activities. He chose instead objects that were useful—chairs, wastebaskets, bedcovers. Detached and abstracted from its original contexts on painted figures and brightly colored objects, Barragán's most important folk art reference appeared as color on the severe planes of his blank walls. Some years later, Esther McCoy observed Barragán's distinctive method of reconstituting associations with folk tradition in favor of the visual over the tactile when she noted that "there is nothing in his buildings to suggest a return to handcrafts. If the hand seems to have smoothed the plaster and the hand to have laid the stones on the floor . . . an eye aware of the history of architecture, and especially of Le Corbusier, has brought them together in something as international as it is purely Mexican."[42] This decontextualization of craft from the people to whom and villages where it was truly native continued in exaggerated form the appropriation of folk art begun by Montenegro and other artists and intellectuals in the 1920s.[43] But through abstraction Barragán also stripped folk art of its potentially political associations. Materials and color were no longer stand-ins for native or mixed-race people who were the subjects of a grand project of cultural integration, or the imagined beneficiaries of architecture. By emphasizing utilitarian rather than decorative objects, he made his work much more accessible to an audience accustomed to thinking of modernism as geometric, hard, useful, and urban, rather than curvaceous, soft, decorative, and rural.

The distinction Barragán made between his and dominant appropriations of folk culture was further underscored by the objects he did collect and display. At various points throughout the house he positioned painted wooden colonial statues of saints or the Virgin, crucifixes, and models of horses' heads. A wooden bookstand evocative of those used to support medieval choir books accented the living room. These ornamental references to colonial Catholicism and hacienda culture, along with the doors and window coverings, oriented vision and movement in the tradition of baroque planning. Understood in the context of Barragán's approach to folk art and its role in modern Mexican architecture, these objects expressed not only their owner's faith but also his approach to history and cultural expression. Since the 1920s architects had used references to indigenous culture to place their work in Mexican architectural history, create symbolic links to provincial Mexico, and acknowledge the social and political concerns behind the commissions. As early as 1956, foreign observers admired the way Barragán disciplined and "civilized" the native associatively by using "stone and wood and concrete with . . . precision and restraint, transmuting the savagery of his materials into an art that is austere, beautiful and urbane."[44] Barragán's abstractions, the notable absence or invisibility of objects such as toys or cookware that might conjure—as Arai did intentionally—the image of indigenous people at work or play, the visibility instead of things useful to their modern owner, excised the indigenous body and native culture from the interior. The presence of the religious sculptures and horse heads further emphasized the colonialism of this approach.

Poniatowska perceived the entwining of religion, control, and even gender in Barragán's house. Fairly or not, since at least 1857, Catholicism and its agents had been viewed with suspicion and blamed for an enormous number of social and political injustices in Mexico. Anticlericalism had waxed and waned since then. Revolutionary ideology, especially under President Calles, and the dominant narrative of national history that emerged with it, along with various manifestations of Marxism, had helped cement antireligious feeling, especially among intellectuals and artists. Barragán's undisguised faith set him apart from his colleagues and many clients he might have shared with them.

For some, it also firmly linked him with patriarchy and male spaces. In 1975 Poniatowska characterized Barragán's house as a "monastery for a single monk," and reflected on the discomfort she ultimately came to feel when she visited him there.[45] He had the appearance, she thought, of "a suave and slightly sinister Franciscan" and being in the house reminded her of making her first communion.[46] She claimed he "believed in house-fortresses to which no rumor of the other arrives."[47] Barragán, she thought, "liked women without chests and without buttocks."[48] After years, she wrote, "I stopped visiting him. I thought, 'Before going to his house I have to lose ten kilos,' because there, among those high and very white walls, any little tire would take on the proportions of the tire of a tractor, black and defiant. His critical, vigilant eye, with an infinite and tortured Franciscan piety, took in every detail of the visitor and immediately her pudgy belly, gaudy sash, acrylic dress, and excessive makeup stood out." Leaving his house and returning to the "common" world of *chicharrón* sellers and miscellany stores on the streets outside, Poniatowska "breath[ed] easy."[49] A longtime friend of the architect, the poet saw

> Within the immaculate Barragánian whiteness of withdrawal, the garden full of crazy herbs, thorny roses and diabolical sensuality, a mix of refinement and mysticism, of perversion and purity which are the essence of Barragán himself, that tortured man who could be taken for a saint, a medieval mendicant, a judge of the inquisition, a counselor to the queen, a leader of the Knights Templar, a missionary of the holy spirit, a camel who crosses the desert, a profane monk, a golden age actor (siglo de oro), an errant Jew, a sheik of Arabia, beautiful, tall, troubling, like the best of his thoughts.[50]

Poniatowska's characterization of the architect as "tortured," her emphasis on his desire to live in an impenetrable, self-denying, self-sacrificing world and the critical perception of her own body that being around him provoked, implied that he wrestled personally with the dynamics of exposure and occlusion that the house suggested spatially. That she experienced stifling qualities in his house like those he had attributed to Guadalajara as a young man suggests that a powerful play of confinement and release animated his thinking for decades. Her comparisons of Barragán to "exotic" Jews and Arab sheiks and conjuring of the medieval near east compounded the idea that he was somehow different, which Villagrán's characterizations of him as being outside the architectural mainstream had introduced. The detailed attention other writers gave to Barragán's body and clothing—topics not often mentioned in discussions of Mexican architects—contributed to it further still. Selden Rodman wrote in 1957 that Barragán was "tall, even taller than [Mathias] Goeritz, thin, with a long bronzed face and a bald dome of a head, his handsome dark eyes under slightly raised eyebrows cased in heavy black-shell glasses. He was superbly dressed in charcoal grays with a shell-pink shirt, gray socks, and well-polished black sport shoes."[51] In 1963 Barragán was "a slender, handsome man in his sixties . . . an excellent horseman, . . . who remains one of the world's most charming and elusive bachelors."[52] Barragán never married, had no children, and appears to have lived alone, circumstances that clearly attracted attention in a country that privileged and prized family, and in which multigenerational cohabitation was common. His appearance and manner drew particular attention, and his personal life did not outwardly resemble the lives of most of his colleagues. The experience of living alone and apart, and his desire for privacy, mixed with a yearning for attention, dominated his approach to his own house in 1947, as well as the image of it and himself that he tried to create.

WALLED IN

Architecturally the desire to not be seen manifest most profoundly in Barragán's large, windowless walls. As Yañez noted, in many new houses architects used native materials expressively to create variety in texture and color and, like Barragán, made gardens and patios important parts of their designs. Many created compositions of planes that appeared to intersect or slide past one another, but almost none visually enclosed their inhabitants so emphatically. Enrique del Moral's own house, which stood just down the street from Barragán's at 5 Francisco Ramírez Street and was built in 1949 offered an especially revealing contrast. Like the house at number 14, del Moral's had wooden, handmade furniture, spacious rooms, was oriented to the outside and enlivened by a play of planes surfaced in a wide palette of materials including volcanic rock, stucco, brick, and wood. In his L-shaped plan, however, del Moral positioned walls to create considerably greater visual movement and flexible circulation than Barragán's plan permitted. Space flowed much more freely in the del Moral house, and in a way much more like that of Miesian buildings than in Barragán's (figure 6.13). The other, even more important difference, was del Moral's prolific use of glass. Throughout the house—even in a bathroom—floor-to-ceiling windows provided views to gardens and patios. Most of these window-walls were shaded and had doors or windows that could be

FIGURE 6.12. Barragán on his roof terrace, 1969. Photograph by Rene Burri.

left open, as is the custom in Mexico City, to allow cool mountain air to permeate the house, even as the rooms were sheltered from strong sunlight. The large planes of glass in the del Moral house, the casual mode of living that the plan and access to the outside seemed to support, made it similar to modern houses in many parts of the world, and to many other new houses in Mexico City, such as those by Mario Pani, Francisco Artigas, Victor de la Lama, and Juan Sordo Madeleno.[53]

Barragán disliked glass intensely and found large expanses of it distasteful and threatening. The high, thick, solid walls he became famous for were at the core of his design process and essential to the manipulation of sight lines and movement. Rather than beginning a project by drawing plans or elevations, he approached it imaginatively and developed it as a painter might a canvas, in a process he recounted to landscape architect Mario Schjetnan in 1980. After envisioning a design, Barragán created small drawings in perspective, which he then gave to an assistant with whom he created blueprints and developed a cardboard model. Next, he sketched the composition of facades and main volumes by drawing outlines and then arranged pieces of black cardboard against the white paper to explore planar relationships, typically developing ten schemes and ultimately selecting the "most compelling" ones.[54] Later, Barragán modified "certain walls by making them wider, lower, higher or eliminating them altogether," believing "that if a painter can completely modify a canvas, an architect should be able to do the same with his work."[55] Color selection came near the end of the process, and was always understood as an element that could be changed repeatedly. After many site visits to see light at different times of the day, consultations with art books (particularly to look again at surrealist paintings), and revisiting Reyes's work, the architect directed painters to develop test colors on pieces of cardboard that were affixed to the walls. He then selected those he liked best and were most effective in visually expanding or shrinking space. Color was a "complement to architecture."[56]

More than any other aspect of his architecture, Barragán's treatment of walls linked his work to colonial and popular forms. Since the sixteenth century, architects and builders had used walls to fortify and symbolize fortification, and as sites for decoration. The streets of countless indigenous villages and Mexican towns were lined with buildings with thick, stuccoed walls that were sometimes painted and had few windows and were heavily fortified.[57] Walls were made of stone, occasionally of adobe, and later of concrete frame with brick or concrete block infill. Whether they were actually old or not, these

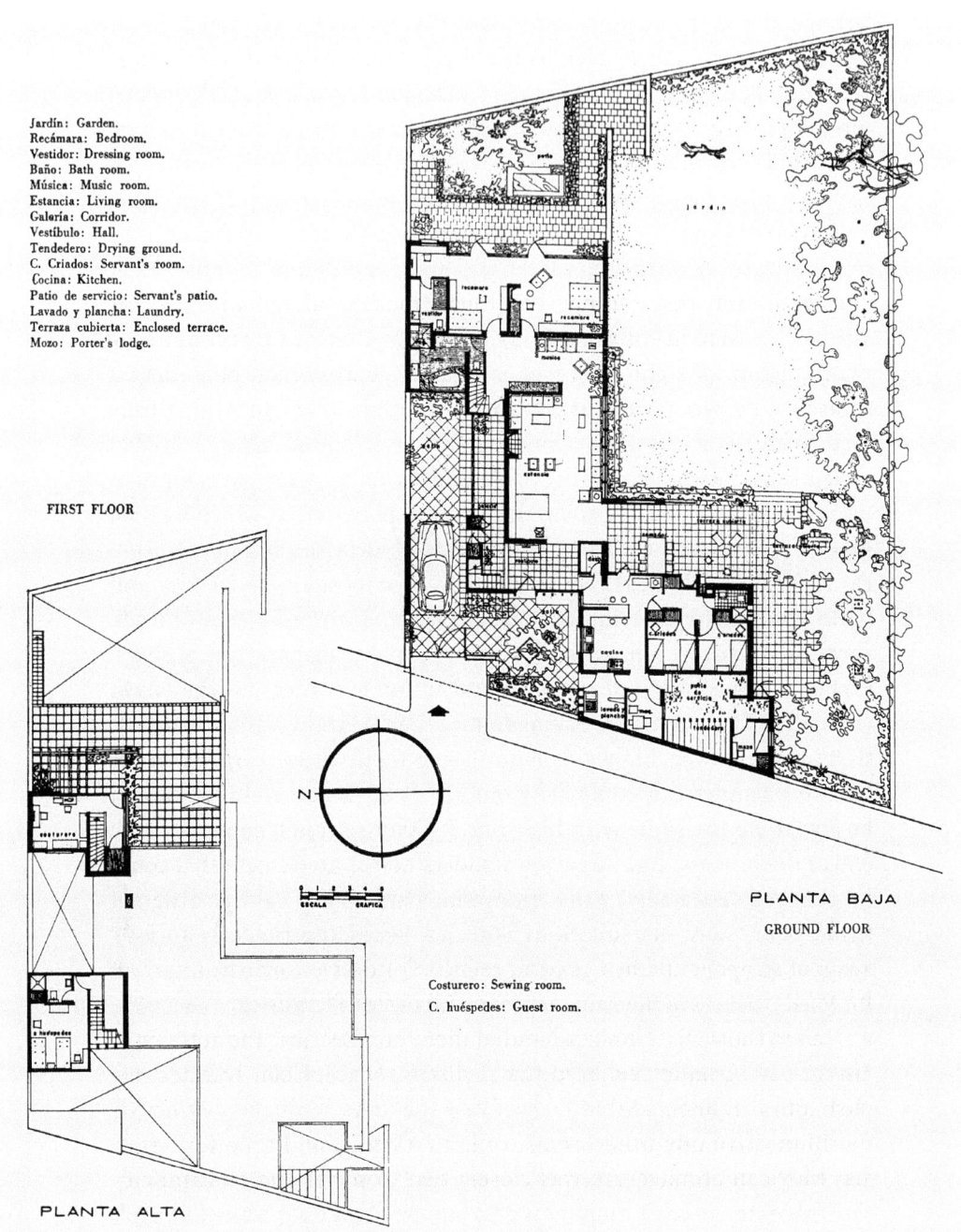

Jardín: Garden.
Recámara: Bedroom.
Vestidor: Dressing room.
Baño: Bath room.
Música: Music room.
Estancia: Living room.
Galería: Corridor.
Vestíbulo: Hall.
Tendedero: Drying ground.
C. Criados: Servant's room.
Cocina: Kitchen.
Patio de servicio: Servant's patio.
Lavado y plancha: Laundry.
Terraza cubierta: Enclosed terrace.
Mozo: Porter's lodge.

FIRST FLOOR

PLANTA BAJA
GROUND FLOOR

PLANTA ALTA

Costurero: Sewing room.
C. huéspedes: Guest room.

FIGURE 6.13. Enrique del Moral, del Moral House, plan, 1948.

character-defining elements gave villages and provincial towns, and even streets in Mexico City, the sense of oldness and "timelessness" that fascinated so many twentieth-century artists, architects, and tourists. As sites of fading customs, the making of folk art, and the front line of the advance of the modernization that had swept the capital, these towns seemed to embody the past. Their walls, which often hid poverty that had been endemic for centuries, contributed to the picturesqueness—in the broadest sense—of provincial Mexico and its quality of seeming particularly and truly "Mexican."

Barragán's reinterpretation of the wall coincided with the growth of interest in Mexican vernacular architecture, when architects began to mine it as a source to help rejuvenate modern design and give it a distinctively national character. The surge of attention it received was most evident in architects' houses and in an exhibition and catalog organized by the National Institute of Fine Arts that brought vernacular buildings into the canon of Mexican art.[58] In 1950 it mounted the "Exposición de arquitectura popular Mexicana," and in 1954 published the bilingual book, *Arquitectura popular de México*, in the forward to which Yañez explained that the curators and authors sought to "reveal the values and constants [in Mexican architecture] that architects can often only feel," and to "enrich modern architecture" and "stimulate Mexican architects" by exposing to them to *cultura popular*."[59] On a journey that recalled the search of Henry Peabody, Sylvester Baxter, and 1920s artists and intellectuals for provincial folk art, photographer Gabriel García Maroto traveled from Mexico City to twenty states to record vernacular architecture for the exhibition and catalog. The buildings he chose included humble structures that could have been built in any century, as well as colonial churches distinguished by sculptural decoration that imitated high-style baroque forms but was clearly made by native artisans. In addition to Yañez's forward, texts were written by the photographer and by the composer Carlos Chávez, who was known for works that integrated themes from Mexican folk music.

Like historians of colonial and modern architecture, the authors of *Arquitectura popular* believed that a distinctive Mexican architecture existed in the past and that it was likely that a new, equally distinctive and impressive one would soon come into being, and they suggested that Mexican architecture was closely tied to social and cultural circumstances particular to Mexico. Unlike the histories, however, *Arquitectura popular* was not primarily concerned with style, periodization, or type, and instead emphasized the qualities of provincial architecture that might rejuvenate contemporary metropolitan architecture. Without specifying architects or buildings, Chávez critiqued modern architecture and alluded to twenty-year-old debates about functionalism, saying, "We are building ugly houses that make ugly cities for purely

FIGURE 6.14. Gabriel García Maroto, vernacular buildings in *Arquitectura popular de México.*

economic reasons, and we will regret it in the long run because it is a
mistake to believe that the functional does not include the aesthetical
sense. . . . Architecture is not always but should always be a fine art."[60]
The pages that followed implied that because of its association with
premodern Mexicans, who, as Baxter had suggested, were themselves
imagined to be instinctive artists, provincial vernacular architecture
might inspire contemporary urban architects to design more beautiful
buildings.

In his photographs García Maroto studiously avoided the picturesque and the touristic, but he also took care to exclude or deemphasize
advertisements, automobiles, and other emblems of modern life to the
greatest extent possible. Most of the images were tightly framed to draw
attention to buildings' surfaces, textures, and materials (figure 6.14).
Attempting to influence contemporary Mexican architecture against
the backdrop of debates about historicity and plastic integration, the
book recalled Baxter's claim that great Mexican buildings were defined
in part, like Churrigueresque architecture, by their relationship to the
other arts and the artistic potential of wall surfaces. An entire section

of *Arquitectura popular* was devoted to "Applied Sculpture," (exemplified by the sixteenth-century portal in Tlaxacala), which, the authors argued, was fundamental to "Mexican" architecture, saying that "Everything concerns our task of integration [of] major plastic arts, understood from their origin and directed towards the achievement of different goals, creative and functional."[61]

Barragán's engagement with provincial and colonial forms was rooted in personal experience and manifest in highly private buildings, but it positioned him in the main currents of Mexican architecture. His explanation of why he used solid walls, and why he hated glass, however, distanced him from them. As they had for Mexicans for centuries, for Barragán, solid walls protected and excluded. Their association with colonial and rural types made them especially effective defensive elements because they could be explained with reference to history and tradition—things that were impersonal and often vague. By 1957 the liberation Barragán had experienced in the streets of Mexico City as a young man had turned into an anxiety about being seen and about maintaining an internal equilibrium, which bordered on elitist agoraphobia. Sitting in his house, he told Rodman:

> I want to be at peace when I come in out of the traffic of Juárez and Madero [streets]! The complete human being is not just physical. You notice how small a proportion of this room is devoted to that single 10' × 10' window? Yet even *that* must be covered with a curtain all day long! The architecture magazines have been a bad influence. Modern architecture looks fine in photographs—but can you *live* in it? A landscape has less value when seen through a plate of glass; through familiarity, by your own constant presence, you reduce its value. I enjoyed Michelangelo's dome most when I saw it, once, through a keyhole. So why open a whole wall to bring a garden into a house? The sense of mystery is important for life, for everyday living, of adventure, promotes life. Only primitives, or very cultivated people, are concerned with beauty. The masses, with their middle-class minds, don't want beauty; they want comfort, security, order, likeness. But all religions make their propaganda through beauty. Architecture today reflects the loss of privacy in modern life. In public, the opportunity to think and to reflect is lost. Houses have become *clubs* where people are no longer alone. The good architect must counter all of this.[62]

Barragán's conviction that glassy modern buildings were not fit to live in, his Loosian belief that beauty was the province of the chosen few and of "primitives," his disparaging reference to "the masses," and the image of him peering at Saint Peter's through a keyhole all suggested that his intense feelings about privacy were entwined with complicated ideas about class, control, and visuality that were quite different from those that underpinned other Mexican architects' engagement with historical and vernacular buildings.

His emphasis on curtains and window coverings of other kinds, and his connection of seeing, degradation, and human presence when speaking of his own house suggested that, despite his efforts, he was not altogether at peace, even at home. It was almost as if the walls of the house functioned as an extension of his body. When discussing vernacular and colonial architecture with Poniatowska, Barragán drew parallels between architecture, anatomy, and buildings' visual and emotional effects. Although he noted his own preference for "rigor, simplicity, and austerity," Barragán liked "overloaded" wall surfaces "when decoration becomes almost a texture or second skin, as in the case of Santa María Tonantzintla or in colonial altarpieces, which are marvelous to me in their baroque-ness, their sugary coating, their volutes, their twists, because the primary emotion is very great and that for me, is the most interesting."[63] The architect read the church and altarpieces, which had long fascinated historians, as works of architecture with covered surfaces, bodies, he suggested, overlaid with sculpture and paint (plate 14). This admiration for historical architecture that "disappeared" or that one could be alone in, and that provoked strong feeling, echoed his interest in seclusion, disappearance, and emotion in his house. Elsewhere he spoke of the wall as an "indispensible coat" that provided "protection."[64] Shadow, like walls, also offered refuge. He believed that humans had a fundamental need to spend time in darkness, that it was part of their spiritual experiences, and that shadows allowed a person "to enter . . . into oneself, into one's problems, or one's own dreams." His belief in the releasing, freeing power of darkness convinced him of the need to "create walls" in order to have corners and "an intimate environment."[65] Years later his client, Francisco Gilardi, recalled Barragán's house as being extremely dark (the main rooms were illuminated only by windows and small lamps) and he imagined that the architect used candles to help light it.[66]

Central to Barragán's work was the fine line between solitude and isolation, which Paz, Arai, and others were exploring in less immediately personal ways at the same time. Barragán repeatedly claimed that his architecture was concerned with solitude, but implied that truly being at home with it was not always easy, and that the seeking of solitude was fundamentally defensive. As if trying to convince himself, he noted in his remarks on winning the Pritzker that "only in intimate solitude

FIGURE 6.15. San Miguel del Arcángel, Huejotzingo, cloister patio, 1544–71.

may man find himself. Solitude is good company and my architecture is not for those who fear or shun it."[67] He said, furthermore, that "serenity is the great and true antidote against anguish and fear, and today, more than ever, it is the architect's duty to make of it a permanent guest in the home." But serenity was ultimately only a guest, and elsewhere Barragán implied that perhaps he had not managed to realize it: "I have frequently visited with reverence the now-empty monumental monastic buildings that we inherited from the powerful religious faith and architectural genius of our colonial ancestors, and I have always been deeply moved by the peace and well-being to be experienced when visiting those uninhabited cloisters and solitary courts. How I have wished that these feelings may leave their mark in my work" (figure 6.15).[68] Barragán's expressions of internal disquiet, his deep need for privacy, "to be don nobody," to find air, but also exclude, and the self-doubt that lurked behind some of his statements suggest that he relied on architecture—its walls and its potential to deflect attention through allusions to historical and vernacular forms—to shield him.

Barragán's desire to retreat, presumably in pursuit of wholeness and plentitude, that underlay his attempt to capture in his own work the "peace and well-being to be experienced" in monasteries and cloisters also echoed that shared by other artists who confronted the disquieting changes brought by the atomic age, rapid industrialization, and urbanization. With this context and knowledge of his religious devotion in mind, it is possible to find in his use of large planes painted in heavily saturated colors parallels to the work of the color-field painters, particularly Mark Rothko, who worked at the same time. Like Barragán's architecture, Rothko's canvases seemed to require stillness, silence, and contemplation to fully experience their visual effects and perceptions of color and space. The similarities between his buildings and color-field painting undoubtedly made Barragán's work more attractive than that of many of his colleagues to international audiences—such as MoMA curators—who admired abstract art. Indeed, in 1984 Dominique de Menil, the patron of the well-known chapel in Houston she had built as a meditative space defined by fourteen Rothko canvases, asked Barragán to design a guest house nearby (plate 18). The project was never realized, but suggested the similarities between his architecture and developments in other media. Barragán's collaboration with Goeritz, and their reference to their work as "emotional" architecture further underscored the parallels between Barragán's buildings and abstract art created abroad, and distanced it from the nationally specific labels some applied to it. Barragán was well-aware of developments in architecture elsewhere that were similarly concerned with nonrational aspects of human experience and that seemed to suggest new directions in design, with which his work was in sympathy. Somewhat deprecatingly, he observed in 1957 that Le Corbusier "has now graduated to making such *emotional* things as the Ronchamps Chapel."[69] Although his "emotional," austere buildings clearly shared a great deal with some other works of avant-garde art, Barragán viewed them as elite agents of self-differentiation. Speaking of his severe, emotional architecture, and its inaccessibility to many, he told Poniatowska, "I belong to a minority, and in that I feel fine, absolutely fine. I love rigor, I love austerity."[70]

THE LANGUAGE OF SILENCE

Barragán's house and his presentation of it in words and images are cast into relief when they are compared to another famous architect's home built at nearly the same time. Philip Johnson's glass house and window-less brick guesthouse in New Canaan, Connecticut, vividly expressed the dynamics of seeing and disappearing in a very different context (figure 6.16). As Alice T. Friedman demonstrated, by cleverly manipulating the tropes and materials of International Style architecture and New England vernacular buildings, Johnson used his design to accommodate public functions and shelter his private life, and to allude to the assumptions latent in postwar American culture about the nature of the family.[71] Barragán visited Johnson's glass house, and, unsurprisingly, hated it. He later recounted being at a dinner party there and admiring the woods and meadows. But, alarmed by the glass walls, as the evening went on, he asked the women guests where they would "like to sit to read or rest, or . . . chat or flee from other people that lived within those four glass walls. The answer was unanimous: in the closet or the bathroom," the only enclosed spaces in the main house.[72] Barragán made no mention of the brick guesthouse—the real place to disappear—and it is unclear whether he saw it or appreciated its significance. Johnson's complex was much more emphatically modernist than Barragán's house and materialized the practical problems that glassy modern architecture presented for private life, but it too carefully controlled visitors' views and movement, not only with walls and sight lines. Steeped in the principles of the Mieisan free plan and Corbusian promenade, where Barragán closed down physical and visual movement with walls and objects, Johnson deftly manipulated plans to orient and organize movement just as carefully, but more subtly.[73] The glass house was positioned so that it was not visible from the road, and the guest

FIGURE 6.16. Philip Johnson, Glass House and Guest House, New Canaan, Connecticut, 1949–51.

house was set at an angle to it, and sited so that visitors arriving in cars would be directed away from it and toward the main house.

Barragán's rhetorical use of architectural history paralleled Johnson's even more than his architecture did. Friedman observed that Johnson used history and wit defensively to inundate critics and historians with information about his house so as to keep them from coming too close. Like Barragán, "Johnson himself established the direction for critical appraising of his house by offering up, in his most polished art-historical manner, a systematic listing of the sources in the history of architecture and design from which he had drawn."[74] Peter Eisenman was among the first to remark on Johnson's distancing in 1978, when he observed that "Johnson is most opaque when he is speaking of himself."[75] Unlike Villagrán, del Moral, and Arai, Barragán resisted theorizing, but in interviews and his Pritzker speech he supplied a long list of historical references to keep scholars busy for years, tracking down references far removed from his personal life. He mentioned Mexican cloisters, churches, and haciendas, specific towns and provinces, vernacular architecture generally, Islamic garden design, Mediterranean architecture, surrealism, Chartres Cathedral, Giorgio de Chirico, Chucho Reyes, Ferdinand Bac, Le Corbusier, Richard Neutra, and Louis Kahn, and he conducted many of his interviews in the Tacubaya house where his large collection of art history books, which impressed so many visitors, served as the backdrop. As a student of art history himself, Barragán, like Johnson, knew well that those who might pry too closely into his work could be easily rerouted when offered a list of precedents and influences. He used historical references to invent a story about his work as he used them in architecture and as he used walls, to attract and then redirect in the service of privacy. Speaking to students, Barragán rhetorically pushed them away and suggested that his architecture emerged from a specific context saying, "Don't ask me about this building or that one, don't look at what I do, see what I saw."[76]

Barragán's insistence that his audience stop talking, *look* away from his work and his life, and *see* their contexts, and his use of the first person underscored the centrality of privacy to his vision. His injunction deflected attention back toward the contextual and historical frameworks through which Mexican architecture had long been understood, but like his house, it also seemed to draw his audience closer by inviting it to ask what he had seen. His list of sources offered one answer, but so too did the many statements by colleagues and critics over the years that defined him as an outsider and his buildings as "sensitive," "decorative," "scenographic," designed when rationalism was canonized as "real" modern architecture. Barragán had once scrawled on a manuscript now in the archives of the Fundación de Arquitectura Tapatía, "Do not ask me what I love and what I believe, Do not go into the depths of my soul."[77] His more publicly stated need to retreat from the world—to get out of the traffic on Juárez and Madero and keep his windows covered constantly—suggested that he felt in some way overwhelmed and threatened by what he saw in the world and what he feared it might see in his house. The many references to silence—to what is unspoken—similarly drew attention to absence and to what could not be known.[78]

REPRESENTING ABSENCE

The urge to silence and to stillness that recurred throughout Barragán's explanations of his architecture manifest as well in the carefully arranged photographs of it that were to be among the most important representations of it. Keith Eggener chronicled Barragán's long and careful collaboration with photographers throughout his career, and argued that photography was integral to his conception of architecture.[79] Eggener has also drawn attention to the parallels between photographs of the buildings, particularly those taken by Armando Salas Portugal, and surrealist paintings, and to the ways in which the Salas Portugal images suggested the silence, stillness, and solitude of which the architect frequently spoke. Noting the theatricality and vague disquiet in many, Eggener highlighted the juxtaposition of the absence of human figures and the viewer's sense that she or he is looking at a place where something has just happened or soon will.[80] Unseen action is the subject of the photographs just as it implicitly was in Barragán's house. It took place behind the curtains and doors, just over and out of view of the high walls—suggested by those that did not quite reach the ceiling and past the narrow door frames, which seemed to hint that someone had just slipped through.

Barragán's silence represented absence in a country where architectural representation implied presence. Although shrouded in historical allusion, his architecture of the unspoken, the unknown, and the unseen was utterly unlike works by his colleagues that relied on representation to assert national distinctiveness and existence in a historical narrative predicated on the presence of mestizos or indigenous people. Barragán's architecture suggested instability and ambiguity, and by its affirmation of absence invited viewers, as the architect did rhetorically, to examine context. His house was not ultimately "postmodern": there was no irony and no joke. It shared with other groundbreaking mid-century works—such as Johnson's glass house/guest house complex and Robert Venturi's house for his mother—a critical distance from the cultural norms of the place and time in which it was created and revealed those norms as such through the deft arrangement of elements drawn from historical, vernacular, and modern architecture. Johnson and Venturi pointed to the confining expectations of U.S. suburban domestic life and high architectural modernism, whereas Barragán's architecture indicated the narrowness of a national architectural history and sociopolitical nationalism predicated on mestizaje. Mexican architectural representation had repeatedly implied the presence of the other, whether colonial or native. Feeling or choosing to be other and outside the norms of his profession, Barragán used the forms that it had made stand for the other and thus for "Mexico," abstractly and at times, disconcertingly, to reveal their tenuousness.

Since the beginning of the twentieth century, Mexican architectural history and many new buildings assumed or projected a trium-

FIGURE 6.17. José
Clemente Orozco,
Cortés and Malinche,
National Preparatory
School, Mexico City,
1926, fresco.

phalist, binary understanding of Mexican history and culture that positioned the fusion of the native and European as the sign of national distinction. In eighteenth-century architecture this had been the Churrigueresque style; in modern architecture it had manifested in the many allusions to folk art and indigenous culture traced in previous chapters. In human terms it was the mestizo person—the child of the European and the native. Procreation, with its implications for domestic life and architecture, thus stood at the core of beliefs about Mexican national specificity. Unmarried and childless, Barragán lived outside of this model, and having matured far from Mexico City and at a distance from the nationalizing dogmas of the postrevolutionary period, he had a particular capacity to recognize the contingent and confining aspects of a binary view of national history, just as his friend and fellow Jaliscan, José Clemente Orozco, did. In the same notes in which Barragán described his feelings of liberation in the anonymity of Mexico City in 1932, he wrote, "Populist indigenism is calming. That is not the national, our yesterday is not a tragic novel of blacks and whites. Orozco has always been right."[81] The architect may well have been referring to conversations with the muralist, but he could also have had in mind Orozco's 1926 fresco in the National Preparatory School in Mexico City, *Cortés and Malinche*, that Barragán would certainly have seen on his visit (figure 6.17). The fresco challenged the ideology of mestizaje by drawing attention to the sexual violence at its core. In Orozco's double portrait, the conquistador and the indigenous woman widely imagined as his native wife and the mother of the first mestizo child, appeared nude and seated. Cortés took her right hand in his right hand while seemingly restraining her with his left arm. Malinche's downcast eyes, tightly clasped knees and ankles, and her apparent unwillingness to take his outstretched hand in her left hand suggested that she was being taken against her will. The fresco is unsettling and filled with ambiguity of a kind that Rivera's work, which was much more readily embraced by the Mexican government and architects including Obregón Santacilia and O'Gorman, seldom included.

Mexican nationalism and, before Barragán, the most canonical forms of Mexican architecture made little space for domestic arrangements and private life not centered on conventional family structures. The concept had literally been built into the walls of the Ministry of Health, reinforced in major works focused on welfare and education, such as the Carranza Center and the elementary schools of the 1930s, and implicitly embodied in the Ciudad Universitaria, with its ambition to create a new kind of citizen who would, presumably, produce the citizens of the future. In arguing that there was no "Mexican" architecture, Barragán created rhetorical space for alternative ways of living and thinking about buildings' purposes and distinctive qualities. Because history in his view was not binary, it, unlike nationalism, could anchor his architecture, and make room for silence and solitude. Although Arai also dealt with themes of alienation and estrangement, in the context of a recent architectural history that had prized representation, mass-legibility, and, by implication, buildings' volubility, Barragán's "silent" works, which seemed to disappear into the city, read as negation and rejection. Barragán privatized architectural history in order not only to disappear into it but also to invite speculation and the possibility of revelation. Unlike his colleagues' facades, with their complicated connections to Mexican architectural history, his seemingly simple ones hid rich, complex interiors. Probing the interior, as Arai and Paz had suggested, might reveal unsettling discoveries—in this case about the core myths of Mexican nationalism and the assumptions that had governed understandings of Mexican architecture since the beginning of the century. In creating an architecture that was perfectly pitched to an international audience that readily interpreted it as "Mexican" and embraced it essentially as a consumer product, but then denying its nationalistic content, and refusing to have it appended to political populism through association with working-class and rural Mexicans, Barragán pointed to the growing alliance between architects and their state clients (which would become vivid in the 1960s), and to the essential fragility of the very idea of "Mexican" architecture.

CONCLUSION

The origins of this book lie in two questions, one about architectural form and the other about history writing. Steeped in the tradition of understanding innovations in plan and section to be chief characteristics of architectural modernism, I was long curious about the absence of attention to these aspects of design in twentieth-century Mexican buildings. Similarly, from my earliest readings of Mexican architectural history, I was struck by scholars' tendency to interpret buildings in terms of social and political conditions framed in national terms, and often as reflections of a rather vague concept of Mexican "identity." These observations generated on the one hand doubts for me about the relevance of Mexican buildings to a broader, international history of architectural modernism, and on the other, a frustration that the nationally specific sociopolitical interpretations, while illuminating in many respects, did not fully explain why buildings looked the way they did. Mindful of injunctions by scholars outside the field to identify the distinguishing characteristics of Mexican modern architecture and to demonstrate its significance, doubt and dissatisfaction became the starting points of my research. When I ceased to see facadism as lesser-than and asked why it has long been so important to the people who have written about them that buildings be "Mexican," I began to get at the common root of both facadism and the privileging of nationalizing narratives, and the idea that linked the buildings I was studying to the widely known story of modern architecture.

That deep engagement with architectural history would be a cornerstone in the development of modern architecture anywhere is unsurprising. What is significant about the example of Mexico is how thoroughly modern architects participated in the construction of that history and how they understood it to intersect with the cultural and social concerns of the colonial era and their own time. Long before social history and architectural history entwined in scholarship on European and U.S. buildings they were inseparable in histories of Mexican architecture. This was not because the authors of those texts were simply parroting official nationalism (Sylvester Baxter's status as foreigner becomes particularly significant when seen in this light), but because the buildings they cataloged did not fit neatly into the stylistic categories developed to organize European buildings. These buildings did make sense when understood contextually in the history of a culture whose most pronounced characteristic was widely judged to be the intermingling of indigenous and European people. The effect of interpreting colonial buildings in this way, perhaps somewhat unintentionally, was to place considerable emphasis on the role of the anonymous craftspeople and builders who actually built the buildings, often over that of the architect or master of works. Authors' attention to craftspeople's contributions was not intentionally Marxist, and it grew from a highly formalist interpretive approach. But it bequeathed to generations of architects a framework that proved useful in the problem of *consciously* shaping buildings that were different from works abroad, yet recognizably related to them and to Mexican architectural history. It also offered a way of talking about the social relevance of buildings in the postrevolutionary era, when so much energy was devoted to presenting Mexico and its government as reflective of and responsive to indigenous culture and citizens. That sociocultural and Marxist-sounding interpretations of architecture are to be found in early twentieth-century histories of colonial Mexican architecture may surprise some architectural historians and raises the question of what other interesting discoveries we might make by looking more widely into our own disciplinary past.

As Rudolph Wittkower famously demonstrated in *Architectural Principles in the Age of Humanism*, examining (or reexamining) architects' own words brings ideas and buildings to life in ways that few other kinds of inquiry can.[1] In the case of modern architecture in Mexico, doing so reveals the existence of an intellectual genealogy that links major architects and buildings and makes clear that there is a great deal more to probe in that history. This is particularly true in the cases of Enrique del Moral, Alberto Arai, and Jesús Acevedo, whose expansive grasp of the ideas at play in Mexican modernism show that new buildings were part of a sophisticated, well-informed international dialogue about the nature of the past, the present, locality, and culture. Architects' involvement in the debates on plastic integration at mid-century invites deeper investigation into the relationships between titanic figures in the arts, such as Mario Pani and José Clemente Orozco. Examining the ways that Luis Barragán used words to avoid saying too much in an architectural culture that cast him as an outsider, and designed a house predicated on disappearance and occlusion, brings to the fore the question of whether he was gay and closeted, which scholars have long discussed with one another in conversation, but almost never print.[2] Although that question is methodologically complicated to research, the issue it raises—the interpretative value of considering homophobia as part of historical context—is more relevant than ever.

Foregrounding the importance of surface to Mexican modernism does not imply that its architecture was superficial, and makes it easier to avoid the intellectual tangle generated by comparisons with buildings in more technologically advanced countries with longer traditions of architectural theory writing. Significantly, in Mexico "surface" tends not to imply an immediate contrast with "depth," as it does in many contexts. One reason for this may be that the country's complicated cultural history is in many respects borne quite literally in the faces of its citizens, which collectively display mestizaje and its absence. As a representational site, the facade was the place where architects could express the yearning to be part of a dynamic, cosmopolitan world alongside the reality of the profound cultural differences that the Mexican Revolution had laid bare. The modern forms that the study of architectural history gave rise to were the means through which architects acknowledged the centuries-old, multidimensional gap that separated Mexico from modern Europe and at the same time bound it to the continent. On new buildings, awareness of the conceptual distance between images or abstract elements and the historical or popular forms that they referenced were analogous to the consciousness of the psychological and experiential gulfs between modern Mexico City dwellers and a host of other groups that animated their imaginations: their colonial forbearers, their contemporaries in industrialized Europe and the United States, and, most often and most profoundly, the indigenous Mexicans with whom they shared historical time and nationality. The many and varied kinds of representation they saw on the walls of modern buildings invited viewers to consider the distance between the image and the original. By encouraging them to ponder the differences between the past and the present all around them by using familiar, seemingly culturally unique forms, architects offered

audiences a window into the very core of modernity, with all its desta-
bilizing implications for individual and collective self-definition.

In Mexico architects made history in words at the same time that
they built in stone, steel, and concrete the buildings that their patrons
intended to be cornerstones of a society defined by its modernity and
cultural uniqueness. They adapted the principles they learned from
their study of architectural history to shape buildings that they consciously envisioned existing in it. From history they had learned that
"Mexican" architecture bore visible traces of indigenous and European
influence, an idea that, in the 1920s, became appealing to patrons who
recognized the considerable political utility of making racial mixing
central to an official definition of national culture. As allusions to historical forms and indigenous culture became commonplace in buildings intended to support reformist policies spearheaded by the national
government, the distinctions between historically referential designs,
politics, and progress became less clear.

By the 1960s modern "Mexican" architecture was in many instances either subsumed within a program directed by the increasingly
autocratic federal government to project official power or into international capitalism. Both of these eventualities were foreshadowed by developments in the 1920s, when governmental patrons forcefully linked
Obregón Santacilia's and Segura's buildings to their reform agendas,
and wealthy Mexicans, along with their counterparts in the southwestern United States, adopted the colonial revival style for expensive
private houses. The propagandistic aspects of the Ciudad Universitaria,
and Barragán's appeal to tastemakers in the United States and Europe
were more immediate antecedents. Both also anticipated the much
greater role interior space played in defining buildings than it had before 1950. As the century wore on, the documentation and publication
of Mexican architectural history became increasingly efficient, institutionalized, and international, and scholars revisited familiar themes.
Once again design and history marched together, now to an increasingly standardized, often official, rhythm.

REWRITING HISTORY

In the 1960s architects and historians published new texts on old buildings at a rate faster than at any time in the century. New books included
surveys and, significantly, for the first time, publications of architects'
writings; *Arquitectura/México* continued to publish stories on colonial
buildings and archaeological sites. In 1955 the National Institute of An-

thropology and History had consolidated its vast photography collection, which included images by Guillermo Kahlo and Luis Márquez, into a single archive organized into sections on colonial architecture, archaeology, and ethnography, making research on pre-Hispanic and colonial architecture easier than ever. Foremost among many new accounts of the art of various indigenous groups by foreign scholars was George Kubler's *The Art and Architecture of Ancient America* (1962), which followed his 1959 history of peninsular and colonial art, *Art and Architecture in Spain and Portugal and Their American Dominions, 1500–1800*. Also in 1962 Joseph Baird published *The Churches of Mexico 1510–1810*; John McAndrew's monumental *The Open-Air Churches of Sixteenth-Century Mexico: Atrios, Posas, Open Chapels, and Other Studies* appeared in 1965. Like their predecessors, historians of modern architecture positioned newer buildings in very long lineages: Mexican architect Max Cetto opened his bilingual *Modern Architecture in Mexico* (1961) with an image of the Temple of the Sun at Teotihuacan and prefaced his typological survey with a discussion of major preconquest and colonial works. In *Architecture of Mexico: Yesterday and Today* (1969), Hans Beacham went further in proposing formal continuities between the very old and very new by juxtaposing photographs of twentieth-century, colonial, vernacular, and preconquest work, documenting the "changing city," and finding "pre-Hispanic vestiges in the Mexican House."[3] In the book's introduction Mathias Goeritz repeated Baxter's central claims that Mexican architecture was exceptional and notable for the ways in which new influences mingled with indigenous ones. In an echo of the arguments made by promoters of the Ciudad Universitaria, he wondered whether the "extraordinary Mexican landscape" had defined national character and identified juxtaposition and "integration" as hallmarks of national architecture: "the forcing together of varied forms and ideas, along with their expression in styles and techniques completely unrelated to each other, results in a paradoxical unity that would be simply impossible in any other culture. In Mexico, a paradox is feasible. The Mexican artistic forms must follow their own special laws of integration, distinct from those of other latitudes, because all elements, ancient and modern, seem to be active."[4] Goeritz's assessment was not an expression of postmodernist pluralism so much as a description of what he, as a European, like so many foreigners, registered as a kind of chaos relative to the apparent order that seemed to govern art and architecture elsewhere. Verna Cook Shipway helped solidify the idea of a "Mexican" house in *The Mexican House, Old and New*, which went through five printings between 1960 and 1965, and in *Mexican Interiors* (with Warren Shipway; 1962). These books, along with Allan W. Kahn and James Norman's *Mexican Hill Town*, about San Miguel de Allende, a colonial town in Guanajuato that was beginning to attract significant numbers of artists and students from the United States, presented "Mexican" architecture as old, picturesque, and romantic—utterly unlike the impression most people had of Mexico City in the 1960s.

Also in the 1960s Mexican architects and scholars began a sustained and far-reaching project of documenting and disseminating the history of modernism in their country at a pace and breadth that paralleled the speed and all-encompassing approach to design that characterized the preparations for the 1968 Olympics that were held in Mexico City.[5] At the center of this effort were the twenty texts published from 1960 to 1966 in the series Cuadernos de Arquitectura under the auspices of the Dirección de Arquitectura of the National Institute of Fine Arts and edited by Ruth Rivera (Diego Rivera's daughter), Salvador Pinocelly, and Ramón Vargas Salguero. In this series, for the first time, theoretical writings by architects including José Villagrán García, Enrique del Moral, and Felix Candela were systematically collected and reprinted.[6]

By far the most important book of the decade was Israel Katzman's *La arquitectura contemporánea mexicana: Precedentes y desarollo* (1964). The first survey of twentieth-century Mexican buildings, it included works outside of Mexico City, and, for the first time, presented buildings in the context of international modernism. In his opening chapter Katzman explained the forms, materials, and principles of modern architecture as they had developed in western Europe and in the practice of Frank Lloyd Wright. He illustrated examples of Art Nouveau, de Stijl, Expressionist, and International Style buildings. In subsequent chapters he retained the national framework inherited from earlier histories of Mexican architecture, but attempted to fuse it with discussions of formal evolution. Each chapter concluded with multiple plates of black-and-white photographs of buildings—most showing facades—organized in rows. The rather visually busy arrangement suggested that a great deal of modern architecture existed in Mexico and that sometimes quite different-looking buildings shared certain qualities. Within chapters additional images appeared, many of unbuilt projects and, significantly, reproductions of plans. Katzman's book presented an unprecedented depth of historical research; he mined journals, newspapers, theoretical writings, and histories from throughout the century. Sources were organized in a bibliography that was, quite unusually, followed by an index—one of the reasons the book remains a standard text. Published by the National Institute of Anthropology and History, *La arquitectura contemporánea mexicana* continued the very long tradition of government-funded texts on Mexican architecture, but introduced to Mexico a new model, more closely based on U.S. and English practice than recent Mexican precedents, of how to write them.

FROM MEXICO TO THE WORLD

Ironically, Arai and Barragán, who found in architectural history lessons about alienation, difference, and solitude, created the works that provided the most significant formal influences for architects who later designed buildings that expressed a unified, collective understanding of national culture and represented the overt politicization of Mexican architecture in the second half of the century. Pedro Ramírez Vázquez and Ricardo Legorreta carried on the tradition of historically engaged facadism that their predecessors established, but embodied the much closer association between architecture and the federal government that characterized the 1960s and 1970s.

Ramírez Vázquez's National Museum of Anthropology (figure C.1), which was built shortly before the Olympics, and Legoretta's Camino Real Hotel, which he designed to house wealthy foreigners coming to the games, continued particularly strikingly the legacies of Arai and Barragán, while their very different historical contexts illustrate the shift that occurred in architecture in the 1960s. One of the world's great museums, the Anthropology Museum served one of the most dramatic state-directed transubstantiations of archaeological artifacts into evidence of national greatness in the twentieth century. Housing works made by people from ancient cultures throughout Mexico, the museum typified the enormous reach of federal power and the centralization of control over what constituted "culture" that O'Gorman's UNAM mosaic referenced and that buildings—from the Ministry of Health to the university campus—embodied successively earlier in the century as they pushed Mexico City farther from its historic center. Architecturally the building also continued the precedents of referencing and representing indigenous cultures materially and pictorially, and alluding to classical traditions. *Tezontle* and marble clad the walls, a giant steel screen designed by the artist Manuel Felguérez and the architect Javier Toussaint evoked pre-Columbian architectural sculpture in the Yucatán Peninsula, and murals with the themes of mestizaje and indigeneity were painted in introductory galleries. In the giant central

FIGURE C.1. Pedro Ramírez Vázquez, National Museum of Anthropology, 1964.

courtyard a massive metal column with bronze reliefs by José Chávez Morado evoked Mesoamerican sculpture and supported the famous giant canopy beneath which water flowed, as if to call to mind watery Tenochtitlan (figure C.2). Influenced by the design of the neoclassical National Gallery of Art in Washington, DC,[7] the space also recalled Mesoamerican plazas and the vast square of the Zócalo.

As the premier luxury hotel for foreign visitors to the Olympics, the Camino Real played a special role as a cultural ambassador. Built near the affluent Polanco neighborhood, at the edge of Chapultepec Park and the Paseo de la Reforma, with the Anthropology Museum, and their predecessors discussed in this book, the hotel continued the shift of the center of culture and activity away from the historic core of the capital. Legorreta fused the lessons of Arai and Barragán to create a building that provided every modern comfort and gave visitors the strong sense of being in Mexico. Like Barragán's house, the hotel was closed to the street by windowless or nearly windowless walls. Allusions to colonial architecture included the spatial arrangement and the naming of wings for

FIGURE C.2. José Chávez Morado, *Fountain*, National Museum of Anthropology, 1964.

FIGURE C.3. Ricardo Legorreta, Camino Real Hotel, lobby, 1968.

saints. Legorreta prioritized interiority and privacy as Barragán had, but of a kind that was ultimately subsumed, as Castañeda has argued, into the larger project of nationalist image projection centered on the Olympics.[8] The surprisingly long shadow of Ferdinand Bac, whose gardens inspired Barragán, materialized in the lattice-like screens that relieved the intensity of continuous wall surfaces, while planes of bright colors—originally red, pink, yellow, orange, brown, and gold—defined interior spaces. Legorreta's hotel, like many of his later buildings, carried on the tradition of using bright pigments on surfaces to evoke folk art, but its abstraction of pre-Hispanic forms and evocations of pre-Columbian planning is indebted to Arai. Organized around two courtyards, one a pentagonal motor court with a giant recessed circular fountain, and the other a large rectangular garden around which wings containing the rooms are arranged, the building seemed knitted into the ground. Inside, the enormous lobby spread out before guests (figure C.3). A textured pattern of small repeated squares on the ceiling made this space seem even more vast than it is and, with the wide, almost ceremonial staircase, the

lobby called to mind not Barragán's rooms for privacy and disappearance, but pre-Columbian plazas. Works of abstract art by leading contemporary artists including Alexander Calder, Anni Albers, and Rufino
Tamayo linked the hotel to the tradition of using the other arts to define
buildings. Mathias Goeritz designed the giant metal lattice at the entrance to the motor court and, with Barragán, the hotel's gardens.[9] In the
wings containing rooms, the twin influences of Arai and Barragán were
evident. Inclined walls, sloped at an angle reminiscent of the talud walls
that fascinated Arai, defined the spaces of private balconies off of each
room, beloved by guests, and repeated in later buildings for the Camino
Real chain, because they completely obscured views from one balcony to
the next.

Both Legorreta's and Ramírez Vázquez's work continued the shift
toward monumentality and the rejection of traditional urban form that
manifested at the Ciudad Universitaria. The dramatic increase in the
scale of buildings and spaces that characterized the UNAM foreshadowed the more general scaling up and walling out that the museum
and hotel typified. In both buildings interior spaces became larger
and more symbolically significant as expressions of state ambition to
shape and control environments fully, than they had been in earlier
institutional works. In keeping with "brutalist" architecture elsewhere
in the 1960s and 1970s, Ramírez Vázquez's buildings, as well as significant ones by Teodoro González de León and Agustín Hernández, were
notable for the ways they conveyed mass and fortification, implicitly
against the growing metropolis. As architects had for several decades,
they used concrete—now often textured—which, when poured in large
abstract forms, created buildings and plazas that evoked preconquest
temples. Fittingly, these buildings' defensive postures had more in
common with those of ancient Mesoamerican cities than with the almost reclusive privatism of Barragán's house. Nevertheless, all of them
suggested that architects and their patrons were increasingly wary of
their context—a city that, by 1970, had nearly seven million people
(many of whom were still quite poor), rapidly deteriorating air quality,
and a perpetually failing system of flood control and water purifica-
tion.[10] In this dense, growing, and largely unplanned metropolis, architects were less influential in shaping urban form and character than
they had been at any time in its history. Although Pani and Villagrán
continued to coordinate and design major new projects, most notably
in Pani's case the vast high-rise housing development at Tlatelolco
(1960), and in Villagrán's ongoing expansions of the medical center,
Mexico City was increasingly defined not by architect-led planning

FIGURE C.4. Augusto Pérez Palacios and Juan O'Gorman, Ministry of Communications and Public Works, 1954.

projects or architect-designed buildings, but by buildings erected hastily by developers or builders, and sometimes by the people who would use them.

Nevertheless, and even as architecture and politics became entwined further, the idea that "Mexican" buildings were visibly related to historical precedents, indigenous culture, and the other arts prevailed and was codified, not just in Mexico City, but in works built abroad. Governments in Mexico and in the United States eagerly appropriated architecture in the service of political and economic programs, further cementing the association between national character and historically informed design. In 1954 O'Gorman created mosaics like those at UNAM to clad Augusto Pérez Palacios's Ministry of Communications and Public Works building, an otherwise fairly typical work of mid-century International Style slab design (figure C.4). Fourteen years later he was sent to San Antonio, Texas, to design yet another, this one on the theme of the "Confluence of Civilizations in the Americas" for the exterior of a building at the HemisFair Exhibition of 1968, an event whose organizers hoped would strengthen the economic and cultural ties between the city and country.

Perhaps the most remarkable example of the legacy of the buildings and ideas discussed in this book is to be found in Legorreta's later work. In the years after he designed the Camino Real, the work of his firm, Legorreta Arquitectos (founded in 1964), began the transformation of a signature style, by then synonymous with "Mexican architecture," into a global brand. Its success and reception abroad underscored the essential flexibility of "Mexican" and the fragility of the idea of a nationally specific idiom. Nearly thirty years after HemisFair, the city of San Antonio hired Legorreta to design the main branch of its public library (plate 19). The result was an enormous building characterized by overscaled Barragánian forms and, on two sides, long blank walls that met the downtown sidewalk in a way that read not as an evocation of Mexican colonial palaces as it might have in Mexico City, but as a hostile posture to pedestrians. Similarly, any likeness to tezontle of the "enchilada red" color of the exterior walls was meaningless to locals, who were alternately delighted and appalled by it. Detractors found the "Mexican" color unrelated to the city's historic fabric, or regarded it as a feeble attempt to acknowledge San Antonio's large Mexican American population using a tired stereotype.[11] The building's six-story central atrium evoked shopping malls more readily than it did the patios of eighteenth-century palaces or soaring nineteenth-century reading rooms.

Having designed buildings on five contents for public and private clients, the firm, which today is called Legorreta + Legorreta, defines itself "as a Mexican firm." In its explanation of its "philosophy" it says that its architects have "been influenced and exposed to Mexican vernacular architecture."[12] Carrying on the tradition associated with Villagrán García (with whom Legorreta worked until 1960), rhetorically at least, and using language familiar from many discussions of Mexican architecture written since the 1930s, the firm says that "architecture should serve society, always above personal interests and false targets,"[13] whatever those might be. Having designed buildings for IBM, Hilton Hotels, Televisa, and outposts of Stanford, Carnegie Mellon, and Texas A&M universities within the Hamad Bin Khalifa University in Doha, along with numerous private houses in Mexico and abroad, Legorreta + Legorreta's success indicates that "Mexican architecture," whatever else it may mean in the twenty-first century, is also a lucrative export product attractive to multinational corporations and wealthy individuals. It suggests as well that the underlying flexibility of terms embedded in the very first histories of colonial architecture and perceptible in later texts not only continues to define major works in the country but also has become, at least in the case of this firm, a critical means of thriving within a national context that still prizes cultural distinctiveness *and* within the global architecture market.

The ways the firm's claims to create an architecture grounded in an ambition to serve society seem to collapse under the evidence of its client list confirms the essential contradiction in the way architecture in Mexico has long been discussed, as some architects began to intuit at mid-century. Fundamentally political and geographic words, like "Mexico," are of limited value in describing visual, spatial, and historical characteristics and phenomena. Legorreta + Legorreta's success reveals the cul-de-sac-like aspects of trying to understand buildings primarily in terms of "national" characteristics without mining what "national" meant to the architects who used the term. Rhetorically, nationalizing architecture distances it from an implied "nonnational" kind, which in the history of modernism has long been taken as the "real" one, to be found chiefly in France and Germany. Although architectural historians have collectively shown the limitations of such a perspective, national frameworks remain in place largely because almost all land is still organized into nation-states and because, when it comes to thinking in terms of comparative geography and culture, most historians and architects perceive themselves as citizens of a particular country. In the case of Mexico, precisely because *patria* has been so central to the political, cultural, economic, and artistic histories of the twentieth century, the meaning of "Mexico" is particularly worth investigating when the protagonists of those histories use it. That "Mexican" has remained a useful means of branding Legorreta + Legorreta's work, and that this brand is desirable to patrons commissioning buildings in countries that include South Korea and Egypt, is itself a fascinating development in the history of "Mexican" architecture. That "Mexican" architectural history and "Mexican" architecture have been bent so readily and so often to fit changing political and commercial needs shows the tenuousness of both ideas and their enduring value to architects and patrons.

The flexibility inherent in the idea of a national architecture; the absence of a long tradition of theoretical writings; an ambition to modify precedents from elsewhere to make them relevant to local contexts: these characteristics defined twentieth century architecture in Mexico, in many ways in contrast to the modernisms of continental Europe. But they link Mexico's modern architectural history to that of its northern neighbor, where it is possible to find a pronounced similarity in the overall trajectory of design in the first half of the century—from a colonial revival style, to a statist modern classicism, to the assimilation of International Style principles, to the rise of "regionalism." Leading modern architects in the United States including Louis Sullivan, Frank Lloyd Wright, Robert Venturi, and Denise Scott Brown also discussed architecture with references to their country and to what they imagined to be distinctive and even native about it—democracy, pluralism, and an (extra)ordinary landscape. By mid-century, Juan O'Gorman, Luis Barragán, Mario Pani, Felix Candela, and many other Mexican architects had direct contact with leading U.S. architects and attended meetings of the American Institute of Architects. O'Gorman cited Wright as a major influence on his own understanding of "organic" architecture and Louis Kahn sought Barragán's advice when he designed the famous court at the Salk Institute.[14] U.S. scholars wrote pioneering accounts of colonial and modern Mexican architecture, and played crucial roles in the development of Mexican archaeology. They were among the first to nationalize the buildings they studied and, with their Mexican colleagues, contributed to the idea that the country's architecture was unique and shaped by its relatedness to racial and cultural mixing.

A history-grounded history of architectural modernism in Mexico not only brings the country's major buildings into dialogue with one another and with the currents of international modernism but also raises the question of whether, given their proximity and historic ties, as the United States and Mexico grow closer together culturally, linguistically, and economically, the time has come to consider how these countries together built an American architectural modernism, one that was related to but distinct from that of western Europe. Such a history might reshape not just the geography of modern architecture, but its definition.

NOTES

INTRODUCTION

1. Sociedad de Arquitectos Mexicanos, *4000 años de arquitectura mexicana* (Mexico City: Libreros Mexicanos Unidos, 1956), 280.

2. A notable exception is Luis Carranza's work on the architecture of the 1920s and 1930s, in which he explores links between politics and architecture, sculpture, muralism, and the Estridentista movement. *Architecture as Revolution: Episodes in the History of Modern Mexico* (Austin: University of Texas Press, 2010).

3. On Ramírez Vázquez and the entwining of architecture and politics: Luis Castañeda, "Beyond Tlaltelolco: Design, Media, and Politics at Mexico '68," *Gray Room* 40 (Summer 2010), 100–126.

4. Johanna Lozoya, *Las manos indígenas de la raza española* (Mexico City: Consejo Nacional para la Cultura y las Artes, 2010); Johanna Lozoya and Tomás Pérez Vejo, eds., *Arquitectura escrita: Docientos años de arquitectura Mexicana* (Mexico City: Instituto Nacional de Antropología e Historia, 2009); Fernanda Canales, *Arquitectura en México, 1900–2010: La construcción de la modernidad, obras, diseño, arte y pensamiento*, exhibition catatalog (Mexico City: Fomento Cultural Banamex, 2013).

5. María Fernández, *Cosmopolitanism in Mexican Visual Culture* (Austin: University of Texas Press, 2014).

6. Luis Castañeda, *Spectacular Mexico: Design, Propaganda, and the 1968 Olympics* (Minneapolis: University of Minnesota Press, 2014).

7. Mauricio Tenorio Trillo, *Mexico at the World's Fairs: Crafting a Modern Nation* (Berkeley: University of California Press, 1996); Fernández, *Cosmopolitanism*, 108–21. In 1929 Manuel Amabilis again made reference to preconquest architecture in his design of the Mexican Pavilion at the Ibero-American Exposition in Seville: Carranza, *Architecture as Revolution*, 86–117.

8. On this topic in the arts: Mary K. Coffey, "The 'Mexican Problem': Nation and 'Native' in Mexican Muralism and Cultural Discourse," in *The Social and the Real*, ed. Alejandro Anreus, Diana L. Linden, and Jonathan Weinberg (University Park: Pennsylvania State University Press, 2006), 43–70.

9. Marilyn Grace Miller, *The Rise and Fall of the Cosmic Race: The Cult of Mestizaje in Latin America* (Austin: University of Texas Press, 2004); Tace Hedrick, *Mestizo Modernism: Race, Nation, and Identity in Latin American Culture, 1900–1940* (New Brunswick, NJ: Rutgers University Press, 2003).

10. William Spratling, "Figures in a Mexican Renaissance," *Scribner's Magazine* (January 1929), 14–21.

11. Edward N. Kaufman, "Architectural Representation in Victorian England," *Journal of the Society of Architectural Historians* 16, no. 1 (March 1987), 30–38.

12. For a general discussion of these themes in the history of modern architecture: Barry Bergdoll, *European Architecture, 1750–1890* (Oxford: Oxford University Press, 2000); Peter Collins, *Changing Ideals in Modern Architecture, 1750–1950*, 2nd ed. (Toronto: McGill-Queens University Press, 1998). On the role of vernacular and folk culture in modern architecture: Barbara Miller Lane, *National Romanticism and Modern Architecture in Germany and the Scandinavian Countries* (Cambridge: Cambridge University Press, 2000).

13. On representation and its role in modern architecture and theory: Neil Levine, *Modern Architecture: Representation and Reality* (New Haven, CT: Yale University Press, 2010).

14. Edward R. Burian, "Postscript," in *Modernity and the Architecture of Mexico*, ed. Edward R. Burian (Austin: University of Texas Press, 1997), 194.

15. Luis Carranza and Fernando Lara, *Modern Architecture in Latin America: Art, Technology, and Utopia* (Austin: University of Texas Press, 2014); *Latin America in Construction: Architecture 1955–1980*, exhibition catalog, ed. Barry Bergdoll et al. (New York: The Museum of Modern Art, 2015).

16. Barry Bergdoll, "Good Neighbors: The Museum of Modern Art and Latin America, 1933–1955, a Journey through the MoMA Archives"; and Ricardo Legorreta, "José Villagrán García and Luis Barragán," in *Modernidad Urbana*, ed. Louise Noelle and Iván San Martín (Mexico City: DOCOMOMO, 2012), 41–75, 125–41.

17. In his preface to the 1934 translation of *Spanish Colonial Architecture in Mexico*, Antonio Castro Leal noted that it was "still the work which covers the history of colonial Mexican architecture with the greatest scope" and that the quantity and quality of its illustrations had not been surpassed. Sylvester Baxter, *La arquitectura Hispano Colonial en México*, trans. Federico E. Mariscal, León Felipe, and Manuel Toussaint (Mexico City: Departamento de Bellas Artes, 1934), i.

18. The phenomenon was most notable in the World's Fair pavilion of 1889. On this and the attention to preconquest culture and indigeneity in Mexican nationalism, Tenorio Trillo, *Mexico at the World's Fairs*.

19. Enrique X. de Anda Alanís, "The Preservation of Historic Architecture and the Beliefs of the Modern Movement, in Mexico, 1914–1963," *Future Anterior* 6, no. 2 (Winter 2009), 58–73.

20. On the centennial celebrations and urban transformations undertaken in preparation for them: Mauricio Tenorio Trillo, "1910 Mexico City: Space and Nation in the City of the Centenario," *Journal of Latin American Studies* 28, no. 1 (February 1996), 75–104.

21. On archaeology and its scholarship, museums and cultural nationalism in nineteenth-century Mexico: Shelly E. Garrigan, *Collecting Mexico: Museums, Monuments, and the Creation of National Identity* (Minneapolis: University of Minnesota Press, 2012).

CHAPTER ONE. HISTORY, PHOTOGRAPHY, AND THE INVENTION OF MEXICAN ARCHITECTURE

Epigraph: Sylvester Baxter, *Spanish-Colonial Architecture in Mexico* (Boston: J. B. Millet, 1901), 1.

1. On Peabody in Mexico: Antonio Saborit, "En busca de la arquitectura hispano colonial: El trabajo de Peabody y Baxter en México," in *Guillermo Kahlo / Henry Greenwood Peabody*, ed. Isabel Garcés and Emma Hernández Tena (Mexico City: Fomento Cultural Grupo Salinas, 2009), 44–57.

2. Benedict Anderson explained this phenomenon in his classic study of nationalism, *Imagined Communities: Reflections on the Origin and Spread of Nationalism* (London: Verso, [1983] 2006).

3. Baxter, *Spanish-Colonial Architecture*, 2.

4. Baxter, *Spanish-Colonial Architecture*, 18, 19, 20.

5. Baxter, *Spanish-Colonial Architecture*, 21, 20.

6. Baxter, *Spanish-Colonial Architecture*, 6.

7. Baxter, *Spanish-Colonial Architecture*, 26. He quotes extensively from Manuel Revilla, *El Arte en Mexico en la Epóca Antiqua y durante el Gobierno Virreinal*, on seventeenth- and eighteenth-century baroque architecture. The 1893 edition of the book (which Federico Mariscal also used) treated pre-Hispanic art and colonial architecture, painting, and sculpture, although the longest chapter of the book was devoted to colonial architecture. The 1893 had no images, although numerous photographs and reproductions of colonial paintings were included in the second edition, which appeared in 1923.

8. Baxter, *Spanish-Colonial Architecture*, 28.

9. Baxter, *Spanish-Colonial Architecture*, 29–30.

10. Revilla, quoted in Baxter, *Spanish-Colonial Architecture*, 35.

11. Revilla, quoted in Baxter, *Spanish-Colonial Architecture*, 34–35.

12. Baxter, *Spanish-Colonial Architecture*, 46.

13. Baxter, *Spanish-Colonial Architecture*, 60.

14. Fernando Mariscal, *La patria y la arquitectura nacional: Resúmenes de las conferencias dadas en la casa de la Universidad Popular Mexicana del 21 de octubre de 1913 al 29 de julio de 1914 por el arquitecto D. Federico E. Mariscal* (Mexico City: Imprenta Stephan y Torres, 1915), 7. Translations are the author's unless otherwise indicated.

15. F. Mariscal, *La patria y la arquitectura nacional*, 9.

16. F. Mariscal, *La patria y la arquitectura nacional*, 10.

17. F. Mariscal, *La patria y la arquitectura nacional*, 10.

18. F. Mariscal, *La patria y la arquitectura nacional*, 11, 7–8.

19. F. Mariscal, *La patria y la arquitectura nacional*, 23, 23–24.

20. On the Ateneo de Juventud: Fernando Curiel, *La revuelta: Interpretación del Ateneo de la Juventud, 1906–1929* (Mexico City: Universidad Nacional Autónoma de México, Centro de Estudios Literarios, Instituto de Investigaciones Filológicas, 1998); on its relationship to the arts: Carmen Gaitán Rojo, Ariadna Patiño Guadarrama, and Julián Martínez González, *El Ateneo de la Juventud y la plástica mexicana* (Mexico City: Consejo Nacional para las Artes y Cultura, Instituto Nacional de Bellas Artes, 2010).

21. Nicolás Mariscal, "El desarrollo de la arquitectura en México," in *Nicolás Mariscal: Arquitectura, arte y ciencia*, ed. Louise Noelle (Mexico City: Consejo Na-

cional para la Cultura y las Artes, Instituto Nacional de Bellas Artes, Dirección de Arquitectura y Conservación del Patrimonio Artístico Inmueble, [1901] 2003), 13.

22. N. Mariscal, "El desarrollo de la arquitectura en México," 14, 2, 3.

23. N. Mariscal, "El desarrollo de la arquitectura en México," 14–15.

24. N. Mariscal, "El arte en México," in *Nicolás Mariscal: Arquitectura, arte y ciencia*, 52, 62.

25. F. Mariscal, prologue to Jesús T. Acevedo, *Disertaciones de un arquitecto* (Mexico City: Ediciones México Moderno, 1920), 19.

26. Acevedo, "La arquitectura colonial in México," in *Disertaciones de un arquitecto*, 137.

27. Acevedo, "La arquitectura colonial in México," 137, 138.

28. Acevedo, "La arquitectura colonial in México," 133.

29. Acevedo, "La arquitectura colonial in México," 130.

30. Acevedo, "La arquitectura colonial in México," 131.

31. Acevedo, "La arquitectura colonial in México," 140, 143, 146–47.

32. Acevedo, "La arquitectura colonial in México," 147.

33. For discussion see Norma Rojas Delgadillo, "Cultural Property Legislation in Mexico: Past, Present, and Future," in *Art and Cultural Heritage: Law, Policy, and Practice*, ed. Barbara T. Hoffman (Cambridge: Cambridge University Press, 2006).

34. These culminated with the founding of the Instituto Nacional de Antropología e Historia (INAH), which controls all archaeological and colonial sites in Mexico today. María del Perpetuo Socorro Villareal Escarrega, "The National Institute of Anthropology and History," in Hoffman, *Art and Cultural Heritage*.

35. Rosa Casanova and Adriana Konzevik, *Mexico, a Photographic History: A Selective Catalogue of the Fototeca Nacional of the INAH* (Mexico City: Consejo Nacional para la Cultura y las Artes; INAH; Editorial RM, 2007), 86.

36. *Guillermo Kahlo: Vida y obra: Fotógrafo, 1872–1941: Catálogo ilustrado* (Mexico City: Consejo Nacional para la Cultura y las Artes, Instituto Nacional de Bellas Artes, 1993), 69.

37. Manrique observed pointedly that the work "was not that of a specialist." Jorge Alberto Manrique, "Guillermo Kahlo, fotógrafo oficial de monumentos," in *Guillermo Kahlo, fotógrafo oficial de monumentos*, ed. David Maawad and Alicia Ahumada (Mexico City: Fototeca del INAH/Casa de las Imágenes, 1992), 16.

38. Genaro García, introduction to *La arquitectura en México: Iglesias* (Mexico City: Talleres de Imprenta y Fotograbado del Museo Nacional de Arqueología, Historia y Etnología, 1914), v.

39. Genero García, "Noticias históricas, generalidades," in *La arquitectura en México: Iglesias*, 1.

40. García, "Noticias históricas, generalidades," 1, 2, 2.

41. In June 1692 Mexico City residents, many of them indigenous artisans and craftspeople, angered by the rising price of maize and seeking to discuss it with a representative of the colonial government, marched to the viceregal palace (having been turned away by the archbishop) and demanded a hearing by the viceroy. He was out of town, and the crowd, doubly infuriated, attacked buildings around the Zócalo.

42. Manuel Alvarez made this point in his study of the history of the Cathedral and the plaza: "La Plaza de La Constitución: Memoria histórica y artística, y proyecto de reformas" (1916). Reprinted in *Manuel F. Alvarez, algunos escritos*, ed. Elisa García Barragán (Mexico City: Secretaría de Educación Pública, Instituto Nacional de Bellas Artes, 1982), 60.

43. Although many of these have been removed it is possible to see where they were replaced by stones whose color varies slightly from the rest of the wall.

44. On Tostado, see Olivier Debroise, *Mexican Suite: A History of Photography in Mexico*, trans. Stella de Sá Rego (Austin: University of Texas Press, 2001), 187.

45. In 2010 the building was acquired by the government of the Federal District to be renovated and reused as the headquarters of the Asociación de Escritores en Lenguas Indígenas.

46. The vogue of colonial revival houses in Mexico was also fueled by the style's popularity in California. On the colonial revival, see Rafael R. Fierro Gossman, *La gran corriente ornamental del siglo XX: Una revisión de la arquitectura neocolonial en la ciudad de México* (Mexico City: Universidad Iberoamericana, 1998), and Clara Bargellini, "La Arquitectura Neocolonial: Historia, Palabras e Identidades," in *Hacia otra historia del arte en México*, vol. 3, ed. Esther Acevedo (Mexico City: Curare, A.C., 2002).

47. Israel Katzman, *La arquitectura contemporánea mexicana: Precedentes y desarrollo* (Mexico City: Instituto Nacional de Antropología e Historia, 1964), 81.

48. On the relationship between architecture and politics: Luis E. Carranza, *Architecture as Revolution: Episodes in the History of Modern Mexico* (Austin: University of Texas Press, 2010), and Luis M. Castañeda, *Spectacular Mexico: Design, Propaganda, and the 1968 Olympics* (Minneapolis: University of Minnesota Press, 2014).

CHAPTER TWO. REPRESENTATION AND REFORM AT THE MINISTRY OF HEALTH

1. William Spratling, "The Public Health Center, Mexico City," *Architectural Forum* (November 1931), 589.

2. Spratling, "The Public Health Center," 593.

3. "El nuevo edificio del Departamento de Salubridad, proyectado y construido por el arquitecto Carlos Obregón Santacilia," *Obras públicas* (August–September 1930), 101.

4. "El Nuevo Edificio del Departamento de Salubridad," 101.

5. For an overview of the cultural and political changes of this period see Mary Kay Vaughan and Stephen E. Lewis, eds., *The Eagle and the Virgin: Nation and Cultural Revolution in Mexico, 1920–1940* (Durham, NC: Duke University Press, 2006).

6. Luis Carranza, *Architecture as Revolution: Episodes in the History of Modern Mexico* (Austin: University of Texas Press, 2010).

7. On the 1921 exhibition: Rick A. López, *Crafting Mexico: Intellectuals, Artisans, and the State after the Revolution* (Durham, NC: Duke University Press, 2010), 76–86; 89–93; on folk art in the postrevolutionary period: James Oles, *South of the Border: Mexico in the American Imagination, 1914–1947* (Washington, DC: Smithsonian Institution Press, 1993), and in the context of U.S. exhibitions: Anna Indych-López, *Muralism without Walls: Rivera, Orozco, and Siqueiros in the United States* (Pittsburgh: University of Pittsburgh Press, 2009).

8. Dr. Atl, *Iglesias de México*, vol. 6 (Mexico City: Publicaciones de la Secretaría de hacienda, 1924–27), 109.

9. Dr. Atl, *Iglesias de México*, 109.

10. Dr. Atl, *Iglesias de México*, 19.

11. Dr. Atl, *Iglesias de México*, 19, 20.

12. Spratling wanted to meet Atl after having read *Iglesias de México* in the "offices of the Journal of the American Institute of Architects in New York, to whom the Mexican Government had given a set." The architect also apparently read "many books on the glories of Spain in the New World," in the National Library in Mexico City. William Spratling, "Figures in a Mexican Renaissance," *Scribner's Magazine* (January 1929), 16.

13. "Primero Renglones," *El arquitecto* 1, no. 1 (September 1923): n.p.

14. Drawings for this project are held in the Carlos Obregón Santacilia archive at the Instituto Nacional de Bellas Artes.

15. He recalled many years later one project, for the entrance to a cemetery, to which students responded in a variety ways using Egyptian, colonial, and gothic forms. Carlos Obregón Santacilia, *50 años de arquitectura mexicana (1900–1950)* (Mexico City: Editorial Patria, 1952), 38

16. Among the earliest European debates about architectural style were those in Germany, most famously that opened by Heinrich Hübsch in "In welchem Style sollen wir bauen?" (1828). For Hübsch's essay and others: Heinrich Hübsch, *In What Style Should We Build? The German Debate on Architectural Style* (Santa Monica, CA: Getty Center for the History of Art and the Humanities; distributed by the University of Chicago Press, 1992).

17. Obregón Santacilia described Ituarte and Macedo y Arbeu as "progressive," in *50 años de arquitectura*, 38.

18. Obregón Santacilia, *50 años de arquitectura*, 39. Information about modern architecture abroad was published in Mexico City in the 1920s in six main sources: *Cemento* and *Tolteca* (published by the cement industry), in the journals *Arquitectura* (1921–23) and *El arquitecto* (1923–25, 1932–36), and in newspapers *El Excélsior* and *El Universal*. For a summary of the reception of European and United States works in that decade: Enrique X. de Anda Alanís, *La arquitectura de la revolución mexicana* (Mexico City: Instituto Nacional de Bellas Artes, Universidad Autónoma de México, 1990), 79–93.

19. Obregón Santacilia, *50 años de arquitectura*, 36.

20. Obregón Santacilia, *50 años de arquitectura*, 37.

21. *Forma* 3 (1927), quoted in Rafael López Rangel, *La modernidad arquitectónica mexicana, antecedentes y vanguardias, 1900–1940* (Azcapotzalco: Universidad Autónoma Metropolitana, 1989), 81–82.

22. Obregón Santacilia, *50 años de arquitectura*, 34.

23. Obregón Santacilia, *50 años de arquitectura*, 35.

24. López Rangel, *La modernidad arquitectónica*, 9.

25. For example see José de Alcíbar, *The Virgin of Guadalupe Venerated by Saint John and Juan Diego*, ca. 1784, oil on canvas.

26. Obregón Santacilia, *50 años de arquitectura*, 69.

27. Mauricio Tenorio Trillo interprets the 1889 pavilion primarily in terms of written histories of Mexico and debates on race and national progress in *Mexico at the World's Fairs: Crafting a Modern Nation* (Berkeley: University of California Press, 1996), 48–124.

28. Secretaría de Industria y Trabajo, *México: Sus recursos naturales, su situación actual; homenaje al Brasil en ocasion del primer centenario de su independencia, 1822–1922* (Mexico City: La Secretaria de Industria, Comercio y Trabajo, 1922), 271–77, 271.

29. Secretaría de Industria y Trabajo, *México: Sus recursos naturales*, 275, 274, 304.

30. On Vasconcelos's involvement and exhibition building, see Tenorio Trillo, "A Tropical Cuauhtémoc: Celebrating the Cosmic Race at the Guanabara Bay," *Anales del Instituto de Investigaciones Estéticas* 65 (1994), 93–137. On the competition, see especially 105–6.

31. Carranza, *Architecture as Revolution*, 14–55.

32. Vasconcelos and his ideas on culture and architecture have been discussed at length and in many sources. For a focused discussion of them vis-à-vis the Rio Pavilion and Ministry of Education, see Tenorio Trillo, "A Tropical Cuauhtémoc," and Carranza, *Architecture as Revolution*, 14–55.

33. Margaret Hutton Abels, "Painting at the Brazil Centennial Exposition," *Art and Archaeology* 16 (Summer 1923), 108–9.

34. Abels, "Painting at the Brazil Centennial Exposition," 108.

35. Alberto Pani, "El gobierno constitucionalista ante los problemas sanitario y educativo de México," talk before the American Academy of Political and Social Sciences and the Society of Arbitration and Peace, Philadelphia, November 10, 1916 (50–51). Alberto J. Pani, *Hygiene in Mexico: A Study of Sanitary and Educational Problems*, trans. Ernest L. de Gogorza (New York: G. P. Putnam's Sons, Knickerbocker Press, 1917).

36. See Anthony J. Mazzaferri's detailed analysis of public health reform and political change in Mexico, "Public Health and Social Revolution in Mexico: 1877–1930" (Phd diss., Kent State University, 1968).

37. The surviving drawings by Obregón Santacilia for the Ministry of Health have not been cataloged and are part of the architect's archive held by the Instituto Nacional de Bellas Artes, Mexico City.

38. On the Reforma monuments and allusions to antiquity: Barbara A. Tenenbaum, "Streetwise History: The Paseo de la Reforma and the Porfirian State, 1876–1910," in *Rituals of Rule, Rituals of Resistance*, ed. William H. Beezley, Cheryl English Martin, and William E. French (Lanham, MD: Rowman and Littlefield, 1994), 127–50. On Mexico City during the Centennial: Mauricio Tenorio Trillo, "1910 Mexico City: Space and Nation in the City of the Centenario," *Journal of Latin American Studies* 28, no. 1 (February 1996), 75–104.

39. T. Philip Terry, *Terry's Guide to Mexico* (Boston: Houghton Mifflin, 1933), 356.

40. Sylvester Baxter, *Spanish-Colonial Architecture in Mexico*, 10 vols. (Boston: J. B. Millet, 1901), 1:117.

41. Federico Mariscal, *La patria y la arquitectura nacional: Resúmenes de las conferencias dadas en la casa de la Universidad Popular Mexicana del 21 de octubre de 1913 al 29 de julio de 1914 por el arquitecto D. Federico E. Mariscal* (Mexico City: Imprenta Stephan y Torres, 1915), 44.

42. Anita Brenner, *Your Mexican Holiday* (New York: Putnam's, 1932), 77.

43. On Art Deco in Mexican architecture: de Anda Alanís, *La arquitectura de la revolución*, 127–56.

44. On the ministry in the context of Art Deco art and architecture in Mexico: de Anda, "El edificio de la Secretaría de Salud: La modernidad frente al Castillo," in *Art Déco: Un país nacionalista, un Méxcio cosmopolita*, ed. Jaime Soler (Mexico City: Instituto Nacional de Bellas Artes, 1997), 86–95.

45. Obregón Santacilia, *50 años de arquitectura*, 48.

46. The Pedregal area south of Mexico City and distinguished by its landscape of volcanic rock is the best known example of a place imagined to be linked to indige-

nous Mexicans because of the material. Keith Eggener, *Luis Barragán's Gardens of El Pedregal* (New York: Princeton Architectural Press, 2001), 16–19.

47. Spratling, "The Public Health Center," 591.

48. Charles A. Hale, *The Transformation of Liberalism in Late Nineteenth-Century Mexico* (Princeton, NJ: Princeton University Press, 1989), 141–47.

49. Bernardo Gastélum, "El espíritu del héroe," *Contemporáneos* 1, no. 1 (June 1928), 13.

50. Bernardo Gastélum, "Democracia asimétrica," *Contemporáneos* 2, no. 6 (November 1928), 245.

51. Gastélum, "Democracia asimétrica," 248–49.

52. Mary K. Coffey, "'All Mexico on a Wall': Diego Rivera's Murals at the Ministry of Public Education," in *Mexican Muralism: A Critical History*, ed. Alejandro Anreus, Leonard Folgarait, and Robin Adèle Greeley (Berkeley: University of California Press, 2012), 56–74, esp. 63–70.

53. Bernardo Gastélum, *La clase, la arquitectura de la comunidad* (Mexico City: n.p., 1928), 9.

54. Gastélum, *La clase, la arquitectura*, 10, 10–11, 19.

55. Mariscal, *La patria y la arquitectura*, 10.

56. Kathryn E. O'Rourke, "Science and Sex in Diego Rivera's Health Ministry Murals," *Public Art Dialogue* 4, no. 1 (2014), 9–40.

57. Obregón Santacilia, *50 años de arquitectura*, 27.

58. On images of food and its cultural significance in Mexican painting: Nina M. Scott, "Measuring Ingredients: Food and Domesticity in Mexican Casta Paintings," *Gastronomica* 5, no. 1 (2005), 70–79; and Edward J. Sullivan, "Naturalezas mexicanas: Objects as Cultural Signifiers in Mexican Art, c. 1760–1875," in *The Lure of the Object*, ed. Stephen W. Melville (Williamstown, MA: Sterling and Francine Clark Art Institute, 2005), 59–71.

59. Karen Cordero Reiman, "The Best Maugard Drawing Method," *Journal of Decorative and Propaganda Arts, Mexico Theme Issue* 26 (The Wolfsonian—Florida International University, 2010), 46.

60. Best Maugard worked closely with anthropologist Manuel Gamio, who introduced him to Franz Boas, whose ideas were influential for him. Cordero Reiman, "Best Maugard Drawing Method," 53–54.

61. On Furness and Sullivan: James F. O'Gorman, *Three American Architects: Richardson, Sullivan, Wright, 1865–1915* (Chicago: University of Chicago Press, 1991), 70–75. On conventionalization and sculpture in Wright's early work: Neil Levine, *The Architecture of Frank Lloyd Wright* (Princeton, NJ: Princeton University Press, 1996), 33–37.

62. As part of the expansion and renovation of the Ministry of Foreign Relations that Obregón Santacilia directed in 1923, Montenegro designed a large stained-glass dome for the main hall. The painter also created two murals in the Benito Juárez School in 1925. On both projects, see Victor Jiménez, *Carlos Obregón Santacila, pionero de arquitectura Mexicana* (Mexico City: Insituto Nacional de Bellas Artes, Consejo Nacional para la Cultura y las Artes, 2001), 30–47.

CHAPTER THREE. FIT AND TRIM

Epigraph: Alfonso Pallares, "Por qué no tenemos una arquitectura nacional? El concurso del Pabellón de México en Sevilla y su significado," originally published May 9, 1926, in *Excélsior*, reprinted in *Ideario de los arquitectos mexicanos*, vol. 2, ed. Ramón

Vargas Salguero and J. Víctor Arias Montes (Mexico City: Instituto Nacional de Bellas Artes, 2010), 116.

1. For example in the *Anuario de la Sociedad de Arquitectos Mexicanos, 1922–23*: Heraclio Cabrera, "El acueducto y las fuentes coloniales de Querétaro," 4–19; Pallares, "Ante el plano de la ciudad de México," 21–32; Antonio Muñoz García, "El Jardin Borda, Cuernavaca," 79–81; Luis Prieto y Souza, "En pro de la ciudad," *El Universal*, November 5, 1927, republished in *Idearios de los arquitectos mexicanos*, 2:140–41.

2. Dina Berger, *The Development of Mexico's Tourism Industry: Pyramids by Day, Martinis by Night* (New York: Palgrave Macmillian, 2006), 11–15. Berger observed that "tourism functioned as a barometer of national development," 13.

3. Federal District publications from the late 1920s and 1930s repeatedly emphasized progress in paving roads and providing sewage systems to the growing city. See Departamento del Distrito Federal, *Atlas general del Distrito Federal* (Mexico City: Department of the Federal District, 1930) and the *Memorias del Departamento del Distrito Federal* from the period. Municipal authorities had been behind in providing services for most of modern Mexican history. See Claudia Agostoni, *Monuments of Progress: Modernization and Public Health in Mexico City, 1876–1910* (Calgary: University of Calgary Press, 2003).

4. "Mexico City to Get Huge Park," *Los Angeles Times*, September 9, 1929, 15.

5. Anita Brenner, *Your Mexican Holiday* (New York: G.P. Putnam's Sons, 1932), 238.

6. In the late 1920s through the 1930s in its annual *Memorias* and other publications the Federal District and the municipal authority that preceded it heavily promoted its infrastructure improvements in the capital and cited them as evidence of its fulfillment of "revolutionary" mandates.

7. On this project, see Natalia de la Rosa de la Rosa, "Mirada dirigida y control del cuerpo: Arquitectura y pintura mural en la escuela Domingo Faustino Sarmiento," in *Encauzar la Mirada: Arquitectura, pedagogía e imágenes en Méxcio, 1920–1950*, ed. Renato González Mello and Deborah Dorotinsky Alperstein (Mexico City: Universidad Nacional Autónoma Méxcio, Instituto de Investigaciones Estéticas, 2010), 75–105.

8. Legarreta's other projects were built in the La Vaquita and San Jacinto developments.

9. Segura, interview with Xavier Guzmán, in "Modernidad en la arquitectura," reprinted in *Modernidad en la arquitectura mexicana (18 protagonistas)*, ed. Pablo Quintero (Mexico City: Universidad Autonoma Metropolitana-Unidad Xochimilco, 1990), 618.

10. Segura interview with Guzmán, 616–17.

11. Antonio Toca Fernández, "Juan Segura: Orígenes de la arquitectura moderna en México," in *El Museo Nacional de Arquitectura* (Mexico City: Instituto Nacional de Bellas Artes, 1990), 234.

12. On the colonial revival style in this context, see Rafael Fierro Gossman, *La gran corriente ornamental del siglo XX: Una revisión de la arquitectura neocolonial en la ciudad de México* (Mexico City: Universidad Iberoamericana, 1998).

13. Enrique X. de Anda Alanís, *La arquitectura de la revolución mexicana* (Mexico City: Instituto Nacional de Bellas Artes, 1990), 106.

14. The most complete account of Segura's oeuvre is "Exposición Juan Segura," in *El Museo Nacional* (Mexico City: Instituto Nacional de Bellas Artes, 1990), 153–250.

15. Earlier histories that cast International Style modernism as the one true modernism or the profusion of International Style buildings at mid-century as the apogee of architectural modernity and thus excluded Segura altogether include Esther Born,

The New Architecture in Mexico (New York: Architectural Record, William Morrow, 1937); I. E. Myers, *Mexico's Modern Architecture* (New York: Architectural Book, 1952); and Sociedad de Arquitectos Mexicanos, *4000 años de arquitectura mexicana* (Mexico City: Libreros Mexicanos Unidos, 1956). In his survey of Mexican architecture from the beginning of the twentieth century Katzman classified Segura's work as part of the "transition" between "nationalism" and the "affirmation of a new esthetic impulse." Israel Katzman, *Arquitectura contemporánea mexicana* (Mexico City: Instituto Nacional de Antropologia e Historia; SEP, 1964).

16. José Villagrán García, *Panorama de 50 años de arquitectura mexicana contemporánea* (Mexico City: INBA, 1950), quoted in Toca Fernández, "Juan Segura," *La arquitectura mexicana del siglo XX*, ed. Fernando González Gortázar (Mexico City: Consejo Nacional para la Cultura, 1996), 152.

17. José Villagrán García, *Panorama de 62 años de arquitectura mexicana contemporánea (1900–1962)* (Mexico City: INBA, 1963), vii.

18. Salvador Pinocelly remarked on Segura's "individualism" with reference to his use of different materials and called his architecture "modern and personal." "Juan Segura, precursor," *Diorama de Excélsior* (Mexico, November 1965), quoted in Toca Fernández, "Juan Segura, orígenes," 241. See also Enrique X. De Anda Alanís, "Tradicionalismo y Modernidad en la obra de Juan Segura," in *Una mirada a la arquitectura mexicano del siglo XX (Diez ensayos)* (Mexico City: Consejo Nacional para la Cultura y las Artes, 2005), 61–71.

19. Jorge Alberto Manrique, "Las cuentas claras en la arquitectura mexicana," *Artes visuales* 2 (Spring 1974), 34.

20. Louis Prieto y Souza, "Sobre la tan debatida cuestión del arte colonial," originally published August 24, 1924, in *El Universal*; reprinted in *Ideario de los arquitectos mexicanos*, 2:129, 130.

21. Prieto y Souza, "Problemas del momento: El mejoramiento matieral y económico de las clases sociales," originally published September 26, 1926, in *El Universal*; reprinted in *Ideario de los arquitectos mexicanos*, 2:137.

22. Prieto y Souza, "Problemas del momento," 137.

23. Luis Carranza, *Architecture as Revolution: Episodes in the History of Modern Mexico* (Austin: University of Texas Press, 2010), 86–117.

24. Pallares, "Por que no tenemos una arquitectura nacional?" 117.

25. Brenner, *Your Mexican Holiday*, 151.

26. Dr. Atl, *Iglesias de México*, vol. 4 (Mexico City: Secretaria de Hacienda, Talleres de la editorial "Cultura," 1925), 5.

27. Dr. Atl, *Iglesias de México*, 4:9.

28. Dr. Atl, *Iglesias de México*, 6:109.

29. Dr. Atl, *Iglesias de México*, 6:140.

30. See Karen Cordero Reiman, "Constructing a Modern Mexican Art, 1910–1940," in James Oles, *South of the Border: Mexico in the American Imagination, 1914–1947*, ed. James Oles (Washington, DC: Smithsonian Institution Press, 1993), 29.

31. Dr. Atl, *Iglesias de México*, 6:140.

32. Dr. Atl, *Iglesias de México*, 6:189.

33. Manuel Romero de Terreros, *The House of Tiles: La Casa de los Azulejos* (Mexico City: Bland Brothers, Printers, 1925); Marion Lucile Arendt, *The Historical Significance of Mexican Art and Architecture* (Mexico City: Secretaría de Educación Pública; Talleres Gráficos de la Nación, 1928).

34. Walter H. Kilham, *Mexican Architecture of the Vice-Regal Period* (New York: Longmans, Green, 1927), 10.

35. Kilham, *Mexican Architecture*, 121.

36. J. M. Puig Casauranc, untitled essay, *Forma* 1, no. 1 (October 1926), 1.

37. Puig Casauranc, untitled essay, 1.

38. Benedict Anderson, *Imagined Communities: Reflections on the Origin and Spread of Nationalism* (London: Verso, 1983).

39. "Revolutionary Birth Feted by Nation at Social Welfare Park," *Excélsior*, November 21, 1929, sec. 2, p. 2.

40. David E. Lorey, "The Revolutionary Festival in Mexico: November 20 Celebrations in the 1920s and 1930s," *Americas* 54, no. 1 (July 1997), 39–82.

41. José Manuel Puig Casauranc, *La obra integral de la revolución mexicana: Discurso pronunciado por el Dr. J.M. Puig Casauranc, el 20 de noviembre de 1929, al inaugurarse el Centro Social y Deportivo para Trabajadores "Venustiano Carranza"* (Mexico City: Departamento del Distrito Federal, Talleres Gráficos de la Nación, 1929), 12. Hereafter, *La obra integral*.

42. "Inauguró ayer el Sr. Presidente E. Portes Gil el centro social y deportivo para trabajadores," *Excélsior*, November 21, 1929, sec. 2, p. 1.

43. Departamento del Distrito Federal, *Centro Social y deportivo para trabajadores "Venustiano Carranza" en el parque de Balbuena; Memoria descriptiva del centro y folleto conmemorativo de los festivales de inauguración, 20 a 24 de noviembre de 1929* (Mexico City: Talleres Gráficos de la Nación, 1929), 15. Hereafter, *Memoria descriptiva del centro*.

44. The theater has been destroyed and few images of it exist.

45. Departamento del Distrito Federal, *Memoria descriptiva del centro*, 16.

46. Toca Fernández, "Juan Segura, orígenes," 231. Images of many different kinds of European modernism arrived in Mexico beginning in the early 1920s in publications that included *Moderne Bauformen*, *L'Architecte*, *Architectural Record*, and *Archittetura e Arti Decorative*, and in the architecture pages of Mexican periodicals; Katzman, *Arquitectura contemporánea mexicana*, 99–100.

47. Barbara Miller Lane has discussed this phenomenon in the context of the national romantic architecture of Germany and Scandinavia built in the late nineteenth and early twentieth centuries. *National Romanticism and Modern Architecture in Germany and the Scandinavian Countries* (Cambridge: Cambridge University Press, 2000), 249–320.

48. Departamento del Distrito Federal, *Atlas general del Distrito Federal*, 223.

49. Departamento del Distrito Federal, *Memoria descriptiva del centro*, 15.

50. Departamento del Distrito Federal, *Atlas general del Distrito Federal*, 224.

51. Lorenzo Fuentes, "La construcción del Centro Social y Deportivo para trabajadores en Balbuena," *Obras Publicas* (January 1930), 18.

52. "Inauguro ayer el Sr. Presidente E. Portes Gil el centro social y deportivo para trabajadores," *Excélsior*, November 21, 1929, sec. 2, p. 1.

53. "Inauguro ayer el Sr. Presidente E. Portes Gil."

54. Gabriel Fernández Ledesma, "Fotografías de deportes," *Forma: Revista de artes plásticas* 3 (1927), 12.

55. On the National Stadium: Valerie Fraser, *Building the New World: Studies in the Modern Architecture of Latin America, 1930–1960* (London: Verso, 2000), 29; Diana Briuolo Destéfano, "El Estadio Nacional: Escenario de la raza cósmica," *Crónicas: El*

muralismo, producto de la revolución mexicana, en América, seminario de investigación no. 2 (May–August 1998), 16–17, 28–30; Rubén Gallo, *Mexican Modernity: The Avant-Garde and the Technological Revolution* (Cambridge, MA: MIT Press, 2005), 209; Sigfried Kracauer, "The Mass Ornament," repr. in *The Mass Ornament: The Weimar Essays*, ed. and trans., Thomas Y. Levin (Cambridge, MA: Harvard University Press, 1995), 75–86.

56. Kracauer, "The Mass Ornament," 76.

57. Kracauer, "The Mass Ornament," 76.

58. For Detlef Mertins, Mies van der Rohe's curtain wall materialized this phenomenon. "Mies's Skyscraper 'Project': Towards the Redemption of the Technical Structure," in *The Presence of Mies*, ed. Detlef Mertins (New York: Princeton Architectural Press, 1996), 48–67.

59. Kracauer, "The Mass Ornament," 77.

60. *Excélsior*, November 21, 1929, sec. 2, p. 1.

61. *Excélsior*, November 21, 1929, sec. 2, p. 1.

62. Marilyn Grace Miller discusses prevailing attitudes in Mexico about racial "weakness" and "depression" in *Rise and Fall of the Cosmic Race: The Cult of Mestizaje in Latin America* (Austin: University of Texas Press, 2004), 34–36.

63. "'El laborillo,' pantomina de una Fiesta popular en Tehuantepec, será representa hoy en el teatro al aire libre del Centro 'Venustiano Carranza,'" *El Universal*, November 23, 1929, sec. 2, p. 1.

64. Departamento del Distrito Federal, *Programa general para los festivales y competencias que se efectuarán en el Centro Social y Deportivo para trabajadores "Venustiano Carranza" durante los dias del 20 al 24 de noviembre de 1929, en ocasión de la inauguración de dicho centro* (Mexico City: Departamento del Distrito Federal, 1929). Hereafter, *Programa general*.

65. Departamento del Distrito Federal, *Memoria descriptiva del centro*, 41.

66. Departamento del Distrito Federal, *Memoria descriptiva del centro*, 42.

67. Departamento del Distrito Federal, *Programa general*, 5.

68. Anita Brenner, "Romance and Realism in a Modern Aztec Theatre," *Art and Archeology* 20, no. 2 (August 1925), 68.

69. Frances Toor, "El Principio de un Teatro Mexicano," *Mexican Folkways* 5, no. 2 (April–June 1929), 61–62.

70. On early twentieth-century outdoor theaters: Frank A. Waugh, *Outdoor Theaters: The Design, Construction, and Use of Open-Air Auditoriums* (Boston: Richard G. Badger, 1917).

71. Brenner, "Romance and Realism," 68.

72. Brenner, "Romance and Realism," 68.

73. Salvador Baguez, "Ancient and Modern Mexican-Indian Folk Lore," *Los Angeles Times*, September 22, 1929, I2.

74. Baguez, "Ancient and Modern Mexican-Indian Folk Lore," I2.

75. Arthur Miller, "Mexico Depicted as Land of Artists," *Los Angeles Times*, September 22, 1929, B11.

76. Brenner, "Romance and Realism," 69. Gamio claimed that "it was a simple step from reality to realism."

77. A photograph that appeared in Brenner's *Art and Archeology* article showed the heads of the audience. Their hats suggested that people from a variety of classes were in the audience: newsboy caps, fedoras, sombreros, and wide-brimmed women's hats appeared.

78. Brenner, "Romance and Realism," 69.

79. Brenner's *Art and Archeology* article included two high-quality photographs of productions at Teotihuacan and a brief discussion by Gamio of the movies made there (Brenner, "Romance and Realism," 69).

80. Barry Bergdoll, *European Architecture 1750–1890* (Oxford: Oxford University Press, 2000), 189.

81. Bergdoll, *European Architecture*, 192.

82. For examples of how these crossed national borders, see Alex Bremmer, *Imperial Gothic: Religious Architecture and High Anglican Culture in the British Empire c.1840–70* (New Haven, CT: Yale University Press, 2013).

83. William J. R. Curtis, *Modern Architecture since 1900*, 3rd ed. (London: Phadion Press, 1996), 561.

84. Alice T. Friedman, *Women and the Making of the Modern House* (New York: Abrams, 1998), 188–213.

85. Robert Venturi, *Complexity and Contradiction in Architecture*, 2nd ed., repr. (New York: The Museum of Modern Art, 1996), 32.

86. Venturi, *Complexity and Contradiction*, 25, 19, 88–90.

87. Venturi, *Complexity and Contradiction*, 104.

CHAPTER FOUR. COMPOSITION AND CONFLICT

1. O'Gorman oversaw the restoration of another twenty-eight schools, helped create the building and curriculum of a new architecture school, and designed eight houses for Mexico City artists and intellectuals, all by 1935.

2. Juan O'Gorman and Antonio Luna Arroyo, *Juan O'Gorman, autobiografía, antología, juicios críticos y documentación exhaustive sobre su obra* (México City: Cuadernos Populares de Pintura Mexicana Moderna, 1973), 94.

3. Luis E. Carranza discusses functionalism from a variety of perspectives as they relate to O'Gorman's development. *Architecture as Revolution: Episodes in the History of Modern Mexico* (Austin: University of Texas Press, 2010), 119–31.

4. Justino Fernández, "The New Architecture in Mexico: An Outline of Its Development," in Esther Born, *The New Architecture in Mexico* (New York: Architectural Record, William Morrow, 1937), 15.

5. O'Gorman and Luna Arroyo, *Juan O'Gorman*, 100.

6. On Mexican education in this period: Mary Kay Vaughan, *Cultural Politics in Revolution: Teachers, Peasants, and Schools in Mexico, 1930–1940* (Tucson: University of Arizona Press, 1997).

7. Carranza called O'Gorman's work and architecture of "quotations" and discussed its revolutionary content at length, *Architecture as Revolution*, 118–67.

8. On "functionalism" in scholarship and criticism, Stanford Anderson, "The Fiction of Function," *Assemblage* 2 (February 1987), 18–31. William J. R. Curtis has drawn attention to Le Corbusier's own tendency to select and compose elements. *Modern Architecture since 1900*, 3rd ed. (London: Phaidon Press, 1996).

9. Valerie Fraser, *Building the New World: Studies in the Modern Architecture of Latin America, 1930–1960* (London: Verso, 2000), 44–45.

10. Adriana Zavala, "Mexico City in Juan O'Gorman's Imagination," *Hispanic Research Journal* 8, no. 5 (December 2007), 491–506.

11. Among these were Alberto Le Duc and Roberto Alvarez Espinosa, *Una casa*

habitación del siglo XVIII en la ciudad de México (Mexico City: Talleres de la Editorial Cultura, 1939); Jorge Enciso and Lauro E. Rosell, *Edificios coloniales artísticos e históricos de la Republica Mexicana que han sido declarados monumentos* (Mexico City: Talleres tipográficos de la editorial Cultura, 1939); José R. Benítez, *Las catedrales de Oaxaca, Morelia y Zacatecas, estudio de arqueografia comparada* (Mexico City: Talleres Gráficos de la Nación, 1934); Manuel Toussaint, *Paseos coloniales* (Mexico City: Imprenta Universitaria, 1939); Manuel Toussaint, Federico Gómez de Orozco, and Justino Fernández, *Planos de la ciudad de México siglos XVI y XVII, estudio histórico, urbanístico y bibliográfico* (México City: Instituto de Investigaciones Estéticas, Universidad Nacional Autónoma, 1939).

12. O'Gorman and Luna Arroyo, *Juan O'Gorman*, 79.

13. O'Gorman and Luna Arroyo, *Juan O'Gorman*, 79, 80.

14. T. Philip Terry, *Terry's Guide to Mexico* (Boston, 1933), 416.

15. O'Gorman and Luna Arroyo, *Juan O'Gorman*, 82. O'Gorman noted with pleasure that after his family sold the house it was renovated by a "professional knowledgeable about colonial architecture" (102).

16. Quoted in Victor Jiménez, "Un arquitecto de nuestro tiempo," in *O'Gorman* (Mexico City: Grupo Financiero Bital; Milan: Américo Arte Editores, 1999), 124.

17. O'Gorman refers to himself as Obregón Santacilia's student in O'Gorman and Luan Arroyo, *Juan O'Gorman*, 89.

18. Jiménez first noted the extent of O'Gorman's involvement in the Ministry of Health project in "Un arquitecto de nuestro tiempo," 121.

19. These drawings are in the Lionel Pries archive at the University of Washington. I am grateful to Juan Manuel Heredia for calling them to my attention.

20. Diego Rivera, "The New Mexican Architecture: A House of Carlos Obregón," *Mexican Folkways* 2, no. 6 (1926), 19–29.

21. One of the best remaining examples was the Casa de Montejo (1549) in Mérida.

22. Rivera, "New Mexican architecture," 22.

23. Rivera, "La nueva arquitectura mexicana." Author's translation.

24. O'Gorman and Luna Arroyo, *Juan O'Gorman*, 100–101.

25. O'Gorman and Arroyo, *Juan O'Gorman*, 94. In the Spanish O'Gorman refers to the famous book as *Hacia una arquitectura*, closer to its French title, *Vers une architecture*, than the most-often-used English translation, *Towards a New Architecture*. Clive Bamford Smith reported that O'Gorman read the book four times before he turned twenty in 1925. *Builders in the Sun: Five Mexican Architects* (New York: Architectural Book. 1967), 18.

26. See Hannes Meyer, "Building," in *Programs and Manifestoes on 20th-Century Architecture*, ed. Ulrich Conrads, 15th ed. (Cambridge, MA: MIT Press, 2001), 117–20. Meyer was most influential as director of the Bauhaus. On his positions regarding functionalism during that period: Barry Bergdoll, "Bauhaus Multiplied: Paradoxes of Architecture and Design in and after the Bauhaus," in *Bauhaus 1919–1933: Workshops for Modernity*, eds. Barry Bergdoll and Leah Dickerman (New York: Museum of Modern Art, 2009), 56–58.

27. O'Gorman and Luna Arroyo, *Juan O'Gorman*, 102.

28. The buildings have been interpreted thus by scholars in different countries and disciplines including Fraser; Hayden Herrera, *Frida, a Biography of Frida Kahlo*, repr. (New York: Perennial, 2002); and Victor Jiménez, *Las casas de Juan O'Gorman para Diego y Frida* (Mexico City: Instituto Nacional de Bellas Artes, Museo Casa-Estudio Diego Rivera y Frida Kahlo, 2001).

29. On the couple and the way they used the buildings: Herrera, *Frida*, 194–96.

30. O'Gorman and Luna Arroyo, *Juan O'Gorman*, 115, 103.

31. "Bridged Domesticity: The Diego Riveras Have Two Roofs and One Menage," *Arts and Decoration* 39 (August 1933), 26–30. In 1937 Esther Born described the buildings as a "studio" and "small house" and did not mention Kahlo. Born, *New Architecture in Mexico*, 89. See also "Diego Rivera's House and Studio on the Outskirts of Mexico City," *American Architect and Architecture* 146 (May 1935), 66.

32. "Bridged Domesticity," 28.

33. "Bridged Domesticity," 30.

34. "Bridged Domesticity," 30.

35. Born, *New Architecture in Mexico*, 87–89.

36. Le Corbusier, *Vers une architecture*, trans. Frederick Etchells (from the 13th ed.) (London: John Rodker, 1927), 81.

37. Le Corbusier, *Vers une architecture*, 81.

38. Le Corbusier, *Vers une architecture*, 31.

39. Le Corbusier, *Vers une architecture*, 37.

40. Le Corbusier, *Vers une architecture*, 153.

41. Le Corbusier, *Vers une architecture*, 288, 289.

42. For example, see "Monsieur Le Corbusier," *Tolteca* (November 1930), 216–17.

43. For discussion of Tolteca's photograph competition and its position on architecture, see James Oles, "Modern Photography and Cementos Tolteca: A Utopian Alliance," in *Mexicana: Fotografía moderna in México, 1923–1940*, ed. Salvador Albiñana and Horacio Fernández (Valencia: Generalitat Valencia, 1998), 273–75.

44. On the competition and images of modern industry in Mexican art, see James Oles, "Industrial Landscapes in Modern Mexican Art," *Journal of Decorative and Propaganda Arts* 26 (Miami Beach: The Wolfsonian—Florida International University, 2010), 128–59.

45. Enrique X. de Anda Alanís, "El proyecto de Juan O'Gorman para el concurso de la 'vivienda obrera' de 1932," *Arquine* 20 (Summer 2002), 71.

46. Nixtamal is treated corn used in making tortillas and other traditional Mexican foods. Oles read the shop as part of an "inventory" of architectural forms from the past to the present. Oles, "Industrial Landscapes," 149.

47. Secretaría de Educación Pública, *Escuelas primarias* (Mexico City: Secretaría de Educación Pública, 1933), 8–9.

48. Secretaría de Educación Pública, *Escuelas primarias*, 10.

49. O'Gorman briefly worked with Villagrán, from whom he learned about rationalist classicism, which Villagrán began to develop in his most important project before the tuberculosis sanatorium, the National Hygiene Institute. On the National Hygiene Institute in relation to O'Gorman's development, see Carranza, *Architecture as Revolution*, 133–35; on the tuberculosis sanatorium at Huipulco, see Kathryn E. O'Rourke, "Guardians of Their Own Health: Tuberculosis, Rationalism, and Reform in Modern Mexico," *Journal of the Society of Architectural Historians* 71, no. 1 (March 2012), 60–77.

50. Secretaría de Educación Pública, *Escuelas primarias*, 14.

51. Juan O'Gorman, "Escuelas Nuevas," *Imagen* 1, no. 11 (September 1933), n.p.

52. O'Gorman, "Escuelas nuevas," n.p.

53. John Mraz, *Looking for Mexico* (Durham, NC: Duke University Press, 2009), 77.

54. Mraz, *Looking for Mexico*, 77.

55. On the relationship between the Estridentistas and architecture: Carranza, *Architecture as Revolution*, 56–85.

56. Frank Yerbury and Willy Boesiger also photographed Le Corbusier's buildings, including the Villa Stein-de Monzie, with a car. On Yerbury: *Frank Yerbury: Itinerant Cameraman, Architectural Photographs, 1920–1935* (London: Architectural Association, 1987). Cars also appeared in early photographs of the Villa Church (Ville d'Avery, 1928) and the Maison Lipchitz and Miestchanninof (Boulogne-sur-Seine, 1923–25) and the Pavillion Suisse (Paris, 1930–31). Reproduced in William J. R. Curtis, *Le Corbusier: Ideas and Forms* (London: Phaidon, 2001), figs. 71, 77, 79, 106.

57. On *Une Maison–Un Palais*, see C. A. Poole, "Theoretical and Poetical Ideas in Le Corbusier's Une Maison–Un Palais," *Journal of Architecture* 3, no. 1 (Spring 1998), 1–30. "Work of Le Corbusier and Pierre Jeanneret," *Die Bauwelt* 20 (1929), 5–7.

58. "Federal Schools of Mexico," *Architectural Record* 75 (May 1934), 444.

59. Anita Brenner, *Idols behind Altars* (New York: Harcourt Brace, 1929), 171, 174.

60. Brenner, *Idols behind Altars*, 174.

61. Brenner, *Idols behind Altars*, 175–76.

62. The pulquerías were Los Fifís, at Calle Manrique (now Republica de Cuba), Entre las Violetas, near La Lagunilla market, and Mi Despacho, at Chapultepec and Insurgentes avenues. All three have been destroyed.

63. O'Gorman and Luna Arroyo, *Juan O'Gorman*, 59.

64. "Pintura de caballete y pintura de pulquería," *El Demócrata: Diario independiente de la mañana* (July 20, 1923), n.p.; Diego Rivera, "Mexican Painting, Pulquerias," *Mexican Folkways* 2, no. 7 (June–July 1926), 6.

65. Rivera, "Mexican Painting, Pulquerias," 8.

66. Rivera, "Mexican Painting, Pulquerias," 8.

67. Rivera, "Names of Pulquerias," *Mexican Folkways* 2, no. 7 (June–July 1926), 16–19.

68. Rivera, "Names of Pulquerias," 17.

69. O'Gorman and Luna Arroyo, *Juan O'Gorman*, 105.

70. For a thorough account of the painters and their work, see Frances Toor, *Frescoes in Primary Schools by Various Artists* (Mexico City: Frances Toor Studios, 1943).

71. Toor, *Frescoes in Primary Schools*, n.p.

72. For discussion of the social context of the schools' construction, see Natalia de la Rosa de la Rosa, "Mirada dirigida y control del cuerpo," in *Encauzar la mirada: Arquitectura, pedagogía e imágenes en México, 1920–1950*, ed. Renato González Mello and Deborah Dorotinsky Alperstein (Mexico City: UNAM, IIE, 2010), 75–107. On the schools in relation to the development of Mexican modernism: Daniel Schávelzon, "Vicente Mendiola: Escuelas al aire libre (1926–1927)," *Traza* 5 (November–December, 1983), n.p.; and Schávelzon, "Los origenes de la arquitectura moderna en México: Las esceulas al aire libre (1925–1927)," *DANA, Documentos de Arquitectura Nacional y Americana* (Argentina) 21 (September 1986), 68–75. On murals in schools and other buildings for education: *Pintura mural en los centros de educación de México* (Mexico City: Secretaría de Educación Pública, 2003).

73. *Las escuelas al aire libre en México* (Mexico City: Secretaría de Educación Pública, 1927), 11.

74. The open air theater, furniture, and clock designed by Leonardo Noriega and Javier Stávoli at the Parque México in the Hipódromo neighborhood are perhaps the best surviving example of this tendency.

75. *Las escuelas al aire libre en México*, 11.

76. *Las escuelas al aire libre en México*, 11–12.

77. Frances Toor, "Los pequeños artistas y la revolución de la pintura," *Mexican Folkways* 4, no. 1 (January–March, 1928), 6–10; Salvador Novo, "Los fines de las escuelas de pintura," *Mexican Folkways* 4, no. 1 (January–March, 1928), 24–27.

78. Toor, "Los pequeños artistas," 17–21.

79. O'Gorman and Luna Arroyo, *Juan O'Gorman*, 92.

80. O'Gorman usually positioned "functional" architecture against classicism, not Mexican revivalist forms, and characterized Zárraga's view similarly: O'Gorman and Luna Arroyo, *Juan O'Gorman*, 93.

CHAPTER FIVE. LANDSCAPE AND SUBJECTIVITY AT THE CIUDAD UNIVERSITARIA

Epigraph: Selden Rodman, *Mexican Journal: The Conquerors Conquered* (New York: Devin-Adair, 1958), 85.

1. Jorge Alberto Manrique, "El futuro radiante: La Ciudad Universitaria," in *La arquitectura mexicana del siglo XX*, ed. Fernando González Gortázar (Mexico City: Consejo Nacional para la Cultura y las Artes, 1996), 195–221.

2. On the significance of the campus in landscape architecture: Mario Schjetnan Garduño, "Ciudad Universitaria y los orígenes del paisaje contemporáneo," *Bitácora arquitectura* 11 (February–April 2004), 10–15.

3. On this shift, particularly as it was embodied by Luis Barragán's work and in relation to international developments: Keith Eggener, "Postwar Modernism in Mexico: Luis Barragán's Jardines del Pedregal and the International Discourse on Architecture and Place," *Journal of the Society of Architectural* Historians 58, no. 2 (June 1999), 122–45.

4. For example, Guillermo Rossell and Lorenzo Carrasco, introduction to *Guía de arquitectura mexicana contemporánea*, ed. Guillermo Rossell and Lorenzo Carrasco (Mexico City: Editorial Espacios, 1952), n.p.; and "Un arquitecto opina . . ." in *Guía de arquitectura mexicana contemporánea*, n.p.

5. Frank Lloyd Wright had been concerned with such matters since at least the early 1910s. Neil Levine, *The Architecture of Frank Lloyd Wright* (Princeton, NJ: Princeton University Press, 1996), esp. 74–111 on Taliesin. Keith Eggener positioned Mexican "regionalism" in Luis Barragán's work in the context of related developments abroad ("Postwar Modernism in Mexico"). In the 1950s U.S. architect Harwell Hamilton Harris used the CU, which he visited before it was completed, in the development of his theories of architectural regionalism: "Regionalism and Nationalism in Architecture," *Texas Quarterly* 1 (February 1958), 115–24.

6. For example, del Moral's discussion of Mexican architecture: "Caracteres y condicionantes de la arquitectura en México" (1949). Reprinted in Enrique del Moral, *El hombre y la arquitectura: Ensayos y testimonios* (Mexico City: Universidad Nacional Autónoma de México, 1983), 45–49.

7. Mary K. Coffey, *How a Revolutionary Art Became Official Culture: Murals, Museum, and the Mexican State* (Durham, NC: Duke University Press, 2012). On the mosaics at the CU, see 109–19.

8. Valerie Fraser suggested that the spatial organization reflected architects' at-

tempts to assert to supremacy of architecture over the other arts. *Building the New World: Studies in the Modern Architecture of Latin America, 1930–1960* (London: Verso, 2000), 75.

9. José Antonio Aldrete-Haas understood the campus as an example of the "Mexicanization" of International architecture and identified in the buildings "three different versions of functionalism . . . all derived from European ideology." "The Search for Roots in Mexican Modernism," in *Latin American Architecture 1929–1960, Contemporary Reflections*, ed. Carlos Brillembourg (New York: Monacelli Press, 2004): 106–7. In Fraser's assessment the Olympic Stadium, fronton courts, and landscape "represent an architecture that is both modern and Mexican, geographically and historically rooted" (*Building the New World*, 71–72).

10. Keith Eggener, "Settings for History and Oblivion in Modern Mexico, 1942–1958," in *Cruelty and Utopia*, ed. Jean-Francois Lejeune (New York: Princeton Architectural Press, 2005), 231. Fraser, *Building the New World*, 73.

11. Luis Castañeda, *Spectacular Mexico: Design, Propaganda, and the 1968 Olympics* (Minneapolis: University of Minnesota Press, 2014), esp. xix–xxi; Barry Bergdoll, "Learning from Latin America: Public Space, Housing, and Landscape," in *Latin America in Construction: Architecture 1955–1980*, exhibition catalog, ed., Barry Bergdoll et al. (New York: Museum of Modern Art, 2015), 16–39.

12. On Mexican political history: Enrique Kruze, *Mexico: Biography of Power, a History of Modern Mexico, 1810–1996*, trans. Hank Heifetz (New York: Harper Perennial, 1997); and Aaron W. Navarro, *Political Intelligence and the Creation of Modern Mexico, 1938–1954* (University Park: Pennsylvania State University Press, 2010).

13. Pani and del Moral wrote an overview of the project many years after it was built: Mario Pani and Enrique del Moral, *La construcción de la Ciudad Universitaria del Pedregal: Concepto, programa y planeación arquitectónica* (Mexico City: Universidad Nacional Autónoma de México, 1979).

14. Christina Bueno, "Teotihuacán: Showcase for the Centennial" and Lisa Pinley Covert, "Colonial Outpost to Artists' Mecca: Conflict and Collaboration in the Development of San Miguel de Allende's Tourist Industry," in *Holiday in Mexico: Critical Reflections on Tourism and Tourist Encounters*, ed. Dina Berger and Andrew Grant Wood (Durham, NC: Duke University Press, 2010), 56–76, 183–220.

15. Kenneth J. Conant, Letter to the Editor, *Magazine of Art* (February 1943), 78.

16. Conant, Letter to the Editor, 78.

17. Richard Grove, "Un escritor opina . . .," in *Guía de arquitectura mexicana contemporánea*, n.p.

18. For example, Gabriel García Maroto, *Arquitectura popular de México* (Mexico City: Instituto Nacional de Bellas Artes, 1954).

19. Grove, "Un escritor opina . . .," n.p.

20. Villagrán was the godfather of one of Pani's sons. Author interview with Enrique Pani and Cathy Pani, October 16, 2014, Mexico City.

21. Texts explaining Villagrán's teachings and based on his teaching were published in *Arquitectura/México* in four installments between 1939 and 1941.

22. Carlos Obregón Santacilia, *50 años de arquitectura mexicana, 1900–1950* (Mexico City: Editorial Patria, 1952), 118–120. See also his *México como eje de las antiguas arquitecturas de las Américas* (Mexico City: Editorial Atlante, 1947), an illustrated history of architecture that related colonial and modern Mexican architecture to preconquest architecture throughout the hemisphere.

23. Obregón Santacilia, *50 años de arquitectura*, 120.

24. In addition to the *Guía de arquitectura contemporánea mexicana* were Luis de Cervantes, *Crónica arquitectónica: Prehispanica, colonial, contemporánea* (Mexico City: Editorial CIMSA, 1952); I. E. Myers, *Mexico's Modern Architecture* (New York: Architectural Book Publishing, 1952); Enrique Yañez, *18 residencias de arquitectos mexicanos* (Mexico City: Ediciones Mexicanas, 1951), and exhibition of the same title; "Exposición de arquitectura contemporánea mexicana," at the annual meeting of the American Institute of Architects, Houston, Texas, April 1949; "Exposición de arquitectura mexicana contemporánea," organized by INBA, held at the Palacio de Bellas Artes, Mexico City, 1950; "Exposición de arquitectura popular mexicana," held at Palacio de Bellas Artes, Mexico City, 1952; García Maroto, *Arquitectura popular de México*; "Arquitectura contemporánea y sus antecedentes históricos," exhibition held at Palacio Bellas Artes, Mexico City, organized by Alberto Arai, 1953–54. Del Moral also participated in public discussions on the status of architecture. See "Contestación a la encuesta de la revista *Hoy*, sobre el 'Balance de Medio Siglo de Arquitectura en México,'" *Hoy* (July 22, 1950); reprinted in del Moral, *El hombre y la arquitectura*, 67–68; and "Encuesta de la revista espacios," the print version of a television interview in 1950; reprinted in *El hombre y la arquitectura*, 63–65.

25. See Arai's long tribute to Villagrán, "José Villagrán García: Pilar de la arquitectura contemporánea de México," *Arquitectura/México* 55, no. 12 (September 1956), 139–62; and Enrique del Moral, "Villagrán García y la evolución de nuestra arquitectura," in the same issue, 131–32.

26. For an overview of Pani's work and biography, see Louise Noelle, ed., *Mario Pani: Arquitecto* (Mexico City: Universidad Nacional Autónoma de México, Instituto de Investigaciones Estéticas, 2008); Salvador Elizondo, "Mario Pani, arquitecto," 15–28; Alejandro Caso, "El hombre," 29–34; Fernando Barbará Zetina, "Mario Pani: Arquitecto, maestro y amigo," 43–54; as well as Graciela de Garay Arellano, *Mario Pani: Vida y obra* (Mexico City: Universidad Nacional Autónoma de México, Facultad de Arquitectura, 2004).

27. On the journal, see George F. Flaherty, "Mario Pani's Hospitality: Latin America through *Arquitectura/México*," in *Latin American Modern Architectures: Ambiguous Territories*, ed. Patricio del Real and Helen Gyger (New York: Routledge, 2013), 253–69.

28. Author interview with Enrique Pani and Cathy Pani.

29. Author interview with Enrique Pani and Cathy Pani.

30. On del Moral: Louise Noelle Merles, *Enrique del Moral, un arquitecto comprometido con México* (Mexico City: Consejo Nacional de la Cultura y las Artes, 1998); Salvador Pinoncelly, *La obra de Enrique del Moral* (Mexico City: Universidad Nacional Autónoma de México, 1983).

31. William J. R. Curtis, "'The General and the Local': Enrique del Moral's Own House, Calle Francisco Ramírez 5, Mexico City, 1948," in *Modernity and the Architecture of Mexico*, ed. Edward R. Burian (Austin: University of Texas Press, 1997), 115–26.

32. Enrique del Moral, "El baroco como fenómeno estilístico, características en Francia y España," (1944–1945) reprinted in *El hombre y la arquitectura*, 15–30; see also "Notas sobre el estilo" (1946), 31–33, and "El tránsito del Churriguera al neoclásico," (1954), 81–94.

33. Enrique del Moral, "Tradición vs. modernidad integración?," *Arquitectura/México* 10 (March 1954), 5–24.

34. del Moral, "Tradición vs. modernidad integración?," 8.

35. del Moral, "Tradición vs. modernidad integración?," 14.

36. On the history of urbanism: Carol McMichael Reese, "The Urban Development of Mexico City, 1850–1930," in *Planning Latin America's Capital Cities, 1850–1950*, ed. Arturo Almandoz (New York: Routledge, 2002), 139–69; on landscape architecture: Kathryn E. O'Rourke, "Gardens and Landscapes of Frida Kahlo's Mexico City," in *Frida Kahlo's Garden*, ed. Adriana Zavala, Joanna Groake, Mia D'Avanza (New York: Prestel, 2015), 86–103.

37. Kirsten Einfeldt discusses explorations of space in landscape painting, muralism, and the UNAM campus in terms of national identity in *Moderne Kunst in Mexiko Raum: Material und nationale Identität*, transcript (Bielefeld: Verlag, 2010), 69–174.

38. In 1928 architects Mauricio Campos and Marcial Gutiérrez Camarena created a project for a University City on a site just to the south of Mexico City in Tlalpan, where Villagrán García's tuberculosis sanatorium was built instead. In 1946 del Moral and Villagrán began developing the CU's program. In 1947 a jury that included Federico Mariscal, the president of the Sociedad de Arquitectos Mexicanos, Guillermo Zárraga, the president of the Colegio Nacional de Arquitectura, and Enrique Yañez, who acted on behalf of the university rector, selected the proposal submitted by del Moral, Pani, and Mauricio Campos on behalf of the Escuela Nacional de Arquitectura.

39. On the symbolic and psychological aspects of the Pedregal: Helen Thomas, "Sublimation (el Pedregal)," in *InterSections: Architectural Histories and Critical Theories*, ed. Iain Borden and Jane Rendell (New York: Routledge, 2000), 109–24.

40. Esther Born, *The New Architecture in Mexico* (New York: Architectural Record, William Morrow, 1937), 2.

41. René Davids, "Mythical Terrain and the Building of Mexico's UNAM," *CLAS Working Papers* (Center for Latin American Studies, University of California, Berkeley, 2008), 1–22; Thomas, "Sublimation (el Pedregal)," 109–24.

42. Carlos Lazo, "Discursos pronunciados en la colocación de la primera piedra de la Ciudad Universitaria" (June 5, 1950), in *Pensamiento y destino de la Ciudad Universitaria de México* (Mexico City: Universidad Nacional Autonóma de México, 1952), 9.

43. Lazo, "Discursos pronunciados," 10–11.

44. On Wright's influence: Eggener, "Towards an Organic Architecture in Mexico," in *Frank Lloyd Wright: Europe and Beyond*, ed. Anthony Alofsin (Berkeley: University of California Press, 1999), 166–83. On Barragán and Neutra: Richard Ingersoll, "In the Shadows of Barragán," in *Luis Barragán: The Quiet Revolution*, ed. Federica Zanco (Milan: Barragán Foundation, 2001), 217–20. O'Gorman discusses the influence of Wright and Gaudí on his later work in Juan O'Gorman and Antonio Luna Arroyo, *Juan O'Gorman: Autobiografía, antología, juicios críticos y documentación exhaustiva sobre su obra* (Mexico City: Cuadernos Populares de Pintura Mexicana Moderna, 1973), 152–56.

45. Kaspé wrote about his student years with Pani in Vladimir Kaspé, "Tiempos de estudiante con Mario Pani," *Arquitectura/México* 67 (September 1959); reprinted in *Mario Pani, arquitecto*, 35–42.

46. See, in addition to del Moral's school and Barragán's Gardens of El Pedregal, O'Gorman's work with Rivera on the Anahuacali Museum and addition to the Kahlo house in Coyoacán.

47. Vladimir Kaspé, "Le Corbusier y la Arquitectura Contemporanea," *Arquitectura/México* 21 (November 1946), 4.

48. Kaspé, "Le Corbusier," 5.

49. Kaspé, "Le Corbusier," 6.

50. Kaspé, "Le Corbusier," 9.

51. The campus was published in journals including *Arquitectura/México, L'architecture d'aujourd'hui, Journal of the AIA,* and *Architecture Record.*

52. On aerial photography and modern architecture in Latin America: Adnan Morshed, "The Cultural Politics of Aerial Vision: Le Corbusier in Brazil (1929)," *Journal of Architectural Education* 55, no. 4 (May 2002), 201–10. Among Mexican architects, Carlos Obregón Santacilia used aerial photographs extensively in two publications: and *El maquinismo, la vida, y la arquitectura: Ensayo* (Mexico City: La Imprenta Universitaria, 1939), and *México como eje.*

53. Velasco won prizes for his painting at the World's Fairs of 1876 and 1893.

54. Author interview with Enrique and Cathy Pani. When they were not in Europe, the Panis lived in the Mexico City neighborhood of Santa Maria la Ribera, where one of Velasco's most significant groups of paintings hung in the Institute of Geology. For the upper floor of the building Velasco painted ten large canvases depicting the evolution of plants and animals from the sea to land.

55. Alfred Barr, Introduction to Juan O'Gorman, "Velazco: Painter of Time and Space," *Magazine of Art* 36, no. 6 (October 1943), 202.

56. Henry Clifford, "Note on Velasco's Paintings," in Philadelphia Museum of Art, Brooklyn Museum, and Mexico, Dirección General de Educación Extra-Escolar y Estética, *José María Velasco, 1840–1912* (Philadelphia and Brooklyn: Philadelphia Museum of Art and the Brooklyn Museum, 1944), 15–16.

57. Juan O'Gorman, "Velazco: Painter of Time and Space," *Magazine of Art* 36, no. 6 (October 1943), 204–6.

58. Carlos Pellicer, "The Valley of Mexico," in *José María Velasco, 1840–1912,* 13.

59. Pellicer, "The Valley of Mexico," 14.

60. Pellicer, "The Valley of Mexico," 14.

61. Juan O'Gorman, "Decoration," *Northwest Architect* 16, no. 5 (September–October 1952), 8.

62. Originally O'Gorman intended the design of the building to evoke a preconquest pyramid. Pani and del Moral rejected this scheme. *La construcción de la Ciudad Universitaria del Pedregal,* cited in Edward R. Burian, "Modernity and Nationalism: Juan O'Gorman and Post-Revolutionary Architecture in Mexico, 1920–1960," in *Cruelty and Utopia: Cities and Landscapes of Latin America,* ed. Jean-Francois Lejeune (New York: Princeton Architectural Press, 2003), 220.

63. Burian has suggested that the mosaic "represented a shift to a didactic, symbolic, allegorical architecture" and that in it O'Gorman "reconnect[ed] . . . a mythical past for political and racial purposes." "Modernity and Nationalism," 220.

64. Kathryn E. O'Rourke, "El pasado y el futuro de la arquitectura 'mexicana' a los mediados del siglo XX," in *Imaginarios de modernidad y tradición: Arquitecturas americanas del siglo XX,* ed. Catherine R. Ettinger (Mexico City: Editorial Porrúa, 2015), 11–32.

65. O'Gorman and Luna Arroyo, *Juan O'Gorman,* 146–51.

66. Henry-Russell Hitchcock said of the Ciuadad Universitaria that "it is with little question the most spectacular extra-urban architectural entity of the North

American continent and has in scale and degree of completion no real rival in the rest of Latin America," *Latin American Architecture since 1945* (New York: Museum of Modern Art, 1955), 45.

67. For a summary of "integración plástica" in relation to twentieth-century Mexican architecture, see Alberto Híjar, "La integración plástica," in *La arquitectura mexicana del siglo XX*, ed. Fernando González Gortazar (Mexico City: Consejo Nacional para la Cultra y las Artes, 1996), 222–30.

68. Scholarly analyses of the shift include Raquel Tibol, "Juan O'Gorman in varios tiempos," *Calli* 29 (1967), 7–10; Eggener, "Contrasting Images of Identity in the Post-War Mexican Architecture of Luis Barragán and Juan O'Gorman," *Journal of Latin American Cultural Studies* 9, no. 1 (2000), 27–45; Luis E. Carranza, *Architecture as Revolution: Episodes in the History of Modern Mexico City* (Austin: University of Texas Press, 2010), 116, 158–67; and Alejandro Hernández Gálvez, "Juan O'Gorman: Architecture and Surface," *Journal of Decorative and Propaganda Arts* 26 (2010), 206–29.

69. Juan O'Gorman, "Espacios pregunta, Juan O'Gorman responde," *Espacios* 25 (June 1955), 20.

70. Juan O'Gorman, "El desarrollo de la arquitectura Mexicana en los ultimos trienta años," *Arquitectura* 23, no. 100 (April and June 1968), 51.

71. Juan O'Gorman, "3 Preguntas a Juan O'Gorman," *Espacios* 14 (March 5, 1953), n.p.

72. O'Gorman, "3 Preguntas," n.p.

73. Juan O'Gorman, "Decoration," 8.

74. Author interview with Enrique Pani and Cathy Pani.

75. In his Benito Juárez housing project, Pani collaborated with artist Carlos Mérida, who designed mosaics installed as panels on building facades in open-air staircases.

76. "Entrevista con el arquitecto Mario Pani, el 1 de octubre de 1979," in *Testimonios vivos 20 arquitectos: 1781–1981, bicentenario de la Escuela de Pintura, Escultura y Arquitectura*, ed. Lilia Gómez and Miguel Angel Quevedo (Mexico City: Secretaria de Educación Pública, Instituto Nacional de Bellas Artes, Mayo–Agosto, 1981), 105–8.

77. Cristina López Uribe, "Los Murales de Chávez Morado, obras que cambian con el paso del tiempo y las modficaciones de CU," *Boletín Universidad Nacional Autónoma de México-DGCS-086 Ciudad Universitaria* (February 10, 2012), accessed May 8, 2014, www.dgcs.unam.mx/boletin/bdboletin/2012_087.html.

78. Gisela Mateos, Adriana Minor, and Valeria Sánchez Michel, "Una modernidad anunciada: Historia del Van de Graaff de Ciudad Universitaria," *Historia Mexicana* 62, no. 1 (July–September 2012), 415–42.

79. Jennifer Jolly, "Art of the Collective: David Alfaro Siqueiros, Josep Renau and Their Collaboration at the Mexican Electricians' Syndicate," *Oxford Art Journal* 31, no. 1 (2008), 129–51.

80. David Alfaro Siqueiros, "Memorial al señor arquitecto Carlos Lazo: Gerente general de las obras en la ciudad universitaria; sobre el problema de mis murales en la rectoría y en la la Facultad de Ciencias Químicas" (1953), in *Palabras de Siqueiros*, ed. Raquel Tibol (Mexico City: Fondo de Cultura Económica, 1996), 367–70; Siqueiros, "Un problema técnico sin precedente en la historia del arte: El muralismo figurativo y realista en el exterior," *Arte público: Tribuna de pintores muralistas, escultores, grabadores y artistas de la estampa en general* 1 (December 1952), 6; Siqueiros, "Arquitectura

internacional a la zaga de la mala pintura," *Arte público: Tribuna de pintores, escultores, grabadores, arquitectos, dibujantes, fotógrafos, criticos de arte* 2, no. 2 (November 1954–February 1955), 36.

81. Siqueiros, "Arquitectura internacional," 36.

82. "City of Culture: The New World's Oldest University Builds a Monument to Modern Education and Ancient Art," *Interiors* (February 1952), 78.

83. Adolf Loos, "Ornament and Crime," (1908) reprinted in *Programs and Manifestoes on 20th-Century Architecture*, ed. Ulrich Conrads, trans. Michael Bullock (Cambridge, MA: MIT Press, 2001), 19–24.

84. Siqueiros, "Arquitectura internacional," 36.

85. Others also interpreted plastic integration at the Ciudad Universitaria historically. In 1953 the influential critic Gabriel García Maroto suggested that the mosaics should be seen in relation to a long national history of plastic integration beginning with preconquest architecture. "Vida y arte: La plástica y su proyección pública; proceso de la integración plastica," *Novedades: México en la cultura* (March 29, 1953), 4–5. As Charles Bullrich suggested, "Mexicans came to the conclusion that [plastic integration] . . . typified pre-Columbian, pre-Cortesian, and colonial architecture. Thus, what seemed to them specifically Mexican did not quite correspond with the sense of rationality that had been expounded by Mexico's leading theorist of the thirties, Villagrán García." Charles Bullrich, *New Directions in Latin American Architecture* (New York: George Braziller, 1969), 28.

86. Siqueiros, "Arquitectura internacional." Siquieros had explained his ideas about plastic integration in relation to history, technology, and politics in an earlier, longer essay: "Hacia una nueva plástica integral," *Espacios* 1 (September 1948), n.p.

87. O'Gorman, "3 Preguntas," n.p.

88. The lecture was published as an essay shortly thereafter as "Tradición vs. modernidad integración?"

89. del Moral, "Tradición vs. modernidad integración?" 15, 16, 20.

90. O'Gorman claimed that he had imagined the library to have mosaics from the beginning and proposed the idea to Lazo in 1949. O'Gorman and Luna Arroyo, *Juan O'Gorman*, 146–47.

91. del Moral, "Tradición vs. modernidad integración?" 24.

92. del Moral, "Tradición vs. modernidad integración?" 24.

93. del Moral, "Tradición vs. modernidad integración?" 8.

94. del Moral, "Tradición vs. modernidad integración?" 11.

95. del Moral, "Tradición vs. modernidad integración?" 20.

96. del Moral, "Tradición vs. modernidad integración?" 20.

97. del Moral, "Tradición vs. modernidad integración?" 20.

98. Hitchcock, *Latin American Architecture*, 26–27.

99. Villagrán, quoted in Clive Bamford Smith, *Builders in the Sun* (New York: Architectural Book Publishing, 1967), 10.

100. Luis E. Carranza, "La arquitectura prehispánica en el imaginario moderno," *Arquine* 38 (Winter 2009), 78–91.

101. Alberto T. Arai, *Caminos para una arquitectura mexicana* (Mexico City: Dirección de Arquitectura de la Instituto Nacional Bellas Artes, 2002), 6.

102. Arai, *Caminos*, 6.

103. Enrique del Moral, "Lo General y lo Local," *Espacios* 2 (October 1948), n.p.

104. Arai, *Caminos*, 32, 1, 24.

105. Arai, *Caminos*, 32.

106. On Gamio: Rick A. López, *Crafting Mexico: Intellectuals, Artisans, and the State after the Revolution* (Durham, NC: Duke University Press, 2010), 127–37.

107. Arai, *Caminos*, 29.

108. Malcolm Clendenin identified this in Hector Guimard's work, which was concerned with nature rather than history. Like Arai, Guimard was politically engaged, concerned with the possibility of creating universal forms, and informed by rationalism. Clendenin, "Hector Guimard, Political Movements, and the Paris Metro: Natural Sympathies, Governing Harmony, and Social Change" (PhD diss., University of Pennsylvania, 2008).

109. Arai, *La arquitectura de Bonampak, ensayo de interpretación del arte maya; Viaje a las ruinas de Bonampak* (Mexico City: Ediciones del Instituto Nacional de Bellas Artes, 1960).

110. Salvador Toscano, "Nota preliminar," in Agustín Villagra Caleti, *Bonampak, la ciudad de los muros pintados* (Mexico City: Instituto Nacional de Antropología e Historia, Secretaría de Educación Pública, 1949), 8.

111. Arai, *Caminos*, 42.

112. Arai, *Caminos*, 42.

113. Arai, *Caminos*, 34

114. Arai, *Caminos*, 34.

115. Arai, *Caminos*, 39.

116. "Mexico's Mammoth Campus," *Architectural Forum* 108, no. 3 (March 1958), 108–13.

117. "Mexico's Mammoth Campus," 111.

118. Octavio Paz, "The Labyrinth of Solitude," in *The Labyrinth of Solitude and Other Writings,* trans. Lysander Kemp, Yara Milos, and Rachel Philips Belash (New York: Grove Press, 1985), 25.

119. Arai, *Caminos*, 46, 47.

120. Adriana Novoa has examined Paz's thinking about spatiality in relation to Eisenstein's work: "In the Borders of Being: Mexico, Space, and Time in Sergei Eisenstein and Octavio Paz," *Atlantic Studies* 7, no. 3 (September 2010), 215–39.

121. Among them was Rufino Tamayo, whose 1952 mural-scaled, but canvas painting, *Birth of Our Nationality* (Palacio de Bellas Artes) depicted the violence of the Spanish conquest using forms reminiscent of Picasso and colors and tones more like Paul Klee's than Diego Rivera's.

CHAPTER SIX. ALONE IN HISTORY

1. Guy Trebay, "Finding Mexico City, and Luis Barragán, Again," *New York Times*, June 13, 2014, http://www.nytimes.com/2014/06/15/travel/finding-mexico-city -and-luis-barragan-again.html?_r=0.

2. Kenneth Frampton notes that "modernity for Barragán was inseparable from the continuity of tradition," in "A Propos Barragán: Formation, Critique and Influence," in *Luis Barragán: The Quiet Revolution*, ed. Federica Zanco (Milan: Barragán Foundation, 2001), 22.

3. Henry-Russell Hitchcock, *Latin American Architecture since 1955* (New York: Museum of Modern Art, 1955), 183.

4. Barragán is often mentioned in conjunction with contemporary writers and intellectuals, especially Octavio Paz and Carlos Fuentes. He was a close friend of Carlos Pellicer. Marc Treib, "A Setting for Solitude: The Landscape of Luis Barragán," in Zanco, *Luis Barragán*, 125–26, 135.

5. Elena Poniatowska, "Luis Barragán: Entrevista," in *Luis Barragán, escritos y conversaciones*, ed. Antonio Riggen Martínez (Madrid: El Croquis Editorial, 2000), 120. Hereafter, Poniatowska interview.

6. Luis Barragán, Acceptance Speech, Pritzker Architecture Prize, Dumbarton Oaks, Washington, DC, 1980, www.pritzkerprize.com/1980/ceremony_speech1, accessed September 10, 2013.

7. On promotion of Pedregal and other work, Keith Eggener, *Luis Barragán's Gardens of El Pedregal* (New York: Princeton Architectural Press, 2001), 63–76.

8. Many of the interviews, along with the architect's few writings were published in Luis Barragán, *Luis Barragán: Escritos y conversaciones*, ed. Antonio Riggen Martínez (Madrid: El Croquis Editoria, 2000).

9. Antonio Riggen Martinez has given perhaps the most attention to the texts: *Luis Barragán: Mexico's Modern Master, 1902–1988* (New York: Monacelli Press, 1996), 159–90.

10. Poniatowska interview, 113.

11. Among them Riggen Martinez, *Luis Barragán: Mexico's Modern Master*; Frampton, "A Propos Barragán," 14–27; Leonardo Diaz-Borioli, "Collective Autobiography: Building Luis Barragán" (PhD diss., Princeton University, 2015).

12. Richard Ingersoll, "In the Shadows of Barragán," in Zanco, *Luis Barragán*, 206–27; Keith Eggener, "Barragán's 'Photographic Architecture': Image, Advertising and Memory," in Zanco, *Luis Barragán*, 178–95; Emilia Terragni, "Art within Architecture," in Zanco, *Luis Barragán*, 236–51.

13. Ingersoll, "In the Shadows of Barragán," 213–14, 218–20; Eggener, *Luis Barragán's Gardens*; Eggener, "Postwar Modernism in Mexico: Luis Barragán's Jardines del Pedregal and the International Discourse on Place," *Journal of the Society of Architectural Historians* 58, no. 2 (June 1999), 122–45; Treib, "A Setting for Solitude."

14. Riggen Martínez, *Luis Barragán*, 183.

15. Scholars have noted it too. Felipe Leal, "Nightless Enclosure: An Afternoon at the Home of Luis Barragán," trans. Roberto Tejada, in *Artes de México* 23 (1994), 3rd ed. (1999), 93–95; Juan Palomar, "The Alchemist of Memory," trans. Carole Castelli, *Artes de México* 23, 76–79.

16. José Villagrán García, "Carta a un amigo," August 2, 1951, quoted in José Antonio Aldrete-Haas, "The Search for Roots in Mexican Modernism," in *Latin American Architecture, 1929–1960: Contemporary Reflections*, ed. Carlos Brillembourg (New York: Monacelli Press, 2004), 107–8.

17. Enrique Yañez, introduction to I. E. Myers, *Mexico's Modern Architecture* (New York: Architectural Book Publishing, 1952), 13.

18. Emilio Ambasz, *The Architecture of Luis Barragán* (New York: Museum of Modern Art, 1976), 107.

19. Eggener, *Luis Barragán's Gardens*, 7–57; Treib, 125–51.

20. *Les Colombières*, Bac's book on the garden in France was also quite influential in shaping Barragán's interest in landscape architecture. Treib has observed that the poetic and philosophical aspects of the books were ultimately far more influential than the gardens themselves. Treib, "A Setting for Solitude," 117.

21. Esther Born, *The New Architecture in Mexico* (New York: Architectural Record, 1937), 40.

22. Poniatowska interview, 120.

23. Barragán also visited the Villa Savoye, in Poissy. He mentions both works in a brief text, "Apuntes de París: Ideas sobre arquitectura contemporánea" (1931), in Barragán, *Luis Barragán: Escritos y conversaciones*, 17.

24. Barragán, "Apuntes de París," 17.

25. Barragán, "Sobre Ferdinand Bac y Guadalajara" (1932), in Barragán, *Luis Barragán: Escritos y conversaciones*, 18.

26. Barragán, "Sobre Ferdinand Bac," 18.

27. Barragán, "Sobre Ferdinand Bac," 18–19.

28. Legarreta was one of the most radical leftists among Mexican architects in the 1930s. Carlos González Lobo, "Juan Legaretta," in *La arquitectura mexicana del siglo XX*, ed. Fernando González Gortázar (Mexico City: Centro Nacional de la Cultura y las Artes, 1994), 110–11.

29. He designed four private gardens on the block at Constituyentes Avenue and Francisco Ramírez Street, and three more on San Jerónimo Avenue between 1943 and 1945. On his first house on Francisco Ramírez: Federica Zanco, "Luis Barragán: The Quiet Revolution," in Zanco, *Luis Barragán*, 80–87.

30. Equipal chairs are traditional, handmade, rustic furniture made of unfinished wood and leather.

31. On controlled views and movement with objects, barriers, and the use of montage, see Zanco, "Luis Barragán: The Quiet Revolution," 96–97.

32. Zanco suggests this is related to marketing the Gardens of El Pedregal, in "Luis Barragán: The Quiet Revolution," 94–95.

33. "Mexico: The Architect at Home," *Harper's Bazaar* (March 1956), 187.

34. Mary Jean Kempner, "In Mexico City—An Eloquent Statement," *House Beautiful* (August 1966), 92.

35. "The New Mexico: Yesterday's Tradition Take on Today's Tempo," *Look* (January 25, 1966), 55.

36. Hitchcock, *Latin American Architecture*, 183.

37. Myers, *Mexico's Modern Architecture*, 82.

38. Enrique Yañez, *18 residencias de arquitectos mexicanos* (Mexico City: Ediciones Mexicanas, 1951), 8.

39. Yañez, *18 residencias*, 8.

40. Yañez, *18 residencias*, 8. For example, the house Mario Pani designed in Cuernavaca. It had stone from Puebla and Oaxaca, wood from the Yucatán jungles, and textiles from the workshop of Eva Galindo.

41. On the importance of the interior to modernism, Beatriz Colomina, *Privacy and Publicity: Modern Architecture as Mass Media* (Cambridge, MA: MIT Press, 1994). She observed that "modernity . . . coincides with the publicity of the private," 9.

42. Esther McCoy, "Designing for a Dry Climate," *Progressive Architecture* 52 (August 1971), 53.

43. By 1950 fascination with folk art was as strong as ever. In 1948 Roberto Montenegro wrote a quatrilingual catalog of the Museum of Popular Arts, *Museo de Artes Populares* (Mexico City: Ediciones de Arte, 1948).

44. "Mexico: The Architect at Home," *Harper's Bazaar* (March 1956), 187.

45. Poniatowska interview, 123.

46. Poniatowska interview, 122–23.

47. Poniatowska interview, 105.

48. Poniatowska interview, 105.

49. Poniatowska interview, 123.

50. Poniatowska interview, 123.

51. Selden Rodman, *Mexican Journal* (New York: Devin-Adair, 1958), 95–96.

52. "Master Designer, Luis Barragán." *Interiors* (December 1963), 84.

53. Abroad, the work of Richard Neutra offered the closest parallels, and the greatest influence. Neutra made several trips to Mexico and Barragán knew him well. Max Cetto, with whom Barragán collaborated in the design of the demonstration house in the Gardens of El Pedregal, had worked with Neutra in California before coming to Mexico.

54. Mario Schjetnan Garduño, "Enclosures and the Open Sky: A Conversation of Forms," trans. Roberto Tejada, *Artes de México* 23 (most of the text is a transcription of Schjetnan's interviews with Barragán in 1980–81), 93. Hereafter, Schjetnan interview.

55. Schjetnan's interviews, 92.

56. Schjetnan's interviews, 93.

57. Barragán described the influence of these buildings on his approach to walls in an interview with Damián Bayón published as "Luis Barragán y el Regreso a las Fuentes" (1975), in Barragán, *Luis Barragán: Escritos y conversaciones*, 99.

58. For example, Enrique de la Mora's house for himself. Myers, *Mexico's Modern Architecture*, 102–3; also Augusto Alvarez's own house in Yañez, *18 residencias*, 79–83.

59. Yañez, forward to Gabriel García Maroto, *Arquitectura popular de México* (Mexico City: Instituto Nacional de Bellas Artes, 1954), n.p.

60. Carlos Chávez, introduction to García Maroto, *Arquitectura popular de México*, 6.

61. García Maroto, *Arquitectura popular de México*, 186.

62. Rodman, *Mexican Journal*, 97.

63. Poniatowska interview, 117.

64. Poniatowska interview, 108.

65. Damián Bayón and Luis Barragán, "Luis Barragán y el regreso a las Fuentes," in Barragán, *Luis Barragán: Escritos y conversaciones*, 98.

66. Francisco Gilardi, interview by Enrique X. de Anda Alanís, Mexico City, August 2, 1989, https://parafernalia.jux.com/950674, accessed April 2, 2014.

67. Barragán, Acceptance Speech.

68. Barragán, Acceptance Speech.

69. Rodman, *Mexican Journal*, 96.

70. Poniatowska interview, 119.

71. Alice T. Friedman, *Women and the Making of the Modern House* (New York: Abrams, 1998), 147–57.

72. Bayón and Barragán, "Luis Barragán y el regreso," 98.

73. Johnson discussed his theory of circulation and orientation years after the glass house was built, in "Whence & Whither: The Processional Element in Architecture," *Perspecta* 9, no. 10 (1965), 167–78.

74. Friedman, *Women and the Making of the Modern House*, 149.

75. Friedman, *Women and the Making of the Modern House*, 150.

76. Quoted in René Burri, *Luis Barragán* (London: Phaidon Press, 2000), 23.

77. Quoted in Riggen Martínez, *Luis Barragán*, 159n1.

78. Riggen Martínez analyzed the implications of negation in "silence" and interpreted Barragán's "silence" as cultural: "Barragán's propensity for silence was born from his refusal to accept the bitterness of the contemporary and expressed his Mexican character." *Luis Barragán*, 163.

79. Eggener, *Luis Barragán's Gardens*, 63–93.

80. Eggener, *Luis Barragán's Gardens*, 79.

81. Barragán, "Sobre Ferdinand Bac," 18.

CONCLUSION

1. Rudolf Wittkower, *Architectural Principles in the Age of Humanism* (London: Warburg Institute, University of London, 1949). On the significance of this book: James S. Ackerman, Book Review, *Art Bulletin* 33, no. 3 (September 1951), 195–200; Henry A. Millon, "Rudolph Wittkower, Architectural Principles in the Age of Humanism: Its Influence on the Development and Interpretation of Modern Architecture," *Journal of the Society of Architectural Historians* 31, no. 2 (May 1972), 83–91; Alina A. Payne, "Rudolph Wittkower and Architectural Principles in the Age of Modernism," *Journal of the Society of Architectural Historians* 53, no. 3 (September 1994), 322–42.

2. Leonardo Diaz-Borioli, "Collective Autobiography: Building Luis Barragán" (PhD diss., Princeton University, 2015).

3. Hans Beacham, *The Architecture of Mexico: Yesterday and Today* (New York: Architectural Book, 1969).

4. Mathias Goeritz, introduction to Beacham, *The Architecture of Mexico*, 8.

5. George F. Flaherty, "Responsive Eyes: Urban Logistics and Kinetic Environments for the 1968 Mexico City Olympics," *Journal of the Society of Architectural Historians* 73, no. 3 (September 2014), 372–97.

6. Louise Noelle provides a historiographic survey of journals: "La arquitectura mexicana en las publicaciones periódicas del siglo XX," *Bitácora* 19 (2009), 14–18.

7. Luis M. Castañeda, *Spectacular Mexico: Design, Propaganda, and the 1968 Olympics* (Minneapolis: University of Minnesota Press, 2014), 78.

8. Castañeda, *Spectacular Mexico*, 175–90.

9. On Goeritz, Barragán, Legorreta, and "emotional" architecture: Castañeda, *Spectacular Mexico*, 175–91.

10. Vera S. Candiani, *Dreaming of Dry Land: Environmental Transformation in Colonial Mexico City* (Redwood City, CA: Stanford University Press, 2014), 315–24.

11. "Library in Texas: A Shade Too Much?" *New York Times*, November 26, 1995.

12. "Firma Perfil, Filosofía," Legorret + Legoretta, http://legorretalegorreta.com/en/perfil/filosofia-firma, accessed June 29, 2015.

13. "Firma Perfil, Filosofía."

14. On Kahn and Barragán at the Salk Institute: Daniel S. Friedman, "Salk Institute for Biological Studies," in David B. Brownlee and David G. De Long, *Louis I. Kahn: In the Realm of Architecture* (New York: Rizzoli and the Museum of Contemporary Art, Los Angeles, 1991), 330–40.

BIBLIOGRAPHY

Abels, Margaret Hutton. "Painting at the Brazil Centennial Exposition." *Art and Archaeology* 16 (Summer 1923), 108–9.

Acevedo, Jesús T. *Disertaciones de un arquitecto.* Mexico City: Ediciones México Moderno, 1920.

Acevedo, Jesús T. "La arquitectura colonial in México." In Acevedo, *Disertaciones de un arquitecto,* 129–55.

Ackerman, James S. Book Review. *Art Bulletin* 33, no. 3 (September 1951), 195–200.

Adrià, Miguel. *Mario Pani: La construcción de la modernidad.* Mexico City: Consejo Nacional para la Cultura y las Artes; Ediciones G. Gili, 2005.

Agostoni, Claudia. *Monuments of Progress: Modernization and Public Health in Mexico City, 1876–1910.* Calgary: University of Calgary Press, 2003.

Agostoni, Claudia. "Popular Health Education and Propaganda in Times of Peace and War in Mexico City, 1890s–1920s." *American Journal of Public Health* 96, no. 1 (January 2006), 52–61.

Aguirre, Enrique C. "Plazas publicas para deportes en el Distrito Federal." *Obras publicas,* February 1930, 115–20.

Aldrete-Haas, José Antonio. "Light in the Labyrinth or the Teachings of Luis Barragán." In Zanco, *Luis Barragán,* 274–83.

Aldrete-Haas, José Antonio. "The Search for Roots in Mexican Modernism." In *Latin American Architecture 1929–1960, Contemporary Reflections,* edited by Carlos Brillembourg, 100–115. New York: Monacelli Press, 2004.

Alfaro, Alfonso. "Quiet Voices of Ink: The Spiritual Itinerary of Luis Barragán." Translated by Lorna Scott Fox. *Artes de México* 23 (1999), 79–90.

Altamirano Piolle, Maria Elena. *National Homage: José María Velasco, 1840–1912.* Mexico City: Amigos del Museo Nacional de Arte, 1993.

Álvarez Noguera, José Rogelio. "Salud y arquitectura moderna y contemporánea en México." In *Salud y arquitectura en México,* edited by José Rogelio Álvarez Noguera, 114–89. Mexico City: Universidad Nacional Autónoma de México, 1998.

Ambasz, Emilio. *The Architecture of Luis Barragán.* New York: Museum of Modern Art, 1976.

de Anda Alanís, Enrique X. *La arquitectura de la revolución mexicana.* Mexico City: Instituto Nacional de Bellas Artes, Universidad Autónoma de México, 1990.

de Anda Alanís, Enrique X. "La identidad nacionalista del estilo neo-colonial y su persistencia en la cultura mexicana contemporánea." In *El neobarroco en la Ciudad de México,* 14–27. Mexico City: Museo de San Carlos, 1993.

de Anda Alanís, Enrique X. "El Déco en México: Arte de coyuntura." In *Art Decó: Un país nacionalista, un México comopolita,* 19–97. Mexico City: Instituto Nacional de Bellas Artes, 1997.

de Anda Alanís, Enrique X. "El edificio de la secretaría de salud: La modernidad frente al Castillo." In *Art déco: Un país nacionalista, un México cosmopolita,* edited by Jaime Soler, 86–95. Mexico City: Instituto Nacional de Bellas Artes, 1997.

de Anda Alanís, Enrique X. *Historia de la arquitectura mexicana.* Mexico City: G. Gili, 2002.

de Anda Alanís, Enrique X. "El proyecto de Juan O'Gorman para el concurso de la 'vivienda obrera' de 1932." *Arquine* 20 (Summer 2002), 64–75.

de Anda Alanís, Enrique X. *Una mirada a la arquitectura mexicana del siglo XX (Diez ensayos).* Mexico City: Arte e Imagen; Consejo Nacional para la Cultura y las Artes, 2005.

de Anda Alanís, Enrique X. "The Preservation of Historic Architecture and the Beliefs of the Modern Movement, in Mexico, 1914–1963." *Future Anterior* 6, no. 2 (Winter 2009), 58–73.

Anderson, Benedict. *Imagined Communities: Reflections on the Origin and Spread of Nationalism.* London: Verso, 2006.

Anderson, Stanford. "The Fiction of Function." *Assemblage* 2 (February 1987), 18–31.

Andrade Briseño, Magdalena. *Utopía, no utopía: La arquitectura, la enseñanza y la planificación del deseo.* Mexico City: Museo Casa Estudio Diego Rivera y Frida Kahlo, Instituto Nacional de Bellas Artes, 2005.

Apuntes para las historia y critica de la arquitectura mexicana del siglo xx: 1900–1980. Mexico City: Secretaria de Educación Pública, Instituto Nacional de Bellas Artes, 1982.

Arai, Alberto T. *Voluntad cinematográfica: Ensayo para una estética del cine.* Mexico City: Editorial Cultura, 1937.

Arai, Alberto T. "José Villagrán García: Pilar de la arquitectura contemporánea de México," *Arquitectura/México* 55, no. 12 (September 1956), 139–62.

Arai, Alberto T. *La arquitectura de Bonampak, ensayo de interpretación del arte maya; viaje a las ruinas de Bonampak.* Mexico City: Ediciones del Instituto Nacional de Bellas Artes, 1960.

Arai, Alberto T. *Caminos para una arquitectura mexicana.* Mexico City: Dirección de Arquitectura de la Instituto Nacional Bellas Artes, 2002.

Arendt, Marion Lucile. *The Historical Significance of Mexican Art and Architecture.* Mexico City: Secretaría de Educación Pública; Talleres Gráficos de la Nación, 1928.

Armando Salas Portugal Photographs of the Architecture of Luis Barragán. Edited by Isabelle Bleecker and Andrea E. Monfried. New York: Rizzoli International, 1992.

Arredondo Zambrano, Celia Ester. "Modernity in Mexico: The Case of the Ciudad Universitaria." In Burian, *Modernity and the Architecture of Mexico,* 91–106.

Atl, Dr. *Las artes populares en México.* Mexico City: Editorial Cultura, 1922.

Atl, Dr., Manuel Toussaint, and José R. Benítez. *Iglesias de México.* Mexico City: Secretaría de Hacienda, Editorial Cultura, 1924–27.

Ayres, Atlee. *Mexican Architecture: Domestic, Civil, and Eccelesastical.* New York: W. Helburn, 1926.

Ayuntamiento Constitucional de México. *Memoria de los trabajos realizados durante en ejercicio de 1926.* Mexico City: Departamento de Publicidad, 1927.

Baguez, Salvador. "Ancient and Modern Mexican-Indian Folklore." *Los Angeles Times*, September 22, 1929, I2.

Baird, Joseph Armstrong. *The Churches of Mexico, 1530–1810.* Berkeley: University of California Press, 1962.

Balderas, Esperanza. *Roberto Montenegro: La sensualidad renovada.* Mexico City: Fondo Editorial de la Plástica Mexicana, 2001.

Barbará Zetina, Fernando. "Mario Pani: Arquitecto, maestro y amigo." In Noelle, *Mario Pani: Arquitecto*, 43–54.

Barbosa, Ana Mae. "The Escuelas de Pintura al Aire Libre in Mexico: Freedom, Form, and Culture." *Studies in Art Education* 42, no. 4 (2001), 285–97.

Bargellini, Clara. "La arquitectura neocolonial: Historia, palabras e identidades." In *Hacia otra historia del arte en México.* Vol. 3, edited by Esther Acevedo, 157–69. Mexico City: Curare, 2002.

Barr, Alfred. Introduction to Juan O'Gorman, "Velazco: Painter of Time and Space." *Magazine of Art* 36, no. 6 (October 1943), 202.

Barragán, Luis. Acceptance Speech. Pritzker Architecture Prize. Dumbarton Oaks, Washington, DC, 1980. Accessed September 10, 2013. www.pritzkerprize.com /1980/ceremony_speech1/.

Barragán, Luis. *Barragán: The Complete Works*, edited by Raúl Rispa. New York: Princeton Architectural Press, 1996.

Barragán, Luis. *Luis Barragán: Escritos y conversaciones*, edited by Antonio Riggen Martínez. Madrid: El Croquis Editoria, 2000.

Barragán, Luis. "Apuntes desde París: Ideas sobre arquitectura contemporánea." In Luis Barragán, *Luis Barragán: Escritos y conversaciones*, 17.

Barragán, Juan José. "Juan José Barragán a Luis Barragán." In Luis Barragán, *Luis Barragán: Escritos y conversaciones*, 140.

Barragán, Luis. "Reflexiones sobre la Arquitectra Moderna en México, DF y EEUU." In Luis Barragán, *Luis Barragán: Escritos y conversaciones*, 20–21.

Barragán, Luis. "Reflexiones sobre los temas: La Belleza, el Artista, la Realidad y el Arte, a partir de la literatura de Oscar Wilde." 1955. In Luis Barragán, *Luis Barragán: Escritos y conversaciones*, 41–49.

Barragán, Luis. "Sobre el Pintor Jesús 'Chucho' Reyes." 1951. In Luis Barragán, *Luis Barragán: Escritos y conversaciones*, 32–35.

Barragán, Luis. "Sobre Ferdinand Bac y Guadalajara." In Luis Barragán, *Luis Barragán: Escritos y conversaciones*, 18–19.

Bartra, Roger. *The Cage of Melancholy: Identity and Metamorphosis in the Mexican Character.* Translated by Christopher J. Hall. New Brunswick, NJ: Rutgers University Press, 1992.

Bassols, Narciso. *Narciso Bassols, pensamiento y acción*, edited by Alonso Aquilar Monteverde. Mexico: Fondo de Cultura Economica, 1995.

Baxter, Sylvester. *Spanish-Colonial Architecture in Mexico.* 10 vols. Boston: J. B. Millet, 1901.

Baxter, Sylvester. *La arquitectura hispano colonial en México.* Translated by Federico E. Mariscal, León Felipe, and Manuel Toussaint. Mexico City: Departamento de Bellas Artes, 1934.

Bayón, Damián, and Luis Barragán. "Luis Barragán y el regreso a las Fuentes." In Luis Barragán, *Luis Barragán: Escritos y conversaciones*, 96–102.

Beacham, Hans. *The Architecture of Mexico: Yesterday and Today*. New York: Architectural Book, 1969.

Beals, Carleton. *Mexico: An Interpretation*. New York: B. W. Huebsch, 1923.

Behne, Adolf. *The Modern Functional Building*. Translated by Michael Robinson. Santa Monica, CA: Getty Research Institute for the History of Art and the Humanities, 1996.

Benítez, José R. *Las catedrales de Oaxaca, Morelia y Zacatecas, estudio de arqueografía comparada*. Mexico City: Talleres Gráficos de la Nación, 1934.

Bergdoll, Barry. *European Architecture, 1750–1890*. Oxford: Oxford University Press, 2000.

Bergdoll, Barry. "Bauhaus Multiplied: Paradoxes of Architecture and Design in and after the Bauhaus." In *Bauhaus 1919–1933: Workshops for Modernity*, edited by Barry Bergdoll and Leah Dickerman, 56–58. New York: Museum of Modern Art, 2009.

Bergdoll, Barry. "Good Neighbors: The Museum of Modern Art and Latin America, 1933–1955: A Journey through the MoMA Archives." In *Modernidad Urbana*, edited by Louise Noelle and Iván San Martín, 41–75. Mexico City: DOCOMOMO, 2012.

Bergdoll, Barry. "Learning from Latin America: Public Space, Housing, and Landscape." In *Latin America in Construction, 1955–1980*, edited by Barry Bergdoll, Carlos Comas, Jorge Francisco Liernur, and Patricio del Real, 16–67. New York: Museum of Modern Art, 2015.

Bergdoll, Barry, Carlos Comas, Jorge Francisco Liernur, and Patricio del Real. *Latin America in Construction, 1955–1980*. New York: Museum of Modern Art, 2015.

Berger, Dina. *The Development of Mexico's Tourism Industry: Pyramids by Day, Martinis by Night*. New York: Palgrave Macmillan, 2006.

Berger, Dina, and Andrew Grant Wood, eds. *Holiday in Mexico: Critical Reflections on Tourism and Tourist Encounters*. Durham, NC: Duke University Press, 2010.

Best Maugard, Adolfo. *Metódo de dibujo: Tradición, resurgimiento y evolución del arte mexicano*. Mexico City: Departamento Editorial de la Secretaría de Educación, 1923.

Bletter, Rosemarie Haag. Introduction. In Behne, *The Modern Functional Building*.

Bliss, Katherine Elaine. *Compromised Positions: Prostitution, Public Health and Gender Politics in Revolutionary Mexico City*. University Park: Pennsylvania State University Press, 2001.

Boissiere, Olivier. "Habitation de M. Francisco Gilard, Mexico; architect: Luis Barragán." *L'Architecture d'aujourd'hui* 208 (January 1980), xix–xxii.

Bonilla, Mario. *París-México: La primera modernidad arquitectónica*. Mexico City: Instituto Francés de América Latina/Colegio de Arquitectos México—Sociedad de Arquitectos Mexicanos/Universidad Autónoma Metropolitana, Xochimilco, 1993.

Born, Esther. *The New Architecture in Mexico*. New York: Architectural Record, William Morrow, 1937.

Bossom, Alfred C. *An Architectural Pilgrimage in Old Mexico*. New York: Scribner's, 1924.

Bremmer, Alex. *Imperial Gothic: Religious Architecture and High Anglican Culture in the British Empire, c. 1840–70*. New Haven, CT: Yale University Press, 2013.

Brenner, Anita. "Romance and Realism in a Modern Aztec Theater." *Art and Archeology* 20, no. 2 (August 1925), 66–73.

Brenner, Anita. *Idols behind Altars*. New York: Harcourt Brace, 1929.

Brenner, Anita. *Your Mexican Holiday*. New York: Putnam's, 1932.

"Bridged Domesticity: The Diego Riveras Have Two Roofs and One Menage." *Arts and Decoration* 39 (August 1933), 26–30.

Britton, John A. "Urban Education and Social Change in the Mexican Revolution, 1931–1940." *Journal of Latin American Studies* 5, no. 2 (November 1973), 233–45.

Briuolo Destéfano, Diana. "El Estadio Nacional: Escenario de la raza cósmica." *Crónicas: El muralismo, producto de la revolución mexicana, en América, seminario de investigación* 2 (May–August 1998), 8–43.

Buchenau, Jürgen. *Plutarco Elías Calles and the Mexican Revolution*. Lanham, MD: Rowman and Littlefield, 2007.

Bueno, Christina. "Teotihuacán: Showcase for the Centennial." In Berger and Wood, *Holiday in Mexico*, 56–76.

Bullrich, Charles. *New Directions in Latin American Architecture*. New York: George Braziller, 1969.

Burian, Edward R., ed. *Modernity and the Architecture of Mexico*. Austin: University of Texas Press, 1997.

Burian, Edward R. "The Architecture of Juan O'Gorman: Dichotomy and Drift." In Burian, *Modernity and the Architecture of Mexico*, 127–50.

Burian, Edward R. "Postscript." In Burian, *Modernity and the Architecture of Mexico*, 191–94.

Burian, Edward R. "Modernity and Nationalism: Juan O'Gorman and Post-Revolutionary Architecture in Mexico, 1920–1960." In *Cruelty and Utopia: Cities and Landscapes of Latin America*, edited by Jean-Francois Lejeune, 210–23. New York: Princeton Architectural Press, 2003.

Burke, Michael E. "The University of Mexico and the Revolution, 1910–1940." *Americas* 3, no. 2 (October 1977), 252–73.

Burri, René. *Luis Barragán*. London: Phaidon Press, 2000.

Bustamante, Miguel E. "La coordinación de los servicios sanitarios federales y locales como factor de progreso higiénico en México." *Gaceta Médica de México* 65, nos. 7–8 (July–August 1934), 179–238.

Canales, Fernanda. *Arquitectura en México, 1900–2010: La construcción de la modernidad, obras, diseño, arte y pensamiento*, exhibition catalog. Mexico City: Fomento Cultural Banamex, 2013.

Candiani, Vera S. *Dreaming of Dry Land: Environmental Transformation in Colonial Mexico City*. Redwood City, CA: Stanford University Press, 2014.

Carranza, Luis E. "Contemplating Reason: Juan O'Gorman and the Dialectics of Modern Architecture." *Casabella* 9 (May 2001), 82–85.

Carranza, Luis E. "La arquitectura prehispánica en el imaginario moderno." *Arquine* 38 (Winter 2009), 78–91.

Carranza, Luis E. *Architecture as Revolution: Episodes in the History of Modern Mexico*. Austin: University of Texas Press, 2010.

Carranza, Luis, and Fernando Lara. *Modern Architecture in Latin America: Art, Technology, and Utopia*. Austin: University of Texas Press, 2014.

Casanova, Rosa. "Guillermo Kahlo: La vision monumental." In *Guillermo Kahlo/Henry Greenwood Peabody: Dos miradas a la arquitectura monumental de México*, edited by Isabel Garcés and Emma Hernández Tena, 108–25. Mexico City: Fomento Cultural Grupo Salinas, 2009.

Casanova, Rosa, and Adriana Konzevik. *Mexico, a Photographic History: A Selective Catalogue of the Fototeca Nacional of the INAH*. Mexico City: Consejo Nacional para la Cultura y las Artes; Instituto Nacional de Antropología e Historia; Editorial RM, 2007.

Caso, Alejandro. "El hombre." In Noelle, *Mario Pani: Arquitecto*, 29–34.

Castañeda, Luis M. "Beyond Tlaltelolco: Design, Media, and Politics at Mexico '68." *Gray Room* 40 (Summer 2010), 100–126.

Castañeda, Luis M. *Spectacular Mexico: Design, Propaganda, and the 1968 Olympics*. Minneapolis: University of Minnesota Press, 2014.

de Cervantes, Luis. *Crónica arquitectónica: Prehispanica, colonial, contemporánea*. Mexico City: Editorial CIMSA, 1952.

Cetto, Max. *Modern Architecture in Mexico*. New York: Praeger, 1961.

Cheney, Sheldon. *The Open-Air Theatre*. New York: Kennerley, 1918.

"Cité Universitaire de Mexico." *Arquitecture d'aujoud'hui* 21, no. 34 (1951), 82–87.

"City of Culture: The New World's Oldest University Builds a Monument to Modern Education and Ancient Art." *Interiors* (February 1952), 78.

Ciudad Universitaria: Crisol del México moderno, edited by Roger Díaz de Cossío. Mexico City: Universidad Nacional Autónoma de México, 2009.

Clendenin, Malcolm. "Hector Guimard, Political Movements, and the Paris Metro: Natural Sympathies, Governing Harmony, and Social Change." PhD dissertation, University of Pennsylvania, 2008.

Clifford, Henry. "Note on Velasco's Paintings." In *José María Velasco, 1840–1912*. Philadelphia and Brooklyn: Philadelphia Museum of Art and the Brooklyn Museum, 1944.

Coffey, Mary K. "The 'Mexican Problem': Nation and 'Native' in Mexican Muralism and Cultural Discourse." In *The Social and the Real*, edited by Alejandro Anreus, Diana L. Linden, and Jonathan Weinberg, 43–70. University Park: Pennsylvania State University Press, 2006.

Coffey, Mary K. "'All Mexico on a Wall': Diego Rivera's Murals at the Ministry of Public Education." In *Mexican Muralism: A Critical History*, edited by Alejandro Anreus, Leonard Folgarait, and Robin Adèle Greeley, 56–74. Berkeley: University of California Press, 2012.

Coffey, Mary K. *How a Revolutionary Art Became Official Culture: Murals, Museum, and the Mexican State*. Durham, NC: Duke University Press, 2012.

Collins, Peter. *Changing Ideals in Modern Architecture, 1750–1950*. 2nd ed. Toronto: McGill-Queens University Press, 1998.

Colomina, Beatriz. "The Split Wall: Domestic Voyeurism." In *Sexuality and Space*, edited by Beatriz Colomina, 73–132. New York: Princeton Architectural Press, 1992.

Colomina, Beatriz. *Privacy and Publicity: Modern Architecture as Mass Media*. Cambridge, MA: MIT Press, 1994.

Connant, Kenneth J. Letter to the Editor. *Magazine of Art* (February 1943), 78.

Cordero Reiman, Karen. "Constructing a Modern Mexican Art, 1910–1940." In *South of the Border: Mexico in the American Imagination, 1914–1947*, edited by James Oles, exhibition catalog, Yale University Art Gallery, 11–48. Washington, DC: Smithsonian Institution Press, 1993.

Cordero Reiman, Karen. "La invención del arte popular y la construcción de la cultura visual moderna en México." In *Hacia otra historia del arte en México*, vol. 3, edited by Esther Acevedo, 67–90. Mexico City: Consejo Nacional para la Cultura y las Artes, 2002.

Cordero Reiman, Karen. "The Best Maugard Drawing Method." *Journal of Decorative and Propaganda Arts, Mexico Theme Issue* 26, 44–79. Miami: The Wolfsonian—Florida International University, 2010.

Cortés, Antonio, and Genaro García. *La arquitectura en México: Iglesias.* Mexico City: Tall. de Impr. y Fotograbado del Museo Nacional de Arqueología, Historia y Etnología, 1914.

Covert, Lisa Pinley. "Colonial Outpost to Artists' Mecca: Conflict and Collaboration in the Development of San Miguel de Allende's Tourist Industry." In Berger and Wood, *Holiday in Mexico*, 183–220.

Cruz González Franco, Lourdes. "Los hoteles para un México moderno." In Noelle, *Mario Pani: Arquitecto*, 183–220.

Cruz Rodríguez, María Soledad. *Crecimiento urbano y procesos sociales en el Distrito Federal (1920–1928).* Mexico City: Universidad Autónoma Metropolitana, 1994.

Curiel, Fernando. *La revuelta: Interpretación del Ateneo de la Juventud, 1906–1929.* Mexico City: Universidad Nacional Autónoma de México, Centro de Estudios Literarios, Instituto de Investigaciones Filológicas, 1998.

Curtis, William J. R. *Le Corbusier: Ideas and Forms.* London: Phaidon Press, 1986.

Curtis, William J. R. *Modern Architecture since 1900.* 3rd ed. London: Phaidon Press, 1996.

Curtis, William J. R. "'The General and the Local': Enrique del Moral's Own House, Calle Francisco Ramírez 5, Mexico City, 1948." In Burian, *Modernity and the Architecture of Mexico*, 115–26.

Damaz, Paul F. *Art in Latin American Architecture.* New York: Reinhold, 1963.

Davids, René. "Mythical Terrain and the Building of Mexico's UNAM." *CLAS Working Papers* (2008), 1–15.

Dawson, Alexander S. "From Models for the Nation to Model Citizens: *Indigenismo* and the 'Revindication' of the Mexican Indian, 1920–1940." *Journal of Latin American Studies* 30 (1998), 279–308.

Debroise, Olivier. *Mexican Suite: A History of Photography in Mexico.* Translated by Stella de Sá Rego. Austin: University of Texas Press, 2001.

Departamento de Educación Pública. *Las escuelas al aire libre en México.* Mexico City: Secretaria de Educación Pública, 1927.

Departamento del Distrito Federal. *Centro social y deportivo para trabajadores "Venustiano Carranza" en el parque de Balbuena; memoria descriptiva del centro y folleto conmemorativo de los festivales de inauguración, 20 a 24 de noviembre de 1929.* Mexico City: Talleres gráficos de la nación, 1929.

Departamento del Distrito Federal. *Programa general para los festivales y competencias que se efectuarán en el Centro Social y Deportivo para Trabajadores "Venustiano Carranza" durante los días del 20 al 24 de noviembre de 1929, en la inauguración de dicho centro.* Mexico City, 1929.

Departamento del Distrito Federal. *Atlas general del Distrito Federal.* Mexico City, 1930.

Departamento del Distrito Federal. *Hamarandecua.* Program. Mexico City: Talleres gráficos de la nación, 1930.

Departamento del Distrito Federal. *Informe Presidencial y Memoria del Departamento del Distrito Federal que rinde el C. Jefe del mismo, Lic. Aarón Sáenz, por el periodo administrativo comprendido entre el 10. de julio de 1933 y el 30 de junio 1934.* Mexico City, 1934.

Derisanty. "La Gran Exposición Internacional de arte moderno industrial y decorativo en Paris." *Cemento* (October–November 1925), n.p.

Diaz-Borioli, Leonardo. "Collective Autobiography: Building Luis Barragán." PhD dissertation, Princeton University, 2015.

Diego Rivera: A Retrospective. Exhibition catalog. Edited by Cynthia Newman Helms. New York: Norton, 1986.

"Diego Rivera's House and Studio on the Outskirts of Mexico City." *American Architect and Architecture* 146 (May 1935), 66.

Dirección de Monumentos Coloniales. *Tres siglos de arquitectura colonial.* Mexico City: Talleres gráficos de la nación, 1933.

Le Duc, Alberto, and Roberto Alvarez Espinosa. *Una casa habitación del siglo XVIII en la ciudad de México.* Mexico City: Talleres de la Editorial Cultura, 1939.

Dussel, Susanne C., and José Morale-Saravia. "The 'Own' and the 'Foreign': Architecture and the Discourses on Identity in 20th-Century Mexico." In *Constructing Identity in Contemporary Architecture: Case Studies from the South*, edited by Peter Herrle and Stephanus Schmitz, 187–50. Berlin: Lit. Verlag Dr. W. Hopf, 2009.

Eggener, Keith L. "Postwar Modernism in Mexico: Luis Barragán's Jardines del Pedregal and the International Discourse on Architecture and Place." *Journal of the Society of Architectural Historians* 58, no. 2 (June 1999), 122–45.

Eggener, Keith L. "Towards an Organic Architecture in Mexico." In *Frank Lloyd Wright: Europe and Beyond*, edited by Anthony Alofsin, 166–83. Berkeley: University of California Press, 1999.

Eggener, Keith L. "Contrasting Images of Identity in the Post-War Mexican Architecture of Luis Barragán and Juan O'Gorman." *Journal of Latin American Cultural Studies* 9, no. 1 (2000), 27–45.

Eggener, Keith L. "Barragán's 'Photographic Architecture': Image, Advertising and Memory." In Zanco, *Luis Barragán*, 178–95.

Eggener, Keith L. *Luis Barragán's Gardens of El Pedregal.* New York: Princeton Architectural Press, 2001.

Eggener, Keith L. "Settings for History and Oblivion in Modern Mexico, 1942–1958." In *Cruelty and Utopia: Cities and Landscapes of Latin America*, edited by Jean-Francois Lejeune, 224–39. New York: Princeton Architectural Press, 2003.

Einfeldt, Kirsten. *Moderne Kunst in Mexiko: Raum, Material und nationale Identität.* Transcript. Bielefeld: Verlag, 2010.

Elizondo, Salvador. "Mario Pani, arquitecto." In Noelle, *Mario Pani: Arquitecto*, 15–28.

de la Encina, Juan. *El Paisajista José María Velasco (1842–1912).* Mexico City: Colegio de México, Fondo de Cultura Económica, 1943.

Encisco, Jorge, and Lauro E. Rosell. *Edificios coloniales artísticos e históricos de la Republica Mexicana que han sido declarados monumentos.* Mexico City: Talleres tipográficos de la editorial Cultura, 1939.

"Entrevista con el arquitecto Mario Pani, el 1 octubre de 1979." In *Testimonios vivos 20 arquitectos*, edited by Lilia Gómez and Miguel Angel Quevedo, 93–110. Mexico City: Secretaría de Educación Pública, Instituto Nacional de Bellas Artes, Mayo-Agosto, 1981.

Escudero, Alexandrina. *Apuntes para la historia crítica de la arquitectura mexicana del siglo XX: 1900–1980.* Mexico City: Secretaría de Educación Pública, Instituto Nacional de Bellas Artes, 1982.

"La Escuela Benito Juárez." *Cemento* 16 (1926), 18–26.

Las escuelas al aire libre en México. Mexico City: Secretaría de Educación Pública, 1927.

Espinosa López, Enrique. *Ciudad de México, compendio cronológico de su desarrollo urbano, 1521–1980.* Mexico City: E. Espinosa López, 1991.

"Exposición Juan Segura." In *El Museo Nacional de Arquitectura*, edited by Instituto Nacional de Bellas Artes, 155–225. Mexico City: Instituto Nacional de Bellas Artes, 1990.

"Federal Schools of Mexico." *Architectural Record* 75 (May 1934), 444–46.

Fernández, Justino. "The New Architecture in Mexico: An Outline of Its Development." In Born, *New Architecture in Mexico*, 14–15.

Fernández, María. *Cosmopolitanism in Mexican Visual Culture.* Austin: University of Texas Press, 2014.

Fernández Ledesma, Gabriel. "Fotografías de deportes." *Forma: Revista de artes plásticas* 3 (1927), 11–12.

Fierro Gossman, Rafael R. *La gran corriente ornamental del siglo XX: Una revisión de la arquitectura neocolonial en la ciudad de México.* Mexico City: Universidad Iberoamericana, 1998.

Flaherty, George F. "Mario Pani's Hospitality: Latin America through *Arquitectura/México*." In *Latin American Modern Architectures: Ambiguous Territories*, edited by Patricio del Real and Helen Gyger, 253–69. New York: Routledge, 2013.

Flaherty, George F. "Responsive Eyes: Urban Logistics and Kinetic Environments for the 1968 Mexico City Olympics." *Journal of the Society of Architectural Historians* 73, no. 3 (September 2014), 372–97.

Fontana, María Celia. "La conversión del churrigueresco en estilo nacional." In Lozoya and Pérez Vejo, *Arquitectura escrita*, 51–63.

Forty, Adrian. "Cement and Multiculturalism." In *Transculturation: Cities, Spaces and Architectures in Latin America*, edited by Felipe Hernandez, Mark Millington, and Iain Borden, 144–54. Amsterdam: Rodopi, 2005.

Frampton, Kenneth. "A Propos Barragán: Formation, Critique and Influence." In Zanco, *Luis Barragán*, 14–27.

Frank Yerbury: Itinerant Cameraman, Architectural Photographs, 1920–1935. London: Architectural Association, 1987.

Fraser, Valerie. *Building the New World: Studies in the Modern Architecture of Latin America, 1930–1960.* London: Verso, 2000.

Friedman, Alice T. *Women and the Making of the Modern House.* New York: Abrams, 1998.

Friedman, Daniel S. "Salk Institute for Biological Studies." In David B. Brownlee and David G. De Long, *Louis I. Kahn: In the Realm of Architecture*, 330–40. New York: Rizzoli and the Museum of Contemporary Art, Los Angeles, 1991.

Fuentes, Lorenzo. "La construcción del Centro Social y Deportivo para trabajadores en Balbuena." *Obras publicas* (January 6, 1930), 18–24.

Fuentes para el estudio de la arquitectura en México, siglos XIX y XX, edited by Louise Noelle. Mexico City: Universidad Nacional Autónoma de México; Instituto de Investigaciones Estéticas, 2007.

Gaitán Rojo, Carmen, Ariadna Patiño Guadarrama, and Julián Martínez González. *El Ateneo de la Juventud y la plástica mexicana.* Mexico City: Consejo Nacional para las Artes y Cultura, Instituto Nacional de Bellas Artes, 2010.

Galguera, Hilario III. "La Ciudad Universitaria y Mario Pani." *Arquitectura/México* 15 (1959), 155–58.

Galindo y Villa, Jesús. *Historia sumaria de la ciudad de México*. Mexico City: Editorial Cultura, 1925.

Gallo, Rubén. *Mexican Modernity: The Avant-garde and the Technological Revolution*. Cambridge, MA: MIT Press, 2005.

Gamio, Manuel. *The Population of the Valley of Teotihuacan: Introductions Synthesis and Conclusions*. Mexico City: Talleres gráficos de la nación, 1922.

de Garay Arellano, Graciela. *La obra de Carlos Obregón Santacilia, arquitecto*. Cuadernos de Arquitectura y Conservación del Patrimonio Artístico, No. 6. Mexico City: Secretaría de Educación Pública, Instituto Nacional de Bellas Artes, 1982.

de Garay Arellano, Graciela. *Mario Pani: Vida y obra*. Mexico City: Universidad Nacional Autonoma de Mexico, Facultad de Arquitectura, 2004.

García, Genaro. *La arquitectura en México: Iglesias*. Mexico City: Talleres de Imprenta y Fotograbado del Museo Nacional de Arqueología, Historia y Etnología, 1914.

García Maroto, Gabriel. "Vida y arte: La plástica y su proyección pública; proceso de la integración plástica." *Novedades: México en la cultura* (March 29, 1953), 4–5.

García Maroto, Gabriel. *Arquitectura popular de México*. Mexico City: Instituto Nacional de Bellas Artes, 1954.

Garrigan, Shelly E. *Collecting Mexico: Museums, Monuments, and the Creation of National Identity*. Minneapolis: University of Minnesota Press 2012.

Gastélum, Bernardo J. *La clase, la arquitectura de la comunidad*. Mexico City, 1928.

Gastélum, Bernardo J. "Democracia asimétrica." *Contemporáneos* 2, no. 6 (1928), 244–56.

Gastélum, Bernardo J. "El espíritu del héroe." *Contemporáneos* 1, no. 1 (1928), 1–14.

Gastélum, Bernardo J. "Pensar en vez de recordar." *Contemporáneos* 6, no. 20 (1930), 8–20.

Gilardi, Francisco. Interview with Enrique X. de Anda. August 2, 1989. paraphernalia .jux.com/950674 (May 30, 2013).

Goldman, Shifra M. "Nationalist and Anti-nationalist Modernisms in Vanguard Mexican Art." *Art Nexus* (January/March 1997), 76–81.

González Gortázar, Fernando. *La arquitectura mexicana del siglo XX*. Mexico City: Consejo Nacional para la Cultura y las Artes, 1996.

González Gortázar, Fernando. "La integración plástica en el trabajo de Mario Pani." In Noelle Merles, *Mario Pani: Arquitecto*, 81–104.

González Lobo, Carlos. "Juan Legaretta." In González Gortázar, *La arquitectura mexicana*, 110–11.

Guillermo Kahlo: Fotógrafo oficial de monumentos, edited by David Maawad and Alicia Ahumada. Mexico City: Casa de las Imágenes, 1992.

Guillermo Kahlo: Vida y obra: Fotógrafo, 1872–1941: Catálogo ilustrado. Mexico City: Consejo Nacional para la Cultura y las Artes, Instituto Nacional de Bellas Artes, 1993.

Hale, Charles A. *The Transformation of Liberalism in Late Nineteenth-Century Mexico*. Princeton, NJ: Princeton University Press, 1989.

Harris, Harwell Hamilton. "Regionalism and Nationalism in Architecture." *Texas Quarterly* 1 (February 1958), 115–24.

Hedrick, Tace. *Mestizo Modernism: Race, Nation, and Identity in Latin American Culture, 1900–1940*. New Brunswick, NJ: Rutgers University Press, 2003.

Hernández Gálvez, Alejandro. "Juan O'Gorman: Architecture and Surface." *Journal of Decorative and Propaganda Arts* 26 (2010), 206–29.

Herrera, Hayden. *Frida: A Biography of Frida Kahlo.* 1981. Reprint. New York: Perennial, 2002.

Hijar, Alberto. "La integración plástica." In González Gortázar, *La arquitectura mexicana*, 222–30.

Hillier, Bevis. *Art Deco.* London: Studio Vista, 1968.

Hitchcock, Henry-Russell. *Latin American Architecture since 1945.* New York: Museum of Modern Art, 1955.

Hitchcock, Henry-Russell, and Philip Johnson. *The International Style.* 1932. New York: Norton, 1995.

Hoffman, Barbara T., ed. *Art and Cultural Heritage: Law, Policy, and Practice.* Cambridge: Cambridge University Press, 2006.

Horn, James J. "The Mexican Revolution and Health Care, or the Health of the Mexican Revolution." *Latin American Perspectives* 10, no. 4 (1983), 24–39.

Hübsch, Heinrich. "In welchem Stil sollen wir bauen?" (1828). *In What Style Should We Build? The German Debate on Architectural Style.* Santa Monica, CA: Getty Center for the History of Art and the Humanities; University of Chicago Press, 1992.

Huntington, Ellsworth. "The Relation of Health to Racial Capacity: The Example of Mexico." *Geographical Review* 11, no. 2 (April 1921), 243–64.

Ideario de los arquitectos mexicanos. Vols. 1–3, edited by Ramón Vargas Salguero and J. Víctor Arias Montes. Mexico City: Instituto Nacional de Bellas Artes y Literatura, 2010.

"Inauguró ayer el Sr. Presidente E. Portes Gil el Centro Social y Deportivo para Trabajadores." *Excélsior,* November 21, 1929.

Indych-López, Anna. *Muralism without Walls: Rivera, Orozco, and Siqueiros in the United States.* Pittsburgh: University of Pittsburgh Press, 2009.

Ingersoll, Richard. "In the Shadows of Barragán." In Zanco, *Luis Barragán,* 206–27.

Jaén, Didier T. Introduction. *The Cosmic Race.* Bilingual edition. Baltimore: Johns Hopkins University Press, 1997.

Jiménez, Victor. *Carlos Obregón Santacila, pionero de arquitectura Mexicana.* Mexico City: Insituto Nacional de Bellas Artes, Consejo Nacional para la Cultura y las Artes, 2001.

Jiménez, Víctor. *Las casas de Juan O'Gorman para Diego y Frida.* Mexico City: Instituto Nacional de Bellas Artes, Museo Casa-Estudio Diego Rivera y Frida Kahlo, 2001.

Jiménez, Víctor. *Carlos Obregón Santacilia: Un precursor de la modernidad mexicana.* Mexico City: Consejo Nacional para la Cultura y las Artes, Dirección General de Publicaciones, 2004.

Jiménez, Víctor, and Alejandra Escudero. *El Palacio de Bellas Artes: Construcción e historia.* Mexico City: Consejo Nacional para la Cultura y las Artes, Instituto Nacional de Bellas Artes, 1994.

Johnson, Philip. "Whence & Whither: The Processional Element in Architecture." *Perspecta* 9, no. 10 (1965), 167–78.

Jolly, Jennifer. "Art of the Collective: David Alfaro Siqueiros, Josep Renau and Their Collaboration at the Mexican Electricians' Syndicate." *Oxford Art Journal* 31, no. 1 (2008), 129–51.

Jones, Owen, and Francis Bedford. *The Grammar of Ornament.* London: Day and Son, 1856.

Juan O'Gorman, 100 Años: Temples, dibjuos y estudios preparatorios, edited by Cándida Fernández de Calderón and Carlos Monroy Valentino. Mexico City: Consejo Nacional para la Cultura y las Artes, Fomento Cultural Banamex, 2005.

Kahn, Allan W., and James Norman. *Mexican Hill Town*. Santa Monica, CA: Fisher-Edwards, 1963.

Kalach, Alberto. "Architecture and Place: The Stadium of the University City." In Burian, *Modernity and the Architecture of Mexico*, 107–14.

Kandell, Jonathan. *La Capital: The Biography of Mexico City*. New York: Random House, 1988.

Kaspé, Vladimir. "Le Corbusier y la Arquitectura Contemporánea." *Arquitectura/México* 21 (November 1946), 3–13.

Kaspé, Vladimir. "Tiempos de estudiante con Mario Pani." *Arquitectura/México* 67 (September 1959); reprinted in Noelle, *Mario Pani: Arquitecto*, 35–42.

Kaspé, Vladimir. *La arquitectura contemporánea mexicana; precedentes y desarrollo*. Mexico City: Instituto Nacional de Antropología e Historia, 1964.

Kaspé, Vladimir. *La arquitectura del siglo XIX en México*. Mexico City: Editorial Trillas, Centro de Investigaciones Arquitectónicas, Universidad Nacional Autónoma de México. 1973.

Katzman, Israel. *La arquitectura contemporánea Mexicana: Precedentes y desarrollo*. Mexico City: Instituto Nacional de Antropología e Historia, 1964.

Kaufman, Edward N. "Architectural Representation in Victorian England." *Journal of the Society of Architectural Historians* 16, no. 1 (March 1987), 30–38.

Kempner, Mary Jean. "In Mexico City—An Eloquent Statement." *House Beautiful* (August 1966), 88–93.

Kilham, Walter H. *Mexican Architecture of the Vice-Regal Period*. New York: Longmans, Green, 1927.

Kismaric, Susan. *Manuel Álvarez Bravo*. New York: Museum of Modern Art, 1997.

Kracauer, Sigrfried. "The Mass Ornament." Republished in *The Mass Ornament: The Weimar Essays*. Edited and translated by Thomas Y. Levin, 75–86. Cambridge, MA: Harvard University Press, 1995.

Kruze, Enrique. *Mexico: Biography of Power, a History of Modern Mexico, 1810–1996*. Translated by Hank Heifetz. New York: Harper Perennial, 1997.

Kubler, George. *The Art and Architecture of Ancient America: The Mexican, Maya, and Andean Peoples*. Baltimore: Penguin Books, 1962.

Kubler, George, and Martin Soria. *Art and Architecture in Spain and Portugal and Their American Dominions, 1500 to 1800*. Baltimore: Penguin Books, 1959.

"'El laborillo,' pantomima de una fiesta popular en Tehuantepec, será representa hoy en el teatro al aire libre del Centro 'Venustiano Carranza.'" *El Universal*, November 23, 1929.

Lane, Barbara Miller. *Architecture and Politics in Germany, 1918–1945*. Cambridge, MA: Harvard University Press, 1965.

Lane, Barbara Miller. *National Romanticism and Modern Architecture in Germany and the Scandinavian Countries*. Cambridge: Cambridge University Press, 2000.

Lazo, Carlos. "Discursos pronunciados en la colocación de la primera piedra de la Ciudad Universitaria" (June 5, 1950). In *Pensamiento y destino de la Ciudad Universitaria de Mexico*. Mexico City: Imprenta Universitaria, 1952.

Leal, Felipe. "Nightless Enclosure: An Afternoon at the Home of Luis Barragán." Translated by Roberto Tejada, in *Artes de México* 23 (1999), 93–95.

Le Corbusier. *Vers une architecture*. 1923. Translated by Frederick Etchells. New York: Dover, 1986.

Legorreta, Ricardo. "José Villagrán García and Luis Barragán." In *Modernidad urbana*, edited by Louise Noelle and Iván San Martín, 125–41. Mexico City: DOCOMOMO, 2012.

Levine, Neil. *The Architecture of Frank Lloyd Wright*. Princeton, NJ: Princeton University Press, 1996.

Levine, Neil. *Modern Architecture: Representation and Reality*. New Haven, CT: Yale University Press, 2010.

Loos, Adolf. "Ornament and Crime." 1908. Reprinted in *Programs and Manifestoes on 20th-Century Architecture*. Edited by Ulrich Conrads and translated by Michael Bullock, 19–24. Cambridge, MA: MIT Press, 2001, 1971.

López, Rick A. "The Noche Mexicana and the Exhibition of Popular Arts: Two Ways of Exalting Indianness." In *The Eagle and the Virgin: National and Cultural Revolution in Mexico, 1920–1940*, edited by Mary Kay Vaughan and Stephen E. Lewis, 23–42. Durham, NC: Duke University Press, 2006.

López, Rick A. *Crafting Mexico: Intellectuals, Artisans, and the State after the Revolution*. Durham, NC: Duke University Press, 2010.

López García, Juan. "El arquitecto Carlos Obregón Santacilia: La tradición arquitectónica mexicana (nacimiento, invención y renovación)." PhD dissertation, Universidad Politécanica de Catalunya, 2002.

López Morales, Fancisco Javier. *Arquitectura vernácula en México*. Mexico City: Editorial Trillas, 1987.

López Rangel, Rafael. *Diego Rivera y la arquitectura mexicana*. Mexico City: Secretaría de la Educación Pública, 1986.

López Rangel, Rafael. *La modernidad arquitectónica Mexicana antecedentes y vanguardias 1900–1940*. Azcapotzalco: Universidad Autónoma Metropolitana, 1989.

López Rangel, Rafael. *La planificación de la ciudad de México, 1900–1940*. Azcapotzalco: Universidad Autónoma Metropolitana, División de Ciencias y Artes para el Diseño, 1993.

López Uribe, Cristina. "Los murales de Chávez Morado, obras que cambian con el paso del tiempo y las modficaciones de CU." *Boletín Universidad Nacional Autónoma de MÉXICO-DGCS-086 Ciudad Universitaria* (February 10, 2012). Accessed May 8, 2014. www.dgcs.unam.mx/boletin/bdboletin/2012_087.html.

Lorey, David E. "The Revolutionary Festival in Mexico: November 20 Celebrations in the 1920s and 1930s." *Americas* 54, no. 1 (July 1997), 39–82.

Lozoya, Johanna. "Usos y desusos de historiografía cultural arquitectónica mexicana." In Lozoya and Pérez Vejo, *Arquitectura escrita*, 9–14.

Lozoya, Johanna. *Las manos indígenas de la raza española*. Mexico City: Consejo Nacional para la Cultura y las Artes, 2010.

Lozoya, Johanna, and Tomás Pérez Vejo, eds. *Arquitectura escrita: Docientos años de arquitectura Mexicana*. Mexico City: Instituto Nacional de Antropología e Historia, 2009.

Maawad, David, and Alicia Ahumada, eds. *Guillermo Kahlo, fotógrafo oficial de monumentos*. Mexico City: Fototeca del Instituto Nacional de Antropología e Historia /Casa de las Imágenes, 1992.

Manrique, Jorge Alberto. "Las cuentas claras en la arquitectura mexicana: Triunfo, venganza y desquiciamiento." *Artes visuales* 2 (Spring 1974), 34–37.

Manrique, Jorge Alberto. "Guillermo Kahlo, fotógrafo oficial de monumentos." In Maawad and Ahumada, *Guillermo Kahlo*, 11–17.

Manrique, Jorge Alberto. "El futuro radiante: La Ciudad Universitaria." In González Gortázar, *La arquitectura mexicana*, 195–221.

Manuel F. Alvarez, algunos escritos, edited by Elisa García Barragán. Mexico City: Secretaría de Educación Pública, Instituto Nacional de Bellas Artes, 1982.

Mario Pani, arquitecto. Mexico City: Universidad Autónoma Metropolitan Atzcapotzalco; Editorial Limusa, 1999.

Mariscal, Federico. *La patria y la arquitectura nacional: Resúmenes de las conferencias dadas en la casa de la Universidad Popular Mexicana del 21 de octubre de 1913 al 29 de julio de 1914 por el arquitecto D. Federico E. Mariscal*. Mexico City: Imprenta Stephan y Torres, 1915.

Mariscal, Nicolas. "El arte en Mexico." In *Nicolás Mariscal: Arquitectura, arte y ciencia*, edited by Louise Noelle, 29–38. Mexico City: Consejo Nacional para la Cultura y las Artes, Instituto Nacional de Bellas Artes, Dirección de Arquitectura y Conservación del Patrimonio Artístico Inmueble, 2003.

Mariscal, Nicolas. "El desarrollo de la arquitectura en Mexico." In *Nicolás Mariscal: Arquitectura, arte y ciencia*, edited by Louise Noelle, 1–17. Mexico City: Consejo Nacional para la Cultura y las Artes, Instituto Nacional de Bellas Artes, Dirección de Arquitectura y Conservación del Patrimonio Artístico Inmueble, 2003.

Martínez, Máximo. *Las plantas medicinales de México*. Vol. 1, 7th ed. Mexico City: Ediciones Botas, 2005.

"Master Designer, Luis Barragán." *Interiors* (December 1963), 84–91.

Mateos, Gisela, Adriana Minor, and Valeria Sánchez Michel. "Una modernidad anunciada: Historia del Van de Graaff de Ciudad Universitaria." *Historia Mexicana* 62, no. 1 (July–September 2012), 415–42.

Mazzaferri, Anthony J. "Public Health and Social Revolution in Mexico: 1877–1930." PhD dissertation, Kent State University, 1968.

McAndrew, John. *The Open-Air Churches of Sixteenth-Century Mexico: Atrios, Posas, Open Chapels, and Other Studies*. Cambridge, MA: Harvard University Press, 1965.

McCoy, Esther. "Ciudad Universitaria de México." *Arts and Architecture* (August 1952), 23, 41.

McCoy, Esther. "Designing for a Dry Climate." *Progressive Architecture* 53 (August 1971), 50–57.

Mérida, Carlos. *Frescoes in Primary Schools by Various Artists: An Interpretative Guide with 16 Reproductions*. Mexico City: Frances Toor Studios, 1943.

Mertins, Detlef. "Mies's Skyscraper 'Project': Towards the Redemption of the Technical Structure." In *The Presence of Mies*, edited by Detlef Mertins, 49–70. New York: Princeton Architectural Press, 1996.

Mexican Art Today. Exhibition Catalog. Philadelphia: Philadelphia Museum of Art and Dirección General de Educación Extra-Escolar y Estetica, México, 1943.

"Mexico: The Architect at Home." *Harper's Bazaar* (March 1956), 186–87.

"Mexico City to Get Huge Park." *Los Angeles Times*, September 9, 1929.

México Moderno, edited by J. Luis Parra. Mexico City: Compañía Editoria de México Moderno, 1924.

"Mexico's Mammoth Campus." *Architectural Forum* 108, no. 3 (March 1958), 108–13.

Meyer, Hannes. "Building." In *Programs and Manifestoes on 20th-Century Architecture*, edited by Ulrich Conrads, 117–20. Cambridge, MA: MIT Press, 2001.

de Michelis, Marco. "The Origins of Modernism: Luis Barragán, the Formative Years." In Zanco, *Luis Barragán*, 42–65.

Mijares Bracho, Carlos G. "The Architecture of Carlos Obergón Santacilia: A Work for Its Time and Context." In Burian, *Modernity and the Architecture of Mexico*, 151–62.

Millan, Verna Carleton. *Mexico Reborn*. Boston: Houghton Mifflin, 1939.

Miller, Arthur. "Mexico Depicted as Land of Artists." *Los Angeles Times*, September 22, 1929.

Miller, Marilyn Grace. T*he Rise and Fall of the Cosmic Race: The Cult of Mestizaje in Latin America*. Austin: University of Texas Press, 2004.

Millon, Henry A. "Rudolph Wittkower, Architectural Principles in the Age of Humanism: Its Influence on the Development and Interpretation of Modern Architecture." *Journal of the Society of Architectural Historians* 31, no. 2 (May 1972), 83–91.

Miranda, F. P. "The Public Health Department in Mexico City." *American Journal of Public Health* 20 (1930), 1125–28.

"Monseiur Le Corbusier." *Tolteca* (November 1930), 216–17.

Montenegro, Roberto. *Museo de Artes Populares*. Mexico City: Ediciones de Arte, 1948.

von Moos, Stanisalus. *Le Corbusier: Elements of a Synthesis*. Cambridge, MA: MIT Press, 1979.

del Moral, Enrique. "Lo General y lo Local." *Espacios* 2 (October 1948), n.p.

del Moral, Enrique. "Tradición vs. modernidad integración?" *Arquitectura/México* 10 (March 1954), 5–24.

del Moral, Enrique. "El tránsito del churrigueresco al neoclásico en México." *Arquitectura/Mexico* 10 (September 1954), 131–45.

del Moral, Enrique. "Villagrán García y la evolución de nuestra arquitectura." *Arquitectura/México* 55, no. 12 (September 1956), 131–32.

del Moral, Enrique. *El hombre y la arquitectura: Ensayos y testimonios*. Mexico City: Universidad Nacional Autónoma de México, 1983.

Morales, Alfonso, and Servando Aréchiga. "Domus Dei, Porta-Coeli." In Maawad and Ahumada, *Guillermo Kahlo*, 21–35.

Morshed, Adnan. "The Cultural Politics of Aerial Vision: Le Corbusier in Brazil (1929)." *Journal of Architectural Education* 55, no. 4 (May 2002), 201–10.

Mraz, John. *Looking for Mexico*. Durham, NC: Duke University Press, 2009.

Mullen, Edward J. "Contemporáneos in Mexican Intellectual History, 1928–1931." *Journal of Interamerican Studies and World Affairs* 13, no. 1 (January 1971), 121–30.

Murales. Mexico City: Universidad Nacional Autónoma Mexicana, 1967.

Mutis, Álvaro. "Three Visits to the Luis Barragán Library." Translated by Roberto Tejada. *Artes de México* 23 (1999), 90–91.

Myers, I. E. *Mexico's Modern Architecture*. New York: Architectural Book, 1952.

Navarro, Aaron W. *Political Intelligence and the Creation of Modern Mexico, 1938–1954*. University Park: Pennsylvania State University Press, 2010.

"The New Mexico: Yesterday's Tradition Takes on Today's Tempo." *Look* (January 25, 1966), 54–57.

Noelle, Louise, ed. *Mario Pani: Arquitecto*. Mexico City: Universidad Nacional Autónoma de México, Instituto de Investigaciones Estéticas, 2008.

Noelle Merles, Louise. *Luis Barragán: Búsqueda y creatividad*. Mexico City: Universidad Nacional Autónoma de México, 1996.

Noelle Merles, Louise. "The Architecture and Urbanism of Mario Pani: Creativity and Compromise." In Burian, *Modernity and the Architecture of Mexico*, 177–90.

Noelle Merles, Louise. *Enrique del Moral, un arquitecto comprometido con México*. Mexico City: Consejo Nacional de la Cultura y las Artes, 1998.

Noelle Merles, Louise. "La revista *Arquitectura/México*." In Noelle, *Mario Pani: Arquitecto*, 317–28.

Noelle Merles, Louise. "La arquitectura mexicana en las publicaciones periódicas del siglo XX." *Bitácora* 19 (2009), 14–18.

Novo, Salvador. "Los fines de las escuelas de pintura." *Mexican Folkways* 4, no. 1 (January–March 1928), 24–27.

Novoa, Adriana. "In the Borders of Being: Mexico, Space, and Time in Sergei Eisenstein and Octavio Paz." *Atlantic Studies* 7, no. 3 (September 2010), 215–39.

"Oaxaca: El valor arquitectonico de las obras del pasado." *Arquitectura* 26 (January 1949), 8–19.

Obregón Santacilia, Carlos. *El maquinismo, la vida y la arquitectura: Ensayo*. Mexico City: Publicaciones Letras de México, 1939.

Obregón Santacilia, Carlos. *México como eje de las antiguas arquitecturas de las Américas*. Mexico City: Editorial Atlante, 1947.

Obregón Santacilia, Carlos. *50 años de arquitectura mexicana (1900–1950)*. Mexico City: Editorial Patria, 1952.

"Observations on Mexico's University City." *Journal of the AIA* (January 1953), 9–13.

Ochsner, Jeffery Karl. *Lionel N. Pries, Architect, Artist, Education*. Seattle: University of Washington Press, 2007.

O'Gorman, James F. *Three American Architects: Richardson, Sullivan, Wright, 1865–1915*. Chicago: University of Chicago Press, 1991.

O'Gorman, Juan. "Escuelas nuevas." *Imagen* 1, no. 11 (September 1933), n.p.

O'Gorman, Juan. "El Departmento Central Inquisidor de la nueva arquitectura." *Frente a Frente* 5 (August 1936), 22.

O'Gorman, Juan. "Velazco: Painter of Time and Space." *Magazine of Art* 36, no. 6 (October 1943), 202–7.

O'Gorman, Juan. "Decoration." *Northwest Architect* 16, no. 5 (September–October 1952), 8.

O'Gorman, Juan. "3 Preguntas a Juan O'Gorman." *Espacios* 14 (March 5, 1953), n.p.

O'Gorman, Juan. "Espacios pregunta, Juan O'Gorman responde." *Espacios* 25 (June 1955), 20.

O'Gorman, Juan. "El desarrollo de la arquitectura Mexicana en los ultimos trienta años." *Arquitectura* 23, no. 100 (April and June 1968), 48–55.

O'Gorman, Juan. "La palabra de Juan O'Gorman." *Platicas sobre arquitectura 1933*, edited by Louise Noelle, 17–33. Mexico City: Consejo Nacional para la Cultura y las Artes, Instituto Nacional de Bellas Artes, 2001.

O'Gorman, Juan, and Antonio Luna Arroyo. *Juan O'Gorman, autobiografía, antología, juicios críticos y documentación exhaustive sobre su obra*. México City: Cuadernos Populares de Pintura Mexicana Moderna, 1973.

O'Gorman, Juan, and Elena Poniatowska. *O'Gorman*. Mexico City: Bital, 1999.

Oles James. *South of the Border: Mexico in the American Imagination, 1914–1947*. Exhibition catalog. Washington, DC: Smithsonian Institution Press, 1993.

Oles, James. "Modern Photography and Cementos Tolteca: A Utopian Aliance." In

Mexicana: Fotografia moderna en Mexico, 1923–40, edited by Salvador Albiñana and Horacio Fernández, 273–75. Valencia: Generalitat Valenciana, 1998.

Oles, James. "Police, Sports and Spectacle: *Festival Militar*, 1931." *Luna Córnea* 16 (September–December 1998), 199–203.

Oles, James. "For Business or Pleasure: Exhibiting Mexican Folk Art, 1820–1930." In *Casa Mañana*, edited by Susan Danly, 11–29. Albuquerque: University of New Mexico Press for the Mead Art Museum, Amherst College, 2002.

Oles, James. "Industrial Landscapes in Modern Mexican Art." *Journal of Decorative and Propaganda Arts* 26 (Miami Beach: The Wolfsonian—Florida International University, 2010), 128–59.

Olivares Correa, Martha. *Primer director de la escuela de arquitectura del siglo XX*. Mexico City: Instituto Politénico Nacional, 2006.

Oropesa, Salvador A. *The Contemporáneos Group: Rewriting Mexico in the Thirties and Forties*. Austin: University of Texas Press, 2003.

O'Rourke, Kathryn E. "Guardians of Their Own Health: Tuberculosis, Rationalism, and Reform in Modern Mexico." *Journal of the Society of Architectural Historians* 71, no. 1 (March 2012), 60–77.

O'Rourke, Kathryn E. "Science and Sex in Diego Rivera's Health Ministry Murals." *Public Art Dialogue* 4, no. 1 (2014), 9–40.

O'Rourke, Kathryn E. "Gardens and Landscapes of Frida Kahlo's Mexico City." In *Frida Kahlo's Garden*, edited by Adriana Zavala, Joanna Groake, and Mia D'Avanza, 86–103. New York: Prestel, 2015.

O'Rourke, Kathryn E. "El pasado y el futuro de la arquitectura 'mexicana' a los mediados del siglo XX." In *Imaginarios de modernidad y tradición: Arquitecturas americanas del siglo XX*, edited by Catherine R. Ettinger, 11–32. Mexico City: Editorial Porrúa, 2015.

Orozco, José Clemente. "José Clemente Orozco a Luis Barragán." In Luis Barragán, *Luis Barragán: Escritos y conversaciones*, 149.

Ortiz Gaitán, Julieta. *Entre dos mundos: Los murales de Roberto Montenegro*. Mexico City: Instituto de Investigaciones Estéticas, Universidad Nacional Autónoma de México, 1994.

Ortiz Macedo, Luis. *Secretaría de Salud: Departamento de Salubridad Pública*. Mexico City: Secretaría de Salud, 1991.

Palomar, Juan. "The Alchemist of Memory." Translated by Carole Castelli. *Artes de México* 23 (1999), 76–79.

Pani, Alberto J. *Hygiene in Mexico: A Study of Sanitary and Educational Problems*. Translated by Ernest L. de Gorgoza. New York: Putnam's, Knickerbocker Press, 1917.

Pani, Mario. "The Overall Plan of the Ciudad Universitaria." *Arts and Architecture* (August 1952), 21, 41.

Pani, Mario, and Enrique del Moral. *La construcción de la Ciudad Universitaria del Pedregal: Concepto, programa y planeación arquitectónica*. Mexico City: Universidad Nacional Autónoma de México, 1979.

Payne, Alina A. "Rudolph Wittkower and Architectural Principles in the Age of Modernism." *Journal of the Society of Architectural Historians* 53, no. 3 (September 1994), 322–42.

Paz, Octavio. "The Labyrinth of Solitude." In *The Labyrinth of Solitude and Other Writings*. Translated by Lysander Kemp, Yara Milos, and Rachel Philips Belash, 7–212. New York: Grove Press, 1985.

Pellicer, Carlos. "The Valley of Mexico." In *José María Velasco, 1840–1912*, 13–14. Philadelphia and Brooklyn: Philadelphia Museum of Art and the Brooklyn Museum, 1944.

Pinoncelly, Salvador. *La obra de Enrique del Moral*. Mexico City: Universidad Nacional Autónoma Mexicana, 1983.

"Pintura de Caballete y Pintura de Pulquería." *El Demócrata: Diario independiente de la mañana* (July 20, 1923).

Pintura mural en los centros de educación de México. Mexico City: Secretaría de Educación Pública, 2003.

Poniatowska, Elena. "Luis Barragán: Entrevista." In Luis Barragán, *Luis Barragán: Escritos y conversaciones*, 105–23.

Poole, C. A. "Theoretical and Poetical Ideas in Le Corbusier's Une Maison–Un Palais." *Journal of Architecture* 3, no. 1 (Spring 1998), 1–30.

"Primero Renglones." *El Arquitecto* 1, no. 1 (September 1923), n.p.

Puig Casauranc, J. M. Untitled essay. *Forma* 1, no. 1 (October 1926), 1.

Puig Casauranc, José Manuel. *La obra integral de la revolución Mexicana: Discurso pronunciado por el Dr. J. M. Puig Casauranc, el 20 de noviembre de 1929, al inaugurarse el Centro Social y Deportivo para Trabajadores "Venustiano Carranza."* Mexico City: Departamento del Distrito Federal, Talleres Gráficos de la Nación, 1929.

Quintero, Pablo, ed. *Modernidad en la arquitectura mexicana (18 protagonistas)*. Mexico City: Universidad Autonoma Metropolitana-Unidad Xochimilco, 1990.

Ramírez, Fausto. "Los saldos de la modernidad y de la revolución." In *Pintura y vida cotidiana en México, 1650–1950*, 143–207. Mexico City: Reproducciones Fotomecánica, Fomento Cultural Banamex, Consejo Nacional para la Cultura y las Artes, 1999.

Reese, Carol McMichael. "The Urban Development of Mexico City, 1850–1930." In *Planning Latin America's Capital Cities, 1850–1950*, edited by Arturo Almandoz, 139–69. New York: Routledge, 2002.

Revilla, Manuel. *El arte en Mexico en la época antiqua y durante el gobierno virreinal*. Mexico City: Librería Universal de Porrúa Hermanos, 1923.

"Revolutionary Birth Feted by Nation at Social Welfare Park." *Excélsior*, November 21, 1929.

Riggen Martínez, Antonio. *Luis Barragán: Mexico's Modern Master, 1902–1988*. New York: Monacelli Press, 1996.

Rivera, Diego. "The New Mexican Architecture: A House of Carlos Obregón." *Mexican Folkways*, no. 9 (October–November 1926), 19–27.

Rivera, Diego. "Los nombres de las pulquerías." *Mexican Folkways* 2, no. 7 (June–July 1926), 16–19.

Rivera, Diego. "La pintura de las pulquerías." *Mexican Folkways* 2, no. 7 (June–July 1926), 6–10, 10–15.

Rochfort, Desmond. *Mexican Muralists*. San Francisco: Chronicle Books, 1993.

Rodman, Selden. *Mexican Journal: The Conquerors Conquered*. New York: Devin-Adair, 1958.

Rodríguez Prampolini, Ida. *Juan O'Gorman: Arquitecto y pintor*. Mexico City: Universidad Nacional Autónoma de México, 1982.

Rogers, Isabel S., and Henry Clifford. Forward and Acknowledgment. In *José Maria Velasco, 1840–1912*, 9–10. Philadelphia and Brooklyn: Philadelphia Museum of Art and the Brooklyn Museum, 1944.

Rojas, Pedro. *La Ciudad Universitaria en la época de su construcción.* Mexico City: Universidad Nacional Autónoma de México, 1979.

Rojas Delgadillo, Norma. "Cultural Property Legislation in Mexico: Past, Present, and Future." In Hoffman, *Art and Cultural Heritage*, 114–18.

Romero de Terreros, Manuel. *The House of Tiles: La Casa de los Azulejos.* Mexico City: Bland Brothers, Printers, 1925.

de la Rosa de la Rosa, Natalia. "Mirada dirigida y control del cuerpo: Arquitectura y pintura mural en la escuela Domingo Faustino Sarmiento." In *Encauzar la mirada: Arquitectura, pedagogía e imágenes en México, 1920–1950*, edited by Renato González Mello and Deborah Dorotinksy Alperstein, 75–108. Mexico City: Universidad Nacional Autónoma de México, Instituto de Investigaciones Estéticas, 2010.

Rossell, Guillermo, and Lorenzo Carrasco. "Un arquitecto opina . . ." In Rossell and Carrasco, *Guía de arquitectura mexicana contemporánea*, n.p.

Rossell, Guillermo, and Lorenzo Carrasco, eds. *Guía de arquitectura mexicana contemporánea.* Mexico City: Editorial Espacios, 1952.

Rykwert, Joseph. "The Ecole des Beaux-Arts and the Classical Tradition." In *The Beaux-Arts and Nineteenth-Century French Architecture*, edited by Robin Middleton, 9–17. Cambridge, MA: MIT Press, 1982.

Saborit, Antonio. "En busca de la arquitectura hispano colonial: El trabajo de Peabody y Baxter en México." In *Guillermo Kahlo/Henry Greenwood Peabody*, edited by Isabel Garcés and Emma Hernández Tena, 44–107. Mexico City: Fomento Cultural Grupo Salinas, 2009.

Salvat, Jorge. "Los Colores de México: Entrevista." In Luis Barragán, *Luis Barragán: Escritos y conversaciones*, 128–31.

Schávelzon, Daniel. "Vicente Mendiola: Escuelas al aire libre (1926–1927)." *Traza* 5 (November–December 1983), n.p.

Schávelzon, Daniel. "Los origenes de la arquitectura moderna en México: Las escuelas al aire libre (1925–1927)." *DANA, Documentos de Arquitectura Nacional y Americana* 21 (September 1986), 68–75.

Schjetnan, Mario. "Ciudad Universitaria y los orígenes del paisaje contemporáneo." *Bitácora arquitectura* 11 (February–April 2004), 10–15.

Schjetnan Garduño, Mario. "Enclosures and the Open Sky: A Conversation of Forms." Translated by Roberto Tejada. *Artes de México* 23 (1999), 92–93.

Schjetnan Garduño, Mario. "El arte de hacer o cómo hacer el arte: Entrevista." In Luis Barragán, *Luis Barragán: Escritos y conversaciones*, 124–27.

Scott, Nina M. "Measuring Ingredients: Food and Domesticity in Mexican Casta Paintings." *Gastronomica* 5, no. 1 (2005), 70–79.

Secretaría de Educación Pública. *Escuelas primarias.* Mexico City, 1933.

Secretaría de Educación Pública. *Escuelas primarias urbanas.* Vols. 1–2, 4–5. Mexico City: Comisión Editora Popular, 1938.

Secretaría de Industria y Trabajo. *México: Sus recursos naturales, su situación actual; homenaje al Brasil en ocasion del primer centenario de su independencia, 1822–1922.* Mexico City: La Secretaria de Industria, Comercio y Trabajo, 1922.

Sedgwick, Eve Kosofsky. *Epistemology of the Closet.* Berkeley: University of California Press, 1990.

Shipway, Verna Cook, and Warren Shipway. *The Mexican House, Old and New.* New York: Architectural Book, 1960.

Shipway, Verna Cook, and Warren Shipway. *Mexican Interiors*. New York: Architectural Book, 1962.

Siqueiros, David Alfaro. "Hacia una nueva plástica integral." *Espacios*, no. 1 (September 1948), n.p.

Siqueiros, David Alfaro. "Un problema técnico sin precedente en la historia del arte: El muralismo figurativo y realista en el exterior." *Arte público: Tribuna de pintores muralistas, escultores, grabadores y artistas de la estampa en general* 1 (December 1952), 6.

Siqueiros, David Alfaro. "Memorial al señor arquitecto Carlos Lazo: Gerente general de las obras en la ciudad universitaria; sobre el problema de mis murales en la rectoría y en la la Facultad de Ciencias Químicas." Mexico City: Sala de Arte Público Siqueiros, 1953.

Siqueiros, David Alfaro. "Arquitectura internacional a la zaga de la mala pintura." *Arte público: Tribuna de pintores, escultores, grabadores, arquitectos, dibujantes, fotógrafos, criticos de arte* 2, no. 2 (November 1954–February 1955), 36.

La situación actual de la historiografía de la arquitectura mexicana, edited by Catherine R. Ettinger McEnulty. Morelia: Universidad Michoacana de San Nicolás de Hidalgo; Universidad Nacional Autónoma de México, 2008.

Sitwell, Sacheverell. *Southern Baroque Art: A Study of Painting, Architecture and Music in Italy and Spain of the 17th and 18th Centuries*. 3rd ed. London: Duckworth, 1931.

Smith, Clive Bamford. *Builders in the Sun: Five Mexican Architects*. New York: Architectural Book, 1967.

Sociedad de Arquitectos Mexicanos. *4000 años de arquitectura mexicana*. Mexico City: Libreros Mexicanos Unidos, 1956.

Socorro Villareal Escarrega, María del Perpetuo. "The National Institute of Anthropology and History." In Hoffman, *Art and Cultural Heritage*, 394–97.

Spratling, William. "Figures in a Mexican Renaissance." *Scribner's Magazine* (January 1929), 14–21.

Spratling, William. "The Public Health Center, Mexico City." *Architectural Forum* (November 1931), 589–94.

Stern, Alexandra Minna. "Responsible Mothers and Normal Children: Eugenics, Nationalism, and Welfare in Postrevolutionary Mexico, 1920–1940." *Journal of Historical Sociology* 12, no. 4 (December 1999), 369–97.

Sullivan, Edward J. "Naturalezas mexicanas: Objects as Cultural Signifiers in Mexican Art, c. 1760–1875." In *The Lure of the Object*, edited by Stephen W. Melville, 59–71. Williamstown, MA: Sterling and Francine Clark Art Institute, 2005.

Tablada, José Juan. *Historia del arte en México*. Mexico City: Compañía Nacional Editora Aguilas, 1927.

Taylor, Tess. "Barragán Revisited: The Menil Collection Takes a Look Back at the 'Humanists' Retreat that Could Have Been." *Metropolis* 23, no. 10 (June 2004), 70.

Tenenbaum, Barbara A. "Streetwise History: The Paseo de la Reforma and the Porfirian State, 1876–1910." In *Rituals of Rule, Rituals of Resistance: Public Celebrations and Popular Culture in Mexico*, edited by William H. Beezley, Cheryl English Martin, and William E. French, 127–50. Wilmington, DE: Scholarly Resources, 1994.

Tenorio Trillo, Mauricio. "A Tropical Cuauhtémoc: Celebrating the Cosmic Race at the Guanabara Bay." *Anales del Instituto de Investigaciones Estéticas* 65 (1994), 93–137.

Tenorio Trillo, Mauricio. *Mexico at the World's Fairs: Crafting a Modern Nation.* Berkeley: University of California Press, 1996.

Tenorio Trillo, Mauricio. "1910 Mexico City: Space and Nation in the City of the Centenario." *Journal of Latin American Studies* 28, no. 1 (February 1996), 75–104.

Terragni, Emilia. "Art within Architecture." In Zanco, *Luis Barragán*, 236–51.

Terry, T. Philip. *Terry's Guide to Mexico.* Boston: Houghton Mifflin, 1933.

Terry, T. Philip. *Terry's Guide to Mexico.* Boston: Houghton Mifflin, 1940.

Thomas, Helen. "Sublimation (el Pedregal)." In *InterSections: Architectural Histories and Critical Theories*, edited by Iain Borden and Jane Rendell, 109–24. New York: Routledge, 2000.

Tibol, Raquel. "Juan O'Gorman in varios tiempos." *Calli* 29 (1967), 7–10.

Toca Fernández, Antonio. *Arquitectura contemporánea en México.* Azcapotzalco: Universidad Autónoma Metropolitana; México City: Gernika, 1989.

Toca Fernández, Antonio. "Juan Segura, orígenes de la arquitectura moderna en México." In *El Museo Nacional de Arquitectura*, edited by Instituto Nacional de Bellas Artes, 227–50. Mexico City: Instituto Nacional de Bellas Artes, 1990.

Toca Fernández, Antonio. "Juan Segura." In González Gortázar, *La arquitectura mexicana*, 102–3.

Toll, Marie-Pierre. "Color as Structure: The Newest House by Luis Barragán." *House and Garden* (September 1981), 134–41, 189.

Toor, Frances. "Maximo Pacheco." *Mexican Folkways* 3, no. 3 (July–September 1927), 132–33.

Toor, Frances. "Por que este tipo de escuelas rurales." *Mexican Folkways* 3, no. 1 (February–March 1927), 41–43.

Toor, Frances. "Los pequeños artistas y la revolución de la pintura." *Mexican Folkways* 4, no. 1 (January–March 1928), 3–23.

Toor, Frances. "El principio de un teatro mexicano." *Mexican Folkways* 5, no. 2 (April–June 1929), 60–65.

Toor, Frances. "Nuevas escuelas y mas frescos." *Mexican Folkways* 7, no. 4 (October–December 1932), 212–13.

Toor, Frances. *Frescoes in Primary Schools by Various Artists.* Mexico City: Frances Toor Studios, 1943.

Topelson Grinberg, Sara, and Raquel Franklin. "El Conservatorio Nacional de Música." In Noelle, *Mario Pani: Arquitecto*, 105–14.

Torre, Susana. "An Aesthetics of Reconciliation: The Nationalist Origins of Modernity in Latin American Architecture." *Center* 24 (June 2003–May 2004), 166–69.

Toussaint, Manuel. *Paseos coloniales.* Mexico City: Imprenta Universitaria, 1939.

Toussaint, Manuel. *Colonial Art in Mexico.* Translated by Elizabeth Wilder Weissman. Austin: University of Texas Press, 1967.

Toussaint, Manuel, Federico Gómez de Orozco, and Justino Fernández. *Planos de la ciudad de México siglos XVI y XVII: Estudio histórico, urbanístico y bibliográfico.* México City: Instituto de Investigaciones Estéticas, Universidad Nacional Autónoma, 1939.

Tovar de Teresa, Guillermo. Prologue to *Guillermo Kahlo/Henry Greenwood Peabody: Dos miradas a la arquitectura monumental de México*, edited by Isabel Garcés and Emma Hernández Tena, 14–17. Mexico City: Fomento Cultural Grupo Salinas, 2009.

Tradición de la cultura: Nacionalismo cultural: Carlos Obregón Santacilia. Mexico City: Colección Forjadores de Mexico, PRI, 1988.

Trebay, Guy. "Finding Mexico City, and Luis Barragán, Again." *New York Times*, June 13, 2014. http://www.nytimes.com/2014/06/15/travel/finding-mexico-city-and-luis -barragan-again.html?_r=0/.

Treib, Marc. "A Setting for Solitude: The Landscape of Luis Barragán." In Zanco, *Luis Barragán*, 114–39.

Vaughan, Mary Kay. *Cultural Politics in Revolution: Teachers, Peasants, and Schools in Mexico, 1930–1940*. Tucson: University of Arizona Press, 1997.

Vaughan Mary Kay, and Stephen E. Lewis, eds. *The Eagle and the Virgin: Nation and Cultural Revolution in Mexico, 1920–1940*. Durham, NC: Duke University Press, 2006.

Venturi, Robert. *Complexity and Contradiction in Architecture*. 2nd ed. Reprint. New York: Museum of Modern Art, 1996.

"La Vida Moderna." *Cemento* (May 1928), 17.

Villagra Caleti, Agustín. *Bonampak, la ciudad de los muros pintados*. Mexico City: Instituto Nacional de Antropología e Historia, Secretaría de Educación Pública, 1949.

Villagrán García, José. *Panorama de 62 años de arquitectura mexicana contemporánea (1900–1962)*. Mexico City: Instituto Nacional de Bellas Artes, 1963.

Vogt, Adolf Max. *Le Corbusier, the Noble Savage: Toward an Archeology of Modernism*. Translated by Radka Donnell. Cambridge, MA: MIT Press, 1998.

Walter, W. E. "Gustav und Hans Pillig: Zwei westfälische Künstler." *Die Wochenschau* 31 (1913), 980–82.

Waugh, Frank A. *Outdoor Theaters: The Design, Construction, and Use of Open-Air Auditoriums*. Boston: Richard G. Badger, 1917.

Wittkower, Rudolf. *Architectural Principles in the Age of Humanism*. London: Warburg Institute, University of London, 1949.

"Work of Le Corbusier and Pierre Jeanneret." *Die Bauwelt* 20 (1929), 5–7.

Yañez, Enrique. *18 Residencias de arquitectos mexicanos*. Mexico City: Ediciones Mexicanas, 1951.

Yañez, Enrique. "Foreword." In I. E. Myers, *Mexico's Modern Architecture*, 9–14. New York: Architectural Book, 1952.

Zanco, Federica. "Luis Barragán: The Quiet Revolution." In Zanco, *Luis Barragán*, 78–105.

Zanco, Federica, ed. *Luis Barragán: The Quiet Revolution*. Milan: Barragán Foundation, 2001.

Zavala, Adriana. "Mexico City in Juan O'Gorman's Imagination." *Hispanic Research Journal* 8, no. 5 (December 2007), 491–506.

ILLUSTRATION CREDITS

INTRODUCTION

Sociedad de Arquitectos Mexicanos, 4000 Años de Arquitectura Mexicana, 1; Juan O'Gorman, © 2016 Artists Rights Society (ARS), New York / SOMAAP, Mexico City, University of Washington Libraries UW36825, 2; Henry Greenwood Peabody, 3.

CHAPTER 1

Antonio Cortés, 8–9; Guillermo Kahlo, 10; Kathryn E. O'Rourke, 7, 8, 11, 13; Henry Greenwood Peabody, 1–5, 12; *Revista Mexicana de Ingeniería y Arquitectura* 7, no. 6 (June 15, 1929), 14.

CHAPTER 2

Archivo DACPAI.INBA, 6–9; *Anuario de la Sociedad de Arquitectos Mexicanos* (1923), 3; *Cemento* 16 (1926), 5; Guillermo Kahlo, 1, 2, 10; Kathryn E. O'Rourke, 12–18, 21–23; *Método de dibujo*, 19–20; Postcard collection of the author, 4, 11.

CHAPTER 3

Archivo de El Palacio de Hierro, S.A., 3; *Art and Archeology* 20, no. 2 (1925), 10, 11; *Atlas General del Distrito Federal*, vol. 1, 8; *Atlas General del Distrito Federal*, vol. 2, 1, 5; bpk, Berlin/Art Resource, 12; *Centro Social y deportivo para trabajadores "Venustiano Carranza" en el parque de Balbuena; memoria descriptiva del centro y folleto conmemorativo de los festivales de inauguración, 20 a 24 de noviembre de 1929*, 6, 7; *Excélsior*, November 24, 1929, 2; *Iglesias de México*, vol. 6, 3; *Los Inicios de México Contemporáneo*, 9; Carol M. Highsmith, 13.

CHAPTER 4

Manuel Álvarez Bravo, Agustín Jiménez, or Luis Márquez, *Escuelas primarias*, 13–17, 19–20, 22, 23, 25–27; Angel Chápero and Julio I. Prieto, *Escuelas primarias*, 18; Le Corbusier, © F.L.C. / ADAGP, Paris / Artists Rights Society (ARS), New York, 2016, 9, 11; Charles Gérard, © F.L.C. / ADAGP, Paris / Artists Rights Society (ARS), New York

2016, 24; Guillermo Kahlo, Digital Image © The Museum of Modern Art/Licensed by SCALA/Art Resource, New York; Juan O'Gorman © Copyright. Kahlo-Rivera House, San Angel, Mexico City, 1933, Gelatin silver print, 8" × 10". Architecture and Design Study Center, 7–8; Vicente Mendiola, *Las Escuelas al Aire Libre en México*, 30; *Mexican Folkways* 2, no. 6 (1926), 5, 6; Tina Modotti, Collection Center for Creative Photography © 1981 Center for Creative Photography, Arizona Board of Regents, 32; *O'Gorman*, 2; Juan O'Gorman, © 2016 Artists Rights Society (ARS), New York / SO-MAAP, Mexico City, 1, 3, 4, 10; Juan O'Gorman, © 2016 Artists Rights Society (ARS), New York / SOMAAP, Mexico City, University of Washington Libraries UW24468z, 3; Juan O'Gorman, © 2016 Artists Rights Society (ARS), New York / SOMAAP, Mexico City, University of Washington Libraries UW36824, 4; Pablo O'Higgins, © 2016 Artists Rights Society (ARS), New York / SOMAAP: 29; Edward Weston, Collection Center for Creative Photography © 1981 Center for Creative Photography, Arizona Board of Regents, 21, 28.

CHAPTER 5

Manuel Álvarez Bravo, 16; AHUNAM Photograph by Saul Molina, Colección Carlos Lazo, paq. 134 3/7, 2; AHUNAM Fondo Construcción de la Universidad 2778, 6; AHUNAM, photograph by Ricardo Salazar, Fondo Construcción de la Universidad 3020, 9; AHUNAM, photograph attributed to Ricardo Salazar, Fondo Construcción de la Universidad 3852, 19; *Bonampak, la Ciudad de los Muros Pintados*, 20, 21; Compañía Mexicana Aerofoto, S.A., Fundación ICA, 3; Gamboa, Postcard collection of the author, 1; Kathryn E. O'Rourke, 4, 5, 10–12; 17, 18; 22; Kathryn E. O'Rourke, © 2016 Banco de México Diego Rivera Frida Kahlo Museums Trust, Mexico, D.F. / Artists Rights Society (ARS), New York, 13, 14; Marius Gravot, Le Corbusier © F.L.C. / ADAGP, Paris / Artists Rights Society (ARS), New York, 2016, 7; Le Corbusier © F.L.C. / ADAGP, Paris / Artists Rights Society (ARS), New York, 2016, 8; Postcard collection of the author, 15; Wallace Litwin, *Architectural Forum* (March 1955), 23; *Viaje a las ruinas de Bonampak*, 21.

CHAPTER 6

Manuel Álvarez Bravo, © 2016 Barragán Foundation, Switzerland / Artists Rights Society (ARS), New York, 4; Luis Barragán, © 2016 Barragán Foundation, Switzerland / Artists Rights Society (ARS), New York, 5; Esther Born, Courtesy Center for Creative Photography, University of Arizona © Esther Born Estate, 11; Rene Burri, Magnum Photos, © 2016 Barragán Foundation, Switzerland / Artists Rights Society (ARS), New York, 6, 12; Carnegie Arts of the United States Collection, Courtesy of Hargrett Rare Book and Manuscript Library/University of Georgia Libraries, 16; Gabriel García Maroto, *Arquitectura Popular de México*, 14; Lucien Hervé. The Getty Research Institute, Los Angeles (2002.R.41) © J. Paul Getty Trust; Le Corbusier © F.L.C. / ADAGP, Paris / Artists Rights Society (ARS), New York, 2016, 7; *Jardins enchantés: Un Romancero*, 2; *Luis Barragán*, © 2016 Barragán Foundation, Switzerland / Artists Rights Society (ARS), New York, 3; Enrique del Moral, *18 Residencias de Arquitectos mexicanos*, 18; Alberto Moreno Guzman, © 2016 Barragán Foundation, Switzerland / Artists Rights Society (ARS), New York, 9; Kathryn E. O'Rourke, 15; Kathryn E. O'Rourke, © 2016 Barragán Foundation, Switzerland / Artists Rights Society (ARS), New

York: 1; Kathryn E. O'Rourke, © Artists Rights Society (ARS), New York/SOMAAP, Mexico City, 17; Armando Salas Portugal, © 2016 Barragán Foundation, Switzerland / Artists Rights Society (ARS), New York, 8; Quintero or L. Limon, *18 Residencias de Arquitectos Mexicanos*, 10.

CONCLUSION

Kathryn E. O'Rourke, 1–3; Mark Turok, postcard collection of the author, 4.

COLOR PLATES

Atlas General del Distrito Federal, vol. 1, 6, 7; Rene Burri, Magnum Photos, © 2016 Barragán Foundation, Switzerland / Artists Rights Society (ARS), New York, 16; *Jardins enchantés*, 15; Alberto Moreno Guzman, © 2016 Barragán Foundation, Switzerland / Artists Rights Society (ARS), New York, 17. *Journal of Decorative and Propaganda Arts*, Juan O'Gorman © 2016 Artists Rights Society (ARS), New York / SOMAAP, Mexico City, 10; *O'Gorman*, Juan O'Gorman © 2016 Artists Rights Society (ARS), New York / SOMAAP, Mexico City: 9; Kathryn E. O'Rourke, 1–5; © Banco de México Diego Rivera Frida Kahlo Museums Trust, México, D.F. / Artists Rights Society (ARS), New York, 12; Kathryn E. O'Rourke, 13–14; 19; Nicolas Sapieha / Art Resource, NY, Rothko, Mark (1903–70), Juan O'Gorman © ARS, NY, 18; *Tasco*, © 2016 Artists Rights Society (ARS), New York / SOMAAP, Mexico City, 8.

INDEX

Note: Page references in *italics* refer to illustrations.

INDEX